PLUTARCH

Lives That Made Greek History

D1473944

PLUTARCH

Lives That Made Greek History

Edited, with Introductions and Notes, by
James Romm

Translated by Pamela Mensch

Hackett Publishing Company, Inc.
Indianapolis/Cambridge

16 15 14 13 12   1 2 3 4 5 6 7

For further information, please address
    Hackett Publishing Company, Inc.
    P.O. Box 44937
    Indianapolis, Indiana 46244-0937

    www.hackettpublishing.com

Cover design by Abigail Coyle
Interior design by Meera Dash
Maps by William Nelson
Composition by William Hartman
Printed at Data Reproductions Corporation

Library of Congress Cataloging-in-Publication Data

Plutarch.
        [Lives. English]
        Plutarch : lives that made Greek history / edited,
    with introductions and notes, by James Romm ; translated
    by Pamela Mensch.
            p. cm.
        Includes bibliographical references and index.
        ISBN 978-1-60384-846-6 (pbk.) —
        ISBN 978-1-60384-847-3 (cloth)
        1. Greece—Biography.   I. Romm, James S.   II. Mensch,
    Pamela, 1956–   III. Title.   IV. Title: Lives that made
    Greek history.
    DE7.P513 2012
    938.009'9—dc23   2012023888

Contents

Introduction

Plutarch's *Lives* provide a different experience of Greek history than can be found elsewhere. The eras Plutarch dealt with, and even the presentation of important episodes, often overlap closely with the eras covered by the works of Herodotus, Thucydides, and Xenophon, for these were his principal sources. But the questions Plutarch asked differed from those of earlier writers. He tried to show how individual character interacts with society and with history, how ethical qualities either thrive or lead to disaster within the maelstrom of events. He was not concerned with creating a record, for others before him had done that. Six centuries of Greek historical writing stretched out behind him, a treasury in which he delved deep to find the material for his *Lives* (as well as for the speeches, dialogues, and essays he wrote throughout his life, collected today under the title *Moralia*).

Plutarch distinguished his character-based approach to history from more traditional narratives in a famous passage at the opening of his *Alexander*. He vows there to capture the soul of the person he studies as a portrait painter captures the face: the limbs and body are not the portraitist's concern, and neither are the mere facts of history Plutarch's. A battle may loom less large in Plutarch's pages than a quip or apothegm in which his subject's spirit stands revealed. Although Plutarch did not ignore any significant action or episode—his readers would be puzzled by such an omission—he felt free to give short shrift where insight into character could not be gleaned.

In his *Parallel Lives of the Greeks and Romans*, a work probably dating from the early second century CE, Plutarch created a set of inquiries into how great leaders succeeded or failed; how they held up under stress of political strife and warfare; what moral lessons can be learned from them; and, not least importantly, how the lives of leaders from two different nations, Greece and Rome, echo or resemble one another. In Plutarch's scheme, as the title *Parallel Lives* indicates, Greek biographies were paired with Roman ones, and most of these pairs were prefaced by a brief essay in which he compared the two figures profiled. In other works written separately, he also produced a handful of unpaired lives, one of which portrayed neither a Greek nor a Roman but a Persian king. Fifty of Plutarch's *Lives* survive, forty-six of which once belonged to the pairs that made up *Parallel*

Lives. At least twelve additional lives are known to have perished; possibly many more, unknown to us even by title, were lost.

Lost, too, are many of the sources Plutarch used for his research, apart from the three great ones mentioned above. Writers who in his day were considered nearly as great did not survive the broad dying-off of ancient literary works that occurred in the European Dark Ages. As a result, Plutarch's *Lives*, though not intended as a historical record, sometimes constitute the best record we have or provide a valuable comparison with the records preserved by others—especially, in the classical Greek context, by Herodotus and Thucydides. In many cases the *Lives* contain information not found in other sources, the precious relics of Plutarch's readings of Theopompus, Ephorus, Hieronymus of Cardia, and others whose writings have since disappeared.

Plutarch expected his audience to be familiar with the events he deals with, so he sometimes makes only passing references to even the most crucial of these or to important secondary characters. Reading the *Lives* without the same degree of familiarity is thus often a frustrating endeavor, but this volume is designed to help. In the footnotes I have tried to restore the historical context that Plutarch often leaves out. I have also tried to clarify the sequence of events, about which Plutarch is often vague, since chronology was not his concern. Cross-references to relevant passages in other *Lives*, or to the works of other authors, help readers to compare available accounts, and bring together information about individuals and episodes into a unified narrative of the classical Greek world.

My interest, as both a teacher and an author, in creating a unified narrative has led me to exclude certain Greek lives from this collection. *Theseus* was severely truncated on the grounds that, as Plutarch himself acknowledged, it does not have the same grounding in recoverable fact as the lives of other figures. Two works dealing principally with Greek Sicily—*Dion* and *Timoleon*—were omitted altogether, as were those lives that take place largely or entirely in the Hellenistic Age, after the death of Alexander the Great (*Eumenes, Pyrrhus, Agis,* and *Aratus*). Also excluded was *Artaxerxes,* a treatise not originally part of *Parallel Lives,* dealing with the life and times of a Persian king. I have tried to focus entirely on the central sphere of action in the Classical Age, the region we now call Greece or the Balkan Peninsula, the territory dominated at various times by Athens, Sparta, or Thebes. The fifteen *Lives* excerpted in this volume center on statesmen from those cities, and, in the case of *Alexander,* on a Macedonian leader who ineradicably changed the destinies of all three.

A gradual shift in the way the *Lives* are read, moving away from the ethical and toward the historical, has been under way for some time. Long ago, the elegant pairings Plutarch strove so hard to create were broken up; Greeks were segregated with other Greeks, Romans with Romans. The Penguin Classics series then further broke up the *Lives* into volumes organized around chronological periods—*The Age of Alexander* and the like—encouraging readers to consider them in a primarily historical context. My edition takes a further step in this direction, by excerpting from the *Lives* the material of greatest historical significance. I have tried to serve the needs of readers exploring ancient history through primary sources, while hopefully also aiding those intrigued by outstanding models of character and behavior.

It has been painful to see some of Plutarch's best anecdotes, apothegms, and moral exempla cast aside in the excerpting process. Yet it is precisely this aspect of his *Lives*, I believe, that deters many modern readers. Punch lines of Plutarchan jests often today require explanation or cannot be understood at all. Although I have excised many of these, I have tried to retain enough to preserve the basic outlines of Plutarch's character portraits, for these are, above all, what make his *Lives* into documents of enduring power and meaning. I can only hope Plutarch would consider my excisions a price worth paying for the sake of gaining a wider modern readership.

In marking excisions, the principle I have followed is to preserve the reader's ability to find his way easily to the parallel passage of a Greek text. Thus, cuts made from the middle of a chapter are marked with an ellipsis (. . .), but those that remove the beginning or end of a chapter, or an entire chapter, are not marked; chapter numbers can in those cases help readers find their way in a companion text. Short excisions from inside a sentence often simply remove a name or term that a modern reader might find unfamiliar. Plutarch loved to heap up parallels and cross-references, counting on his readers to quickly shift frameworks and recognize a wide array of historical and literary figures. But students striving to master the cast of characters in a single *Life* can feel discouraged, even betrayed, if new names, belonging to an entirely different cast, are thrown at them out of nowhere. I have tried to eliminate such disruptions where possible, or else I have used the footnotes to ease their disorienting effect.

I have made few efforts to eliminate repetition between the
Lives of contemporaneous figures, for Plutarch often retells stories but seldom in quite the same way. It is fascinating to see how
his treatment changes, for example, when recounting the rivalry
between Themistocles and Aristides from the perspective first of
Themistocles, then of Aristides. Stories that overlap with those found
in other ancient authors' works are also retained here, with the sole
exception of Nicias' conduct of the Sicilian expedition, which closely
and at great length replicates the account of Thucydides. Cross-
references will help the curious reader compare different versions,
which sometimes illustrate Plutarch's license as an adapter of his
sources, at other times the range of competing and diverging traditions within the wide spectrum of readings he consulted.

The influence of Plutarch's *Lives* on Western literature and
thought has been enormous. In the Renaissance, Jacques Amyot's
French translation of Plutarch's works sparked the imagination of
Michel de Montaigne, and Sir Thomas North's English version
supplied Shakespeare with the plots of *Julius Caesar*, *Antony and
Cleopatra*, and *Coriolanus*, as well as short episodes in numerous other
plays. In the seventeenth century the poet and critic John Dryden
supervised an elegant translation of the *Lives* that is still in print
today. The American founding fathers were avid readers of Plutarch,
as were the transcendentalists of the nineteenth century, especially
Ralph Waldo Emerson. "Go with mean people and you think life
is mean," Emerson wrote. "Then read Plutarch, and the world is a
proud place, peopled with men of positive quality, with heroes and
demigods standing around us, who will not let us sleep."

Plutarch might not accept the phrase "men of positive quality," for his *Lives* capture roguish and amoral behavior as well as
virtuous deeds. But he would certainly endorse the idea that one's
view of the world, even one's actions, are influenced by what one
knows of great individuals of the past. He created an unforgettable
gallery of portraits in his *Lives*, and he expected that his readers
would be morally wiser as a result of spending time there. This edition of the *Lives*, in the stately new translation of Pamela Mensch, is
offered in the hopes that he was right.

James Romm

Bibliography

Duff, T. *Plutarch's* Lives: *Exploring Virtue and Vice*. Oxford: Oxford University Press, 1999.

Gianakaris, C. J. *Plutarch*. New York: Twayne, 1970.

Jones, C. P. *Plutarch and Rome*. Oxford: Oxford University Press, 1971.

Lamberton, R. *Plutarch*. New Haven, CT: Yale University Press, 2001.

Momigliano, A. *The Development of Greek Biography*. 2nd ed. Cambridge, MA: Harvard University Press, 1993.

Mossman, J. M., ed. *Plutarch and His Intellectual World*. London: Duckworth/Classical Press of Wales, 1997.

Pelling, C. B. R. *Plutarch and History: Eighteen Studies*. Swansea: Classical Press of Wales, 2002.

Russell, D. A. *Plutarch*. London: Duckworth, 1973.

Scardigli, B., ed. *Essays on Plutarch's Lives*. Oxford: Clarendon Press, 1995.

Stadter, P., ed. *Plutarch and the Historical Tradition*. London: Psychology Press, 1992.

Wardman, A. *Plutarch's* Lives. London: Elek, 1974.

Life Spans of the Subjects of Plutarch's *Lives*

SOLON

ARISTIDES

THEMISTOCLES

CIMON

PERICLES

NICIAS

ALCIBIADES

LYSANDER

AGESILAUS

PELOPIDAS

PHOCION

DEMOSTHENES

ALEXANDER

700 BCE

600 BCE

500 BCE

400 BCE

300 BCE

PERSIAN WARS (490–479)

PELOPONNESIAN WAR (432–404)

THEBAN HEGEMONY (371–362)

REIGN OF ALEXANDER (336–323)

xi

The Greek World

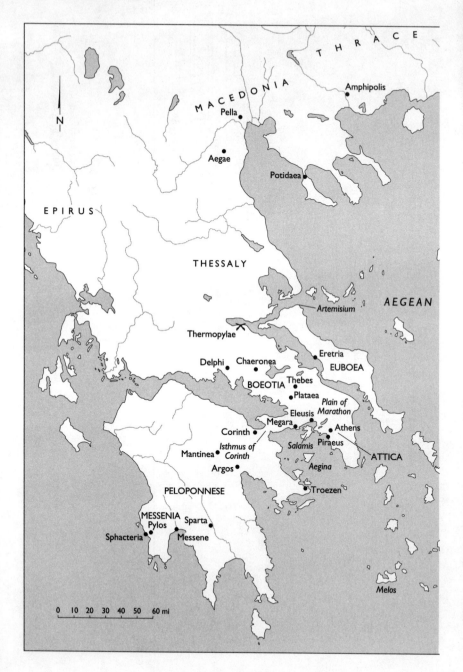

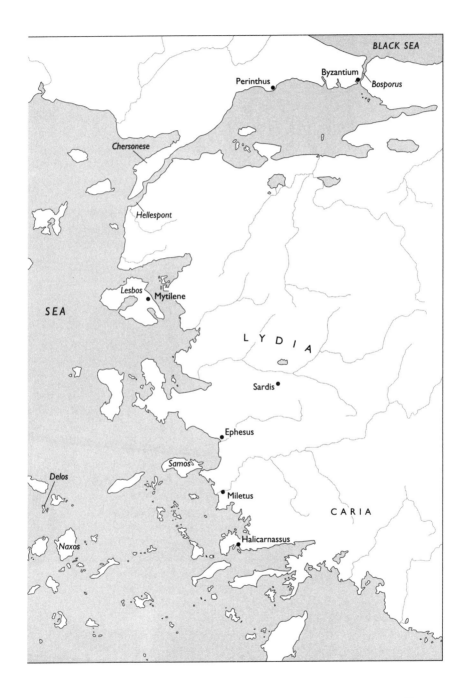

BLACK SEA

Byzantium

Perinthus

Bosporus

Chersonese

Hellespont

Lesbos
Mytilene

SEA

L Y D I A

Sardis

Ephesus

Samos

Delos

Miletus

CARIA

Naxos

Halicarnassus

Persian Invasions of Greece, 490–480 BCE

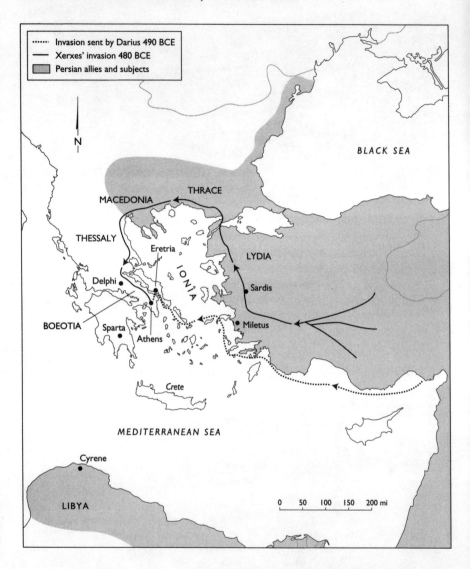

The Persian Empire and the Route of Alexander's Campaigns

SCYTHIA
Danube
MACEDONIA
THRACE
Delphi
Athens
Sparta
Crete
Sardis
LYDIA
Miletus
BLACK SEA
Halys
Tigris
Nineveh
Euphrates
Babylon
CASPIAN SEA
Aral Sea
SOGDIANA
BACTRIA
MEDIA
Choaspes
Susa
PERSIS
Persepolis
INDIA
Indus
GEDROSIA
PERSIAN GULF
ARABIAN SEA
RED SEA
Nile
Thebes
Elephantine
EGYPT
Memphis
Shrine of Ammon
LIBYA
Cyrene
MEDITERRANEAN SEA
Syracuse

—N—

500 miles

0

Persian allies and subjects

Theseus

Plutarch's Life *of the Athenian hero Theseus is represented here only by a few brief selections, since its content is overwhelmingly mythical rather than historical. Nonetheless it preserves important ideas the Athenians held about their own early history, especially the notion of Theseus' unification of Athens into a centralized society. This* sunoikismos *or "aggregation of settlements," as the Greeks called it, was the closest thing Athens had to a foundation, and in Plutarch's account it is followed by the bestowal of the city's name. In fact, the unification of Athens probably took place slowly, over centuries, but it is conceivable that one visionary leader gave it a strong push at some early stage.*

The time frame of Plutarch's Life of Theseus *is hard to establish, but it is several centuries earlier than the next earliest life, that of Lycurgus. The myth of Theseus' voyage to Crete and slaying of the Minotaur seems to recall an early phase of Greek history when Minoan civilization, centered on Crete, dominated much of the Greek mainland. The idea that Athens once paid human tribute to Crete but then freed itself from subjugation perhaps contains a distant memory of the collapse of Cretan society in the fifteenth century BCE. Theseus, on this reading, was not only Athens' first unifier but also the first of many fighters who stood up to foreign despots and kept the city free. Certainly that is how his later countrymen regarded him, and they made his grave a place of sanctuary for all those fleeing the abuses of power.*

[3] On his father's side, Theseus' family goes back to Erechtheus[1] and Athens' original inhabitants, while on his mother's side he was related to Pelops. Now Pelops was the most powerful of the kings in the Peloponnese, as much because of the number of his progeny as the greatness of his wealth; for he had given many daughters in marriage to the noblest men, and had dispersed many sons among the cities as rulers. One of these was Pittheus . . . who settled the smallish city of Troezen and enjoyed the highest renown for being well-versed in the lore of his own day and supremely wise. . . .

They say that Aegeus, who desired children, received from the Pythian priestess[2] the well-known oracle in which she urged him

---

1. Erechtheus was the legendary first king of Athens, a man supposedly sprung from Earth itself.

2. Priestess of Apollo at Delphi, called "Pythian" because a monstrous serpent called Python had once dwelled on the spot where the oracle was founded.

to have intercourse with no woman until he reached Athens. But
Aegeus thought her utterance rather obscure, which was why, when
he reached Troezen, he communicated to Pittheus the response of
the god, which ran thus:

> Loose not the jutting neck of the wine skin,
> Great ruler of men, until you reach the city of Athens.

Pittheus apparently understood the response, and either persuaded
or tricked Aegeus into sleeping with his daughter Aethra. When
Aegeus, having done so, learned that he had slept with the daughter
of Pittheus and suspected that she was pregnant, he left behind a
sword and sandals, hiding them under a huge stone that lay over a
hollow just large enough to contain what had been placed there. He
told no one but Aethra, and urged her, if she bore him a son, and if
on reaching manhood he was able to lift up the stone and remove
what had been left there, to send the boy to him with these objects,
in perfect secrecy, and taking every possible precaution to conceal
his journey from everyone. For he greatly feared the Pallantids,[3] who
were plotting against him and who despised him for his childlessness,
since fifty children had been born to Pallas. Aegeus then departed.

[4] When Aethra gave birth to a son, some say he was immediately named Theseus because of the *placing* of the tokens, while others
say he received the name later, in Athens, when Aegeus *acknowledged*
him.[4]

[6] When Theseus was a lad, and displayed, along with bodily
strength, great courage, and a proud spirit united with intelligence
and sagacity, Aethra led him to the stone and told him the truth about
his birth. She urged him to take up the paternal tokens and sail to
Athens. Slipping his shoulder under the rock, he easily raised it up,
but he refused to travel by sea, though this was the safer course, and
his grandfather and mother begged him to do so. For the road to
Athens was difficult to travel on foot, since no part of it was safe or
free from bandits and ruffians.

For that age produced men who, in skill of hand and speed of
foot and strength of body, were extraordinary and tireless, but who
applied their natural gifts to nothing that was decent or useful.
Instead they delighted in arrogant violence, and took advantage of

---

3. A rival faction of the royal line at Athens.

4. Both italicized words translate Greek words derived from *tithemi*, a verb
that shares an important root with the name *Theseus*.

their power to exercise an inhuman cruelty, mastering and coercing and destroying everything they encountered. As for reverence, justice, equality, and generosity, they believed that most men praised these things because they lacked the courage to injure others or from fear of being injured themselves, and considered them of no value to men whose might gave them the upper hand. Heracles cut off and killed some of these men on his travels, while those who escaped his notice cowered, drew back, and by behaving humbly were overlooked. . . . The journey was therefore treacherous for those who traveled on foot from the Peloponnese to Athens. And Pittheus, by describing at length every sort of rascal one might encounter, and the way such a fellow treated strangers, tried to persuade Theseus to travel by sea. But it seems that the renown of Heracles' courage had long been secretly inflaming Theseus.

Plutarch here describes the feats Theseus performed en route to Athens, cleansing the countryside of monsters, bandits, and evildoers in much the same way as Heracles was thought to have done earlier. Theseus arrived safely in Athens and was reunited with his father Aegeus, who immediately proclaimed him his heir. This set off a war with the Pallantids, a rival faction who had hoped to inherit the throne, thinking that Aegeus would die childless. Theseus and his supporters prevailed in that war and secured rule for the line of Aegeus.

[15] Shortly thereafter, the tribute-collectors arrived for the third time from Crete. Most writers agree that because Androgeos was thought to have been treacherously killed in Attica, his father Minos waged a grievous and protracted war on the region's inhabitants,[5] and the gods themselves also ravaged their country, since there was famine and widespread disease, and its rivers failed. It is also reported that when the god proclaimed that if the Athenians appeased Minos and were reconciled with him the gods' anger would abate and their troubles would come to an end, the people sent heralds to Crete with their supplications and entered into an agreement to send Minos seven youths and seven maidens as a tribute every nine years.

---

5. Minos, ruler of Crete, had according to legend lost his son Androgeos near Athens at the hands of Aegeus. Minos then invaded and besieged Athens, demanding that the Athenians send selected youths to Crete every nine years to feed the Minotaur (a monstrous creature engendered when Minos' wife Pasiphae mated with a bull).

[17] When the time came for the third tribute, and the fathers of unmarried sons had to provide the allotted number, Aegeus again found himself maligned by the citizens, who were grieved and vexed that he, who was the cause of all their troubles, was the only one who had no share in the punishment, but was bequeathing his empire to an illegitimate and foreign son,[6] and allowing *them* to be deprived of their legitimate offspring and left without children. This troubled Theseus; and thinking he ought not to ignore, but to share in his fellow citizens' fortunes, he came forward and offered himself without drawing any lot. The citizens admired his resolve and were delighted with his fellow feeling; and when Aegeus, though he begged and pleaded with Theseus, saw that his son was immovable and unalterable, he chose the other young people by lot.

Previously there had been no hope of deliverance, which is why they used to send the ship with a black sail, since their misfortune was foreseen. But this time, as Theseus sought to hearten his father and boasted that he would overpower the Minotaur, Aegeus gave the helmsman a different sail, a white one, and ordered him to raise the white sail if Theseus were returning safely, but if not, to raise the black sail and thereby give notice of their misfortune.

[18] When the lot was cast, Theseus took those on whom the lot had fallen from the town hall, and on reaching Delphinium he dedicated his olive branch to Apollo on their behalf. (This was a bough of the sacred olive tree, wreathed with white wool.) After making his vows, he went down to the sea on the sixth day of the month of Munichion.

[19] According to most of the tales and songs, when Theseus sailed to Crete he received the thread from Ariadne, who had fallen in love with him. Taught how to make his way through the winding passages of the labyrinth, he killed the Minotaur and sailed away, taking Ariadne and his young comrades with him. And Pherecydes says that Theseus bored holes in the hulls of the Cretans' ships, thereby hindering the pursuit. And Demon says that Taurus, Minos' general, was killed in a naval battle in the harbor as Theseus was sailing away.[7]

[22] As they were approaching Attica, both Theseus and the helmsman completely forgot, in their joy, to raise the sail with which

6. Meaning Theseus. Because the young man had wandered into Athens from Troezen, the Athenians did not trust the story of his parentage.

7. The author of this version of the legend, Demon, was apparently looking ahead to the days when Athens would base its military power on its navy.

they were to make their deliverance known to Aegeus; and thus the king, in despair, hurled himself down from the cliff and perished.[8]

[23] The vessel in which Theseus sailed with his young comrades and safely returned—a thirty-oared ship—was preserved by the Athenians down to the time of Demetrius of Phalerum.[9] They would routinely remove the ancient planks and replace them with fresh, strong timber, and consequently the boat became an illustration for the philosophers in the controversial debate about growth, some saying that it remained the same boat, others arguing that it was not the same.

[24] After the death of Aegeus, Theseus conceived of a great and wonderful project. He settled the inhabitants of Attica together in one city, and made them one people and the residents of one city, though they had been scattered formerly and could not easily be assembled to address their common interest; at times they had even quarreled and gone to war with one another. He now approached and sought to persuade them, village by village and clan by clan. Private citizens and poor folk readily welcomed his appeal.[10] To the powerful he offered a government without a king, and a democracy that would use him only as a leader in war and a guardian of the laws,[11] while in all other spheres everyone would be on an equal footing. (Some persons were actually persuaded, while others, who feared his daring and his power, which was already enormous, preferred to be persuaded rather than compelled to accept these measures.) He then eliminated the town halls, council chambers, and offices that had existed in each separate community, and made one common town hall and council

8. The death of Aegeus in the sea off Attica has forever given that body of water its name, the Aegean Sea.

9. That is, until the late fourth century BCE. Unfortunately, Plutarch does not explain why the ship, so carefully preserved for many centuries, suddenly disappeared.

10. Theseus is here cast in the political mold of Athens' most important later leaders, that is, as a champion of the more populous lower classes against the interests of the aristocracy. Cleisthenes, Themistocles, and Pericles all came to power by this means.

11. Plutarch uses the word "democracy" very loosely here, as it would be many centuries before Athens would experiment with true democracy. It appears that what Theseus offered was a very limited monarchy, in which he, as king, would hold sway only over military ventures—something like the kingship that later evolved at Sparta.

chamber where the city now stands. He named the city Athens, and made the Panathenaea[12] a festival in which they all shared.

[25] Wishing to make the city even larger, Theseus invited all men there on equal terms, and they say that the proclamation "Come hither, all people" came into use when Theseus had established a city that in some sense belonged to all the people. Yet he did not let the democracy develop in a disorderly manner or permit the throngs who streamed to it to be mixed together indiscriminately. He began by distinguishing the nobles, the landowners, and the artisans, granting the nobles the administration of religious affairs, the choice of magistrates, the teaching of the laws, and the interpretation of matters sacred and divine, while establishing among the other citizens a balanced polity in which the nobles were thought to prevail in renown, the landowners in utility, and the artisans in numbers. That Theseus was the first to be favorably disposed to the common people, as Aristotle says, and to renounce monarchy, is also affirmed by Homer in the catalogue of ships, where only the Athenians are referred to as a "people."[13]

[26] Theseus sailed into the Black Sea, as Philochorus and some others say, and after joining forces with Heracles against the Amazons,[14] received Antiope[15] as a prize of valor. But most writers . . . say more persuasively that Theseus sailed in his own ship, after the time of Heracles, and that he captured the Amazon as a prisoner of war. For none of his comrades-in-arms is said to have taken an Amazon captive. Bion even says that Theseus tricked Antiope into departing with him. For the Amazons, as they were naturally friendly

12. A festival of athletic and arts competitions, culminating in a magnificent procession in honor of Athena. There were scaled-down versions of the Panathenaea every year, but bigger and more elaborate ones every fourth year.

13. The reference is to Homer's *Iliad* 2.546, where the Athenians in the Greek expedition against Troy are referred to as a *demos*. The word *demos*, part of our word "democracy," was the common term in Athenian politics for the broad mass of the citizen body, "the people."

14. Heracles had been instructed, as one of his twelve labors, to fetch the magic girdle worn by Hippolyta, queen of the Amazons. The legendary Amazons, a race of warrior women who excluded men from their society, were thought to dwell in the far northeast of the world known to the Greeks.

15. Antiope was Hippolyta's sister. Some ancient writers transposed the names and recorded that Theseus had married Hippolyta, not Antiope, and this is the version Shakespeare followed in *A Midsummer Night's Dream*.

to men, did not flee from Theseus when he put ashore at their country, but actually sent him gifts of friendship. Theseus invited the Amazon who brought him the gifts to board his vessel, and when she had done so he put out to sea.

[27] This, at any rate, was the pretext for the Amazons' war, and it appears that the engagement was by no means paltry or womanish.[16]

Plutarch goes on to relate several more mythic stories about Theseus and his friend and companion Pirithous. These adventures take the intrepid pair to many distant parts of the earth and even down to Hades, the land of the dead. Theseus is brought back from that grim place by Heracles, but Pirithous remains stuck there forever.

[35] Theseus returned to Athens, where his friends had not yet been utterly overpowered. . . . Wishing to rule again as before, and to manage the state, he became embroiled in strife and troubles, finding that those who had hated him when he went away had now added fearlessness to their hatred.[17] He also saw that many of the common people had been corrupted, and that they preferred to be coaxed into following orders instead of doing so in silence. When he attempted to overpower his opponents by force, he was defeated by demagogues and factions, and finally, despairing of his political ambitions, sent his children away secretly to Euboea . . . while he himself, calling down curses on the Athenians at Gargettus, where even today there is a place called Araterion, "the place of cursing," sailed away to the island of Scyros, where the people were friendly to him, as he thought, and where he had ancestral estates.

Lycomedes was then king of Scyros. Theseus approached him, seeking to recover his estates, since he intended to settle there, though some say that he urged Lycomedes to lend him aid against

16. Plutarch here refers to an important episode in Athenian mythic history. The Amazons were thought to have entered the Greek world and besieged Athens in an effort to retrieve Antiope, and to have actually sacked parts of the city, until Theseus led a successful counterattack. The "Amazonomachy" scenes that can still be seen on several Greek temples commemorated this mythic war.

17. Plutarch casts the overthrow of Theseus as a political struggle rather than a dynastic one. Other writers make Menestheus, a royal rival who had occupied the throne while Theseus was away on his adventures, responsible for the coup.

the Athenians. But Lycomedes . . . led Theseus to the heights of the country (ostensibly to point out his property from there) and killed him, thrusting him down from the cliffs, though some say that Theseus slipped and fell by himself when taking his customary walk after dinner. In the immediate aftermath, no one took any account of his death. Menestheus[18] became king of the Athenians, and Theseus' sons joined Elephenor as private citizens on the expedition to Troy. But after Menestheus died there, they returned and recovered the sovereignty.

Much later, it occurred to the Athenians, for various reasons, to honor Theseus as a hero,[19] particularly because no small number of those who fought the Persians at Marathon[20] thought they saw an apparition of Theseus in arms, rushing ahead of them against the barbarians.

[36] After the Persian wars, during Phaedo's archonship,[21] the Pythian priestess advised the Athenians who consulted her to retrieve the bones of Theseus, deposit them honorably in their city, and keep watch over them. But owing to the harshness and inhospitality of the Dolopians, who inhabited the island, it was difficult to find his grave and get possession of his bones. When Cimon[22] had captured the island, as has been recorded in my account of his life, and was eager to find Theseus' grave, he spotted an eagle striking a mound-like place, as they say, and tearing up the ground with its beak and talons; and by some divine chance Cimon was inspired to dig there. The grave of a tall corpse was found; and a bronze shield and sword lay beside the body. When these were brought home by Cimon on his trireme, the delighted Athenians welcomed them with brilliant parades and sacrifices, just as if Theseus himself were returning to

18. See note 17.

19. The word "hero" here should be taken in its original Greek sense to mean a semidivine being whose gravesite receives cult worship.

20. For the battle of Marathon in 490 BCE, see *Aristides* 5 (in this volume) and Herodotus, *Histories* 6.102–24.

21. 476 or 475 BCE.

22. Cimon was the Athenian leader most in command of policy during the aftermath of the Persian wars (see *Cimon* in this volume). The return of Theseus' skeleton, or whatever bones were taken for it, was no doubt a huge boost to Cimon's political fortunes and provided a rallying point for Athenian national pride in the aftermath of the city's naval victories over the Persians.

the city. And today he lies buried in the middle of the city, near the present gymnasium, and his tomb is an asylum for household slaves and for all the lowly who fear the more powerful, since Theseus was a champion and protector of such men and responded generously to their appeals. They perform the most important sacrifice in his honor on the eighth of Pyanepsion, on which date he returned with his young comrades from Crete.

Lycurgus

Plutarch's Life of Lycurgus *is unique among the* Lives *in this collection, since it concerns a man about whom very little was known. Instead of a true biography, then, this* Life *is largely a record of Spartan laws and institutions, since Lycurgus, according to semimythic Greek traditions, devised these on his own sole authority. Perhaps there is truth behind these myths, and a lawgiver named Lycurgus did indeed reform the Spartan constitution in the eighth century BCE; modern historians are unsure. But Plutarch has used the legend as a hook on which to hang a portrait of classical Sparta—a society very much weakened and transformed in his own day but depicted here in more detail than in any contemporary source.*

According to Plutarch, Lycurgus was a member of one of Sparta's two royal families but was not in the direct line of succession. (From earliest times Sparta's governments had been headed by two kings who provided checks on one another's power; eventually they were further weakened by the oversight of public officials called ephors.) When one of the city's two thrones became vacant, Lycurgus briefly occupied it, but he willingly stepped down when he learned that his sister-in-law was pregnant with a more legitimate heir. Lycurgus then served as regent, wielding power on behalf of his infant nephew, but he came under suspicion (as most regents do) of wanting to rule in his own name. To allay these suspicions, Lycurgus chose to remove himself from Sparta by traveling abroad.

[4] Sailing away, Lycurgus traveled first to Crete. Studying the forms of government there, and becoming acquainted with the most reputable men, he admired and adopted some of their laws, intending to carry them home with him and put them into effect. . . . From Crete Lycurgus sailed to Asia, where he reportedly wished to compare the extravagance and luxury of Ionia with the Cretan way of life, which was frugal and austere, just as a doctor compares unsound and diseased bodies with healthy ones.[1] . . . The Egyptians think that Lycurgus also visited *them*, and that as he particularly admired the separation of their soldiery from the other classes of society,[2] he

---

1. This is the first of many metaphors in which Plutarch compares Lycurgus to a doctor curing a patient. Greek writers often equated social ills, in particular luxuriousness, with disease.

2. In contrast to modern nation-states, most Greek city-states did not have professional soldiers or standing armies but instead drafted ordinary citizens for limited periods of time or when a conflict required their service. Sparta

carried that practice back to Sparta, and by excluding the craftsmen and artisans from participation he made his polity truly refined and pure. Some of the Greek writers confirm the Egyptians' claims.

[5] The Spartans yearned for Lycurgus when he was away, and sent for him often, in the belief that their kings, despite their renown and eminence, were really no different from most people, whereas Lycurgus possessed a natural talent for command and an ability to lead. And the kings were not averse to having him at home, but hoped that in his presence the people would treat them with less insolence. Accordingly, upon returning to citizens so well-disposed to him, he at once tried to alter existing conditions and change the form of government, thinking there was no point or advantage in changing the laws one by one, but that he must act as a doctor would with a patient who was ill and afflicted with all sorts of diseases, lowering and changing the existing temperature by means of drugs and purges, and instituting a new and different regimen. . . .

Lycurgus tried to enlist the best men and encouraged them to help him, explaining his undertaking first to his friends, and then little by little engaging others and uniting them to put his program into effect. When the critical moment came, he ordered thirty of them to take up arms, go to the marketplace at dawn, and strike fear and astonishment into their opponents.[3] . . . Among Lycurgus' many innovations, the first and most important was the establishment of the council of elders,[4] which, as Plato says, by being combined with the inflamed rule of the kings,[5] and by having an equal vote with them in the most important matters, produced stability and moderation. For

---

was the first and, for a long time, the only Greek state to maintain what we would call career soldiers.

3. Even a divinely inspired sage such as Lycurgus, in Plutarch's view, needed armed force behind him in order to effect dramatic social change.

4. The Greek word translated as "council of elders" is *gerousia*, the name of an essential organ of the Spartan government. The *gerousia* consisted of twenty-eight men over the age of sixty, chosen by the citizens' assembly (see chapter 6) from a small group of noble families and serving for life. They formed both a kind of Spartan supreme court as well as a steering and governing body for the assembly. Since they had the power both to try the kings for abuses and to negate acts of the assembly, Plutarch regards them as a moderating force between the two extremes of autocracy and mob rule.

5. Continuing the medical metaphor of the previous paragraph, Plutarch speaks of the Spartan kingship as though it were an infected wound in want of cleansing.

the polity had veered between tyranny and democracy, inclining now to the kings, now to the multitude. But now, by making the council of elders a central weight, like a ship's ballast, which always provides equilibrium, the state achieved the safest arrangement and order, the twenty-eight elders always taking the kings' side against democracy, but at the same time strengthening the people to resist encroaching tyranny. The number of elders was established at twenty-eight.

[6] So eager was Lycurgus to establish this government that he brought from Delphi a prophecy about it, which they call a *rhetra*.[6] It runs thus: "Once you have erected a shrine of Zeus Syllanius and Athena Syllania, divided the people into classes and subclasses, established a council of thirty elders with the help of the leaders,[7] hold an assembly of the people from time to time between Babyca and Cnacion, where you will introduce and rescind motions; but the people must have the deciding voice and power." . . . The Babyca is today called Cheimarrus, and the Cnacion Oernus. . . . Between these two places the Spartans held their assemblies, though there were no porticoes or any other sort of building. For Lycurgus thought that such things did nothing to enhance soundness of judgment, but rather undermined it by filling the minds of the assembled citizens with foolish and frivolous thoughts as they sat gazing steadfastly at statues and paintings, theatrical backdrops, or the elaborately constructed roofs of council chambers.

When the people had assembled, none of them was permitted to make a motion, though the assembly had the authority to decide for or against a motion proposed by the elders and the kings. Later on, however, when by subtractions and additions the people warped and distorted the motions, Kings Polydorus and Theopompus[8] subjoined

6. The Greek term *rhetra* here is left untranslated because there is no good English equivalent; it signifies a law or decree given in spoken rather than written form. Wherever this *rhetra* originated (probably it was not in fact generated by the oracle of Apollo at Delphi, though it was in Lycurgus' interest to make it appear so), it represents the oldest known constitutional document in the Greek world. It also contains the oldest establishment of a sovereign people's assembly, with the power to pass motions put to it by the kings. Historians often refer to it as the Great Rhetra.

7. The "leaders" are *archēgetai* in Greek, one of several obscure and antiquated terms used in this *rhetra*. In context, it must refer to the two Spartan kings, as Plutarch clarifies below.

8. Their reigns probably fell in the early seventh century BCE, about a century after the time assumed for Lycurgus.

the following clause to the *rhetra*: "But if the people adopt a crooked measure, the elders and leaders have the power to dissolve an assembly," meaning that the elders and kings should not ratify the measure, but should simply dismiss and dissolve the assembly if the people were distorting and altering the motion contrary to the city's best interests.[9]

[7] Though Lycurgus thus tempered his commonwealth, the men who came after him, seeing the oligarchy still "untempered and fierce," as Plato says, "imposed the power of the ephors upon it as a curb."[10] Roughly 130 years after Lycurgus, the first ephors[11]— Elatus and his colleagues—were appointed during the reign of Theopompus. It is said that Theopompus was reproached by his wife because the royal power, when he handed it over to his sons, would be weaker than when he received it, to which he replied, "On the contrary, stronger, since it will last longer." For in fact, by throwing off its excesses and jealousies, the Spartan sovereignty escaped danger, and consequently the Spartan kings did not suffer the fate that the Messenians and Argives inflicted on *their* kings,[12] who were unwilling to yield in any way or to relax their power for the people's benefit.

[8] Lycurgus' second and extremely bold political measure was his redistribution of the land. For there was a terrible disparity in this regard, since many propertyless and poor people were becoming a burden to the city, and wealth was flowing wholly to a few. Aiming to rid the polity of violence, envy, malice, and luxury, and the more longstanding and graver afflictions, namely wealth and poverty, Lycurgus persuaded the people to pool all their territory and let a new distribution be made, and to live together on an equal footing, each man possessing equal means of subsistence and seeking preeminence on the basis of virtue alone, it being assumed that there was no other difference or inequality between one man and the next

9. This serious limitation on the power of the assembly probably came in response to some policy error or military reverse, possibly during the Messenian wars that dominated the later part of the eighth century BCE.

10. *Laws* 692a.

11. Sparta had five ephors elected annually by the people's assembly. The ephors served as a check on the kings, against whom they were empowered to bring charges. No one could hold the office of ephor more than once.

12. Argos and Messenia, territories neighboring Sparta, did away with their monarchies during the Archaic Age.

than that which was established by blame for shameful actions and praise for honorable ones.

Acting on his proposal, he distributed the rest of the Laconian territory to the "free inhabitants," in thirty thousand lots, and divided the share belonging to the city of Sparta into nine thousand lots, as that was the number of Spartan citizens. . . . Each man's lot was of a size to produce seventy bushels of wheat for a man, and twelve for his wife, and a proportionate quantity of liquid measures. For he thought that a lot of that size would suffice them, since they needed sustenance enough to maintain vigor and health, and nothing else.

[9] When he tried to divide up their movable property as well, so that inequity and inequality might be eliminated, he saw that the people balked at its outright confiscation. He therefore took a different course and attacked greed by enacting political measures. First, after canceling the value of all gold and silver currency, he ordered the citizens to use iron exclusively. Then he assigned a very small value to a bulky, weighty mass of it, so that the iron equivalent of ten minas[13] required a large storeroom at home and a yoke of oxen if it were to be transported. When this law went into effect, many sorts of wrongdoing disappeared from Lacedaemon. For who was likely to steal, or take as a bribe, or rob, or plunder a thing that could neither be hidden, nor creditably possessed, nor was even of value when cut in pieces? For it is said that by quenching the red-hot iron with vinegar Lycurgus spoiled it for any other purpose, since it became brittle and could not be worked.

He then rid the city of useless and superfluous crafts and manufacture. Most of these crafts would probably have disappeared along with the common coinage even if no one had outlawed them, since their products could not be sold. For the Spartans could not carry their iron money to other parts of Greece, and it had no value there; indeed, it was even ridiculed. And consequently the Spartans could not purchase any foreign goods or small wares, and no merchant shipped cargo into Spartan harbors. No sophist set foot on Laconian[14] soil, no vagabond soothsayer, no keeper of prostitutes, no fashioner of gold or silver ornaments, since there was no money there.

13. Ten minas equaled about 1,000 drachmas, or a sixth of a talent. The daily wage of a well-off Athenian in the Classical Age was about a drachma, so ten minas would be the equivalent of about three years' decent salary.
14. Laconia was the region surrounding Sparta.

[10] With the intention of further attacking luxuriousness and undermining the zeal for wealth, he introduced his third and noblest political measure, namely the institution of public meals, so that the citizens might eat together in companies, consuming a fixed menu of meats and grains, and not spend their time reclining on couches at extravagant tables, growing fat by night at the hands of servants and chefs, like gluttonous animals, and ruining their bodies along with their characters by devoting the former entirely to appetite and satiety, which require prolonged naps, warm baths, extended idleness, and, in some sense, daily nursing. This was indeed a great achievement, but even greater was his making wealth "an object of no desire," as Theophrastus[15] says, and even creating "freedom from wealth" by their communal meals and the frugality of their way of life.

[11] They say it was because of this political measure that the well-to-do were harshly disposed to Lycurgus. Banding together against him, they assailed him with angry shouts and cries; and at last, pelted with stones, he was forced to run from the marketplace. He fled to the temple ahead of all the others except Alcander, a youth by no means without ability, but hasty and passionate, who pursued and attacked him. When Lycurgus turned around, Alcander struck him with a cane and put out his eye. Lycurgus, however, undaunted by the accident, confronted his fellow citizens, showing them his face stained with blood and his sight destroyed. And they were so overcome with shame and sorrow at the sight that they delivered Alcander into his hands and escorted him to his house, all of them indignant on his behalf. Commending his fellow citizens for their conduct, Lycurgus dismissed them, but brought Alcander inside. There he did the boy no harm by word or deed, but after sending away his familiar servants and attendants, ordered Alcander to minister to his needs. The young man, who was not ill-bred, performed his duties in silence. Abiding with Lycurgus and sharing his daily life, and coming to understand the gentleness and serenity of his soul, the austerity of his way of life, and the dauntlessness he brought to his labors, Alcander grew deeply devoted to him and told his acquaintances and friends that the man was not harsh or willful, as he had supposed, but the mildest and gentlest character in the world.

[12] The Cretans call their common meals "mens' table," while the Spartans call it "meager table.". . . Each [Spartan] table group included roughly fifteen men. Each member would contribute a

---

15. A philosopher and scientist of the fourth century BCE.

bushel of barley meal each month, eight measures of wine, five minas of cheese, five half-minas of figs, and, in addition to these items, some very small sum of money for the purchase of fish or other relish. Besides this, a member who had performed a sacrifice would send along first-fruits,[16] and one who had gone hunting would send a portion to the common mess. For a man who had sacrificed or had returned late from hunting was permitted to dine at home, but all the others had to attend the mess. . . . Boys, too, used to visit the common messes, as if they were attending schools of self-discipline. They would listen to political discussions and observe men who could teach them how a freeborn man conducts himself. . . . Of their dishes, the most famous is their black broth. Their older men do not even ask for a slice of meat; they leave the meat for the young men, and dine only on the broth. . . . After drinking moderately, they depart without a torch. For the Spartans are not allowed to walk with a light, on this or any other occasion, so that they may accustom themselves to marching boldly and fearlessly at night. Such is the fashion of their common messes.

[13] Lycurgus did not commit his laws to writing, and in fact one of the *rhetras* forbids it. . . . Another was directed against extravagance. It required that every house have a roof fashioned by the axe, and doors by the saw only, and no other tool. . . . A third *rhetra* of Lycurgus . . . discourages the people from frequently waging war against the same enemies, lest the latter, becoming accustomed to defending themselves often, become skilled warriors. It was chiefly on this ground that they later denounced Agesilaus, their king, who by launching prolonged and frequent invasions and campaigns against Boeotia made the Thebans a match in battle for the Spartans. That was why, when Agesilaus had been wounded, Antalcidas said to him, "You are certainly receiving handsome tuition fees from the Thebans, having taught them to fight despite their reluctance and ignorance."[17]

[14] When it came to education, which he considered to be the greatest and noblest task of the lawgiver, Lycurgus began so far back as to regulate all that concerned marriages and births. . . . He saw to it that the girls took physical exercise—in races, wrestling, and

16. The best portion of the sacrificial offering was rendered first.
17. See *Agesilaus* 26 in this volume. Agesilaus, a Spartan king of the late fifth and early fourth centuries BCE, led numerous campaigns against Thebes.

hurling the discus and javelin—so that their embryos, implanted firmly in firm bodies, might develop more healthily, and so that the women themselves, enduring their pregnancies with fortitude, might struggle successfully and easily with the pains of childbirth. . . . The baring of the girls' bodies involved nothing shameful, since modesty attended them, and wantonness was dispelled.[18] On the contrary, it implanted habits of simplicity and a zeal for bodily vigor, and gave womankind a taste of noble high-mindedness, since they were participating no less than the men in the pursuit of excellence and honor. And this was why their women were moved to speak and think in the manner attributed to Gorgo, the wife of Leonidas. For it seems that when some foreign woman said to her, "You women of Sparta are the only ones who rule their men," Gorgo replied, "Yes, since we alone give birth to men."

[15] These measures were also intended to foster marriage—I mean the young women's processions, their disrobing, and the fact that their contests were attended by the young men, who were drawn there, as Plato says, "not by geometric, but by erotic necessity."[19] Moreover, Lycurgus imposed a certain dishonor on those who did not marry. For these persons were barred from viewing the gymnastic exercises, and in winter they were commanded by the magistrates to go around the marketplace in a circle, lightly clad and singing a song about bachelors to the effect that they were justly punished for disobeying the laws. . . .

The Spartans married by abducting their brides, who were not small and immature, but in their full bloom and ripeness. When the bride had been carried off, her so-called bridesmaid received her, cropped her hair short all around, dressed her in a man's cloak and sandals, and laid her down on a pallet, alone in the dark. Then the groom, not drunk or even tipsy, but sober after dining as usual in the common mess, stole in, loosened her maiden girdle, raised her in his arms, and carried her to the bed. After spending very little time with her, he departed discreetly to his usual quarters, to sleep among the other young men. And so he continued to do from then on. Spending his days with his age-mates and sleeping among them, he would visit

18. Spartans were famous among other Greeks for being unembarrassed by nakedness; see, for example, Thucydides, *The Peloponnesian War* 1.6.
19. *Republic* 458d, in a description of the life of the guardians, the elite warrior class of the ideal state. Plato fashioned the upbringing and social customs of the guardians after those of the Spartans.

his bride cautiously and in secret, ashamed and fearful lest anyone indoors notice him. And likewise his bride would conspire with him to arrange opportune times when they could meet without being detected. . . . Such a sexual life not only fostered self-restraint and moderation, but brought husbands and wives to their union when their bodies were healthy and vigorous and their affections fresh and new, rather than sated or exhausted by unrestrained intercourse, and kept alive a spark of desire and mutual delight.

Having given marriage such a modest and orderly character, Lycurgus nonetheless abolished vain and womanish jealousy by making it honorable, while keeping marriage free of all promiscuity, for worthy men to share their wives for the purpose of begetting children; and he ridiculed those who consider such sharing intolerable and resort to murders and wars rather than consent to it. . . . For, in the first place, Lycurgus did not regard children as the property of their fathers, but rather of the commonwealth, and therefore would not have his citizens produced by random couplings, but by the best that could be arranged.[20]

[16] It was not for the father to decide whether the child was reared. He had to carry it to a place called Lesche, where the elders of the tribes would conduct a careful examination of the newborn. If it was sturdy and strong, they ordered the father to rear it, and allotted it one of the nine thousand parcels of land. If it was unsound and ill-shaped, they would send it away to the so-called Apothetae, a pitlike place near Mount Taygetus, in the belief that a life not endowed by nature at the outset with health and vigor was of no advantage either to the child itself or to the city. And for the same reason, the women used to bathe their newborns not with water, but with wine, as a way of testing their constitutions. For it is said that epileptic and sickly infants are thrown into convulsions by the unmixed wine[21] and lose consciousness, while healthy ones, on the contrary, are steeled and strengthened by it. . . .

But Lycurgus would not entrust the children of Spartans to purchased or hired tutors,[22] nor was each father permitted to rear and

20. Further points on which the life of the Spartans served as a model for the guardians of Plato's ideal state in the *Republic*.
21. Ancient wine was very strong and was usually mixed with water before being drunk.
22. *Paidagogoi* or "child minders," usually slaves, would look after the sons of well-off citizens in other Greek cities.

educate his son as he liked. Instead, as soon as the children were seven years old, Lycurgus ordered that they be taken and enrolled in companies, where they lived under the same discipline and nurture and grew accustomed to studying and playing together. The boy who excelled in judgment and warlike spirit was made captain of his company, and the others would look up to him, obey his orders, and submit to his punishments, with the result that their education was a training in obedience. The elders would observe the boys as they played, and by frequently involving them in battles and competitions, gained accurate knowledge as to which boy would endure, and which would shirk in their contests.[23]

The children learned to read and write only for practical purposes.[24] All the rest of their education was intended to make them obey commands, endure hardship, and prevail in battle. That was why, as time went on, they increased the boys' training, cut their hair short, and accustomed them to going barefoot and playing for the most part without clothes. After the age of twelve, they were no longer given tunics to wear, received one cloak a year, and had hard, dry bodies and little experience of bathing and unguents;[25] they indulged in such amenities only on certain days of the year. They slept together, in companies and bands, on beds that they collected for themselves, breaking off by hand, without an iron tool, the tops of the rushes that grew by the Eurotas.[26]

[17] When the boys reached this age, reputable youths consorted with them as lovers.[27] The older men also kept an eye on them, coming more often to the gymnasia and observing their contests of strength and wit, not casually, but with the idea that all of them were in some sense the fathers, tutors, and governors of all the boys.

23. Further points that inspired Plato when he was composing the *Republic*, though in that work's scheme, children are examined by judges at a much younger age, to determine which belong to the silver class and which to the bronze.

24. Presumably the main purpose a Spartan would have for letters was to send and receive military orders.

25. Most Greek men used olive oil to cleanse and soften the skin.

26. A river in the vicinity of Sparta.

27. Xenophon, who himself spent much time in Sparta and had his two sons educated there, contradicts Plutarch on this point, claiming that Lycurgus banned all homosexuality among males and made it equivalent to incest. But Xenophon also admits that few Greeks of his time believed this (*Constitution of the Spartans* 2.12–14).

And thus, on every occasion and in every place a boy who erred had someone to correct and chastise him. Moreover, a supervisor of their education was appointed from among the noblest citizens, and the boys themselves always chose as leaders of their bands the most prudent and warlike of the so-called *eirens*. (The young men who are two years past boyhood are called *eirens;* the senior boys are called *melleirens*.) Now the *eiren*, at twenty years of age, commands his charges in their war games, and at home makes them serve at table. He orders the stout ones to fetch wood, the smaller ones vegetables. And they fetch by stealing, some going to the orchards, others slipping into the men's common messes very craftily and cautiously; for if a boy is caught he receives many lashes with the whip for being an inept and careless thief. The boys also steal whatever food they can and learn to be adept at taking advantage of people who are sleeping or keeping careless watch. For the boy who is caught is punished with a beating and by having to go hungry. Their meals are meager, in order that the boys may exert themselves to stave off hunger and thus be forced to become bold and intrepid.

[18] The boys took their thieving so seriously that one of them, who had stolen a fox's whelp and was hiding it under his threadbare cloak, and whose belly was being torn by the animal's claws and teeth, is said to have endured—and died—in order to escape detection. And one may well believe it, judging by the Spartan youths of our own day, many of whom we have seen dying under the lash at the altar of Orthia.

The *eiren*, reclining after supper, would order one of the boys to sing, and would ask another a question requiring a clever answer, as, for example, "Who is the noblest among our citizens?" or "What do you think of his conduct?" By this practice the boys were accustomed to judge soundly and to be interested, from an early age, in their fellow citizens. For if, when asked who was a good citizen, or who a disreputable one, the boy was at a loss to answer, the Spartans considered it the sign of a sluggish mind, and one that did not aspire to moral excellence. And the boy's answer, which had to include a reason and a proof, also had to be expressed briefly and concisely. As punishment for an inadequate answer, the boy was bitten on the thumb by the *eiren*. . . . Lovers shared in their beloved's reputation, for good or ill, and it is even reported that on one occasion the lover of a boy who, while fighting, let out an ignoble cry, was fined by the magistrates. Being in love with the young was so approved among them that even the most respectable women fell in love with young girls.

[19] The boys were trained to develop a speaking style in which pungency was combined with grace, and acute insights were tersely expressed.[28]

[21] Training in song and lyric poetry was assigned as much importance as the cultivation of a speaking style that was correct and pure. And their songs had the capacity to stir the spirit and rouse impulses both enthusiastic and energetic.[29] . . . Pindar declares that the Spartans were highly musical and at the same time highly warlike;

For swordsmanship vies with exquisite harp-playing,

as their poet[30] has said. For just before their battles their king offered sacrifices in honor of the Muses, reminding his warriors, as it seems, of their training and their firm resolves, so that they might be ready to face the worst and perform soldierly deeds worthy of some record.

[22] In time of war, too, they also relaxed the rigor of the young men's training, and no one hindered the soldiers from adorning their hair and attending to the good order of their weapons and cloaks, rejoicing to see them, like horses, prancing and neighing eagerly before their races. That was why, as soon as Spartans reached manhood, they let their hair grow, and would take care, especially in times of danger, that their hair appear sleek and well-parted,[31] recalling Lycurgus' remark about hair, that it makes the handsome appear even more distinguished, the ugly more fearsome. They trained more lightly during their campaigns, and in other respects their daily routines were less restrictive, and the young men themselves were less likely to be called to account for their conduct. And thus these were the only men for whom war itself brought a respite from the training for war. Once their phalanx[32] had been drawn up and the enemy was

28. Numerous anecdotes attest to the Spartan dislike of excess verbiage; see, for example, Herodotus, *Histories* 3.46. Today the English adjective "laconic," based on the place-name Laconia (the region around Sparta), refers to this quality.

29. The verses of Tyrtaeus and Alcman, the best-preserved Spartan poets, deal principally with martial themes.

30. Alcman, a lyric poet of the seventh century BCE.

31. See Herodotus 7.208, the episode of the last stand of the Spartan 300, for a famous instance.

32. The phalanx was the standard formation of Greek infantry warfare throughout the Archaic and Classical Ages. Armed warriors, called hoplites, formed a cohesive unit by standing together in rows and files. In this

at hand, the king sacrificed the she-goat,[33] commanded everyone to
don garlands, and ordered the pipers to play the song of Castor;[34]
then he himself began the marching paean, and it was a vision both
awesome and striking when they marched onward to the rhythm
of the flute, keeping their phalanx compact, their souls untroubled,
and their spirits mild and merry as they moved with the music into
deadly combat.

[24] The training of the Spartans continued into their mature
years. For no one was permitted to live as he liked; in their city,
as in a camp, they had an organized routine and civic duties, the
citizens thinking that they belonged not to themselves but to their
country. And if no other duty was assigned to them they spent their
time looking after the children, teaching them something useful, or
receiving instruction themselves from their elders. And indeed one
of the noble and blessed things Lycurgus gave his fellow citizens was
their abundant leisure, since they were not allowed to engage in any
base manufacture whatsoever, and there was no need for moneymaking, with its toilsome amassing and busyness, since wealth no longer
excited envy or honor. The helots worked their land, paying them
the appointed produce.[35] When a Spartan visiting Athens while the
courts were in session learned that a certain Athenian had been fined
for idleness and was being escorted home by his dismayed friends and
receiving their consolation, the Spartan asked the bystanders to point
out to him who it was that had been fined for living like a free man.
So slavish did the Spartans deem the lack of leisure associated with
manufacture and moneymaking. Lawsuits, as it seems, completely
disappeared along with coinage, since instead of greed or want, there
was equality, ease, and leisure based on thrift. Whenever they were

---

way they could lock shields together to form a nearly impenetrable barrier
against the enemy.

33. Evidently a customary prebattle ritual.

34. Castor and Pollux, twins also known as the Dioscuri, were thought to
be native Spartan deities.

35. An important point, though it is raised for the first time only here.
The helots were Greeks from the province of Messenia, an agriculturally
rich territory adjoining that of the Spartans. After the Spartans conquered
the Messenians in a series of wars, they reduced the native population to
the status of forced agricultural labor. The helots raised food on their own
land but were required to donate most of their produce to the Spartan state.
Only in this way was the Spartan military system, which required full-time
training and drill of male citizens, able to function.

not on campaign, all their time was occupied in dancing, good cheer, feasting, and activities associated with hunting, physical exercise, and conversation.

[25] In general Lycurgus accustomed the citizens neither to desire nor even know how to live for themselves. Instead, like bees that are naturally communal and constantly swarm together around their ruler, the citizens of Sparta, practically ecstatic in their enthusiasm and public spirit, belonged wholly to their country.

[26] The elders[36] were at first appointed by Lycurgus himself, as has been mentioned, from among those who shared his counsels. Later he arranged for any vacancy arising from an elder's death to be filled by the man over the age of sixty who had been judged worthiest. . . . The election was carried out in the following way. When an assembly was held, selected men were confined in a little room nearby. Out of sight, and unable to see, they merely heard the shout sent up by the assembled citizens. For as in other competitions, the contestants were judged by acclamation. The candidates were not introduced all together, but each man, chosen by lot, was brought in and made his way in silence through the assembly. The confined men, who had small tablets, distinguished in each instance the loudness of the shout that went up, without knowing for whom it was raised; they knew only the place in the sequence—first, second, third, and so on—of those being introduced. They publicly announced the election of the man for whom the loudest and most thunderous shout was raised. After placing a wreath upon his own head, the victor visited the temples of the gods, escorted by many young men, who congratulated and exalted him, and many women, who sang the good man's praises and called his life blessed.

[27] And Lycurgus filled the city with good examples, whose constant presence and society necessarily exerted a formative influence on those who were walking the path of honor. That was why he did not give his permission when citizens wished to travel abroad and wander in foreign lands, where they might adopt foreign ways and imitate the lives of uneducated peoples who lived under alien forms of government. He even expelled those who streamed into the city and congregated for no useful purpose, not because he feared that they would become imitators of his constitution and learn useful lessons about virtue, as Thucydides says, but rather so that they might not become teachers of anything base. For foreign persons are necessarily

36. See chapter 5 and note 4.

accompanied by foreign ideas; and novel ideas bring novel decisions, with the result that many attitudes and points of view come into being that mar the harmony of the established political order. He therefore thought it more necessary to prevent bad habits from entering and filling the city than it was to keep out infectious diseases.

[28] The so-called secret service[37] of the Spartans, if it is one of Lycurgus' political measures, . . . functioned as follows. From time to time the magistrates would send their brightest young men into the countryside, providing them with daggers and necessary food, but nothing else. During the day, the youths would scatter to unseen places, conceal themselves, and sleep. But at night, coming down to the roads, they would cut the throat of any helot they caught. Often they would even go into the fields and kill the strongest and most powerful of them. And Thucydides, in his *Peloponnesian War*,[38] reports that the helots whom the Spartans had judged to be conspicuously brave decked their heads with garlands to show that they had been freed, and visited the temples of the gods; but shortly afterward they all vanished—more than two thousand men—and neither then nor later could anyone say how they had been slain. And Aristotle in particular adds that the ephors, when they first entered office,[39] declared war on the helots, so that it might be lawful to kill them.

They treated the helots harshly and cruelly in other ways as well. After forcing them to drink too much unmixed wine, they would admit them into the common messes in order to show the young men what it was to be drunk. They would also order the helots to sing songs and dance dances that were ignoble and ridiculous, but would not allow them to perform the nobler kind. . . . But I presume that such instances of harshness occurred later among the Spartans, particularly after the great earthquake,[40] during which the helots and Messenians are said to have jointly attacked the Spartans, devastated the countryside, and placed the city in the gravest danger.

[29] Lycurgus convened everyone in the assembly and said that everything else was progressing fairly and adequately with regard to the city's prosperity and virtue, but that there was one matter of great

37. The Greek word, *krypteia*, literally means "hidden things."
38. 4.80.
39. That is, once each year.
40. In 464 BCE much of Sparta was destroyed by an earthquake, and the helots used the opportunity to launch a revolt; see *Cimon* 16 in this volume, and Thucydides 1.101–2.

importance that he could not reveal to them until he had consulted the god. Accordingly, they must abide by the established laws and not alter or change them until he himself returned from Delphi, at which time he would do whatever the god thought best. When they had agreed to everything and urged him to set off, and he had received sworn promises from the kings, the elders, and all the other citizens that they would uphold and make use of the established constitution "until Lycurgus returned," he departed for Delphi.

When he had arrived at the oracle and sacrificed to the god, he asked whether the laws he had established were sound, and sufficient to ensure the city's prosperity and virtue. When the god replied that the laws were sound, and that the city would continue to be held in the highest esteem while it used the constitution of Lycurgus, he had the prophecy written down and sent to Sparta. And when he had again sacrificed to the god, and had embraced his friends and his son, he decided not to release his fellow citizens from their oath, but to freely end his life there, having reached an age when one might live longer or not, according to one's preference, and when his family and dependents appeared to be prospering sufficiently. Accordingly, he ended his life by abstaining from food, thinking that the death of a statesman should not be a private matter; that the end of his life need not be ineffectual, but might serve as an example of virtue. For his own part, since he had brought the noblest tasks to fulfillment, the end of life would be a consummation of his happiness, while for his fellow citizens it would be a guardian of the blessings he had secured for them during his lifetime, since they had sworn to use his constitution until he returned. And his calculations did not prove false; for the city held first place in Greece for good order and renown, abiding for five hundred years by Lycurgus' laws.

[30] When Agis was king,[41] gold and silver began to flow into Sparta; and with the introduction of money, greed and a zeal for wealth prevailed thanks to Lysander,[42] who, though not corruptible himself, filled his native land with love of wealth and luxuriousness by bringing back gold and silver from the war,[43] thereby undermining the laws of Lycurgus. But while these remained in effect, Sparta had the character not of a city systematically governed, but of a wise

41. The end of the fifth century BCE, the era in which Sparta had to rely on Persian funds to build and staff a navy for its war against Athens.
42. See *Lysander* in this volume.
43. The Peloponnesian War, between Athens and Sparta (431–404 BCE).

and disciplined individual; or rather, just as the poets say of Heracles that with only his club and lion's skin he traveled the world punishing the lawless and savage tyrants, so the city of Sparta, with only a staff and threadbare cloak, ruled over a Greece ready and willing to be so ruled, deposing the unjust dynasties and tyrannies in her various states, acting as a mediator in wars, and bringing civil strife to an end, often without putting a single spear in motion, but merely by sending one ambassador, whose orders everyone instantly obeyed, just as bees, when their ruler appears, swarm to him and array themselves in order. To such a degree did the city's good order and just dealing inspire respect.

[31] But it was not Lycurgus' chief purpose then to leave his city in command of a great many others; he thought rather that the happiness of an entire city, like that of an individual, depends on moral excellence and inner harmony. His aim, therefore, in all his arrangements, was to make his fellow citizens free-minded, self-sufficient, and self-controlled, and keep them so for as long as possible. For Plato took this to be the purpose of Lycurgus' form of government, as did Diogenes and Zeno and all who are praised for their treatises on these matters,[44] though these men left behind them only letters and speeches. But Lycurgus, because he produced not letters and speeches but an inimitable polity, and because he gave to those who assume that the so-called disposition to wisdom is imaginary an example of an entire city in love with wisdom, has fairly surpassed in renown all who have ever created polities among the Greeks. And that is why Aristotle says that Lycurgus obtained fewer honors than he deserved in Lacedaemon, though he enjoys the highest. For there is a shrine in his honor, and they sacrifice there every year as to a god.[45]

---

44. All three of these philosophers wrote treatises describing the ideal composition of a Greek city-state. Diogenes and Zeno both lived slightly later than Plato, in the late fourth century BCE; Diogenes belonged to the Cynic school of philosophy, whereas Zeno is considered the founder of Stoicism.
45. Herodotus 1.66.

Solon

Solon's political career at Athens, in the first decades of the sixth century BCE, falls much later than that of Lycurgus at Sparta. Athens already had written laws and a highly developed constitution in Solon's time, but these had ceased to function well as a result of economic and social strains in the evolving city. Solon was called upon to fix these problems, and should thus be seen as a political reformer rather than, as Lycurgus was (if he in fact existed), a true lawgiver.

Although Solon (c. 640–560) apparently possessed moderate wealth and came from a noble family, he rose to political prominence, to judge by Plutarch, on his reputation for wisdom and fairness. These qualities certainly shine through in his preserved poems (many of which are known only from quotations in this Life*), and also in the unforgettable portrait painted by Herodotus near the outset of his* Histories *(1.29–33). The Greeks classed Solon among the Seven Wise Men, the great sages of the archaic world.*

[2] Because Solon's father, as Hermippus[1] tells us, had depleted his estate by various philanthropic projects and charities, Solon would not have lacked persons willing to assist him. But since he was ashamed to accept help (belonging as he did to a family that had been accustomed to helping others), he embarked, when still a young man, on a career in trade. Yet some say that Solon traveled more for the sake of wide experience and knowledge than for profit, since by common consent he was a lover of wisdom; for even when he was elderly he would say that he "grew older each day, and learnt something new." And he did not admire wealth. He even said that the two men were equally wealthy, both the man

> who has plenty of silver
> And gold and plains of wheat-bearing land,
> Horses and mules, and he who possesses the mere comforts
> Of food, clothing, and shoes,
> Delight in his child and wife, when these blessings come,
> And a suitable span of years in which to enjoy them.[2]

---

1. One of many writers now lost whom Plutarch consulted. Hermippus of Smyrna was a Greek biographer of the third century BCE.

2. The verses are Solon's own composition. Solon was a poet as well as a political leader.

[3] That he classed himself among the poor rather than the wealthy is evident from these verses:[3]

> Many of the wicked are rich, while the good are often in need;
> But we shall not exchange our virtue for their riches,
> Since virtue endures, while wealth is always changing hands.

At first Solon assigned no importance to his poetry; he seems to have treated it as an amusement and a diversion for his leisure hours. Later, however, he put his philosophical views into verse, and incorporated many of his political ideas in his poems, not simply to record and preserve them, but because they contained justifications of his acts, and occasional exhortations, warnings, and rebukes for the Athenians.

[8] When the Athenians had worn themselves out fighting a long and difficult war with the Megarians over the island of Salamis,[4] they passed a law forbidding anyone, on pain of death, to write or say that the city should lay claim to Salamis. Indignant at the disgrace, and seeing that many of the young men wanted someone to start the war, but lacked the confidence to initiate anything themselves because of the law, Solon pretended to be out of his mind, and a rumor spread from his household to the city that he was showing symptoms of insanity. After secretly composing an elegy and practicing it so that he could recite it from memory, he rushed out suddenly to the marketplace with a cap on his head. When a large crowd had assembled, he mounted the herald's stone and recited the elegy that begins,

> As a herald come I from lovely Salamis,
> With a stately song in place of a rant.

This is the poem "Salamis," an utterly charming composition of one hundred lines. When the ode had been chanted and Solon's friends had begun to sing its praises, and Pisistratus in particular was cheering the citizens on and urging them to be persuaded by Solon's words, they repealed the law and resumed the war under Solon's command.

[11] In the aftermath of these events, Solon grew famous and powerful.

---

3. Plutarch says only that Solon claimed to be poor, not that he actually was so. In chapter 14 Plutarch mentions that he was in fact prosperous.

4. Lying in the Saronic Gulf between Attica and the Peloponnese (see Map: The Greek World), Salamis was contested by cities on both shores.

[12] The curse of Cylon[5] had for a long time perturbed the city, ever since the archon Megacles[6] had persuaded Cylon and his confederates, who had approached the goddess Athena as suppliants, to come down and stand trial. These men fastened a linen thread to her statue and clung to it.[7] But when they reached the temple of the Furies on their way down, and the thread spontaneously broke, Megacles and his colleagues rushed to arrest the suppliants, claiming that the goddess was rejecting their prayers. Some of the band were stoned to death outside the precinct, and those who fled for refuge to the altars had their throats cut. Only those who appealed to the archons' wives were set free. Thereafter the archons, who were called "the accursed," were hated. And when the survivors of Cylon and his confederates again became powerful, they continued to quarrel with the descendants of Megacles.[8]

When the current civil strife had become severe and the citizens had taken sides, Solon, who was now held in esteem, stepped in with the noblest of the Athenians, and by entreating and enjoining "the accursed" persuaded them to stand trial and accept the verdict of three hundred jurors of noble birth. Prosecuted by Myron of Phlya, the men were convicted. The living were banished, and the corpses of the dead were dug up and thrown beyond the city limits.[9]

[13] When the disturbance caused by Cylon had been brought to an end and "the accursed," as has been noted, had departed, the Athenians resumed their age-old quarrel about their form of government, the city being split into as many factions as there were

5. About 636 BCE, Cylon, an Athenian nobleman, tried to take over Athens by force and establish himself as sole ruler. He and some supporters seized the Acropolis, but after popular support failed to materialize, Cylon found himself besieged. The subsequent events are related by Plutarch. Thucydides' *Peloponnesian War* gives a slightly different account of the episode at 1.126.

6. An archon is an Athenian magistrate. Megacles, the grandfather of a more famous man also named Megacles, was a member of the Alcmaeonid family, the wealthy, politically active clan that later included Cleisthenes and Pericles.

7. Touching the altar of a god, either directly or through some linking medium, was thought to grant divine protection to a suppliant.

8. The curse of Cylon was felt to be still alive in 432 BCE, two centuries after it began, according to Thucydides (1.126).

9. Ejection of the dead was a way of cleansing the city, which was thought to be tainted by the mere presence of their bodies.

differences in its terrain. The hill-men leaned toward democracy, the plains-men toward oligarchy;[10] and the third party, the coast-dwellers, by espousing a moderate and mixed form of government, hindered the other two and prevented either from gaining the upper hand. At that period, as the disparity between rich and poor had reached a critical point, the city was in danger on every front. It seemed that its turmoil would only be calmed and brought to an end if a tyranny[11] came into being. For all the common people were in debt to the rich. They either farmed their land, paying a sixth of what they produced . . . or, having borrowed money by pledging their own persons,[12] were liable to be delivered into slavery by their creditors, some serving as slaves at home, others being sold abroad. And many were forced to sell their own children (since no law prevented it) and to flee the city because of the cruelty of their creditors. The majority and the ablest-bodied stood together and encouraged one another not to permit this, but to choose a trustworthy man as their leader, liberate the defaulters, redivide the land, and thoroughly reform the government.

[14] At that point the wisest of the Athenians, noting that Solon alone had kept clear of misconduct and was associated neither with the injustice of the rich nor the exigencies of the poor, asked him to step forward and put an end to the city's strife. . . . He was elected

10. Since almost every Greek city except Sparta had eliminated hereditary monarchy, the two remaining choices of government, according to ancient thinking, were oligarchy and democracy. The first system concentrated power in the hands of a few wealthy individuals; the second diffused it widely among a larger spectrum of participants (though still excluding women and noncitizens). Athenian political sentiment was at this time closely linked to geography, as indicated by the names of the rival parties.

11. Our word "tyranny," conveying as it does a cruel and despotic regime, does not translate the Greek word *tyrannis*, but there is no better word, just as "tyrant" often has to serve for *tyrannos*. (If we could use "prince" as Machiavelli did, rather than conveying the idea of a king's son, that word might work for *tyrannos*, an experiment tried by David Grene in his translation of Herodotus.) Greek political thought allowed that sole rule by an individual who was neither elected nor empowered by constitutional authority might, in certain circumstances, be acceptable or even beneficial. Thus a *tyrannos* was not inherently evil.

12. That is, by mortgaging their own freedom against their debts, a common practice at this time.

archon after Philombrotus[13] and made mediator and legislator as well, the rich ready to embrace him because he was prosperous, the poor because he was honorable. It is said that a comment of his which had gone the rounds earlier, to the effect that equality breeds no war, pleased both the affluent and the indigent, the former expecting to enjoy an equality based on rank and prestige, the latter on proportion and number. Since hope was high on both sides, the party chiefs pressed Solon to accept an absolute sovereignty, recommending that he seize the city more boldly now that he had it in his power. And many citizens of moderate views, seeing that it would be a toilsome and difficult business to effect change by argument and law, were not reluctant to put one man, the most just and wise, in charge of their affairs.[14] . . . Solon reportedly told his friends that a tyranny was a lovely spot, but there was no route down from it. And in the poems written to Phocus he says,

> If I spared my
> Country, and stayed my hand from tyranny and implacable violence,
> Declining to defile and disgrace my good name,
> I am not ashamed; for thus shall I
> Win greater renown from all mankind.

[15] Though he had rejected absolute rule, his manner of governing was not especially mild. He was no faint-hearted legislator: he neither yielded to the powerful nor courted the pleasure of those who had elected him. Where existing institutions were excellent he introduced no correction or innovation, fearing that if he dismantled everything and unsettled the city, he would lack the strength to restore and harmonize its institutions on the soundest basis. But where he hoped to find the citizens amenable or submissive, he achieved his ends, as he himself said, "by a combination of force and justice." Accordingly, when he was asked later on whether he had written the best laws for the Athenians, he replied, "The best they would accept."

Solon . . . called the cancellation of debts a "shaking off of burdens." For his first public measure was the enactment that canceled all current debts and prohibited future loans secured on the person of

---

13. Solon's election to the archonship can be dated precisely to 594 BCE, but there is some question as to whether his reforms of Athens' laws came well after this, perhaps in the 570s. Plutarch speaks as though Solon enacted his reforms during his one-year archonship.

14. Perhaps influenced by the example of Sparta; see *Lycurgus* in this volume.

the borrower.[15] But some writers—Androtion is one—have said that the poor were relieved not by a canceling of debts, but by a lowering of the interest rate on those debts, and that *that* was the benefaction they referred to as the "shaking off of burdens," together with the augmentation of measures and the revaluing of money that accompanied it. For he made the mina, previously worth seventy-three drachmas, worth one hundred, so that by paying back an identical amount of money, but the money itself being worth less, those who had heavy debts were benefited, while those to whom the debts were repaid suffered no harm.[16]

[16] Yet Solon satisfied neither side. He displeased the wealthy by canceling their loan contracts, and vexed the poor even more, since he did not effect a redistribution of land as they had expected him to do, nor did he make everyone's way of life level and equal, as Lycurgus had done. But Lycurgus, who was an eleventh-generation descendant of Heracles,[17] and had reigned over Lacedaemon for many years, had great prestige, friends, and influence, which served him well when he set about reforming the commonwealth. Resorting to force more than persuasion (to the extent that he even lost an eye in the struggle),[18] Lycurgus made the city surpassingly secure and harmonious by seeing to it that no citizen was either poor or rich. Solon, on the other hand, since he was a moderate and a man of the people, did not aspire so far in his polity, though he did not act short of his real power, depending as he did solely on the wishes of the citizens and their willingness to trust him.

[17] He began by repealing the laws of Draco[19] (except for all the homicide laws) because of their harshness and the stiff penalties they imposed.

[18] Next, wishing to leave all the magistracies in the hands of the wealthy, as they already were, but to give the rest of the government,

15. That is, loans that resulted in enslavement in the case of default.

16. Inflating one's way out of debt is a strategy still used by many nations today.

17. Spartans believed that their kings, and indeed all people of Dorian stock, could trace their ancestry back to Heracles.

18. See *Lycurgus* 11.

19. Draco apparently lived in the late seventh century BCE, if he is more than a mere legend. Athenians thought he had been their first official to set down laws in writing and that he had set up stern penalties for criminal offenses (in many cases, the death penalty).

in which the common people had had no share, a mixed character, Solon instituted a valuation of the citizens' property. He assigned to the first class those citizens whose lands yielded five hundred measures, both dry and wet, and called them *pentakosiomedimnoi*.[20] The second class consisted of those citizens who were able to maintain a horse or whose land yielded three hundred measures; these citizens he called knights, as they paid a knight's taxes. Citizens of the third class, whose land produced two hundred measures, both wet and dry, were called *zeugitai*.[21] All the other citizens were called *thētes*.[22] *Thētes* were not permitted to hold any office; they participated in the government only as members of the assembly and as jurors.[23] The latter privilege at first seemed insignificant, but later proved to be immensely important, since the majority of disputes ultimately came before the jurors,[24] and all the lawsuits the magistrates were permitted to try could be appealed in court if anyone so desired.

But still thinking he should do more to remedy the weakness of the multitude, he granted to each citizen the right to file suit on behalf of anyone who had suffered an injury. So if a man was beaten, wronged, or injured, anyone who had the ability or desire could indict the malefactor and prosecute him, the legislator rightly accustoming the citizens, like members of the same body, to identify and sympathize with one another. And a saying of Solon's that is consistent with this law is remembered. It seems that when he was asked what city was best to live in he said, "That in which those who have suffered no injury, no less than the injured, prosecute and punish malefactors."

20. A *medimnos* is a Greek measure of grain, roughly twelve gallons, sometimes translated (inaccurately, regarding quantity) as "bushel." The *pentakosiomedimnoi* owned enough land to produce five hundred of these per annum. Later, after more Athenians became wealthy through trade and manufacture, a cash equivalent was presumably substituted.

21. A *zeugos* is a yoke, such as that used for a team of oxen; the *zeugitai* were sufficiently well-off to own such a team.

22. Related to the Greek word for a hired laborer.

23. Later, in the fifth century BCE, other offices were extended to the *thētes* as well. The archonship, which later led to membership in the Council of the Areopagus (see next chapter), was restricted in Solon's time to the top two property classes.

24. After the reforms of Ephialtes in 461 BCE (see *Pericles* 7), which gave vastly greater jurisdiction to the court system. Athenian juries were huge by modern standards.

[19] After establishing the council of the Areopagus,[25] all of whose members had served annual terms as archons (on which account he himself, having so served, was a member), Solon observed that the common people had grown restless and confident as a result of their release from debt, and he therefore established a second council, called the boulē, choosing one hundred men from each tribe (of which there were four),[26] whom he ordered to frame resolutions before they were debated by the people,[27] and to allow no measure to be introduced in the assembly that had not first been submitted to the council. He made the upper council an overseer of all public affairs and a guardian of the laws, as he supposed that the city, moored by two councils as by anchors, would be less subject to rolling, and would keep the people calmer.

[21] He also enacted a law that restricted women's processions, their mourning, and their festivals, with an eye to preventing any disorderly or unbridled behavior. He forbade women to go out wearing more than three garments, carrying food or drink worth more than one obol,[28] or holding a basket more than a cubit high.

[22] Seeing the city constantly filled with people streaming into Attica from all sides for security,[29] and noting that most of the land was barren and poor, and that seafarers were not in the habit of shipping merchandise to people who had nothing to give in return, he directed the citizens toward manufacture of goods,[30] and wrote a

---

25. Plutarch goes on to say, in a passage not included here, that he has contradictory evidence on this point, some of it suggesting (as is in fact the case) that the council of the Areopagus predated Solon's time. The Areopagus ("hill of Ares") was the place where the council met to consider judicial verdicts and make other policy decisions.

26. The boulē (pronounced as two syllables, *boo-lāy*; literally, "council"), later to become Athens' most powerful organ of government, was expanded to five hundred under Cleisthenes, compared to Solon's four hundred.

27. That is, to compose the motions that would come before the assembly. Because it controlled the deliberations and votes of the assembly, the boulē was the closest the Athenians had to an executive branch.

28. An obol was the smallest unit of Athenian currency. Six obols equaled one drachma.

29. Thucydides' *Peloponnesian War* (1.2) notes that Attica, being undesirable on account of its poor soil, experienced less strife than other parts of Greece and so became a haven for refugees.

30. "Manufacture" is a very imprecise translation of the Greek word *technē*, denoting all sorts of craft and production. Athenians early on developed an

law stating that a son who had not been taught a trade was under no obligation to support his father. It was one thing for Lycurgus, who inhabited a city free of a crowd of foreigners, and who possessed a country "large for many, ample for twice as many," as Euripides says[31]—a country, moreover, that harbored a mass of helots,[32] whom it was better not to leave at leisure, but to keep constantly occupied and humbled by hard toil—it was all very well for *him* to release the citizens from laborious and menial pursuits, and to keep them occupied with arms and devoted to that trade only. But Solon, who was adapting his laws to his circumstances, not his circumstances to his laws, and who saw that the produce of the country, scarcely nourishing the farmers, could not support an idle and leisurely throng, conferred prestige upon the tradesmen and ordered the council of the Areopagus to examine how each man made his living and to punish the idle.

[23] But on the whole, Solon's laws pertaining to women seem very odd. For the man who caught an adulterer was permitted to kill him; but if someone abducted and raped a free woman, he was merely required to pay a fine of one hundred drachmas; if he had seduced her, the fine was twenty drachmas, unless the woman was one of those who sell themselves openly (that is, the prostitutes, who consort openly with men who pay for their favors). Moreover, a man is forbidden to sell a daughter or sister unless he finds that she is not a virgin.

[25] All of Solon's laws were meant to be in force for one hundred years. They were written on *axones*, wooden tablets that revolved in oblong frames, small fragments of which have been preserved to this day in the Prytaneum.[33] . . .

After the laws had been published, people took to visiting Solon day after day, either to commend or criticize his wording, or to recommend insertions or deletions, though most of his visitors came to question and interrogate and to urge him to explain and clarify each law's meaning and purpose. Seeing that it would be absurd to do so, but that to refuse would create ill will, and wishing to extricate

---

expertise in pottery, producing famously beautiful vases that were exported far and wide. The income from such trade enabled Athens to buy (or barter for) the food it could not grow on poor native soil.

31. The source of the quote is not known.

32. See *Lycurgus* 24 with n. 35. Helots were Sparta's enslaved agricultural laborers.

33. A state building set aside for use by the boulē.

himself from these difficulties entirely and to escape the citizens'
displeasure and their delight in finding fault (since "in important
affairs it is hard to please everyone," as Solon himself has said), he
made his possession of a ship an excuse for traveling, and sailed away
after asking the Athenians for a ten-year leave of absence.[34] For he
expected that in that period they would become accustomed to his
laws.

[29] While Solon was abroad, the citizens again fell to quar-
reling amongst themselves. Lycurgus[35] led the party of the plain,
Megacles son of Alcmaeon the party of the coast,[36] and Pisistratus
the hill-dwellers,[37] the latter party including most of the *thētes*, who
were particularly vexed by the rich. As a result, though the city still
abided by Solon's laws, everyone now expected a revolution and
longed for a change of government. People no longer hoped merely
for equality, but looked to gain more power by the change and to
get the better of their opponents in everything. Affairs were in this
state when Solon returned to Athens. Though honored and revered
everywhere, he was no longer as able to speak and act in public as
formerly, nor did he wish to do so, since he was now an old man. But
he met privately with the heads of the parties and tried to reconcile
and unite them. Pisistratus appeared to pay him more heed than
the others. For Pisistratus' conversation had a flattering and good-
natured character. He was ready to help the poor and was reasonable
and moderate in his enmities. As for the qualities in which he was
naturally deficient, by imitating them he was more trusted than men
who actually embodied them. He was seen as a circumspect and well-
behaved man, one who loved equality above everything and would
be vexed if anyone disturbed or sought to change the existing order.
In these matters he thoroughly deceived the multitude. Solon soon
discerned his true character and was the first to detect his designs.

34. It was during this ten-year sojourn abroad, according to Herodotus
(1.29), that Solon came to the court of Croesus at Sardis in Lydia, though the
chronology of Solon's life makes an actual meeting with Croesus unlikely.

35. A different person from the Spartan lawgiver of the same name.

36. On Megacles and the Alcmaeonids, see note 6 above.

37. According to Plutarch's own formulation in chapter 6, these three
parties represent the supporters of oligarchy, mixed constitution, and
democracy, respectively. Pisistratus, here portrayed as the people's champion, would one day (as so many people's champions have done) become an
autocrat, founding a dynastic tyranny that endured for most of the sixth
century BCE.

He by no means hated Pisistratus, but he tried to temper the man's character and admonish him, and he told him and others that if anyone could extract from Pisistratus' soul the passion to be preeminent, and cure his desire for absolute rule, no other man would have a greater aptitude for virtue, or be a better citizen.

Thespis[38] at that time was inventing tragedy, which on account of its novelty was attracting many spectators, though it had not yet become a matter of competition. Solon, who was naturally fond of hearing and learning, and in his old age gave himself up even more to leisure and amusement, not to mention wine and music, went to see Thespis performing in one of his own plays, as was the custom among the ancients. After the performance, Solon accosted Thespis and asked him whether he was not ashamed to speak so falsely before so large an audience. When Thespis declared that there was nothing so terrible in saying and doing such things in play, Solon struck the ground fiercely with his cane and said, "Yet if we praise and honor this sort of play, we may find it in our covenants."

[30] When Pisistratus, after wounding himself, was brought to the marketplace in a chariot,[39] and sought to incite the people by claiming that he had been plotted against by his enemies because of his policy, and soon had many people angry and shouting, Solon approached, stood beside him and said, "You are not playing the part of Homer's Odysseus very well, son of Hippocrates. For when *he* wounded himself he was tricking his enemies, whereas *you* are misleading your fellow citizens." The multitude was now ready to fight on Pisistratus' behalf, and the citizens gathered in the assembly. When Ariston had proposed that Pisistratus be given a bodyguard of fifty club-bearers, Solon spoke against the measure. He rose and made many points similar to those he had made in his poems:

> You look with admiration upon the language and words of a wily man.
> Each of you follows in the footsteps of a fox,
> Empty-minded, all of you.

Seeing that the poor were in an uproar and eager to gratify Pisistratus, while the rich, flinching from danger, were running away, Solon departed, saying that he was wiser than the former, though braver than the latter: wiser than those who did not understand what was

---

38. A person about whom little is known, and who may in fact be a legend. Our word "thespian" comes from his name.

39. See Herodotus 1.59 for this episode, though Herodotus' account does not give a role to Solon.

being done, and braver than those who, though they understood, were afraid to oppose the tyranny. When the people had ratified the measure, they set no miserly limit on the number of Pisistratus' club-bearers, but let him keep as many as he liked and lead them about in public, until he seized the Acropolis.

When this was done, and the city was thrown into confusion, Megacles quickly fled with the other Alcmaeonids. But Solon, though he was then quite elderly and had no protectors, came out to the marketplace and argued with the citizens, partly reproaching them with their thoughtlessness and softness, partly spurring them on and urging them not to lose their liberty. It was then that he made the remark that has come down to us, that it had lately been quite easy for them to thwart the tyranny while it was still taking form; but it would be greater and more glorious to sever and destroy it now that it was rooted and growing. As no one was brave enough to listen to him, he went home. And on taking up his weapons and placing them on his porch, he said, "I have done what I could to aid my country and its laws."

[31] When, in light of this, many people warned him that he would be put to death by the tyrant, and asked him what it was he trusted to that he had lost all sense of fear, he replied, "Old age." Yet when Pisistratus had seized control of the government, he won Solon over so completely by honoring him, treating him affectionately, and sending for him, that Solon became his adviser and approved of many of his acts. For Pisistratus preserved most of Solon's laws, abiding by them himself and requiring his friends to do likewise.

Themistocles

Themistocles opens after a gap of nearly a century after the end of Solon. *Plutarch's surviving* Lives *do not include any figures from the middle and late decades of the sixth century BCE. This was the time of the tyranny at Athens founded by Pisistratus and continued by his son Hippias, and of the coup that overthrew Hippias (508 BCE), and of the democratic reforms of Cleisthenes—events narrated in brief by Herodotus,* Histories *5.62–70. Plutarch's* Lives *give us little insight into these events, or into the rise of the Achaemenid Persian empire and its first conflicts with the Greeks, the subject of Herodotus' first five books. At the start of* Themistocles, *those Perso-Greek conflicts are already well under way, and Athens stands directly in the cross-hairs of the Persian war machine, having helped the Greeks in Asia launch a revolt from Persia in 499.*

Plutarch took his cue from Herodotus and Thucydides in his portrait of Themistocles (c. 528–462). Both historians admired Themistocles as a self-made man, a political climber, and a brilliant strategist whose sole determination to fight the Persian navy at Salamis in 480 turned the tide of the conflict. But both were also aware that Themistocles' patriotism could not be easily disentangled from his intense interest in self-advancement and self-enrichment. Plutarch's portrait of Themistocles, like those of his two main sources, reveals a complex blend of heroism and self-serving machination.

[1] The family of Themistocles was too obscure to enhance his reputation. His father was Neocles, a man of no great distinction at Athens. . . . And as these lines tell us, Themistocles was the son of a foreign-born mother:[1]

> Abrotonon, a Thracian born and bred, though I
> Claim to have borne the Greeks mighty Themistocles.

Since the offspring of foreigners used to gather at Cynosarges, a gymnasium of Heracles outside the gates (for Heracles, too, was not native-born among the gods, but was held to be of foreign birth because his mother was mortal), Themistocles persuaded some of the well-born youths to go out to Cynosarges and exercise with him; and

---

1. These humble origins would have made a political career unthinkable for any ordinary Athenian at this time. Despite the reforms of Cleisthenes in 508 BCE, when Themistocles was around twenty, leadership of Athens was still heavily dominated by the aristocracy.

by this clever stroke he is thought to have removed the distinction
between the foreign- and native-born.

[2] It is agreed that as a boy he was impulsive, by nature astute,
and by choice ambitious and political. For in his hours of leisure and
during rests from studying, he did not play or idle away his time like
other boys, but would be found composing and privately rehearsing
speeches in which he either accused one of the boys or argued on his
behalf. And consequently his teacher was in the habit of saying to
him, "You'll be no minor figure, lad, but immensely powerful, either
for good or ill." . . . Later on, when he attended gatherings graced
by the so-called liberal and urbane pastimes, and was mocked by
men who considered themselves cultivated, he was forced to defend
himself rather bluntly by saying that though he did not know how to
tune a lyre or play a harp, he could take a small and obscure city and
make it famous and important. . . .

In his first youthful efforts he was inconsistent and unsteady,
since he relied solely on his natural impulses, which, without the
control of reason and training, veer erratically in the pursuit of their
ends and often lapse into disorder.

[3] Soon, however, politics laid firm hold of Themistocles, and
the strong drive for renown overpowered him. That was why, right
from the start, he was eager to be first, and why he boldly faced
the hostility of the city's most powerful citizens, particularly that of
Aristides, son of Lysimachus,[2] who constantly opposed him. . . . For
Aristides was mild by nature and upright in character, and as he conducted the government not for the sake of winning favor or renown,
but with a view to shaping the best policy consistent with safety and
fairness, he was often compelled to resist Themistocles (on many
occasions the latter stirred the people up by introducing important
innovations) and to oppose his growing influence. For it is said that
Themistocles was so carried away by his desire for renown, and that
his ambition inspired him with such a passion for grand exploits,
that though he was still a young man when the battle against the
barbarians was fought at Marathon and Miltiades' generalship was
celebrated,[3] Themistocles was often seen to be deep in thought. He
lay awake at night and declined to attend his friends' drinking parties,

2. See *Aristides* in this volume.
3. In 490 BCE, when Themistocles was in his mid-thirties. The battle of
Marathon was Athens' first great victory over the Persians, and the beginning of a long conflict. See *Aristides* 5.

and told those who questioned him and who marveled at the change in his way of life that Miltiades' trophy would not let him sleep. For whereas others thought the defeat of the barbarians at Marathon had put the quarrel behind them, Themistocles regarded it as the beginning of more important struggles; and to these he dedicated himself on behalf of Greece as a whole and kept the city in training, since he foresaw from afar what lay ahead.

[4] His first effort concerned the revenues from the silver mines at Laurion,[4] which had customarily been distributed among the Athenians. Themistocles alone ventured to come before the people and say that they should forgo the distribution and instead use the money to build triremes[5] for their war with the Aeginetans.[6] For that war was at its height in Greece, and the islanders, who had a great many ships, had thereby gained control of the sea. Themistocles easily persuaded the Athenians, not by holding Darius[7] or the Persians out as a threat (for these were far away, and excited no great fear of their coming), but by making timely use of the citizens' resentment of the Aeginetans and their eager rivalry. And thus the Athenians used those funds to build a hundred triremes, with which they later fought at sea against Xerxes.

After this, Themistocles gradually enticed the city, drawing her down toward the sea. Arguing that with their infantry the Athenians were no match even for their neighbors, whereas their naval prowess made them strong enough to ward off the barbarians and hold sway in Greece, he made them sailors and seafarers, instead of "steadfast hoplites," as Plato refers to them, and laid himself open to the charge that "Themistocles deprived the citizens of the spear and shield, and reduced the people of Athens to the rower's cushion and oar." He achieved this over Miltiades' objections, as Stesimbrotus[8] says.

4. Laurion was a district of Attica rich in silver, mined both by private citizens and the Athenian state. In the mid-480s a new vein of silver was discovered in one of the state-run mines, creating a rich source of revenue.

5. Greek warships of the Classical Age.

6. Aegina, an island off the coast of Attica, had engaged in a long commercial rivalry with Athens that often reached the level of military hostilities.

7. Darius I was the Persian king who engineered the invasion of Attica that was defeated at Marathon. He seems, in fact, to have died before the silver strike at Laurion, and to have handed power down to his son Xerxes.

8. A prose writer of the mid-fifth century BCE whose works have been lost.

Now whether or not, in doing so, Themistocles harmed the discipline or purity of their public life is a question for a more philosophical writer to consider;[9] but that the Greeks' salvation at that period depended on the sea, and that those triremes restored the city of Athens, the behavior of Xerxes himself, among other things, bears witness. For though his infantry stood by unscathed, Xerxes fled after his naval defeat, understanding that his men were not a match for the Greeks in battle; and he left Mardonius behind, in my opinion, more to prevent the Greeks from pursuing him than to try to enslave them.[10]

[5] Themistocles made himself popular with the common people, partly by knowing each citizen's name by heart, and partly by showing himself an unerring settler of contract disputes. . . . Growing in power, and pleasing the common people, he eventually formed an opposition party and managed to have Aristides banished by ostracism.[11]

[6] When the Persians[12] were already descending upon Greece, and the Athenians were deliberating about the choice of a general, everyone else, they say, willingly shunned the office, as they were intimidated by the danger; but Epicydes, son of Euphemidius, a politician who spoke cleverly but was soft in spirit and open to bribery, was eager to obtain the post and would probably have prevailed in the vote. As Themistocles was afraid that their undertaking would be utterly ruined if the command fell to Epicydes, he bought off the man's ambition with bribes.

---

9. Plutarch implicitly answers Plato, who in a passage of the *Laws* (706c ff., the source of the "steadfast hoplites" phrase quoted above) argued that strength in naval warfare, as compared with infantry, corrupts and weakens a city's moral fiber.

10. Plutarch looks ahead to the events of 480–479 BCE, the main episodes of Themistocles' career (see chapters 11–18).

11. Probably between 485 and 482 BCE. The institution of ostracism was a unique feature of the Athenian constitution. If a large number of citizens voted to hold an ostracism in any given year, then one man, the recipient of a majority of ballots, was forced to leave the city for ten years. Plutarch explains the process in detail at *Aristides* 7.

12. The term translated as "Persians" here (and at several points below) is actually "Medes." Although the Medes were a different people than the Persians, the two groups had become closely intertwined by the fifth century BCE, so that the Greeks often used the names interchangeably.

He is also praised for the action he took against the bilingual man in the delegation sent by the King to demand earth and water.[13] He had the interpreter arrested and put to death by decree for daring to issue barbarian orders in the Greek language. . . . But greatest among all his achievements was that he ended the Greek wars and reconciled the cities with one another, having persuaded them to suspend their enmities because of the war.[14]

[7] As soon as Themistocles assumed the command,[15] he at once made every effort to embark the citizens on their triremes, and tried to persuade them to leave the city and meet the barbarian at sea, as far from Greece as possible. But when many resisted the plan, he led a large army to Tempe[16] with the Spartans, in order to make a stand there in defense of Thessaly, which was not yet thought to be siding with the Persians.[17] But when they retired without having accomplished anything, and the territory as far as Boeotia had sided with the Persians (the Thessalians having gone over to the King),[18] the Athenians paid more heed to Themistocles' desire to fight at sea, and he was sent with a fleet to guard the narrows at Artemisium.

There the Greeks were urging Eurybiades[19] and the Spartans to take command, though the Athenians, since they were contributing more ships than all the other cities combined, thought it unseemly

13. The giving of earth and water was a symbolic expression of submission to the Persian empire. As always in this volume, "King" when capitalized refers to the Great King of Persia.

14. Herodotus (7.145) reports a general conference of the Hellenic states aimed at resolving differences, in 481 BCE, but does not record that Themistocles played any major role.

15. Plutarch only later (chapter 10) narrates the story, which chronologically occurs here, of how Themistocles won out in the assembly with his interpretation of an ambiguous oracle.

16. The vale of Tempe, formed by the Peneius River, gives an easy entry route into northern Greece from the coast, since it cuts through the high mountains that otherwise bar passage.

17. See note 12.

18. Confirmed by Herodotus (7.173–74).

19. Eurybiades was the Spartan admiral chosen to command the collective Greek fleet. Though Athens had contributed by far the largest share of warships, the Greeks felt it was important that a single city hold command of both land and sea forces, and therefore Sparta was the only logical choice. Plutarch makes this selection seem to come from Themistocles, in contrast to Herodotus, who depicts it as the consensus of the Greek states.

for them to obey others. Perceiving the danger, Themistocles ceded his command to Eurybiades and conciliated the Athenians by promising them that if they proved brave in the war, he would see to it that the Greeks willingly obeyed *them* in future. And that is why Themistocles is thought to be most responsible for the deliverance of Greece and for leading the Athenians to the renown of surpassing their enemies in courage and their allies in judgment.

When the barbarian fleet reached Aphetae, Eurybiades was astounded by the number of ships at the mouth of the river.[20] And when he learned that two hundred more were sailing around above Sciathus, he wanted to proceed southward in Greece to the Peloponnese and surround the infantry with his ships,[21] as he believed that the King's prowess at sea was utterly irresistible. Meanwhile the Euboeans, fearing that the Greeks might abandon them, entered into secret discussions with Themistocles, having sent Pelagon to him with a large sum of money. Themistocles took the money, as Herodotus reports,[22] and gave it to Eurybiades.

Among his fellow citizens, Themistocles met with most opposition from Architeles, the captain of the sacred ship.[23] Lacking funds to furnish his sailors with supplies, Architeles was eager to sail away; but Themistocles so incensed his crew against him that they banded together, rushed at him, and stole his supper. Architeles took this hard and grew dejected, whereupon Themistocles sent him a box containing a supper of bread and meat under which he had placed a talent of silver, and urged him to eat now, and take care of his seamen in the morning; otherwise he said he would denounce him before the assembled Greeks for being in possession of money from the enemy. This incident has been recorded by Phanias of Lesbos.

20. Plutarch says "river" even though he really refers to the straits at Artemisium, between the northern tip of Euboea and the Greek mainland. Aphetae was a city on the mainland across the straits from Artemisium.

21. Plutarch here gives a hazy description of the Spartan fallback strategy: to defend the Peloponnese with a land-and-sea barricade at the Isthmus of Corinth but surrender all territory to the north (see chapter 9).

22. Herodotus 8.4–5, but the story there does less credit to Themistocles, who is said to have pocketed much of the money himself.

23. Probably meaning the *Paralus*, one of two state triremes reserved for special functions. Architeles is otherwise unknown.

[8] The engagements that then took place against the barbarian ships near the narrows[24] were not decisive, but the Greeks benefited enormously from the experience, since they were taught by their actual exploits in the face of danger that neither large numbers of ships, nor brilliantly decorated ensigns, nor boastful shouts, nor barbarian war cries held any fear for men who know how to come to blows and dare to fight; instead they must despise such things and simply attack their enemies directly,[25] grapple with them, and fight to the finish.

[9] But when the news about Thermopylae was brought to Artemisium, and the Greeks learned that Leonidas was slain[26] and that Xerxes was in control of the passes, they withdrew into Greece, the Athenians keeping guard over the entire force because of their valor, and taking great pride in what they had accomplished. As Themistocles sailed along the coast, wherever he saw necessary landing-places and refuges for the enemy he engraved clear messages on the stones (finding some by chance, and standing others near the safe anchorages and watering-places), enjoining the Ionians, if they could, to change sides and join the Greeks,[27] who were their ancestors, and who were braving danger on behalf of their freedom. But if this was not possible, he urged them to undermine the barbarians' cause in the battle and throw them into confusion. He was hoping that these messages would either move the Ionians to change sides, or cause trouble by making the barbarians more suspicious of them.[28]

When Xerxes invaded from above, through Doris into Phocis, and burned and destroyed the Phocians' cities, the Greeks did not come to their aid, though the Athenians begged the allies to confront the barbarians in Boeotia before they reached Attica, just as they

24. The battle of Artemisium, 480 BCE; see Herodotus 8.10–18.

25. Plutarch says "attack their very bodies," perhaps a metaphor from wrestling, or perhaps referring to the corps of armed troops each trireme carried for the purpose of boarding an enemy vessel.

26. Leonidas, a Spartan king, was leader of the famous band of three hundred that died defending the pass of Thermopylae. The naval defense of Artemisium was coordinated with the land defense of Thermopylae, since the Greeks recognized that it would be best to stop the Persian army and fleet at about the same point.

27. The Greeks of the Ionian cities, on the coast of Asia Minor, had been forced to join Xerxes' invasion forces. Their geographical location gave them little choice.

28. See Herodotus 8.19 and 8.22.

themselves had sailed to Artemisium to aid others. But no one would
listen to them. All were intent upon the Peloponnese and were eager
to collect all their forces within the Isthmus, which they were fortifying from coast to coast.[29] Anger at the betrayal seized the Athenians,
as well as despair and dejection at being left destitute.

[10] Thereupon Themistocles, at a loss how to persuade the people by any human reasoning, resorted to a device of the tragic stage
and brought divine signs and oracles to bear on them. He took as an
omen the incident of the serpent, which was thought to have disappeared at about that time from the sacred enclosure. The priests,
finding untouched the first-fruits they used to put out for it day after
day, reported to the people (Themistocles giving them the story)
that the goddess had abandoned the city, as she was leading them to
the sea.[30] Then he persuaded the people to accept his interpretation
of the oracle, saying that its "wooden wall" meant nothing but the
ships;[31] and that this was why the god referred to Salamis as "divine,"
rather than "terrible" or "wretched," since the word revealed that the
island would be a great boon to the Greeks. Having won them over to
his view, he wrote a decree[32] requiring that the city be entrusted to
Athena, their patroness, and that all eligible citizens embark on their

29. Since the Spartans were in control of grand strategy, they naturally
favored this fallback to an isthmus wall, which had some hope of saving the
Peloponnese from invasion. Attica and Boeotia, however, would be sacrificed
in such a strategy.

30. Herodotus (8.41) records the story without involving Themistocles.
Apparently the Athenians believed that a snake, which they considered an
incarnation of a god, lived in a sanctuary on the Acropolis, so they left out
a honey cake for it at regular intervals. When one day the cake was not
consumed, it appeared to them that the god had departed.

31. As often, Plutarch assumes his readers know the fuller version of the
story and truncates his account. The oracle given at Delphi, to Athenian
envoys inquiring how they should respond to the Persian invasion, is
reported in full by Herodotus (7.141). It referred to "a wooden wall" that
would protect the Athenians from harm and ended with an invocation
to "divine Salamis," referring to the island off the coast of Attica. Most
Athenians thought the "wooden wall" referred to the palisade surrounding
the Acropolis, according to Herodotus, until Themistocles pointed out it
could also mean the sides of a trireme.

32. A stone tablet containing a decree much like this was found in 1959 near
the site of Troezen. It has since become known as the Themistocles Decree,
but scholars are divided on the question of its authenticity.

triremes, each man having provided as best he could for the safety of his children, womenfolk, and slaves. When the decree had been ratified, most of the Athenians carried their parents and wives safely away to Troezen,[33] the Troezenians welcoming them very creditably. Indeed, they voted to support the Athenians at public expense, giving each citizen two obols, and allowing the boys to pick from the ripe crops everywhere.

[11] These were important accomplishments on Themistocles' part; and when he perceived that the citizens were yearning for Aristides, and were fearful that this man might, in anger, attach himself to the barbarian and ruin the affairs of Greece (for Aristides had been ostracized before the war, when Themistocles' party overpowered his own), Themistocles wrote a decree stating that those who had temporarily emigrated were permitted to return and to devote themselves, in word and deed, to serving the Greek cause along with their fellow citizens.

Because of Sparta's standing, Eurybiades was posted as commander in chief of the naval forces. But as he was faint-hearted in time of danger, and willing to put to sea and sail to the Isthmus, where the infantry of the Peloponnesians had also assembled, Themistocles spoke out in opposition.[34] It was then that Themistocles' memorable remarks are said to have been made. For when Eurybiades said to him, "Themistocles, in races they flog those who start before the signal is given," Themistocles replied, "Yes, but they don't award crowns to those who lag behind." And when Eurybiades raised his cane as if to strike him, Themistocles said, "Strike, then, but listen." Astonished by Themistocles' mildness, Eurybiades urged him to speak, whereupon Themistocles tried to bring him over to his own view. But when someone said that it was not right for a man without a city to instruct others to desert and abandon their native places, Themistocles turned to him and said, "But of course we have abandoned our houses and walls, poor fool, since we disdain to be slaves of soulless things. But we *have* a city, the greatest in Greece: our two hundred triremes, which stand ready for you, if you wish

33. Herodotus reports, rather, that most of the Athenians were transported to Salamis, but the Themistocles Decree (see note 32) favors Plutarch's version.

34. This memorable confrontation, which took place at Salamis in a strategy conference of the Greek commanders, is more fully described by Herodotus (8.62–63).

to be saved by them; but then again, if you betray us a second time and depart, many a Greek will soon hear that the Athenians have acquired a free city and a country no worse than the one they lost." When Themistocles had said this, Eurybiades was seized with fear at the thought that the Athenians might forsake them and depart. And when the Eretrian tried to say something to him, Themistocles said, "After all, what notion can *you* have about war—you who, like the cuttlefish, have a blade but no heart?"[35]

[12] Some writers say that while Themistocles was speaking of these matters from the upper deck of his ship, an owl was seen flying from the right[36] through the fleet and alighting on their mastheads, and that this omen, more than anything, inspired them to adopt Themistocles' plan and prepare to fight at sea. But when the enemy fleet, attacking the coast of Attica all the way to Phalerum, concealed the neighboring shores from view,[37] and the King himself, coming down to the coast with his infantry, was seen with all his assembled forces, the land and naval divisions coming into view simultaneously, Themistocles' counsels were forgotten and the Peloponnesians again gazed with longing toward the Isthmus and raged at anyone who said anything different. They decided to withdraw that night, and gave the pilots their sailing orders. It was then that Themistocles, distressed that the Greeks might desert their advantageous position at the narrows[38] and disperse to their various cities, took counsel and devised the stratagem associated with Sicinnus.

Sicinnus was a Persian by race.[39] Though a prisoner of war, he was well-disposed to Themistocles and served as his children's

35. The cuttlefish has a flat piece of hard cartilage running down the length of its body, which the Greeks called *machaira* or "sword." According to popular belief, mollusks in general had no heart or lungs (see Aristotle, *History of Animals* 1.11–12).

36. In ancient divination, the direction of flight of a notable bird gives important clues about the will of the gods. A bird flying into view from the right is a favorable sign.

37. That is, the Persian ships were so numerous as to fill the horizon. For their numbers, see note 42.

38. The Greeks derived advantage from the narrowness of the strait of Salamis, since the Persians could bring only a portion of their more numerous fleet into play.

39. The Persian origins of this slave are not attested by Herodotus (8.75) and must be considered unlikely, but the idea that a Persian had helped defeat the Persians improves the story.

tutor. Themistocles sent him in secret to Xerxes, ordering him to say, "Themistocles, the Athenian commander, having espoused the King's cause, reports, before anyone else, that the Greeks are running away, and urges him not to let them escape but to attack while they are in distress and separated from their infantry, and to destroy their naval forces."

Xerxes, who assumed the message was sincere, was delighted, and immediately told his fleet's commanders to man their other ships at leisure, but to send out two hundred at once, in order to surround the strait, including the islands, so that no enemy ship might escape.

When these orders had been carried out, Aristides, son of Lysimachus, who was the first to notice the deployment, came to Themistocles' tent, though he was not the man's friend, but had in fact been ostracized through his machinations, as has been mentioned. When Themistocles came forth, Aristides told him of the encirclement. Aware of the man's perfect integrity, and pleased with his arrival just then, Themistocles told him about the Sicinnus affair and urged him to second his efforts and help persuade the Greeks, who he admitted were more likely to trust Aristides, that they should fight in the narrows. Aristides, accordingly, after praising Themistocles for his stratagem, went around to the other generals and captains, spurring them on to battle. While they were still expressing their incredulity, a Tenian trireme[40] that had deserted from the enemy came into view. Its captain, Panaetius, reported the encirclement, whereupon the Greeks, overtaken by necessity, set out whole-heartedly to confront the danger.

[13] At dawn Xerxes was seated at a height overlooking the naval force and its battle array, above the Heracleum[41] . . . where the island is separated from Attica by a narrow strait.

[14] As for the numbers of barbarian ships, the poet Aeschylus, speaking in his tragedy the *Persians*, as though he has positive knowledge, says,

---

40. From one of the Greek cities in Asia that had been forced to fight on Xerxes' side.

41. The Heracleum was a temple of Heracles situated on the high ground above the strait of Salamis. Xerxes reportedly seated himself on a lofty throne there to watch the battle unfold, both because he anticipated victory and because he wanted to record which ships fought well or poorly on his behalf.

Xerxes, I know, had a thousand ships
Under his command; but vessels superior in speed
Numbered two hundred and seven;[42] such was the reckoning.

Of the Attic ships, which numbered 180, each had eighteen men
fighting from the deck, four of whom were archers and the rest
hoplites.

Themistocles is thought to have succeeded just as well in determining the exact time for the battle as he had in choosing its location. For he took care not to stand his ships prow to prow with the
barbarians' until the hour that usually brought a clear breeze from
the open sea and a swell through the narrows. The breeze did no
harm to the Greek ships, as they had shallow drafts and low pro-
files; but it doomed the slower-moving, high-roofed barbarian ships,
with their lofty prows and decks. Falling on *them*, the wind turned
them broadside to the Greeks,[43] who attacked eagerly and paid close
attention to Themistocles, since he could best spot advantageous
openings, and because Ariamenes, Xerxes' admiral, a brave man and
the strongest and most honorable of the King's brothers, with his
large ship confronting that of Themistocles, was firing arrows and
javelins, as though from a fortress. Ameinias of Decelea and Socles
the Paeanian, whose ship was close by, went after Ariamenes. And
when their ships met prow to prow, collided, and were pierced by one
another's bronze beaks, Ariamenes tried to board the other trireme.
Standing their ground and striking him with their spears, the captains hurled him into the sea. Artemisia,[44] pointing out Ariamenes'
body floating among the other wreckage, had it carried to Xerxes.

[15] At that point in the struggle, they say that a great light
shone forth from Eleusis,[45] and that a voice resounded and filled the
Thriasian plain as far as the sea. . . . And from the shouting mass a
cloud seemed to rise gradually from the earth and then to sink down
and settle over the triremes. Others thought they saw apparitions and

42. Herodotus 7.89 gives the exact same number, but that does not mean
the number has any authority. Probably both authors consulted a common
source, or Herodotus got the number from Aeschylus. The actual fleet was
most likely less than half this size.

43. A very dangerous orientation, allowing the enemy to ram easily.

44. A Carian queen who fought courageously in Xerxes' forces; one of
Herodotus' most memorable characters.

45. A sacred site near Athens, the center of the mystery cult that was especially patronized by Athenians.

phantoms of armed men from Aegina stretching out their hands to defend the Greek triremes; these, it was supposed, were the sons of Aeacus,[46] whose aid they had invoked before the battle. The first man to capture a ship was Lycomedes, one of the Athenian captains. . . . When the other Greeks became equal in number to the barbarians, who were attacking by turns in the narrow strait and falling foul of one another, they routed them, though the barbarians resisted until evening.[47]

[16] After the sea battle, Xerxes, still enraged at his failure, set about building moles, so that by blocking up the strait he could lead his infantry against the Greeks on Salamis. Themistocles now sounded Aristides and broached his plan of sailing with the fleet to the Hellespont and breaking up the bridge of ships, "in order," as he said, "to capture Asia in Europe."[48] But Aristides disliked the plan and said, "Up to now, the barbarian we have fought has been richly supplied. But if we confine him in Greece and reduce to fearful necessity a man who is master of such resources, he will no longer sit still under a golden canopy and survey the battle at his ease, but will risk his all. Overseeing everything in person because of his danger, he will mend his ways and take better counsel on behalf of his affairs in general. So we should not destroy the bridge that is already in existence, Themistocles, but should if possible build another, and swiftly drive the man out of Europe." "Well, if that seems best," said Themistocles, "it's time we all take thought and devise a way for Greece to be rid of him as soon as possible."

When this policy had been adopted, Themistocles sent one of the king's eunuchs, whom he had found among the prisoners of war— the man's name was Arnaces—to tell the King that the Greeks had resolved, now that they had prevailed in the naval battle, to sail up to the Hellespont,[49] where the strait was spanned, and demolish the bridge; but that Themistocles, out of concern for the King, advised him to hasten to his own sea and cross over to Asia. Themistocles,

46. Aeacus was a mythic Greek hero, a son of Zeus who became king of Aegina.

47. The battle of Salamis took place in the autumn of 480 BCE. It can be followed in much closer detail in Herodotus 8.84–99.

48. That is, to trap the Persian forces on the European side of the straits.

49. The Hellespont is today the strait of Dardanelles. Xerxes had bridged it in order to bring his army into Europe, by tying together more than three hundred warships stationed side by side.

meanwhile, would contrive various delays for the allies and thereby postpone the pursuit.[50] On hearing this, the barbarian grew fearful and hastened to retreat. And the prudence of Themistocles and Aristides was vindicated in the battle at Plataea, where Mardonius, though he commanded a force many times smaller than that of Xerxes, put the Greeks in danger of losing everything.[51]

[19] In the aftermath of the achievements here related, Themistocles immediately tried to rebuild and fortify Athens— by bribing the ephors[52] not to stand in his way, according to Theopompus,[53] though most say that he merely misled them. For he came to Sparta ostensibly on an embassy, and when the Spartans charged that the Athenians were fortifying their city[54] . . . Themistocles denied it and urged them to send observers—not only because this delay would give his fellow citizens time to complete the fortification, but also because he wanted the Athenians to hold these ambassadors as hostages for him. And that is what happened. When the Spartans realized the truth, they did Themistocles no harm, but suppressed their anger and sent him away.

He then equipped the Piraeus,[55] since he had noticed the favorable configuration of its harbors and wished to orient the entire city toward the sea and thereby reverse, in some sense, the policy of the ancient Athenian kings. For they, as it is said, attempted to draw the citizens away from the sea and accustom them to making their living

50. The point of sending this false message is revealed in chapter 28.

51. Plutarch looks ahead by a year to the final battle for control of Europe, the land battle at Plataea (479 BCE). Mardonius, the Persian commander left in Greece after Xerxes' departure, had a fair chance of winning that battle, Plutarch implies; hence, the naval forces commanded by Themistocles might well have lost, had they forced the Persians into a corner.

52. The ephors are government officials of Sparta, the city to which the scene has now shifted. See *Lycurgus*, n. 11.

53. An important historical writer of the fourth century BCE, whose work is now lost.

54. Athens had always had city walls, but the Persians had largely wrecked them during their occupation of Athens. Sparta, as the only unwalled city in southern Greece and its leading land power, had an interest in preventing Athens from refortifying and indeed reportedly proposed a pact to the Athenians whereby *all* Greek cities would pull down their walls.

55. The Piraeus was a set of fine natural harbors a few miles west of Athens, in the Saronic Gulf. The Athenians had long used it as a transit point for shipping but had not before this time thought to fortify it as a naval base.

not by sailing but by agriculture. . . . Themistocles did not, as the comic poet Aristophanes says, "knead the Piraeus onto the city,"[56] but he fastened the city to the Piraeus, and the land to the sea. He thereby exalted the common people in relation to the nobility, and filled them with confidence, since power was now coming to sailors, signalmen, and pilots.[57] It was for this reason too that the dais built on the Pnyx,[58] which had faced toward the sea, was later turned by the Thirty[59] to face the land, since they thought that the maritime empire had been the wellspring of democracy, and that tillers of the soil were less hostile to oligarchy.

[20] But Themistocles harbored even more grandiose plans for their naval supremacy. When the Greek fleet, after Xerxes' departure, put into Pagasae and passed the winter there, Themistocles addressed the Athenian assembly and said he had a plan that would be beneficial to them and their security, but which should not be revealed to the multitude. When the Athenians urged him to disclose it only to Aristides, and, if *he* approved of it, to put it into effect, Themistocles told Aristides that he proposed to burn the Greeks' dockyards.[60] Aristides then came before the people, and said of Themistocles' proposal that nothing was more advantageous—or more unjust. After that the Athenians ordered Themistocles to abandon it.

At the Amphictyonic council,[61] the Spartans proposed that the cities that had not fought together against the Persians be excluded from membership. At this Themistocles grew alarmed, imagining that the Spartans, if they expelled the Thessalians, Argives, and Thebans from the council, would gain complete control of the votes and see to it that their views prevailed. So he spoke on the cities'

56. *Knights* 815.

57. Military service in Athens was organized by economic class, since citizens supplied their own armor and weaponry. Those who could afford neither a horse nor hoplite gear were consigned to naval service.

58. The Pnyx was the meeting-place of the assembly, the organ of government where the poor played the biggest role.

59. The oligarchic rulers installed by Sparta after the defeat of Athens in 404 BCE; see *Lysander* 15.

60. A proposal paralleling that of the Spartans to pull down all Greek city walls (see note 54). Since Athens had attained naval supremacy, it was in the city's interest to prevent all other cities from building up navies.

61. The governing board that supervised the site of the Delphic oracle, composed of representatives from many states.

behalf and changed their deputies' minds. He explained that only thirty-one cities had taken part in the war, and most of these were very small; it would therefore be intolerable if the rest of Greece should be excluded and the league be dominated by the two or three largest cities. It was for this reason, chiefly, that he incurred the resentment of the Spartans, who now sought to promote Cimon[62] for public honors and make him Themistocles' political rival.

[21] Themistocles also made himself offensive to the allies by sailing around to the islands and trying to exact money from them. For example, Herodotus says that when Themistocles asked the Andrians for money, the following exchange took place. Themistocles said that he had come bringing two gods, Persuasion and Force. To this the Andrians replied that they, too, had two powerful gods, Poverty and Helplessness, who prevented them from giving him money.[63]

Despite his role in the Greek defeat of the Persians, or perhaps because of it—for envy was a powerful political force in Athens—Themistocles fell into disfavor in the 470s, accused of bribe-taking and megalomania.

[22] The Athenians, accordingly, ostracized Themistocles,[64] curtailing his rank and preeminence, as they were in the habit of doing in the cases of all who were felt to be oppressively powerful and at odds with democratic equality. For the ostracism was not a punishment, but a means of mitigating and soothing that jealousy that delights in humbling the eminent, and by imposing such a disgrace vents its ill will.

[23] When he had been banished from the city and was living in Argos, the scandalous doings of Pausanias furnished Themistocles' enemies with grounds against him. . . . For Pausanias, while

62. See *Cimon* in this volume for more on the leading political opponent of Themistocles in the postwar period.

63. Herodotus 8.111. Plutarch retells the story without looking it up in his source, and so alters it a little: In Herodotus Themistocles claims to have "Persuasion and *Necessity*" as his deities. In either version, the tale anticipates Thucydides' exploration of imperial strong-arm tactics in the so-called Melian dialogue (*The Peloponnesian War* 5.84ff.).

64. The date of the ostracism is uncertain, but 473 or 472 BCE is the most likely. On ostracism see note 11 and *Aristides* 7.

pursuing his treasonous scheme,[65] had previously concealed it from Themistocles, though the two men were friends. But when he saw Themistocles banished from public life and in an indignant state of mind, he made so bold as to invite him to take part in his activities, showing him a letter he had received from the King and stoking his anger against the Greeks for their base ingratitude. Themistocles rejected Pausanias' entreaty and wholly renounced the association; but he told no one of Pausanias' proposals, nor did he expose his traitorous scheme, as he assumed either that Pausanias would desist of his own accord or that he would somehow be found out, since he was senselessly grasping at absurd and perilous objects.

When Pausanias had been killed,[66] certain letters and documents pertaining to these matters were found that threw suspicion on Themistocles. The Spartans denounced Themistocles, and the citizens who envied him accused him in his absence, though he defended himself in writing, particularly against the earlier accusations. He pointed out that he had been vilified by his enemies for always seeking to rule, and for being naturally unable and unwilling to *be* ruled; but if that were the case, he would never have sold himself along with Greece either to barbarians or to enemies. But the people, persuaded by his accusers, dispatched men with orders to arrest him and bring him up to be tried before a council of the Greeks.[67]

[24] Learning of this in advance, Themistocles crossed over into Corcyra, where the city was beholden to him. . . . From there he fled to Epirus. And then, pursued by the Athenians and the Spartans, he indulged in desperate and impracticable hopes by fleeing for refuge to Admetus, the king of the Molossians,[68] who had once asked some favor of the Athenians and been offensively rebuffed by Themistocles, then at the height of his power, and had remained angry with him and would clearly take vengeance if he caught him. But in his present predicament, since Themistocles dreaded the

---

65. See Thucydides 1.128–34. Pausanias, a Spartan king and leader of the collective Greek forces at Plataea, apparently let glory go to his head and began colluding with the Persian king, offering to help him subdue the Greek world in exchange for sovereignty over it.

66. By officials at Sparta who had uncovered his plot.

67. The story that follows was taken principally from Thucydides, 1.135ff., but Plutarch has added generous details from other sources. The flight of Themistocles should probably be dated to 470 or 469 BCE.

68. A marginally Greek people, living in what is now Albania.

recent ill will of his own people more than a king's long-standing resentment, he went to Admetus and approached him as a suppliant in a unique and distinctive manner. For he took hold of the king's son, a mere boy, and prostrated himself at the hearth, the Molossians regarding this as the greatest and almost the only undeniable form of supplication. Some say that it was Phthia, the king's wife, who suggested this mode of supplication to Themistocles and seated her son with him at the hearth; others, that Admetus, in order to justify himself to Themistocles' pursuers, imposed on himself the necessity of *not* surrendering him by staging the supplication scene and taking part in it himself.

It was there that Themistocles received his wife and children, who had been spirited out of Athens and sent to him by Epicrates of Acharnae. (Cimon later condemned Epicrates for this and had him put to death, as Stesimbrotus[69] reports.)

[25] Thucydides says that after traveling across Greece to the Aegean, Themistocles sailed from Pydna, and that none of his fellow passengers knew who he was until a gale had carried his vessel down to Naxos, which was then being besieged by the Athenians. Taking alarm, he revealed himself to the shipmaster and the helmsman, and by pleading and threatening to denounce and malign them to the Athenians (he said he would claim that they had not been ignorant when they took him aboard, but had been bribed from the outset), he compelled them to sail on and make for Asia. Most of his money was secretly conveyed away by his friends and sent by sea to Asia. But the sum total of that which came to light and was confiscated for the public treasury amounted to one hundred talents, according to Theopompus (eighty, according to Theophrastus), though Themistocles' fortune had not amounted to three talents before he entered public life.

[26] When he landed at Cyme[70] and learned that many were keeping watch at the coast in order to seize him, and especially Ergoteles and Pythodorus (for the hunt seemed worthwhile to those who embrace any opportunity to turn a profit, the King having offered two hundred talents as a reward for his capture), he fled to Aegae, a small Aeolic town, unrecognized by everyone but his guest-friend Nicogenes, the wealthiest property holder in Aeolia, who was

---

69. An Athenian writer, Stesimbrotus was roughly contemporary with Cimon.

70. A city in Asia Minor, on the west coast of what is now Turkey.

well-acquainted with men of influence in the interior. Themistocles concealed himself with Nicogenes for a few days. . . . Themistocles was sent on his way by Nicogenes, who had devised the following stratagem. Most barbarian races, and particularly the Persians, are naturally savage and cruel in their jealousy where women are concerned. They keep close watch not only over their wedded wives but also over their prostitutes and concubines, making sure that they are seen by no outsiders. At home these women spend their lives in seclusion, and even on journeys their covered carriages are screened with curtains on all sides. Such a wagon was prepared for Themistocles, who slipped inside and journeyed on, his attendants telling those who met and questioned them that they were conducting a young Greek woman from Ionia to one of the King's courtiers.

[27] When Themistocles appeared at that fateful moment, he met first with the chiliarch Artabanus[71] and said that he was a Greek, and that he wished to meet with the King[72] about important matters that were of particular interest to him. Artabanus replied, "The customs of mankind, friend, vary considerably. Different peoples regard different things as noble. But everyone considers it noble to honor and preserve his own ways. It is said that you Greeks especially admire liberty and equality; but for our part, while we have many fine laws, the finest is this: to honor the King, and to make a ritual bow[73] to him as to an image of god, who preserves all things. If, accordingly, approving our customs, you will make this bow, it will be possible for you to see and address the King; if you are otherwise disposed, you may employ others to convey your message to him. For it is not the custom here for the King to listen to a man who has not made obeisance." Themistocles replied, "Well, I have come, Artabanus, with the intention of increasing his fame and power. I shall obey your laws,

71. A chiliarch was a Persian officer who served as the King's right-hand man, sometimes also called a vizier.

72. Here and in what follows, Plutarch declines to use the name of the Persian king, since he has admitted (in a passage not given here) to uncertainty as to whether Xerxes was still on the throne or had been succeeded by Artaxerxes I.

73. The Greek term Plutarch uses, *proskynēsis*, was a highly formalized gesture of submission, seen by the Greeks as a shameful self-prostration. Herodotus reports that two Spartan envoys refused to perform the ritual even under threat of execution. Later, in the time of Alexander the Great, a Greek philosopher vigorously protested Alexander's plan to introduce the ritual at his own court.

since this accords with the will of the god who exalts the Persians. And through *my* having done so, many others will make obeisance to the King. So let this not stand in the way of the conversation I wish to have with him." "Which of the Greeks," said Artabanus, "shall we say has arrived? For your turn of mind resembles that of no ordinary man," to which Themistocles answered, "No one should learn this, Artabanus, before the King himself."

[28] When he was brought before the King, and after making his ritual bow stood in silence, the King ordered the interpreter to ask who he was, and when the interpreter asked, he said, "Themistocles the Athenian has come to you, sire, as an exile, pursued by the Greeks; and to me the Persians are indebted for many evils, but for many more benefits, since I prevented the pursuit as soon as Greece was out of danger and my security at home enabled me to oblige you. Of course, nothing will surprise me in my current predicament, but I have come prepared to receive the favor of one who graciously offers reconciliation, and to entreat away the anger of one who recalls the wrongs done him. Regard my enemies as witnesses of the good I have done Persia, and make my misfortunes the occasion for a display of your virtue, rather than for the satisfaction of your anger. For you may either save your suppliant, or destroy an enemy of the Greeks." So saying, Themistocles alluded to divine influences . . . and remarked that, as he was commanded to proceed to the god's namesake, he concluded that he was being sent to *him*, as both are great and are called "Great King."

On hearing him out, the Persian made no reply to Themistocles, though he was astonished at the man's intelligence and boldness. But among his friends he congratulated himself on what he regarded as the greatest good fortune, and prayed to Arimanius[74] to always dispose his enemies to drive away their best men; he then sacrificed to the gods and embarked at once on a carousal. And during the night, when he was fast asleep, it is said that he thrice sent up the joyous shout, "I have Themistocles the Athenian."

Themistocles won the favor of the King, in part by learning the Persian language and adapting to Persian customs. He was given a high administrative post in the Persian empire, in which he served the King ably for several years.

74. Arimanius is apparently Plutarch's version of the name Ahriman, the deity representing the forces of evil and darkness in the Zoroastrian faith. Much of the Persian nation at this time was Zoroastrian, but it is doubtful that Persians would pray to Ahriman in this way.

[31] Themistocles was not wandering about Asia, but was living in Magnesia, receiving lavish gifts, and being honored as highly as the foremost Persians. He lived for a long time without worry, as the King was paying no heed to Greek affairs, preoccupied as he was with internal matters.

But when Egypt revolted with Athenian aid,[75] and Greek triremes had sailed as far as Cyprus and Cilicia, and Cimon, holding the upper hand at sea, had forced the King to resist the Greeks and to hinder the growth of their power against him, forces were finally deployed, and generals dispatched here and there, and messages were reaching Themistocles saying that the King commanded him to fulfill his promises and apply himself to the Greek problem. Now Themistocles' anger had not been roused against his fellow citizens, nor was he puffed up by the great honor and power he was to have in the war, though he may have thought his task impracticable, since Greece now had other great generals, and Cimon was then enjoying remarkable success against his enemies. But principally out of respect for himself and for his record of achievements and earlier triumphs, he determined that his best course would be to bring his life to a fitting end. On sacrificing to the gods, assembling his friends, and clasping their hands, he drank bull's blood,[76] as the popular account has it, though some say he took a drug that would act the same day, and ended his life in Magnesia, having lived for sixty-five years, most of which he had spent as a leading statesman. When the King learned of the cause and manner of his death, it is said that he admired the man more than ever and continued to support his friends and family.

75. In 460 or 459 BCE, after Themistocles had been almost a decade in Asia. The Egyptians had long chafed at their subjection to Persia, and Athens was all too eager to help the enemies of their enemies; see *Cimon* 18.
76. Widely thought by the Greeks to be poisonous.

Aristides

Aristides (c. 530–c. 467 BCE) will be forever tagged with the epithet the Athenians gave him, "the Just." He was celebrated in his own lifetime for fairness and upright conduct, and he demonstrated these traits quite memorably at the battle of Salamis, according to both Herodotus and Plutarch. But Aristides never really rose to a leadership position in Athens. In the end the Athenians preferred the cunning, conniving Themistocles to straight-arrow Aristides.

In much of this Life, *Plutarch gives Aristides a far bigger role in events than Herodotus does, even while relying on Herodotus as his principal source. Frequently one can compare the two texts and see just how Plutarch has tried to foreground his main character, by attributing to him actions and speeches that Herodotus assigns to the Athenians generally. In most cases the license does not do violence to the historical record, but it should serve to remind readers that in the* Lives *Plutarch was composing character studies and moral paradigms, not history as we know it.*

[2] Aristides became a friend of the Cleisthenes who organized the government after the expulsion of the tyrants.[1] He also emulated and admired Lycurgus the Spartan[2] beyond all other statesmen. He therefore embraced an aristocratic policy and had an entrenched opponent in Themistocles, son of Neocles, the people's champion. Some say that even as boys and schoolmates they were always, from the outset, in deed and word, whether serious or playful, at odds with one another, and that their natures were revealed at once by that rivalry: the one being unscrupulous, reckless, crafty, and quickly and easily carried into every undertaking;[3] the other grounded by a steady character, intent on justice, and admitting no falsehood, buffoonery, or deceit of any kind, even in jest.

[3] As Themistocles had embarked on a course of reckless agitation and was resisting and thwarting his every political initiative,

---

1. In 508 BCE Cleisthenes reorganized the Athenian constitution along democratic lines, after the Pisistratids, the family who had ruled Athens for decades, were driven out.

2. See *Lycurgus* in this volume.

3. As often in the *Lives*, Plutarch changes perspective depending on whose life he is examining. The portrait of Themistocles advanced here is less positive than that in *Themistocles*.

Aristides himself was in some sense compelled, partly in self-defense, and partly in order to curb Themistocles' power, which was increasing through the favor of the multitude, to oppose behind the scenes what Themistocles was trying to do, thinking it better that some advantages should escape the people than that Themistocles should become so powerful as to prevail in everything. Finally, on one occasion when he opposed and defeated Themistocles (though the latter was trying to do something useful), Aristides could not contain himself but said as he was leaving the assembly that there was no safety for Athenian affairs unless they threw both Themistocles and himself into the pit.[4] . . . Through all the vicissitudes of public life, Aristides displayed an admirable steadiness. Honors did not elate him, and he remained calm and mild in adversity, believing that on all occasions alike he had a duty to serve his country freely and without any reward, either in money or even in prestige. And consequently, it appears that when the following verses, composed by Aeschylus about Amphiaraus,[5] were recited in the theater,

> For he wants not to seem, but to *be* just,
> Reaping the harvest from a deep furrow in his mind,
> From which wise counsels spring forth,

everyone gazed at Aristides, thinking that he possessed that integrity in the highest degree.

[5] When Darius[6] dispatched Datis, ostensibly to punish the Athenians for burning Sardis,[7] but actually to subjugate the Greeks, Datis landed at Marathon with his entire fleet and set about plundering the countryside. Of the ten generals the Athenians had appointed for the war, Miltiades held the highest rank; holding second place for renown and influence was Aristides. And on that occasion, since

---

4. The *barathron* was a pit below the Acropolis into which criminals were hurled to their death.

5. Amphiaraus was a mythic hero, subject of a now-lost tragedy by Aeschylus.

6. Persian king of the late sixth and early fifth centuries BCE; Datis was one of his generals. The events referred to in this paragraph took place in 490, the date of the first Persian invasion of European Greece.

7. Athens contributed a small contingent to the Ionian Revolt, an uprising of Greek states in Asia that were subject to Persia. The rebels began by marching to Sardis, capital of Lydia, and torching it, in 499 BCE; Athens soon thereafter withdrew its forces.

he embraced Miltiades' views about the impending battle,[8] Aristides
did much to tip the scales in its favor. For command passed each day
from one general to the next; but when it came around to Aristides,
he surrendered it to Miltiades, explaining to his co-commanders that
to obey and follow men of sense was not shameful, but honorable and
beneficial. And by thus appeasing their rivalry and persuading them
to embrace a single policy, namely the soundest, he strengthened
Miltiades with an authority that no longer passed from one general
to the next. For now each man, when it was his day to command,
yielded his authority to Miltiades.[9]

In the battle,[10] the Athenian center was pressed the hardest; it
was there that the barbarians held out the longest against the tribes
Leontis and Antiochis.[11] And there Themistocles and Aristides
fought superbly, posted side by side, as one was a Leontid, the other
an Antiochid. When the Athenians had routed the barbarians and
driven them onto their ships and saw them sailing not for the islands,
but carried by wind and sea toward Attica, they grew fearful that the
barbarians might seize Athens, which was then bereft of defenders.
Hastening there with nine tribes, they reached the city on the same
day. Aristides, left behind at Marathon with his own tribe to guard
the prisoners and spoils, did not prove false to his reputation. Though
heaps of silver and gold lay at hand, and all sorts of garments and
untold stores of other wealth in the tents and captured vessels, he had
no wish to touch it, nor did he permit anyone else to do so, unless
certain persons helped themselves without his knowledge.

[6] Of all his virtues, it was Aristides' justice that made the
strongest impression on the multitude, because he exercised it con-
tinually and with the public good in mind. And as a result, though
poor and a man of the people, he acquired the most majestic and
sacred name—"the Just."

8. Miltiades was in favor of giving battle immediately, rather than waiting,
as the others preferred; his strategy was widely credited for the Athenian
victory.

9. Herodotus (*Histories* 6.109–10) tells a similar story but without mentioning Aristides; instead it is a man named Callimachus who cedes authority to Miltiades.

10. The battle of Marathon; see Herodotus 6.109–17.

11. "Tribes" here refers to the ten groups into which the Athenian population was divided. Originally based on kinship ties, the tribes by this time
were purely political groupings.

[7] Accordingly, it befell Aristides to be beloved at first because of his nickname, but envied later on, especially when Themistocles spread word among the people that Aristides had destroyed the law courts by trying and judging all cases privately,[12] and had managed, imperceptibly and without a bodyguard, to build himself a monarchy. For by then the common people, priding themselves on their victory and thinking they deserved the highest honors, were vexed at those who enjoyed a renown and reputation that surpassed their own. Assembling in the city from all directions, they ostracized Aristides,[13] terming their envy of his renown "fear of tyranny."

For ostracism was not a punishment for baseness, but was speciously said to be a humbling and curtailing of oppressive pride and power. It was actually a benign means of relieving the spirit of envious hostility, which thus vented itself not in the infliction of some incurable harm, but simply in a ten-year banishment. But when this penalty began to be imposed on people who were base or ill-born they discontinued the practice, Hyperbolus being the last to be ostracized.[14] . . . The procedure—to give a sketch—was as follows. Each man took a potsherd, wrote upon it the name of the citizen he wished to see banished, and brought it to an area in the marketplace that was fenced by a railing. First, the magistrates would count the total number of potsherds. For if they numbered less than six thousand, the ostracism was canceled. Then, after sorting the potsherds by name, they would proclaim that the man whose name appeared on the greatest number was banished for ten years, though he continued to enjoy the income of his property.

At the time I am speaking of, when the voters were writing names on their potsherds, it is said that an illiterate rustic gave his potsherd to Aristides, taking him for a common citizen, and asked him to write down Aristides' name. Aristides was taken aback, and when he asked whether Aristides had done him any harm, the man said, "None at all. I don't even know the man. But I'm tired of everywhere hearing him called 'the Just.'" Aristides, on hearing this, made no reply, but wrote his name on the potsherd and handed it back.

12. An ingenious way to turn Aristides' reputation for justice against him. Since the poor and unemployed of Athens most benefited from jury service, it would gall them to think that their main means of earning a living was being subverted.
13. This ostracism is variously dated between 485 and 482 BCE.
14. See *Alcibiades* 13, *Nicias* 11. The ostracism of Hyperbolus took place about 415 BCE.

[8] But two years later, when Xerxes was marching through
Thessaly and Boeotia against Attica,[15] the Athenians repealed their
law and voted to recall the citizens who had emigrated. They were
especially afraid that Aristides, if he associated himself with the
enemy, might corrupt many citizens and induce them to side with
the barbarian. For they had no true conception of the man, who
even before the public decree was constantly inciting and urging
the Greeks to defend their freedom. And after the decree, when
Themistocles was serving as commander in chief, Aristides supported
his every action and counsel—exalting, for the sake of their common
deliverance, the renown of his worst enemy. For when Eurybiades
was planning to leave Salamis,[16] but the barbarian triremes, putting
out to sea at night, surrounded the strait and got possession of its
islands, and no one knew of the encirclement, Aristides arrived, having recklessly sailed through the enemy's line from Aegina. Coming
by night to Themistocles' tent, and calling him out alone, he said, "If
we are sensible, Themistocles, we will now drop our vain and childish
quarrel, and begin a beneficial and honorable rivalry, vying with one
another to save Greece, with you as ruler and commander, I as helper
and counselor. For even now I hear that you alone are embracing the
best policy, since you are urging the Greeks to fight in the narrows
as soon as possible. And though the allies are seeking to oppose you,
the enemy appears to be lending you a hand. For around and behind
us the sea is now filled with enemy ships, so that even the unwilling have no choice but to be brave men and to fight. For no route
of escape is left." To this Themistocles replied, "I would not have
wished, Aristides, to have you outdo me here, but I will try to rival
your sound beginning, and to surpass you in my actions."

15. In the great Persian invasion of Greece, 480–479 BCE. Xerxes, son of
Darius, used as his pretext that he was seeking to complete the punishment
of Athens for participating in the Ionian Revolt (see note 7); hence he was
marching, primarily, against Attica, but he really planned to conquer all of
European Greece.

16. Plutarch has skipped over other battles against the Persians to reach the
battle of Salamis. Eurybiades was the Spartan admiral in charge of the Greek
fleet stationed at Salamis, and Themistocles, who headed the Athenian contingent, was vigorously opposing his strategy—which would have brought
the fleet south to the Isthmus of Corinth to defend the Peloponnese. See
Themistocles 11ff. (in this volume) and Herodotus 8.74ff.

[10] Thereafter Xerxes, greatly alarmed, headed straight to the Hellespont,[17] while Mardonius was left behind with the best part of the army, a force of nearly three hundred thousand men. A formidable commander, who expected great things of his infantry, Mardonius wrote the Greeks a threatening letter: "With your wooden ships you have conquered landsmen who are unskilled at plying the oar. Now, however, we have the broad land of Thessaly and the Boeotian plain[18]—a fine battlefield for brave horsemen and hoplites." But on his own account he sent the Athenians letters and proposals from the King,[19] promising to restore their city, give them vast sums of money, and make them supreme among the Greeks if they took no part in the war.

On learning of this, the Spartans grew fearful and sent envoys to Athens, beseeching the Athenians to send their children and wives to Sparta, and to accept provisions from them for their elderly.[20] For the people of Athens were in great want, having lost both their city and country. After listening to the envoys, the Athenians gave a marvelous reply, on Aristides' motion. They said they could pardon their enemies for believing that anything could be bought with wealth and money, since these men had no conception of anything more important; but they were angry with the Spartans for seeing only the poverty and destitution now prevailing at Athens, and for being so oblivious of the Athenians' courage and love of honor as to urge them to fight on behalf of Greece merely for the sake of food. On making this motion, Aristides brought the envoys into the assembly and urged them to tell the Spartans that there was no amount of gold, either above ground or below it, which the Athenians would accept in return for the freedom of the Greeks. And in replying to the messengers from Mardonius he pointed to the sun and said, "As long as

17. That is, after losing the sea battle, which Plutarch here has omitted since Aristides played no part.

18. Since Thebes had gone over to the Persian side, Mardonius could consider Boeotia to be *his* ground.

19. As always in this volume, "King" when capitalized refers to the Great King of Persia.

20. Herodotus (8.142) reports that the Spartans offered to feed, not to take in, the civilian population of Athens. The Athenians were at this point in exile on Salamis and in Troezen, having fled from their own city (see *Themistocles* 10).

Helios[21] continues to wend his way, the Athenians will wage war with the Persians on behalf of their ravaged country and the temples that have been burned and desecrated." He also wrote a decree stating that the priests were to call down curses on anyone who negotiated with the Medes or abandoned the Greek alliance.

When Mardonius invaded Attica for the second time,[22] the Athenians again crossed over to Salamis. Dispatched to Sparta, Aristides accused the Spartans of tardiness and negligence, since they were again abandoning Athens to the barbarian, and demanded that they hasten to rescue what still remained of Greece. On hearing this, the ephors,[23] while it was day, made a show of festivity and enjoyment of a holiday, since their Hyacinthia[24] was in progress. But that night they selected five thousand Spartans, each of whom was attended by seven helots,[25] and sent them off without the Athenians' knowledge. When Aristides again approached and accused the ephors, they laughed and said he was talking drowsy nonsense, since the army was already at Oresteum on its march against the foreigners (they referred to the Persians as foreigners).[26] Aristides replied that their pleasantry was ill-timed, as they were deceiving their friends instead of their enemies.[27]

[11] Elected as general with full powers for the battle,[28] Aristides took eight thousand Athenian hoplites and marched to Plataea. Pausanias, as commander of the entire Greek force,[29] joined him there with his Spartans, and other Greek forces were streaming in. As

21. Another name for the sun. Again Plutarch's version of events seems liberally adapted from Herodotus, who reports a speech (8.143) much like that given here, but attributes it to the Athenian people, not to Aristides.

22. In the spring of 479 BCE, after spending winter in camp.

23. A board of five officials at Sparta, responsible for many policy decisions.

24. An important Spartan religious festival in early summer.

25. Helots were the Messenian Greeks enslaved by Sparta and used as the labor force supporting its war machine. See *Lycurgus* 24, n. 35.

26. Other ancient writers confirm that the Spartans called the Persians *xenoi*, "foreigners," while other Greeks called them *barbaroi*, "barbarians."

27. This story by Plutarch again takes events narrated by Herodotus (9.6–11) and inserts Aristides as the leading figure.

28. Confirmed by Herodotus at 9.28.

29. A Spartan king had been placed in charge of the coalition Greek land forces, just as, at Salamis, a Spartan admiral (Eurybiades) had charge of the collective Greek navy.

for the barbarians, because of their vast numbers there was virtually
no limit to their camp, which extended alongside the river Asopus;
and they built a square wall, more than a mile long on each side,
around their baggage train and main headquarters.

[12] Challenging the Athenians about their position in the line,
the Tegeans demanded that whereas the Spartans, as always, held
the right wing, they themselves should hold the left,[30] and cited,
in support of their claim, many praiseworthy actions performed
by their ancestors. The Athenians were indignant, and Aristides
came forward[31] and said, "This is surely not the proper moment
for contending with the Tegeans about noble birth and valor. But
we say to you, Spartans, and to the other Greeks, that one's place
in the line of battle neither gives a man courage nor robs him of it.
Whatever post you assign to us we will try to maintain in a worthy
manner, and thus guard against dishonoring our earlier contests. For
we have come not to quarrel with our allies but to fight the enemy;
not to praise our forefathers, but to show ourselves brave on behalf
of Greece. And this contest will show how much any city or commander or ordinary citizen is worth to Greece." On hearing this, the
commissioners and leaders decided in favor of the Athenians, and
gave them the other wing.

[14] Thereafter Mardonius, deploying what was thought to constitute his greatest asset, made trial of the Greeks, sending his cavalry in close order against them where they had encamped in rocky,
defensible positions at the foot of Mount Cithaeron—all except the
Megarians. These men, three thousand strong, were encamped on
the plain, and that was why they suffered cruelly at the hands of
the cavalry, which charged at them and attacked from all directions.
They quickly sent a messenger to Pausanias, urging him to come to
their aid, since on their own they were unable to hold out against
the barbarians' numbers. When Pausanias heard this, and saw the
Megarians' camp already obscured by the rain of flying javelins and
arrows, and the Megarians themselves cowering together in a small
space, he could not himself ward off the horsemen with his phalanx of

30. It was a much-sought honor to hold one of the extreme positions
("wings") in the line of battle, since that implied great prowess. The Spartans
were always awarded the right wing, by far the more prestigious of the two
assignments, whenever they joined with other cities to fight a battle.
31. Yet again, Plutarch has made Aristides the principal agent in an episode
where Herodotus (9.27) speaks rather of the collective Athenian people.

heavy-armed Spartans; but to the other generals and Greek captains who surrounded him he proposed, as a chance to demonstrate their valor and ambition, that some of them volunteer to aid and defend the Megarians. When the others hesitated, Aristides, undertaking the exploit on behalf of the Athenians, dispatched his bravest captain, Olympiodorus, with the three hundred selected men and some archers under his command.[32] These men arrayed themselves quickly and attacked on the run. And when the barbarian cavalry commander Masistius, a man remarkable for his valor, his stature, and the surpassing beauty of his physique, caught sight of them, he wheeled his horse about and charged toward them. A desperate struggle took place between those who resisted and those who attacked, since they regarded their combat as a trial run for the larger battle. But when his horse was shot with an arrow and Masistius was thrown, he found it hard to move, owing to the weight of his armor, and impossible to fight off the Athenians who were assaulting and striking him. For not only his chest and head, but his limbs as well were armored in gold, bronze, and iron. He was finally slain when someone struck him with the spike of a javelin through his helmet's eyehole, at which point the other Persians abandoned his corpse and fled. The magnitude of their success was recognized by the Greeks not from the number of the corpses, as few men had fallen, but by the barbarians' mourning. For they cut their hair—and that of their horses and mules—in honor of Masistius. Wailing and sobbing filled the plain, as they had lost the man who, after Mardonius, was by far their bravest and most powerful warrior.

[15] After the cavalry engagement, both sides refrained from battle for a long time, since from the sacrifices the seers were predicting, for Persians and Greeks alike, a victory for the side that fought defensively, and a defeat for the aggressors. [16] The Greeks then took counsel and decided to change their camp to a more distant position and to occupy an area that had a good supply of water, since the nearby streams had been sullied and defiled by the barbarian cavalry.

[17] When night came on and the commanders tried to lead their men to the appointed encampment, most of the soldiers were not at all eager to follow them or keep together. Instead, when they

32. Herodotus (9.20–23) confirms the role of the three hundred Athenians at Plataea and the other features of this chapter but does not mention Aristides.

rose from their first defenses, most of them streamed into the city of Plataea, where an uproar arose as the men dispersed and encamped in no sort of order. It happened that the Spartans, against their will, were left alone behind the others. For Amompharetus, a courageous and danger-loving man, who had long been frantic for battle and resented the many delays and postponements, now denounced the change of position as an escape and flight and said he would not leave his post, but would stay there with his fellow soldiers and resist Mardonius. When Pausanias came to him and said that they were acting in accordance with the decision and vote of the Greeks in council, Amompharetus raised an enormous rock in both hands, threw it down before Pausanias' feet, and said that that was *his* vote on the war.[33] He added that he had no use for the cowardly counsels and opinions of the others. At a loss what to do, Pausanias sent word to the Athenians, who had already departed, asking them to wait and march with him. He then led the rest of his forces to Plataea, hoping he would thus prompt Amompharetus to move.

At that point day overtook them, and Mardonius, who had been aware that the Greeks were leaving their camp, drew his forces up in battle array and attacked the Spartans, the barbarians raising a great shout and clamor, since they assumed that there would be no battle, but that they would pick off some of the Greeks as they fled. And this very nearly came to pass. For when Pausanias noticed what was happening, he halted the march and ordered each man to take his position for battle; but either because of his anger at Amompharetus or because he was distracted by the speed of the enemy, he forgot to give the signal to the Greek allies. And for that reason they did not come to his aid immediately or in a body, but in small, scattered bands when the battle was already in progress.

[18] When the order had been given to all the troops to range themselves against the enemy, the phalanx suddenly assumed the appearance of a single wild animal, bristling up to defend itself. The barbarians then recognized that their contest would be with men fighting to the death, which was why they held their wicker shields before them and shot their arrows into the ranks of the Spartans. But these kept their shields locked together as they advanced, attacked the enemy, and thrust away their wicker shields. Then, stabbing with their spears at faces and chests, they struck down many Persians,

33. The gesture is meant as an exaggerated version of the standard Greek method of voting, by dropping pebbles into an urn.

though the latter fought well and courageously before they fell. For they grasped the Greeks' spears with their bare hands and shattered many of them. They then made effective use of their swords; wielding daggers and scimitars, they wrested the Spartans' shields from them, engaged the enemy in close fight, and resisted for a long time.

The Athenians, meanwhile, stood still, waiting for the Spartans; but when they heard loud shouting, as of men engaged in combat, and a messenger, it is said, came from Pausanias to report what was happening, they hastened to the rescue as fast as they could. But as they were advancing across the plain toward the noise, they were attacked by the Greeks fighting for Persia.[34] As soon as Aristides caught sight of *them*, he came forward, far ahead of the others, and shouted out to them, in the name of the gods of Greece, to refrain from battle, and urged them not to oppose or hinder those who were going to aid the foremost defenders of Greece. But when he saw that they were paying him no heed, and were arrayed for battle, he turned aside from the rescue of the Spartans and engaged them, though they numbered nearly fifty thousand. Yet most of them gave way at once and retired, since the barbarians had also retreated. The battle is said to have been fought principally against the Thebans, whose most important and distinguished citizens were then eagerly siding with the Persians and leading the multitude, though the people went along not by choice, but at the bidding of the oligarchs.

[19] With the battle thus joined in two places, the Spartans were the first to repel the Persians; and a Spartan named Arimnestus killed Mardonius, striking his head with a rock. . . . The Spartans, meanwhile, drove the fleeing Persians inside their wooden fort.

Shortly afterward, the Athenians routed the Thebans, slaughtering three hundred of their finest and most distinguished citizens in the battle itself. When the rout had occurred, a messenger reached the Athenians with the news that the barbarian forces, trapped in their fort, were being besieged. And thus the Athenians, letting the other Greeks see to their own escape, hastened in aid to the fort. Joining the Spartans, who were wholly inexperienced and unskilled in siege warfare, they captured the camp by slaughtering enormous numbers of the enemy. For of the three hundred thousand, only forty thousand are said to have fled with Artabanus; of those who contended on behalf of Greece the fallen numbered 1,360 in all.

34. The Persians had compelled their Greek subjects, those living on the coast of Asia, to contribute troops to their invasion force and had also made allies of the Thebans and other Boeotians.

[21] Thereafter a general assembly of the Greeks was held, and Aristides wrote a decree stating that the deputies and ambassadors from Greece were to come together at Plataea every year, and that games—the Eleutheria—were to be held every fifth year; that a standing Greek force was to be enlisted, consisting of ten thousand infantry, one thousand cavalry, and one hundred ships, to make war on the barbarians; and that the Plataeans were to be exempted from military service and consecrated to the service of the gods, performing sacrifices on behalf of Greece.

[22] When the Athenians had returned to their city, Aristides saw that they were eager to restore the democracy. Believing that the common people, because of their bravery, were worthy of consideration, and realizing at the same time that they could not easily be forced out, since they were able warriors and prided themselves on their victories, Aristides wrote a decree stating that all might share in the government and that the archons be chosen from the entire body of Athenian citizens.[35]

When Themistocles told the people that he had a plan that should not be revealed to the multitude, though it was beneficial to the city and its security, they ordered Aristides alone to hear and consider it with him. And when Themistocles told Aristides that he intended to burn the Greek allies' naval station, since by that means the Athenians would be supremely powerful,[36] Aristides came before the people and said that nothing was more advantageous than Themistocles' proposal—and nothing more unjust. On hearing this, the Athenians ordered Themistocles to desist. So devoted to justice were the people, and so trustworthy and true to them was Aristides.

[23] When sent out as general along with Cimon to prosecute the war,[37] Aristides saw Pausanias and the other Spartan commanders treating the allies with oppressive harshness; and by treating them

35. This statement is inaccurate if it means what it seems to. The Athenians, according to Aristotle (*Constitution of the Athenians* 26), only extended the archonship to the third of their four property classes in 457 BCE, well after the time referred to here; and the lowest class was never eligible. Plutarch seems to have trusted a source that was eager to promote Aristides as a friend of democracy.

36. By having the only dockyards, Athens would maintain its naval supremacy. The same story is told in *Themistocles* 20.

37. Though the battle of Plataea (479 BCE) ended the Persian invasion of Greece, the war for control of the Aegean Sea and the western coast of Asia continued thereafter.

gently and generously himself, and seeing to it that Cimon accommo-
dated them and took part in their campaigns, he succeeded, without
the Spartans' realizing it, in stealing away the chief command—not
by means of weapons, ships, or horses, but by sound sense and policy.
For the Athenians had already endeared themselves to the Greeks
by Aristides' fairness and Cimon's good sense; Pausanias' rapacity
and arrogance only made Athenian leadership more desirable. For
Pausanias always dealt angrily and harshly with the allies' commanders, and he punished many men with beatings, or by forcing them
to stand all day long with an iron anchor on their shoulders. And it
was impossible to get hold of straw for bedding or even fodder, or
for anyone who went to a well to draw water ahead of the Spartans,
since their servants, holding whips, would drive away those who
approached. On one occasion, when Aristides had decided to confront and try to reason with him about this, Pausanias scowled, said
he had no time, and would not listen.

After this, the Greek admirals and generals came forward—
especially the Chians, Samians, and Lesbians—and tried to persuade
Aristides to accept the chief command and seek the support of the
allies, who had long wished to be rid of the Spartans and to transfer
their allegiance to the Athenians. When he replied that he saw the
urgency and justice of their proposals, but that as a guarantee of their
fidelity some deed was needed, the performance of which would not
allow the multitude to change sides again, Uliades of Samos and
Antagoras of Chios conspired together and rammed the trireme of
Pausanias near Byzantium, pinning it between their ships as it sailed
out ahead of the rest. When he caught sight of them, Pausanias leaped
up and angrily threatened to make it clear before long that they had
rammed not merely his ship, but their own countries. In reply, they
urged him to depart and be thankful for the luck that had attended
him at Plataea. For it was only their respect for that, they said, that
kept the Greeks from inflicting the punishment he deserved. In the
end, they departed and rejoined the Athenians.

And then Sparta's remarkable high-mindedness showed itself.
For when the Spartans realized that their commanders were being
corrupted by the greatness of their power, they voluntarily renounced
the chief command and stopped sending generals to the war, choosing rather to have their citizens exercise self-control and remain true
to their customs than to hold sway over all of Greece.

[24] The Greeks had been paying a certain tax for the war under
the Spartans' leadership, but as they wanted to be assessed propor-
tionally, city by city, they asked the Athenians to send Aristides, and

charged him with the task of inspecting their territory and revenues and determining the tax according to each city's worth and ability to pay. But though he had become master of such power, and had in a sense been given sole authority over everything Greece possessed— poor as he was when he went forth, he returned poorer still, having performed the assessment not only honestly and justly, but in such a way as to make himself appreciated and beloved by all. For just as the ancients sang the praises of the age of Cronus,[38] so did the Athenians' allies call the assessment in the era of Aristides a kind of windfall for Greece, especially since it was soon doubled and later tripled.

[25] Aristides made the Greeks swear an oath, and he himself took the oath on the Athenians' behalf, casting a mass of red-hot metal into the sea.[39] But later on, it would seem, when their affairs had to be managed more aggressively,[40] he urged the Athenians to lay the blame on *him* for their perjury and to act with an eye to their own advantage. Theophrastus says that on the whole this man, who in private life was exceedingly just to his fellow citizens, often acted in public life with a view to his country's policy, which required many unjust acts. He says, for example, that when the transfer of funds from Delos to Athens, contrary to the covenants, was being debated, and the measure was actually proposed by the Samians, Aristides said that it was unjust but advantageous.[41]

[26] Some say that Aristides died in Pontus,[42] after sailing there on public business, while others claim that he died of old age in Athens, honored and admired by his fellow citizens.

38. The era in which Cronus, father of Zeus, was king of the gods, the earliest era of humankind, was supposedly a Golden Age.

39. The point of this gesture lay in the accompanying oath, which was that the alliance—known to historians as the Delian League, because its treasury was initially housed on the island of Delos—would endure until the metal floated to the surface. Why the lump of metal was heated before this ritual is unclear.

40. A euphemism for the pattern that soon set in, whereby Athens attacked those who sought to withdraw from the league.

41. Somewhat the reverse of his dictum on Themistocles' proposal to burn the Greek dockyards; see chapter 22. Aristides was not so "just" as to ignore self-interest entirely.

42. That is, in the Black Sea region.

Cimon

The life span of Cimon the Athenian (c. 510–450 BCE) overlaps closely with that of Themistocles, and the two men were rivals during much of their political careers. But Cimon came from a much more aristocratic background than Themistocles, being the son of wealthy and influential Miltiades, the hero of Marathon. As was true of many in Athens' upper crust, Cimon was conservative in temperament and leaned toward both oligarchic government and, in foreign policy, friendship with Sparta. These views put him at odds with Themistocles, who focused on building up Athenian strength even at the cost of alienating Sparta, and on enlarging the navy, the branch of the armed forces in which the poor played the biggest role. Cimon proved the winner in the contest with Themistocles, but he was himself brought down by the same populist forces that had once put Themistocles in power.

[4] The mother of Cimon, son of Miltiades,[1] was Hegesipyle—a Thracian by race, and the daughter of King Olorus. . . . Miltiades, who had incurred a fine of fifty talents,[2] was detained pending payment in full. He died in prison, leaving behind Cimon, still a mere lad, with his sister, a young girl still unmarried. Cimon was at first held in low esteem in the city. He was maligned for being unruly, a heavy drinker, and similar in nature to his grandfather . . . whom they say was nicknamed Booby because of his simplicity. . . . Cimon was susceptible to the erotic charms of women. For the poet Melanthius, making fun of Cimon in his elegies, mentions Asteria of Salamis, and then a certain Mnestra, as having been courted by him. And it is clear that he was unusually devoted to Isodice, the daughter of Euryptolemus and granddaughter of Megacles, who lived with Cimon as his lawful wife,[3] and that he deeply grieved her death, if one must rely for evidence on the elegies written to console him in his grief.

1. Cimon's father was the same Miltiades whose leadership had helped win the battle of Marathon; see *Themistocles* 3, *Aristides* 5.

2. Miltiades failed to take the island of Paros in 489 BCE after urging Athens to let him attack it, and his political enemies pounced on him (Herodotus, *Histories* 6.133–39).

3. By marrying Isodice, granddaughter of Megacles, Cimon had become allied with the Alcmaeonids, a family even more wealthy and powerful than his own prominent clan, the Philiads.

[5] All of Cimon's other traits of character were admirable and noble. For he fell short neither of Miltiades in courage nor of Themistocles in sagacity, and it is generally agreed that he was more fair-minded than both and in military expertise not even slightly inferior to them, while it is impossible to conceive how far he surpassed them in political skill when he was still a young man and without experience in war. . . .

Tall as he was and with an abundant crop of long curly hair (as the poet Ion tells us), no fault was to be found with his appearance. Cutting a brave and brilliant figure in the struggle at Salamis,[4] he soon won renown and good will, and many flocked to him, urging him to conceive and carry out exploits worthy of Marathon. When he embarked on his political career, the people welcomed him gladly. Sated as they were with Themistocles,[5] they promoted Cimon to the highest honors and offices in the city; for he was amenable, and his mildness and simplicity won him many friends. And not least among those who exalted him was Aristides, son of Lysimachus,[6] who recognized the natural goodness of his disposition and set him up to rival the cleverness and daring of Themistocles.

[6] When the Persians had fled from Greece, Cimon was posted as a commander,[7] though the Athenians did not yet hold sway at sea, but were obeying Pausanias[8] and the Spartans. From the start Cimon always furnished their expeditions with citizens whose orderly conduct commanded admiration, and who far surpassed the others in zeal. Later, when Pausanias was conversing treasonably with the barbarians,[9] writing letters to the King,[10] treating the allies harshly

4. Herodotus does not record any deeds of Cimon's at the battle of Salamis, though it is nearly certain that he fought there, being then about thirty years old.

5. See *Themistocles* 22. The Athenians ostracized Themistocles shortly after the end of the Persian wars, in part because he had shown too much pride in his role in their victory.

6. See *Aristides* in this volume.

7. According to Plutarch (*Aristides* 23), Aristides served alongside Cimon as a leader of the mopping-up operations in the Aegean following the Greek defeat of the Persians.

8. A Spartan king who had leadership of the collective Greek forces fighting the Persians.

9. See *Themistocles* 23 and Thucydides, *The Peloponnesian War* 1.128–34.

10. As always in this volume, "King" when capitalized refers to the Great King of Persia.

and willfully, and often insolently abusing his authority and displaying a foolish self-importance, Cimon received the injured parties
mildly, treated them humanely, and imperceptibly assumed the role
of commander—not through force of arms, but by virtue of his manner of speaking and his character.[11] For most of the allies attached
themselves to him and to Aristides, as they found Pausanias' harshness and arrogance insufferable. As soon as they had taken charge of
these allies, Cimon and Aristides wrote to the ephors and told them
to recall Pausanias, since Sparta had lost prestige and Greece was in
trouble.

It is said that Pausanias, harboring a shameful purpose, sent for
a girl from Byzantium named Cleonice, who came from an illus-
trious family. Her parents, though fearful, were forced to comply,
and abandoned their daughter to her fate. The girl asked the men
standing before his bedroom to put out the light. As she approached,
in darkness and silence, the couch on which Pausanias had already
fallen asleep, she fell and overturned the lamp-stand. Disturbed by
the noise and drawing the dagger that lay beside him, thinking that
an enemy was approaching, Pausanias struck and killed the girl.
Thereafter, though dead, she allowed Pausanias no rest, but visited
him nightly in his sleep as a phantom, angrily uttering this verse:

> Draw near for punishment; their wanton violence leads men into
> direst evil.[12]

Incensed beyond measure by this incident, the allies joined forces
with Cimon to drive Pausanias from the city.

[7] When the allies had joined him, Cimon sailed as commander
to Thrace, having learned that some distinguished Persians and
kinsmen of the King had occupied the city of Eion, on the river
Strymon, and were harassing the Greeks who lived in the neighborhood. He soon prevailed over the Persians in battle and confined
them in the city. Then, driving from their homes the Thracians
who dwelt beyond the Strymon, from whom the Persians had been
importing grain, he kept the entire country under guard and reduced
the besieged Persians to such straits that Butes, the King's general,
despairing at his predicament, set the city on fire and destroyed himself along with his friends and property. On seizing the city, Cimon

11. Thucydides 1.95–98.
12. This verse is in dactylic hexameter as though quoted from an epic poem,
but its source is unknown.

gained no other advantage worth mentioning, since almost everything had been burned with the barbarians. But as the country was surpassingly fair and fertile, he gave it to the Athenians to inhabit.[13]

[8] The Athenians also occupied Scyros, which Cimon had captured. . . . And when Cimon learned that in ancient times Theseus, son of Aegeus,[14] had fled from Athens to Scyros, but had been put to death by King Lycomedes, who feared him, Cimon was eager to find his grave. For an oracle had commanded the Athenians to bring Theseus' ashes back to the city and offer him a hero's honors. But the Athenians had not known where he lay buried, and the Scyrians would neither admit that the story was true, nor allow them to conduct a search. Now, though, as Cimon's ambition was fired, he exerted himself, found the sacred precinct, placed the bones in his own trireme, and on arranging a magnificent display conveyed them back to Theseus' native city after nearly four hundred years. It was for this deed, more than for any other, that he won the people's hearts.

[11] The allies[15] continued to pay their assessments, but would not furnish men and ships as ordered. Weary by then of military service, they had no use for war, but were eager to farm and live quietly. As the barbarians had retired and were not troubling them, the allies neither manned their ships nor sent out men. The other Athenian generals tried to force them to do so;[16] and by prosecuting the delinquents and punishing them, these generals were making their authority burdensome and painful. But Cimon, taking the opposite course when serving as general, exerted pressure on none of the Greeks, but accepted funds and empty ships from those who had no wish to serve, and allowed the allies, seduced by their foolish love of ease and comfort, to stay at home and become farmers and unwarlike merchants instead of warriors. Meanwhile, he embarked many of the Athenians, one crew relieving another, and worked them hard

13. The Athenians used a system called cleruchy to spread their empire. Lands won in military expeditions were divided into lots and given out for free to Athenian citizens willing to emigrate.

14. A mythic hero and legendary king of Athens. See *Theseus* in this volume.

15. That is, the Greek cities that had joined together to resist the Persian invasion, or had become part of the security organization formed after its defeat. This organization, called the Delian League because its treasury was initially kept on Delos, required member states to contribute either money or ships.

16. See *Themistocles* 21, for example.

in the campaigns. And soon, by means of the wages they received from their allies, he made the Athenians the masters of those who were paying them. For those who avoided service grew accustomed to fearing and flattering those who were constantly serving at sea, bearing arms, and being trained and drilled, and thus became, without realizing it, tribute-paying subjects rather than allies.[17]

[12] And in fact no one did more than Cimon to humble the Great King himself and subdue his pride. For when the King left Greece,[18] Cimon did not let him go quietly, but followed close on his heels, as it were; and before the barbarians halted to catch their breath, Cimon in some instances plundered and subjugated the local peoples, in others persuaded them to revolt and come over to the Greeks, with the result that from Ionia to Pamphylia he completely rid Asia[19] of Persian arms. When he learned that the King's commanders were lying in wait near Pamphylia with a powerful army and a large fleet, Cimon wanted to make them utterly afraid to sail into the sea west of the Chelidonian islands, and he set out from Cnidus and Tropium with thirty ships. These had originally been outfitted by Themistocles for optimal speed and maneuverability, though Cimon now made them broader and gave them gangways along their decks, so that large numbers of hoplites could attack the enemy more effectively.[20] Landing at Phaselis, which was a Greek city but refused to receive the fleet or revolt from the King, Cimon plundered its countryside and assaulted its walls. But the Chians, who were sailing with him and had from ancient times been friendly with the Phaselitans, tried to allay Cimon's enmity; and meanwhile, by shooting arrows over the walls—arrows to which they had attached messages—they passed intelligence to the men of Phaselis. At last

17. Though at first many Delian League members contributed ships to the collective forces, so that they continued to maintain an active fleet with experienced rowers, before long only three member states, Lesbos, Chios, and Samos, chose to do so. The rest gave tribute payments, meaning that they essentially paid the Athenians to serve in their stead.

18. After the battle of Salamis in 480 BCE, Xerxes returned to Asia with the Persian navy. The land army, left in Greece under the command of Mardonius, followed him after the battle of Plataea the next year.

19. "Asia" here refers only to the west coast of Anatolia, as often in ancient Greek.

20. Boarding of enemy vessels was a common tactic in ancient naval warfare.

Cimon made peace with them on condition that they pay him ten talents and serve in his expedition against the barbarians.

Callisthenes[21] says that Ariomandes, son of Gobryas, the Persian commander in chief, was holding the fleet at anchor near the river Eurymedon and that he was not eager to fight with the Greeks, but was waiting for 80 Phoenician ships from Cyprus to join him. Wishing to anticipate their arrival, Cimon put out to sea, ready to force the Persians to fight if they would not do so willingly. At first, to avoid being forced to engage, the Persians ran their fleet into the river. But when the Athenians approached, the Persians sailed out against them with 600 ships, according to Phandemus, though Ephorus says there were 350. At sea, however, they achieved nothing worthy of their power. Immediately returning to shore and abandoning their ships, the foremost Persians fled to the infantry that was stationed nearby; but those who were caught were destroyed with their ships.

[13] The barbarian infantry marched down to the sea against the Greeks. Cimon imagined it would be an enormous task to force a landing and lead his weary Greeks against an unwearied enemy many times more numerous. But when he saw that his men were excited by their own strength and by pride in their victory, and were eager to come to blows with the barbarians, he disembarked the hoplites,[22] still heated from their struggle in the sea battle, and they advanced on the run, raising a shout. Since the Persians stood their ground and bravely awaited the attack, a fierce battle was fought, and brave Athenians—distinguished men who had been prominent in public life—were slain. But after a long struggle they routed the barbarians and slaughtered them. They then seized the survivors and their camp, which was full of all sorts of treasure.

But though like a formidable athlete Cimon had prevailed in two contests in one day, and though he had surpassed the victory at Salamis with an infantry battle, and the victory at Plataea with a sea fight, he went on to compete with his own victories. Informed that the eighty Phoenician triremes, absent from the battle, had put into Hydrus, he sailed in haste, since their generals had not yet obtained reliable intelligence about the larger force, but were still doubtful and in suspense. And consequently, caught off-guard, they lost all

21. A historian and philosopher of the fourth century BCE, and a companion of Alexander the Great.

22. Hoplites are armed infantrymen, clad in metal helmets and breastplates. Each Greek warship carried small contingents of them on its deck.

their ships, and most of their men were slaughtered. This action so humbled the King's conceit that he negotiated the notorious peace, according to which he would always keep between himself and the Greek sea the distance a horse can travel in a day, and would not sail west of the Cyanean and Chelidonian islands with a brazen-beaked warship. Callisthenes, however, denies that the barbarian agreed to these terms, though the King's fear of that defeat had a practical consequence: he withdrew so far from Greece that Pericles, with fifty ships, and Ephialtes, with only thirty, sailed beyond the Chelidonians and encountered no barbarian naval force.[23]

[14] Now some of the Persians refused to abandon the Chersonese,[24] and called in the Thracians from the interior, showing their contempt for Cimon, who had sailed out from Athens with very few triremes. But on setting out against them with four ships, Cimon seized thirteen of theirs, and when he had expelled the Persians and overpowered the Thracians, he appropriated the entire Chersonese for Athens.[25] After this, when the Thasians revolted from Athens, and Cimon conquered them in a sea battle, he seized thirty-three ships and besieged their city, acquired for Athens the gold mines on the mainland opposite, and took possession of the territory controlled by the Thasians.

From there Cimon might easily, it was thought, have invaded and cut off a great part of Macedonia, and when he declined to do so he was accused of having taken bribes from King Alexander[26] and was prosecuted by his enemies.

[15] Cimon was acquitted of that charge. And throughout the remainder of his public career, when he was at home, he overpowered and humbled the common people whenever they encroached on the nobles or tried to draw all the authority and power to themselves. But when he again sailed away on campaign, the people finally broke loose and destroyed the established political order and the traditions they had formerly observed, their chief Ephialtes stripping the council of

---

23. The battle of the Eurymedon is variously dated to 469 or 466 BCE. Historians believe that the "treaty" Plutarch here refers to, with some doubt, did not in fact exist.

24. Modern Gallipoli.

25. An important development, since Athens was dependent on grain shipments that moved through the Hellespont and past the Chersonese.

26. Not Alexander the Great but one of his ancestors, Alexander I, who reigned in the early fifth century BCE.

the Areopagus of all but a few of its cases. Making themselves masters of the law courts, the people transformed the city into an absolute democracy, since Pericles was by then in power and siding with the multitude.[27] That was why when Cimon, on his return, deplored the undermining of the council's prestige, and tried to restore its jurisdiction and reawaken the aristocratic spirit of Cleisthenes' day, they banded together to shout him down, and sought to incite the people against him by reviving the old scandal about his sister[28] and charging him with being a Spartan sympathizer.

[16] Now Cimon *was*, from the beginning, fond of the Spartans. At any rate, he named one of his twin sons Lacedemonius, and the other Eleius.[29] . . . Cimon was held in high esteem by the Spartans, who were soon in conflict with Themistocles[30] and preferred that Cimon, despite his youth, wield power and influence in Athens. The Athenians were pleased with this at first, as they derived no small advantage from the Spartans' good will toward him. While they were growing in power, and busy forming alliances, they were not vexed by the honor and favor the Spartans bestowed on Cimon. For he managed most of their state affairs, dealing gently with the allies and amicably with the Spartans. Later, however, when the Athenians had grown more powerful and noticed that Cimon was warmly devoted to the Spartans, they were vexed. For on every occasion he would hold Sparta up as an example to the Athenians, especially when he had occasion to censure or provoke them. Then, as Stesimbrotus reports,[31] he was in the habit of saying, "Well, the Spartans would never behave in such a way." He thus incurred the ill will and hostility of his fellow citizens.

But the gravest slander against him had the following cause. In the fourth year of the reign of Archidamus, son of Zeuxidamus, king of Sparta, the land of Sparta was torn asunder by the greatest earthquake in human memory.[32] A number of crests broke off from Mount

27. The constitutional reforms of Ephialtes, backed by Pericles, took place in 461 BCE. See *Pericles* 7, n. 10.

28. Cimon was very close with his sister Elpinice, and the two might have been suspected of incest.

29. Both names are based on place-names in the region of Sparta.

30. See *Themistocles* 20.

31. A Greek prose writer of the fifth century BCE whose works are now lost.

32. About 464 BCE. See Thucydides 1.101–2.

Taygetus, and the entire city was destroyed except for five houses. The rest were demolished by the quake. . . . Archidamus quickly realized from the present danger that which was sure to follow. Seeing the citizens trying to convey their most valuable possessions safely from their houses, he gave orders for the trumpet to sound the signal that an enemy was invading, so that they might assemble before him with their weapons as soon as possible. And in fact it was this measure alone that saved Sparta at that critical moment. For the helots[33] from the fields ran together from all sides, intending to carry off those Spartans who had been saved. But finding them armed and drawn up in battle array, the helots withdrew to their cities and made war on Sparta openly, persuading no small number of their neighbors to join them. The Messenians, too, joined the attack upon the Spartans.

The Spartans, accordingly, sent Pericleidas to Athens to request aid. In one of his comedies Aristophanes describes Pericleidas as "sitting at the altars, pale-faced, in a red cloak, requesting an army."[34] When Ephialtes tried to hinder the Athenians, and protested that they should not aid or restore a city that was Athens' rival, and urged the people to let the arrogance of Sparta be trampled underfoot, Critias says that Cimon, deeming his country's rise less important than the Spartans' safety, persuaded the people to go out to aid them with many hoplites. Ion even recalls the expression with which Cimon most effectively roused the Athenians: he urged them "not to let Greece be lamed, nor leave the city bereft of its yokefellow."[35]

[17] The Spartans again called the Athenians in against the Messenians and helots at Ithome.[36] But when the Athenians arrived, the Spartans, fearing their daring and brilliance, sent them back— only the Athenians, among the allies, were thus rebuffed—on the grounds that they were subversive. Returning home in a rage, the Athenians vented their fury openly on those who sympathized with

33. The helots were Greeks, originally inhabitants of Messenia, who had been enslaved by the Spartans for centuries. They served as the agricultural labor and servant class that supported the Spartan war machine. See *Lycurgus* 24, n. 35.

34. *Lysistrata* 1138ff.

35. The idea behind "lamed" was that Athens and Sparta constituted two equally powerful "legs" on which the Greek world stood.

36. The rebel helots had taken up position around Mount Ithome, in a stronghold the Spartans could only take by siege. Since Sparta had very limited experience of siege warfare as compared with Athens, the city called on the Athenians for help. See Thucydides 1.102.

the Spartans. Seizing on some trivial pretext, they banished Cimon by ostracism for ten years. (For that was the established term of banishment for all who were ostracized.)

But soon, when the Spartans were on their way home after freeing the Delphians from the Phocians, and had encamped at Tanagra, the Athenians confronted and sought to engage them in battle.[37] Cimon then came in arms to join his own tribe, the Oenids, as he was eager to avenge himself on the Spartans with his fellow citizens. But when the Council of Five Hundred was informed of Cimon's presence, they grew alarmed (since the man's enemies were accusing him of wanting to throw the phalanx into confusion and lead the Spartans into the city) and would not permit the commanders to receive him. As Cimon departed he entreated Euthippus, son of Anaphlystus, and his other comrades, who were particularly suspected of siding with the Spartans, to contend manfully against the enemy, and to prove by their exploits that the people's charge was groundless. Taking his armor, they placed it in their company, stood resolutely together, and fell, one hundred men in all, leaving the Athenians with a deep sense of loss, and repentance for having suspected them unjustly. Accordingly, they did not remain angry with Cimon for long, partly, as was likely, because they remembered how well he had treated them, and partly from the pressure of circumstances. For they had been defeated in a great battle at Tanagra, and since they expected an army of Peloponnesians to march against them in the spring, they recalled Cimon from exile, Pericles himself writing the decree calling for his return. Quarrels in those days were generally political in character, whereas personal feelings were moderate and easily recalled to conform with the public good. And ambition, which surpassed all other passions, gave ground when the country's welfare was at stake.

[18] As soon as Cimon returned from exile, he ended the war and reconciled Athens and Sparta.[38] When peace was made, however, he saw that the Athenians were unable to keep quiet, but wished to be active and to increase their power by means of military campaigns. Concerned that they might unduly trouble the other Greeks,

---

37. See *Pericles* 10, Thucydides 1.107–8. The date of the events at Tanagra is 457 BCE, while Cimon was still living in exile.
38. About 451 BCE; see Thucydides 1.112. Plutarch passes over the disastrous Athenian intervention in Egypt in the mid-450s; it was the defeat of Athens in Egypt, more than Cimon's influence, that made the city willing to negotiate a treaty with Sparta.

or by maintaining a large naval presence in the islands or near the
Peloponnese might incur blame for internecine wars, or provoke their
allies to lodge complaints against the city, he manned two hundred
triremes, intending to make another expedition against Egypt and
Cyprus. For he wanted to keep the Athenians in training by their
contests with the barbarians, and enable them to enrich themselves
honestly by bringing into Greece the wealth taken from their natural
enemies.

When all was ready and the army about to embark, Cimon had
a dream. He imagined that an angry dog was barking at him, and
that mingled with the barking a human voice uttered these words,
"Come along; for you'll be a friend both to me and my puppies." As
the dream was hard to interpret, Astyphilus of Posidonia, a man
who possessed the prophetic faculty and was a friend of Cimon's,
declared that it foreshadowed Cimon's death, interpreting it thus:
a dog is an enemy of the man it barks at; and to an enemy, no one
can become a friend more than by dying; and the mixed character
of the voice suggests that the enemy is the Persian, since the army
of the Persians includes a mixture of Greeks and barbarians. . . . But
since he could not withdraw from the expedition, he set sail, sending sixty of his ships to Egypt; with the rest he sailed once more to
Cyprus.[39] And after he had defeated the royal fleet of Phoenicians
and Cilissians in a sea battle, he recovered the nearby cities and lay in
wait near Egypt with no trivial end in view, but planning the destruction of the King's entire power, chiefly because he had learned that
Themistocles enjoyed great renown and influence among the barbarians and had promised the King that when the Greek war was sparked
he would serve as commander. But it is said that Themistocles, principally because he despaired of his Greek enterprises, since he could
not surpass Cimon's good fortune and prowess, took his own life.[40]

While laying plans for great actions and holding the fleet near
Cyprus, Cimon sent men to Ammon[41] to consult the god on some
secret matter. For no one knew the object of their mission, nor did
the god give them a response. Instead, as soon as the messengers

39. An island of mixed Greek and Phoenician population, at this time part
of the Persian empire.

40. See *Themistocles* 31.

41. Ammon was an Egyptian god whom the Greeks equated with Zeus.
The shrine of Ammon in the desert west of Egypt was thought to have
oracular powers.

came forward, he ordered them to depart, saying that Cimon himself was already with him. On hearing this, the messengers journeyed down to the sea, and when they reached the Greek camp, which was then near Egypt, they learned that Cimon had died. And when they counted back the days to the oracle, they realized that the man's death had been hinted at, since he was already with the gods.

[19] Most people say that Cimon fell ill and died while besieging Citium, though some say he succumbed to a wound he had sustained in a battle with the barbarians. As he was dying, he ordered his officers to sail away at once and to conceal his death.[42] And thus it turned out that neither the enemy nor the allies knew what had happened, and the force was brought safely back "under the command of Cimon," as Phanodemus[43] says, "though he had been dead for thirty days."

After his death, no Greek general achieved any brilliant exploit against the barbarians. Instead the Greeks were turned against one another by demagogues and warmongers, since no one stepped in to keep them apart. Wars broke out between them, and this afforded the King a respite, but did unspeakable harm to Greek power. Much later, Agesilaus headed an expedition to Asia[44] and engaged in a brief war against the King's generals at the coast. But before they had achieved anything important or brilliant, he and his forces were overwhelmed by the Greeks' internal conflicts and troubles and were denied a second empire. And when they departed, they left in the midst of the allies and allied cities the Persian tax-collectors, not one of whose letter carriers had traveled down to the sea—nor had even one of their horses been seen within fifty miles of it—when Cimon held command.

That his remains were conveyed back to Attica, the funeral monuments, which to this day are called Cimonian, bear witness. And the people of Citium honor a certain tomb of Cimon, as the orator Nausicrates says, since at a period when their land was afflicted with pestilence and barrenness, the god had ordered them not to neglect Cimon, but to revere and honor him as a superior being. Such was the Greek leader.

---

42. So that the enemy would not be emboldened to attack.

43. Phanodemus was a historian of Athens who wrote during the fourth century BCE.

44. See *Agesilaus* 7–15.

Pericles

Plutarch's Pericles *is one of our most important sources for the history of mid-fifth-century Athens, the Athens of the Golden Age. The* Life *takes much of its inspiration from Thucydides, sharing that author's admiration for the lofty, confident, sober-minded style of Pericles' leadership. But it also reveals a darker side in the traditions about Pericles (c. 495–429 BCE), especially the suspicions that the statesman's personal ambitions, and protectiveness of his friends, played an outsized role in his policy choices.*

The chronological scheme of Pericles *is unusually complex even for a Plutarchan* Life. *Plutarch here narrates many events out of chronological sequence, as part of his plan to foreground the key themes in Pericles' career and personality. An effort has been made in the notes to date these events so as to permit a reordering, as well as to correlate them with other extant ancient sources.*

[4] Pericles attended the lectures of Zeno of Elea,[1] who like Parmenides wrote treatises about nature and had perfected a technique of cross-questioning that used contradiction to reduce his opponent to utter perplexity. . . . But the man who consorted most with Pericles, and did most to confer dignity upon him and a purpose weightier than that of a demagogue, and who wholly exalted and elevated the quality of his character, was Anaxagoras of Clazomenae,[2] whom people at the time called Mind.

[5] Admiring this man immensely, and being gradually filled with the so-called higher learning and elevated discourse, Pericles apparently acquired not only a proud spirit and a manner of speaking that was sublime and unsullied by pandering or clever buffoonery, but also a studied expression of countenance not liable to break into laughter, a gentle carriage, a dignity in his attire, which nothing

---

1. Little remains of the writings of this Zeno, but they became famous in antiquity for their mode of argumentation by way of refutation and logical paradox, as Plutarch reveals.

2. Anaxagoras was a cosmologist and natural scientist who came to live in Athens around 480 BCE. He was reportedly the first philosopher to take up residence there and begin teaching (formerly all such thinkers had resided in Miletus and other Ionian cities). His friendship with Pericles made him a target for Pericles' political enemies, and he was put on trial for impiety and forced to leave Athens in the mid-fifth century (see chapter 32).

could disturb while he was speaking, and an eloquence free of bombast—all of which excited everyone's astonished admiration.

[6] But these were not the only benefits Pericles derived from Anaxagoras' society. He also appears to have become superior to superstition, which is produced when amazement at astronomical phenomena seizes the minds of those who, ignorant of their causes, are confused, owing to inexperience, about supernatural matters. The rational account of nature, on the other hand, delivers one from fearful and heated superstition, replacing it with the unfaltering reverence that is accompanied by good hope.

[7] As a young man, Pericles was exceedingly wary of the common people, since in appearance he was actually thought to resemble the tyrant Pisistratus;[3] and as he had a pleasant voice and a quick and nimble tongue, the old men were quite amazed at the similarity. Since he possessed wealth, a brilliant family, and friends who were enormously influential, he was afraid of being ostracized,[4] which was why he abstained from politics, though on military campaigns he proved brave and venturesome. But after Aristides had died and Themistocles had been banished,[5] and the campaigns frequently kept Cimon away from Greece,[6] Pericles at last came forward and devoted himself to the people. And rather than adopt the cause of the rich and few, he adopted that of the many and poor, contrary to his own nature, since he was hardly a man of the people. But since he was evidently afraid of falling into the arrogance of tyranny, and saw that the aristocratic Cimon was beloved by the "noble and good,"[7] he insinuated himself into the common people's good graces, thereby ensuring his own safety and securing the power to oppose his rival.

---

3. Pisistratus and his sons had ruled Athens as tyrants throughout much of the sixth century BCE; see *Solon* 29–30. Though Pisistratus did much good for the city, his son Hippias turned cruel and oppressive and was eventually thrown out by a Spartan-assisted uprising.

4. On the process of ostracism, see *Aristides* 7. It may seem odd to a modern reader that good family background and other political advantages could lead to ostracism, but part of the purpose of that process was to remove men who could otherwise amass too much power.

5. About 471 BCE; see *Themistocles* 22.

6. That is, his many military incursions into Asia or Egypt, to oppose the Persians; see, for example, *Cimon* 12, 18.

7. The Greek term *kaloi kai agathoi* is a common expression denoting the Athenian aristocracy.

He soon reordered his way of life. For in town he was seen walking on one street only—that which led to the marketplace and the council chamber—and he gave up accepting dinner invitations and all such friendly intercourse and society, so that during the long period when he headed the government he never dined with any of his friends except when his cousin Euryptolemus was married, on which occasion he remained until the toasts were made and then immediately rose and departed. For friendly gatherings tend to defeat all posturing, and in the society of one's acquaintances it becomes hard to preserve the lofty air one has assumed for the sake of appearances. . . . In seeking to avoid the satiety that develops with prolonged familiarity, Pericles would approach the people[8] at intervals, as it were, not speaking on every subject, nor coming forward on every occasion, but reserving himself, like the ship *Salaminia*,[9] as Critolaus says, for important business, and on other occasions sent friends and other orators to advance his policies. One of these surrogates, they say, was Ephialtes, who destroyed the power of the council of the Areopagus,[10] and according to Plato poured out too much "unmixed freedom" for the citizens, under the influence of which the people grew restive, like a horse, and, as the comic writers say, "no longer deigned to obey those in authority."

[8] And by way of providing himself with a speaking style attuned, like an instrument, to his way of life and the grandeur of his high purpose, he often interlarded his speech with Anaxagoras'[11] doctrines, infusing his rhetoric, as it were, with the dye of natural philosophy. For it was from natural philosophy, as the divine Plato says, "that he acquired his high-mindedness and consummate expertise, in addition to his natural gifts";[12] and when he had drawn from

---

8. That is, by speaking in the assembly. Here, as often, the term "the people" refers to the entire Athenian citizen body, especially those gathered for an assembly session; but it can also denote "the common people," in contrast to the *kaloi kai agathoi*.

9. One of two ships in the Athenian navy set aside for special missions, including those connected to religious observances.

10. Ephialtes, a political ally of Pericles, sponsored the sweeping constitutional reform of 461 BCE that stripped power from the Areopagus, a judicial body that had long been a stronghold of aristocratic privilege. He was assassinated the following year.

11. On Anaxagoras, see note 2.

12. *Phaedrus* 270a.

it what was suitable for his oratory, he far outshone all other speakers. That was how he reportedly came by his epithet "the Olympian,"[13] though some think it was earned by reason of the works with which he adorned the city, others by reason of the power he wielded in the government and on his campaigns. And it is not at all unlikely that his reputation was based on a combination of his talents. Yet the comedies of those who wrote at the time and who hurled many cutting remarks at him,[14] both in earnest and in jest, make clear that he came by this surname mainly because of his speaking style, since they describe him as "thundering" and "hurling lightning" whenever he spoke in the assembly, and as "bearing a dreadful thunderbolt in his tongue."

[9] Thucydides suggests that the polity of Pericles had an aristocratic character—that it was "a democracy in name, but in reality rule by the foremost man,"[15] though many others say that it was through Pericles' agency that the populace was first made eligible for allotments of land, subsidies for attending theaters, and payments for performing public duties, and under the influence of his policies developed bad habits and became extravagant and undisciplined, rather than sensible and self-reliant. Let us examine the cause of this change by considering the actual events.

At first, as has been mentioned, Pericles set himself up to oppose Cimon's renown, and tried to ingratiate himself with the people. Lacking the wealth and money with which Cimon had won over the poor[16] by providing a daily meal to any Athenian in need of one, and by clothing the elderly and removing the fences from the fields so that anyone who wished might gather fruit—outshone as he was by these popular measures—Pericles turned his hand to distributions of public funds. . . . And soon, having thoroughly bribed the multitude with theater seats, jury pay, other stipends, and sponsorships of the public choruses,[17] he turned the people against the council

13. The epithet "Olympian" ("of Mount Olympus") was otherwise applied mainly to the god Zeus.

14. See, for example, Aristophanes' *Acharnians* 530–31.

15. Thucydides, *The Peloponnesian War* 2.65.

16. After his victories over the Persians at the Eurymedon (see *Cimon* 12), Cimon brought wealthy spoils back to Athens, with which he was able to subsidize public works and welfare.

17. All these measures constitute ways of giving paid work and artistic entertainment to the poor. "Theater seats" and "sponsorship of the public

of the Areopagus, to which he did not himself belong, since he had never been appointed by lot either archon, or junior archon, or king archon, or polemarch.[18] For these offices had been filled by lot from ancient times; and through them men who had been tested ascended to the Areopagus. That was why, when Pericles had acquired sufficient popular support, he directed his party against the council, with the result that it was stripped of most of its cases by Ephialtes,[19] and Cimon was ostracized for being sympathetic to the Spartans and hostile to the common people,[20] though he was no man's inferior in wealth or birth, had won highly honorable victories over the barbarians, and had filled the city with vast amounts of money and spoils, as has been recorded in my account of his life. So great was Pericles' authority among the people.

[10] Persons banished by ostracism were required by law to remain in exile for a period of ten years. But in the middle of his term of exile, when the Spartans invaded the district of Tanagra with a large army, and the Athenians immediately rushed out against them, Cimon returned to bear arms in a regiment of his fellow tribesmen,[21] hoping to dispel the charge that he was sympathetic to Sparta by sharing the dangers of his fellow citizens. But Pericles' friends, banding together, drove him away on the grounds that he had been banished (which is why Pericles is thought to have contended with extraordinary vigor in that battle and to have fought with a surpassing and conspicuous disregard for his own danger). Without exception, all of Cimon's friends, whom Pericles had also accused of Spartan sympathies, fell in the battle; and the Athenians

---

choruses" refer to the state-run festivals at which tragedy and comedy were performed in the Theater of Dionysus. "Jury pay" refers to the daily wage of two obols (a bare sustenance; the obol was Athens' smallest unit of currency) introduced by Pericles. Jury service employed a huge number of citizens in Athens, since juries often numbered in the hundreds or even more than a thousand. "Other stipends" is unclear. Plutarch may be thinking of a salary for assembly attendance that was introduced well after Pericles' time.

18. The offices named are four of the nine magistracies at Athens called archonships. Only former archons were entitled to membership in the council of the Areopagus, which they then retained for life.

19. See note 10. The reforms of 461 BCE were threatening enough to members of the Athenian upper class that (according to our very inadequate sources) they engineered Ephialtes' assassination; see chapter 10.

20. See *Cimon* 16–17.

21. See *Cimon* 17.

were seized by a terrible remorse and a longing for Cimon, now that
they had been defeated at the borders of Attica and were expecting a
grievous war in the spring. Perceiving this, Pericles did not hesitate
to gratify the multitude: for he himself wrote the decree recalling
Cimon home. And on his return, Cimon made peace between the
cities. For the Spartans were as friendly to him as they were hostile
to Pericles and the other popular leaders. . . . As for Ephialtes, who
alarmed the oligarchs by relentlessly investigating and prosecuting
those who wronged the people, his enemies plotted against him and
had him secretly murdered by Aristodicus of Tanagra, as Aristotle
has said;[22] and Cimon died while serving as admiral in Cyprus.

[11] Year after year Pericles sent out sixty triremes,[23] on which
many of the citizens, in receipt of pay for eight months,[24] practiced
and honed their nautical skills. In addition, he sent a thousand
cleruchs[25] to the Chersonese, five hundred to Naxos, half that number to Andros, a thousand to Thrace to dwell with the Bisaltae, and
others to Italy (where Sybaris had been settled) to found the colony
they called Thurii. Pericles thus lightened the city of its throng of
idlers and busybodies,[26] remedied the people's poverty, and, by way
of discouraging rebellious impulses, instilled fear and watchfulness
in their allies.

[12] But that which brought the most delight and beauty to
Athens, and the greatest astonishment to the rest of mankind, and
which now provides Greece with the only evidence that her storied
power and ancient wealth was no false tale—that is, her program
of public works[27]—was particularly disparaged and scorned in the

22. *Constitution of the Athenians* 25.4.

23. Triremes were the warships on which Athenian naval power relied.

24. Athenians probably started receiving pay for military service under
Pericles, but the evidence is unclear. Since the rowers in the navy were
generally poor men (those who could not afford infantry armor), the advent
of state wages for service was a great boon.

25. A cleruch was given a free allotment of land in a foreign possession
of the Athenian empire. He retained Athenian citizenship though living
abroad.

26. Unlike other Greek cities, Athens had an unemployment problem. The
city's imperial wealth helped increase its population beyond its labor needs.

27. In particular, the building program on the Acropolis; the site had been
left a rubble heap after the Persian invasion of 480 BCE. In Plutarch's time,
the Parthenon and other Acropolis structures retained the grandeur of

assemblies by the enemies of Pericles' policy, who cried out that the
city had lost her good name and was maligned for having transferred the common funds of Greece from Delos to Athens,[28] and
that the most respectable of the excuses that they had been able to
offer their accusers, namely that out of fear that the barbarians might
take them from the island they were guarding the common funds in a
safe place, had had its hollowness revealed by Pericles. "Viewed now
as the object of a terrible insult and a flagrant tyranny, Greece sees
that, with her enforced contributions for the war,[29] we are gilding
our city and tricking her out, like a shameless woman, with precious
stones, expensive statues, and temples costing thousands of talents."[30]

But Pericles informed the people that they owed the allies no
account of their funds, since Athens was fighting on their behalf
and holding off the barbarians, whereas the allies were contributing
not a single horse or ship or hoplite, but only money, which belongs
not to those who give it but to those who receive it, if in return for
it they supply the purchased goods. And it was proper, once the city
was sufficiently equipped with what was needed for prosecuting the
war, that she apply any surplus to projects that, when they came to
fruition, would bring a deathless renown, and while in progress provide immediate prosperity, since an array of activities and demands
arise that bring every craft into play, put every hand in motion, and
provide almost the entire city with employment, so that she both
adorns and maintains herself from her own resources.

Athens' greatest days, though the city as a whole had shrunk and lost all its
former power.

28. The contributions of the states constituting the Delian League, the
security organization founded by Greeks attempting to keep the Persians
out of the Aegean, were initially kept in a common treasury on the island of
Delos, a central location. However, Athens controlled their disbursement
and in 454 BCE physically moved the treasury to the Athenian Acropolis.
The move was regarded by other league members as a form of subjugation.

29. It is interesting that Pericles' nameless critic uses the term "war" to
refer to the relations between Greeks and Persians in the mid-fifth century.
According to some sources a peace treaty had been signed, probably in the
460s, setting limits on Persia's territory and ending hostilities. But historians
disagree as to whether this treaty, the Peace of Callias, did in fact exist, and
in any case low-level hostilities were ongoing throughout the period.

30. Chief among these adornments was the Parthenon, built, at Pericles'
urging, using huge amounts of league money.

[13] The works going up were of imposing size and inimitable in their form and grace, the craftsmen competing to surpass themselves in beauty of workmanship, though it was their speed that was most astonishing. . . . Pericles' overseer for all the works, and the man who superintended everything that was built, was Phidias, though the buildings had important architects and artisans. . . .They say that the Odeum,[31] whose interior arrangement included many seats and columns, and whose roof, sloping steeply, had been made from a single crest, was a replica of the King's tent.[32] This work, too, was overseen by Pericles, which is why Cratinus, in his *Thracian Women*,[33] again makes fun of him:

> Squill-head Zeus draws near,
> Wearing the Odeum on his head,
> Since the ostracism's come and gone.

Ambitious as ever, Pericles then passed a resolution, the first of its kind, to the effect that a contest in music and the arts was to be held at the Panathenaea.[34] And he himself, elected as judge, determined the manner in which the contestants were to play the flute, sing, or play the harp. These contests in the arts were presented then and thereafter in the Odeum.

The Propylaea[35] of the Acropolis, designed by the architect Mnesicles, was completed within five years. . . . Phidias sculpted the golden statue of the goddess,[36] and his name has been inscribed on the pillar as its maker. Almost everything had been entrusted to him;

31. A building for musical performances that once occupied the south slope of the Acropolis, now totally vanished. The Odeum of Herodes Atticus seen in Athens today is a much later structure.

32. The tent used by Xerxes in his invasion of Greece in 480 BCE was famous for its extravagance. As always in this volume, "King" when capitalized refers to the Great King of Persia.

33. An Athenian comedy, now lost.

34. A yearly Athenian festival featuring a religious procession and athletic games.

35. The gatelike structure, still largely standing, through which visitors entered the Acropolis structure. It was begun in the mid-430s BCE.

36. The colossal image of a standing Athena housed inside the Parthenon, bedecked not only with gold but ivory as well. Now lost, this statue was considered a masterwork of sculpture. Its precious surface layer was detachable, so that Athens could use it as state revenue in an emergency.

and as we have said, he was put in charge of all the artisans because of his friendship with Pericles.

[14] When the orators in Thucydides'[37] camp denounced Pericles for throwing away money and wasting their revenues, he asked the people in the assembly if they thought he had spent too much. When they replied that he had spent a great deal, he said, "Very well. Then let it not have been spent on your account but on mine, and I will make the votive offerings' inscription a personal one." When Pericles had said this, the people, either out of admiration for his generosity, or envy at his getting the credit for their public works, raised their voices and loudly urged him to use the public funds and spare no expense. Finally, after hazarding everything and prevailing against Thucydides in an ostracism,[38] Pericles secured his rival's banishment and crushed the political party that had opposed him.

[15] When its political conflicts had been entirely dispelled and the city became, as it were, a smooth and united whole, Pericles brought Athens under his personal control along with all the affairs that depended on the Athenians—tribute money, armies, triremes, the islands, the sea, vast power, much of which had come through the Greeks, much also through the barbarians, and a hegemony well-fortified with subject tribes, royal friendships, and alliances with potentates. But Pericles was no longer the same man as before: he was not as submissive to the people, nor did he yield easily or give in to the desires of the multitude as one gives way to blasts of wind. Instead, in place of a leadership that had been relaxed, like a florid and tender melody, and in some respects remiss, he presided over a taut, aristocratic, and regal administration, and conducted the government with an eye to what was best, in an upright and unswerving manner. He led the people by instructing them; and though they often followed his lead willingly, there were times when, despite their hostility, he restrained and subdued them, forcing them to submit to what was for their advantage,[39] exactly as if he were imitating a doctor, who through a patient's long and changeful illness, knows

37. Not Thucydides the historian, but a politician by the same name, one of Pericles' most determined opponents.

38. This ostracism of Pericles' leading opponent is attested only here. It should probably be dated to the early 440s BCE.

39. Plutarch no doubt relied heavily here on Thucydides' famous eulogy of Pericles at 2.65.

precisely when to provide harmless pleasures, and when to insist on performing painful operations and administering lifesaving drugs.

[17] When the Spartans began to be vexed at the growth of Athenian power, Pericles stirred up the populace to be even more high-minded and to think itself worthy of great accomplishments. He passed a decree[40] to invite all the Greeks living anywhere in Europe or Asia, in cities small or large, to send representatives to a conference in Athens, where they would deliberate about the Greek shrines the barbarians had burned down,[41] and about the sacrifices they owed on behalf of Greece, which they had vowed to perform when they fought the barbarians, and about the sea, so that all might sail it without fear and keep the peace. . . . But nothing came of it, nor did the cities' representatives even assemble, owing to the Spartans' opposition,[42] it is said, since the attempt was first baffled in the Peloponnese.

[18] In his campaigns[43] Pericles particularly distinguished himself for his caution, since he neither willingly engaged in a battle that entailed considerable uncertainty or danger, nor did he envy or imitate those who took great risks, enjoyed brilliant luck, and were therefore admired as great generals. He always told the citizens that as far as it depended on him they would remain immortal for all time.

When he saw that Tolmides son of Tolmaeus,[44] who because of his previous good fortune and the outstanding honors he had been accorded for his martial exploits, was preparing, inopportunely, to invade Boeotia, and had persuaded the best and most ambitious of his contemporaries to serve voluntarily (these numbered a thousand apart from the rest of the force),[45] Pericles tried to restrain him,

40. Plutarch is our only source for this decree. If it was in fact passed by Pericles—since Thucydides does not mention it, there is some doubt about its authenticity—it should probably be dated to the early 440s BCE.

41. In the invasion led by Xerxes, 480–479 BCE.

42. Presumably Sparta did not want Pericles, or any Athenian, asserting a Panhellenic leadership role.

43. It should be remembered that Pericles' official position in government was not primarily political but military. He was elected *stratēgos*, one of a board of ten generals, on numerous occasions during the 440s and 430s BCE. Because the *stratēgoi* were chosen from among the leading citizens, however, they also exercised great influence in the assembly and other political bodies.

44. One of the Athenian generals (*stratēgoi*) prominent during this period.

45. Thucydides 1.113 describes this unfortunate campaign.

and appealed to him in the assembly, making the remark that has been remembered, that if Tolmides could not persuade Pericles, he would not err if he awaited the wisest adviser: time. This remark brought Pericles only moderate esteem at the moment; but a few days later, when word came that Tolmides himself was dead after being defeated in battle near Coroneia,[46] and that many brave citizens had also died, it brought Pericles great renown as well as good will among the people for his wisdom and patriotism.

[19] Of all his campaigns, the one to the Chersonese[47] was especially admired, since it proved the salvation of the Greeks who resided there. For not only did he strengthen their cities with an abundance of men by bringing them a thousand Athenian colonists, but he also enclosed the isthmus with bulwarks and barriers, fortified it from sea to sea against the raids of the Thracians who crowded around the Chersonese, and shut out a perpetual and grievous war in which the country had been engulfed throughout that period, surrounded as it was by barbarian neighbors, and full of brigands who roamed the region and its frontiers.[48] Pericles was also admired and talked of by foreigners for his circumnavigation of the Peloponnese,[49] when he embarked from Pegae in Megara with one hundred triremes. For he not only plundered much of the coast, as Tolmides had done earlier, but also marched from the sea into the interior with the hoplites from his ships, and drove inside their walls all the peoples who feared his approach, except the Sicyonians in Nemea; and when they held their ground and joined battle, he routed them by main force and erected a trophy. Recruiting troops from Achaea, an Athenian ally, and embarking them on his triremes, he proceeded with the fleet to the mainland opposite. When he had sailed up the Achelous, he

46. In 447 BCE Tolmides, trying to defend Athenian interests in Boeotia, encountered an army of enemy forces at Coroneia and was soundly defeated.

47. Attested only here, probably dating to 447 BCE. The Thracian Chersonese (modern Gallipoli) was an important Athenian sphere of influence because it dominated the Hellespont, the straits through which much of Athens' food imports had to be shipped.

48. The narrowest point of the Chersonese peninsula is about four miles across. The Athenians had tried since the time of Miltiades to defend the peninsula against incursions from barbarians outside it (see Herodotus, *Histories* 6.36).

49. In 454 BCE, during the so-called First Peloponnesian War; see Thucydides 1.111.

overran Acarnania and confined the Oeniads behind their walls.[50] After plundering and devastating their territory, he sailed for home, having shown himself formidable to his enemies, and at the same time safe and energetic to his fellow citizens. For no harm, even from bad luck, befell the men who served in his campaign.

[20] After sailing into the Black Sea with a large and brilliantly appointed fleet,[51] he performed the services the Greek cities requested, and treated them generously, while to the surrounding barbarian tribes and their kings and potentates he displayed the vastness of his forces, their fearlessness, and the confidence with which they sailed wherever they pleased and brought the entire sea under their control. He also left the Sinopeans thirteen ships of war, with soldiers under Lamachus'[52] command, to aid them against the tyrant Timesileos. When Timesileos and his confederates had been expelled, Pericles passed a decree calling for six hundred Athenian volunteers to sail to Sinope and live with the Sinopeans, inhabiting the houses and territory formerly occupied by the tyrants.

In other matters he did not give in to the citizens' impulses, nor was he carried along when, elated by their power and extraordinary good luck, they sought to reclaim Egypt and to raid the coastal areas of the King's empire.[53] Many were already smitten by that lovesick and ill-starred desire for Sicily that was later inflamed by the orators of Alcibiades' circle. And some even harbored a vision of Tuscany and Carthage—a vision by no means implausible given the breadth of their present supremacy and the prosperous course of their affairs.

50. In standard land warfare of this period, an invading army would ravage the agricultural land in the territory of an enemy in order to force a battle. If the city that was thus invaded felt outmatched and declined a fight, its population would retreat inside the city walls and await the departure of the invader.

51. Only Plutarch mentions this campaign, and its purpose is unclear. Probably it should be dated to the mid-430s.

52. The Athenian Lamachus was frequently elected general during the Peloponnesian War, and he served as one of the three leaders appointed to head the Sicilian expedition (see *Alcibiades* 20).

53. In the 450s Athens attempted a daring foreign intervention by sending a huge fleet to Egypt. The ruler there, Inaros, was attempting to rebel against the Persian empire, Athens' age-old foe. Athens' expeditionary force spent several years fighting the Persians in the Nile delta and vicinity but was finally nearly completely destroyed in 454.

[21] But Pericles sought to check this impulse of theirs, to curtail their meddlesomeness, and to direct their power principally to securing and consolidating what they had already acquired.[54] He thought it important to keep the Spartans in check, and he opposed them covertly on every occasion.

[22] The events that followed proved that Pericles had been right to keep the Athenian forces in Greece. First the Euboeans revolted, and he crossed with a force against them. Soon it was reported that the Megarians had become hostile to the Athenians and that an enemy army was at the border of Attica under the command of Pleistoanax, the king of the Spartans.[55] Accordingly, Pericles hurried back from Euboea for the war in Attica. He did not venture to join battle with the many brave hoplites who had been called up, but he noticed that Pleistoanax was very young, and that, among his advisers, he relied most on Cleandrides, whom the ephors had sent as a guardian and coadjutor because of the king's youth. Pericles made secret overtures to this man, swiftly corrupted him with bribes, and persuaded him to lead the Peloponnesians out of Attica.[56]

When the army had departed and disbanded, its contingents dispersing to their respective cities, the Spartans, who were extremely indignant, imposed a fine on the king; but since he lacked the funds to pay it in full, he emigrated from Sparta.[57] On Cleandrides, who had fled into exile, they imposed the death sentence. This man was the father of Gylippus, who vanquished the Athenians in Sicily.

[24] Thereafter, when the Athenians and Spartans had concluded a thirty-year truce,[58] Pericles had a decree enacted for his

---

54. Plutarch again relies on Thucydides for the main themes of his portrait of Pericles. In a famous speech to the assembly, Pericles, in Thucydides' account, told the Athenians not to expand their imperial holdings while still facing a threat from Sparta (1.144).

55. The revolt of Euboea from Athenian control in 446 BCE posed a grave threat to the Athenian empire. That threat became much greater when Megara launched a rebellion at nearly the same moment and called in Spartan aid. Pericles had to hasten from one theater of war to the other (see Thucydides 1.114).

56. Thucydides says only that the Spartans returned home from Megara; he does not mention bribes. Probably the story about bribery arose from speculation about a retreat that had no obvious explanation.

57. He later returned to Sparta and reigned from 427 until his death in 408 BCE.

58. The Thirty Years' Peace was signed at the end of 445.

expedition against Samos,[59] alleging that though the Samians had been ordered to desist from their war with the Milesians, they had not complied.

Since he is thought to have launched the expedition against the Samians to please Aspasia, this might be an opportune moment to discuss the difficult questions associated with this woman, and to consider what great art or power she possessed that she had the foremost statesmen at her beck and call, and gave the philosophers occasion to discuss her in detail and at length. It is agreed that she was Milesian by birth, the daughter of Axiochus. . . . Some say that Aspasia was courted by Pericles for her astute grasp of politics. For Socrates occasionally visited her with his disciples, and his intimate friends brought their wives to listen to her, though she had charge of a business that was anything but seemly or even respectable, since she supported and trained adolescent courtesans.[60] And Aeschines says that Lysicles the sheep dealer, a man naturally base and ignoble, attained preeminence in Athens because he lived with Aspasia after Pericles' death. And Plato's *Menexenus*, even if its opening section was written in jest, contains relevant information, at least insofar as it mentions that Aspasia associated with many of the Athenians as a teacher of rhetoric. Yet it appears that Pericles' love for Aspasia had a markedly passionate character. For his own wife, who was a kinswoman, had previously been married to Hipponicus, to whom she had borne Callias the Rich; to Pericles she bore Xanthippus and Paralus. But later, as their married life was not agreeable to them, he gave her, with her consent, to someone else, whereupon he himself took Aspasia, of whom he was exceedingly fond. For they say that day after day, on going out or returning from the marketplace, he would salute her with a warm kiss. In the comedies she is called the young

---

59. In 440; see Thucydides 1.115. The war that resulted was the start of a long, close-fought engagement between Athens and Samos.

60. In other words, she was a "madam," though it is impossible to equate the social circumstances of the ancient Greek *hetaira* with that of the modern prostitute. In a society where respectable married or marriageable women had little freedom, social status, or power, the *hetaira*, despite her dependency on male patrons, enjoyed a remarkable degree of "liberation." She stood outside the strict codes that bound a legitimate wife to the demands of the household.

Omphale, and Deianira, and even Hera.[61] Cratinus flatly called her
a whore in these verses:

> To be his Hera, Unnatural Lust bore Aspasia,
> A dog-eyed whore.

And Pericles' illegitimate son[62] is thought to have been her child,
about whom Eupolis, in his *Demes*, portrays Pericles as asking,

> Does my bastard live?

To which Myronides replies,

> He does, and would long have been a man,
> Had he not feared the disgrace of his harlot-birth.

[25] Most of the responsibility for the war against the Samians
is assigned to Pericles, who passed the decree at Aspasia's request on
behalf of the Milesians.[63] For the two cities[64] were waging war near
Priene, and when the Samians had gained the upper hand and the
Athenians ordered them to desist and let their dispute be adjudicated,
they would not obey.

[28] When he had subjugated Samos and returned to Athens,
Pericles honored those who had died in the course of the war with
notable funeral rites; and for his oration, which he delivered, as
was customary, at their tombs,[65] he was regarded with awe and
admiration.

*Plutarch's lengthy account of Pericles' Samian operations in 440–439 BCE
is here omitted.*

61. Three mythic women famous for the power they wielded over men;
Omphale and Deianira were the lover and wife of Heracles, Hera the wife
of Zeus.

62. Also named Pericles, one of the unfortunate generals later found guilty
and executed in the aftermath of the battle at Arginusae (see Xenophon,
Hellenica 1.7, and note 92 below). The Athenians granted him citizenship
out of esteem for his father, though, as the son of a noncitizen mother, he
was not eligible (see chapter 37).

63. As a native of Miletus, Aspasia evidently felt compelled to aid her home
city.

64. That is, Samos and Miletus.

65. Athens held a state-organized funeral oration in each year that the
city was at war, commemorating the war dead. The speech recorded by
Thucydides in book 2, also delivered (though probably not in the form
Thucydides records) by Pericles, is the most famous example.

Ion says that Pericles thought very highly of himself for having defeated the Samians, seeing that it had taken Agamemnon ten years to capture a barbarian city, whereas *he* had conquered the greatest and most powerful of the Ionians in nine months. And his prestige was not undeserved, since the war had truly entailed great uncertainty and danger, if in fact, as Thucydides says, the city of Samos came within an ace of depriving the Athenians of their supremacy at sea.[66]

[29] Thereafter, with the Peloponnesian War already brewing, Pericles persuaded the people to send aid to the Corcyraeans, who were attacked by the Corinthians, and to secure an island that possessed a powerful naval force, since the Peloponnesians were by then practically at war with them.[67] . . . The Corinthians, who were furious with the Athenians and were lodging accusations against them in Sparta, were joined by the Megarians, who alleged that contrary to common rights and the solemn oaths of the Greeks, they had been excluded and driven away from every marketplace and from all the harbors controlled by the Athenians.[68] And the Aeginetans, thinking that they were being injured and outraged, complained in secret to the Spartans, since they did not dare to accuse the Athenians openly.[69] At that point Potidaea, a city obedient to Athens, though a Corinthian colony, revolted and was besieged,[70] a development that hastened the outbreak of the war.

Yet, since embassies were being dispatched to Athens, and since Archidamus, the king of the Spartans, tried to resolve most of the disputes and to pacify his allies, it seems unlikely that the war would have fallen upon the Athenians for any remaining reasons had they been persuaded to cancel their decree against the Megarians and be reconciled with them. And that is why, since Pericles was especially opposed to such a step, and urged the people to persist in their contention with the Megarians, he alone was responsible for the war.[71]

---

66. See Thucydides 8.76.

67. The episode recounted by Thucydides at the outset of his narrative, 1.24ff.

68. Pericles had been instrumental in passing the Megarian Decree in 432 BCE, an embargo on all Megarian trade within the Athenian empire.

69. See Thucydides 1.67.

70. Thucydides' second major episode, 1.56ff.

71. The causes of the Peloponnesian War are here radically simplified, though there is no doubt that war might have been postponed, perhaps even avoided, had Pericles taken a more accommodating stance. Thucydides

[30] They say that when an embassy sent from Sparta to address these matters reached Athens, and Pericles cited a law that made it illegal to take down the tablet on which the decree was inscribed, Polyalces, one of the envoys, said, "Don't take it down, then, but turn it inward; for surely there's no law forbidding that."[72] Though the speech was witty, Pericles would not yield anything more.

[31] Now how the decree originated is not easy to determine, but everyone holds Pericles responsible for its not being repealed. Yet some say that his stiff resistance was highly principled, that it reflected what he felt to be for the best, and that he regarded the statute as a test of the city's submissiveness, and its compliance as a confession of weakness; others, however, maintain that it was more out of arrogance and an ambitious zeal to display his power that he defied the Spartans.

But the worst charge of all, which is confirmed by the most witnesses,[73] is to this effect: Phidias the sculptor, as had been mentioned, was the contractor for the statue. And by becoming a friend of Pericles and acquiring great influence with him, he made a number of enemies, some of whom merely envied him, while others, fastening on him as a way to test the populace and find out what sort of judge it would be of Pericles, persuaded Meno, one of Phidias' colleagues, to sit as a suppliant in the marketplace and request immunity[74] in the event he should give information and lodge charges against Phidias. . . . Phidias, accordingly, was led off to prison, where he fell ill and died, though some say that he died from poisons administered by the enemies of Pericles, who sought to cast suspicion on him. As for the informer Meno, on Glycon's motion the people granted him exemption from public duties, and ordered the generals to ensure his safety.

---

famously attributed the start of the war to Spartan fear of Athenian power, not to any of Pericles' policies. At the end of chapter 32 Plutarch expresses doubt as to how much Pericles was responsible or what his motives were.

72. That is, though the stone could not be removed, it could be reversed so that the decree inscribed on it was not visible and could not be followed.

73. It is not clear who these "witnesses" are or what Plutarch thinks of their testimony. One was surely Aristophanes, the comic playwright, whose *Acharnians* (523–39) explained the start of the war in terms of Pericles' troubles in his personal life. But such lampoons were part of the technique of Old Comedy.

74. The implication being that the powerful Pericles would have him punished otherwise.

[32] At about this time Aspasia was put on trial for impiety, Hermippus the comic poet serving as her prosecutor and alleging, in addition, that she received freeborn women at a trysting-place for Pericles.[75] And Diopeithes passed a resolution to censure persons who did not believe in gods, or expounded doctrines about the heavens, directing suspicion against Pericles by means of Anaxagoras.[76] . . . At the trial Pericles gained pardon for Aspasia, according to Aeschines,[77] by shedding many tears on her behalf and by pleading with the jurors; and as he feared for Anaxagoras, he sent him out of the city.[78] And because he had clashed with the people in Phidias' case and feared the jury in his own, he kindled the imminent and smoldering war, hoping thereby to dispel the accusations and allay the people's ill will, since the city, when confronted with great affairs and dangers, entrusted herself solely to him, by reason of his prestige and power. These, then, are said to be Pericles' reasons for not allowing the people to yield to the Spartans; but the truth is not clear.

[33] Realizing that if Pericles were deposed they would find the Athenians more tractable in every way, the Spartans ordered them to drive out the Cylonian pollution,[79] in which the family of Pericles' mother was implicated, as Thucydides has reported. But their attempt had the opposite of its intended effect; in place of suspicion and slander, Pericles won even greater trust and honor among his fellow citizens, on the grounds that their enemies hated and feared him above all other men. And that was why, before Archidamus invaded Attica with the Peloponnesians, Pericles proclaimed to the Athenians that in the event Archidamus, when devastating other places, spared Pericles' property out of regard for their personal friendship, or in

75. That is, that she procured sex partners for him. The damning part of the charge is contained in the phrase "freeborn women."

76. The natural philosopher who had been Pericles' teacher; see chapter 4.

77. Not the famous orator of the same name but a Socratic philosopher, who wrote a dialogue with the title *Aspasia*.

78. Anaxagoras ended up at Lampsacus and taught there until the end of his days.

79. See *Solon* 12 with n. 5. After Cylon had tried to take over rule of Athens by force, some two centuries before Pericles' time, the ruling magistrates promised him amnesty if he surrendered but then killed him anyway. The betrayal was thought to have incurred a religious curse that was inherited from one generation to the next.

order to supply his enemies with a pretext for slander, he would deed his lands and farmstead to the city.[80]

Accordingly, the Spartans and their allies invaded Attica under the command of King Archidamus. And when they had plundered the countryside they advanced to Acharnae and set up camp, imagining that the Athenians would not stand for it, but would fight with them out of anger and pride. But Pericles thought it would be dangerous to engage in battle, jeopardizing the city itself, against sixty thousand Peloponnesian and Boeotian hoplites (as that was the size of the first invading force),[81] and he tried to appease those who wished to fight, and who were impatient with how things were going, by saying that trees, when they are cut and pruned, grow back quickly, but men, once slain, cannot easily be recovered. And he would not convene the people into an assembly, fearing he would be forced to act against his better judgment. Instead, like the helmsman of a ship, who, when a wind comes sweeping over the open sea, applies his skill to taking all proper precautions and battening down his equipment, and ignores the tears and pleas of his seasick and frightened passengers, Pericles shut the city's gates and posted guards everywhere for security, relying on his own judgment and paying little heed to those who protested and complained. Yet many of his friends urgently entreated him, and many of his enemies threatened and denounced him, and choruses sang humorous ditties to disgrace him, insulting his strategy as unmanly, since it yielded ground to the enemy. And by now Cleon[82] was attacking him, using the citizens' anger to further his own progress toward the leadership of the people.

[34] But Pericles was moved by none of this. He endured the disgrace and the hatred calmly and quietly, and dispatched a force of one hundred ships against the Peloponnese. He did not sail out with the fleet, but remained at home, keeping the city well in hand until the Peloponnesians withdrew. Seeking to soothe the majority, who were distressed by the war, he placated them with distributions of money and proposed allotments of conquered land; for after he

80. See Thucydides 2.13.

81. The actual numbers could not have been even as much as half this figure.

82. Cleon, a popular leader and (according to our sources, anyway) a histrionic demagogue, came to dominate the assembly after Pericles' death. This passage gives our only evidence for his earlier career.

had expelled all the Aeginetans,[83] he apportioned their island among the Athenians by lot. And some consolation was to be had from what the enemy suffered. For the naval force that sailed around the Peloponnese plundered considerable territory and destroyed many villages and small cities, and Pericles himself, invading by land, thoroughly devastated the plain around Megara. This made it clear that though their enemies did the Athenians great harm by land, they also suffered much at their hands by sea, and would not have protracted the war to such a length, but would quickly have renounced it, as Pericles had foretold from the start, had not some divine influence been thwarting human calculations.

It was then that the plague[84] first attacked and ravaged those who were in the vigorous prime of life. Afflicted in body and soul, the citizens were utterly enraged at Pericles, and like people who have been deranged by illness, and who come to resent a doctor or a father,[85] they tried to injure him, persuaded by his enemies that the disease had been caused by bringing the throng of country folk into the city, where, in the summer season, crowds of men were forced to lead a stay-at-home and idle life, huddled together in small houses and stifling huts, instead of the clean life they had previously lived out in the open. Pericles was held responsible, since on account of the war he had poured masses of people from the country within the walls, and then provided no employment for that multitude, but allowed them, like penned cattle, to fill one another up with pestilence, and afforded them no change or relief.

[35] Wishing to remedy these matters and also to harass the enemy, he set about manning 150 ships. When he had embarked many brave hoplites and cavalrymen, he was about to put out to sea, the size of the armament giving great hope to his fellow citizens and no less alarm to the enemy. But when the ships were already manned and Pericles had embarked on his own trireme, a solar eclipse occurred and darkness fell, and everyone was struck with amazement

---

83. In 431 BCE; see Thucydides 2.27. The Aeginetans were hostile to Athens, though part of its empire, and hence were deemed a security threat.

84. See Thucydides 2.47ff. The "plague" described here should not be confused with the bubonic plague that ravaged medieval Europe; probably it was an epidemic of smallpox.

85. The relationship of the sick patient and his caregiver is Plutarch's favorite analogue for the body politic and its leaders, given more point here because Athens had become literally sick.

as at a grave portent. Noticing that his helmsman was terrified and perplexed, Pericles held his cloak up in front of the man's eyes, and on covering them asked him if he thought it anything dreadful or a portent of anything dreadful. When the man said no, Pericles said, "Then how does this differ from that, except that the object which has caused the darkness is somewhat larger than my cloak?" This story is told in the philosophers' schools.[86]

Though he sailed out, Pericles appears not to have accomplished anything worthy of his preparation. After besieging sacred Epidaurus,[87] which raised a hope that he would capture it, he failed to do so because of the plague. When it came, the plague destroyed not only the Athenians but anyone who had had any contact with the army. After this, finding the citizens exasperated with him, Pericles tried to appease and encourage them. But he did not dispel their anger or change their attitude before they had taken their ballots in hand and asserted their authority. They stripped him of his command and punished him with a fine. The amount of it was fifteen talents, according to those who give the lowest figure, and fifty, according to those who give the highest. Cleon was the prosecutor of record, according to Idomeneus, though Theophrastus says it was Simmias, Heracleides Ponticus that it was Lacratidas.

[36] Pericles' public troubles, accordingly, were soon likely to come to an end, since the populace, unsparing in its anger, had not only stung him, but had also, as it were, left its stinger in him. . . . He was never seen to weep, or to mourn, or even to attend the burial of any of his relatives, until at last he lost his only remaining legitimate son Paralus. Though brought low, Pericles tried to preserve his character and maintain his greatness of soul. But as he was approaching the corpse with a garland, he was so overcome by emotion at the sight that he broke into sobs, and shed a great many tears, though he had never done such a thing in his life before.

[37] The city put its other generals and orators to the test for the conduct of the war, but when no one appeared to have the same gravity or the prestige equal to so important a command, the people

86. Since the eclipse is dated to 431 BCE and the naval expedition to 430, this incident could not have happened as Plutarch relates it. He says himself he heard it in the philosophic schools of his day, a reminder that his sources are not always historically reliable.

87. "Sacred" was an epithet given to Epidaurus much later than Pericles' time. The city had a famous sanctuary of Asclepius, the god of healing.

longed for Pericles and summoned him to the dais[88] and the generals' headquarters. Though disheartened and lying sorrowfully at home, he was persuaded by Alcibiades[89] and his other friends to come forth. When the people had apologized for their unfairness to him, and he had again taken charge of their affairs and been elected general, he requested that the law pertaining to illegitimate sons be repealed—a law that he himself had previously introduced—in order that the name and descent of his family might not die out altogether for lack of an heir.

The circumstances of this law were as follows. When Pericles was at the height of his power in the city—this was many years earlier—and had sons, as has been mentioned, who were legitimate, he wrote a law stating that only those persons whose parents had both been Athenians were Athenian citizens.[90] Thereafter, when the king of the Egyptians had sent the Athenian people a gift of forty thousand measures of wheat, and this had to be shared out among the citizens, many lawsuits were filed against persons who, according to Pericles' law, were not legal citizens, but had hitherto escaped notice and been overlooked; and many persons were subjected to false accusations. And consequently, nearly 5,000 persons were convicted and sold into slavery, while those who remained in the body of citizens and had been deemed true Athenians were found to number 14,040.[91] It was therefore a serious matter that the law that had been enforced against so many should be revoked by the man who had enacted it. But Pericles' present domestic distress, which was regarded as the penalty he had paid for his haughtiness and arrogance, moved the Athenians to pity him. Thinking that he had suffered retribution and that it was only human for him to make such a request, they agreed to let him enroll his illegitimate son in the register of his phratry and to give the boy his own name. It was this son who, after conquering

88. The raised stones from which speakers addressed the assembly.

89. Alcibiades, just now reaching adulthood, was a relative of Pericles and had been brought up by him after his own father's death. See *Alcibiades* 1.

90. This law can be dated to 451 BCE.

91. This number has been widely debated by historians investigating ancient demography. To most, it seems low for the mid-fifth century. It should be remembered that "citizens" includes only adult males and not their wives, children, or slaves, so the actual population of Athens would be many times this large.

the Peloponnesians in a sea battle at Arginusae, was put to death by the people along with his fellow commanders.[92]

[38] At that time, it would seem, the plague seized Pericles,[93] not with an acute or severe attack, as it did others, but with a mild, lingering illness, attended by a variety of changes that gradually wasted his body and undermined his judgment.

[39] The progress of their affairs produced in the Athenians a quick appreciation and a keen longing for Pericles. And indeed, people who, when he was alive, had been oppressed by his power, thinking it made *them* obscure, and who made trial, as soon as he was out of the way, of other orators and popular leaders, agreed that no man's character was by nature more moderate in its dignity, or more august in its mildness. And that odious power of his, which they had previously called monarchy and tyranny, now appeared to have been a safe bulwark for the citizenry, so heavily were their state affairs afflicted by the corruption and rampant baseness that he had kept weak and humble, thereby keeping it out of sight and preventing it from becoming incurably powerful.

92. In 406 BCE, well after the death of Pericles, his sole surviving son (also named Pericles) was among the generals commanding the Athenian fleet at Arginusae. The fleet was victorious in a battle against the Spartans but failed to retrieve its dead in the battle's aftermath. All ten generals were sentenced to death for this impiety, and though some escaped, Pericles was executed.

93. Thucydides does not say that Pericles died of the plague, and Plutarch is our only authority for that notion. In fact, the symptoms Plutarch reports here, as he notes himself, differ from those of ordinary plague victims.

Nicias

Plutarch's portrait of Nicias (c. 470–413 BCE), the pious, cautious leader who came to prominence in Athens after the death of Pericles, is taken largely from Thucydides. Both writers admired Nicias as a sober, steady, thoughtful man but found fault with his poor decisions as leader of Athens' expedition to Sicily in 415–413, his greatest and most consequential undertaking. Nicias was unquestionably ill-suited for this job, especially after the defection of Alcibiades, with whom he was initially teamed, left him in nearly sole command. The story of Nicias thus reads, in both Plutarch and Thucydides, as the tragedy of a good man appointed to the wrong post, and as a critique of the democratic processes that brought about that appointment.

[2] Nicias . . . had made a certain name for himself even during Pericles' lifetime; he had served as his co-commander,[1] and had often held sole command. And when Pericles died, Nicias was at once brought forward to hold first place, especially by the wealthy and notable, who made him a political force to counteract the coarseness and daring of Cleon,[2] though Nicias also enjoyed the common people's good will and sympathy. For Cleon had won great influence by "humoring the old folks and offering regular paid employment," but the majority of the very people whose favor he courted observed his greed and bold effrontery and tended to side with Nicias. For Nicias' dignity was not too harsh or oppressive, but was blended with a certain caution, and made him popular, since he was thought to fear the people.[3] Though he was naturally melancholy and unhopeful, good luck had masked his faint-heartedness on the military campaigns,

---

1. Pericles' office during most of his years as Athenian leader was *stratēgos*, one of the ten generals elected annually at Athens to lead military maneuvers. From this position it was easy to also gain political influence, since in the assembly, where anyone could speak, a *stratēgos* was assured of getting a respectful hearing. Plutarch is here noting that Nicias had often been among the board of ten *stratēgoi* in the same year that Pericles was.

2. Cleon, in contrast to Pericles and Nicias, was a politician who achieved influence only through his speaking style and force of personality, not by holding the office of *stratēgos*. His demagogy appealed particularly to the lower classes, prompting the wealthy to look to Nicias as a counterweight.

3. "The people" (*dēmos* in Greek) often means the Athenian assembly or the body of adult male citizens who were eligible to vote there.

since as a general he enjoyed consistent success; and in political life his timidity, and the ease with which he could be confused by accusers, endeared him to the people, who are inclined to fear those who despise them and to exalt those who fear them. For the highest honor the common people can receive from their betters is not to be treated with contempt.

[3] Now it was by his genuine prowess and eloquence that Pericles led the city; he needed no pretense or persuasive power to move the multitude. But as Nicias was inferior in these qualities, though superior in wealth, he made use of his money to win favor with the people. And since he lacked the confidence to compete successfully with the agile buffoonery by which Cleon pandered to the Athenians,[4] Nicias tried to win their favor by sponsoring public choruses, gymnastic competitions, and other such expensive public spectacles,[5] which in their extravagance and elegance surpassed those of all his predecessors and contemporaries.

[4] One may rest assured that Nicias' tendency to indulge and gratify the people stemmed from his piety. For he was one of those persons who are awestruck by divine manifestations, and "heavily influenced by superstition," as Thucydides says.[6] In one of Pasiphon's dialogues it says that day after day Nicias used to offer sacrifices to the gods; and as he kept a seer in his household, he pretended to be constantly consulting him about public matters, though he mainly sought advice about his private affairs, especially about his silver mines. For Nicias had acquired many in Laurion, and they produced vast revenues, though the operations were hazardous. He maintained a multitude of slaves there, and most of his wealth was in silver.

[5] Wary as he was of common informers, he neither dined with any of his fellow citizens nor attended discussions or social occasions. In fact he had no leisure for such pastimes: as a commander he remained until dark at the generals' meeting place, and when attending the boulē[7] he was the last to depart, the first to arrive. If he had

---

4. According to Thucydides, Cleon's speaking style was highly histrionic and accompanied by dramatic gestures, a judgment confirmed by Aristotle (*Constitution of the Athenians* 28.3). See chapter 8.

5. Wealthy Athenians voluntarily supplied the funds for the events Plutarch mentions; at this time Athens had few government subsidies for the arts.

6. An exact quote from Thucydides, *The Peloponnesian War* 7.50.

7. The boulē was the Council of Five Hundred at Athens that served as an executive board setting business for the assembly.

no public business to transact, he was unsociable and unapproachable, remaining at home behind locked doors. Encountering persons who had come to visit him, his friends would beg them to pardon Nicias, since he was even then engaged in public business and not at leisure. [6] Nicias sought to avoid difficult and prolonged military campaigns. But whenever he did hold command he advocated caution and brought most of his ventures to a successful issue, as was to be expected. And he attributed his successes not to any wisdom, power, or prowess of his own, but credited them to luck and took refuge in the divine, preferring to yield part of his glory rather than incur the gods' envy.

Events justified his prudence; for though the city, at that period, met with many reverses, none of them involved Nicias. When the Athenians were defeated by the Chalcidians,[8] Calliades and Xenophon were in command; the misfortune in Aetolia took place under Demosthenes' leadership[9] . . . and Pericles incurred the utmost blame for the plague, since during the war he had confined the throng from the country in the city, changing both their place of residence and their normal way of life.[10] But Nicias remained free of blame for all of these misfortunes. And meanwhile, as general he captured Cythera,[11] an island lying just off Laconia and settled by Spartan colonists; he seized many of the Thracian towns that had revolted, and brought them over to his side; and after forcing the Megarians to take refuge in their city, took immediate possession of the island of Minoa.[12] And soon, using the island as a base, he got control of Nisaea, descended into Corinthian territory, and prevailed in battle, slaughtering many Corinthians including Lycophron, their general.

But then it happened that the corpses of two of his men had been left behind, overlooked when the dead were gathered up. When he realized this, he immediately halted his force and sent a herald to the enemy to request their return. But according to custom and

8. A battle fought in 432 BCE; see Thucydides 1.63–65.

9. In 426 BCE; see Thucydides 3.96–98. The Demosthenes mentioned here and elsewhere in this life, a general of the late fifth century, must be distinguished from the orator of the fourth century who is dealt with in *Demosthenes* later in this volume.

10. See *Pericles* 34.

11. In 424 BCE, during the Peloponnesian War; see Thucydides 4.54.

12. In 427 BCE; see Thucydides 3.51.

convention, the side that obtained a retrieval of corpses under a truce was thought to have renounced the victory and could not lawfully erect a trophy; for those who held the field were regarded as the victors, whereas their petitioners did *not* hold the field, since they were unable to get what they wanted. Despite this, Nicias was willing to yield victory and glory rather than leave two of his fellow citizens behind unburied.

[7] When Demosthenes had fortified Pylos,[13] the Peloponnesians advanced against him with infantry and ships. And when a battle took place, and nearly four hundred Spartans were confined on the island of Sphacteria, the Athenians thought their capture would be a great achievement, as indeed it was. But the siege proved difficult and troublesome, as the region lacked water. And since the transporting of supplies, which in summer was time-consuming and expensive, was unsafe and utterly impracticable in the winter, the Athenians were distressed, and regretted having rejected the embassy of Spartans that had come to negotiate a truce and peace treaty. They had rejected the embassy because Cleon, mainly on Nicias' account, was opposed to it. For Cleon was hostile to Nicias, and when he saw the man eagerly cooperating with the Spartans he persuaded the people to reject the treaty. Then, when the siege was prolonged and the Athenians learned that terrible hardships were afflicting the army, they grew angry with Cleon.

When this man, placing the blame on Nicias, charged that through cowardice and softness he had let the men escape, and claimed that had *he* been in command they would not have held out for so long, it occurred to the Athenians to say, "No time like the present! Why not sail against these men yourself?" Nicias then stood up, relinquished his command at Pylos in favor of Cleon, and urged him to take with him as large a force as he liked, and not to parade his boldness in talk that brought no danger, but to furnish the city with an exploit worthy of serious consideration. At first Cleon hesitated, since he was thrown into confusion by the proposal's unexpectedness;

---

13. In 425 BCE. The episode of Pylos and Sphacteria, as it is often termed, forms one of the early turning points in the Peloponnesian War. Demosthenes decided on his own initiative to build a fort at Pylos, an abandoned harbor on the coast of the Peloponnese, as a base from which to mount raids on Spartan territory. The plan took on much bigger implications, however, when a Spartan force trying to take the fort became cut off on an island offshore, Sphacteria. Plutarch's account of the action is closely based on Thucydides 4.4ff.

but with the people urging him on as well, and Nicias railing at him, Cleon's ambition was excited and inflamed and he not only accepted the command but asserted that within twenty days of sailing he would either slay the men on Sphacteria or bring them alive to Athens. This aroused great laughter among the Athenians, rather than belief; for by then they were used to Cleon's levity and regarded his inspired frenzy in a humorous and not unpleasant light. (It is said that on one occasion when the assembly was in session and the people, seated on the Pnyx, had been waiting for him a long time, he finally appeared, crowned with a garland, and urged them to postpone the assembly until the next day. "For I am not at leisure today," said he, "as I'm about to entertain guests and have just sacrificed to the gods." Thereupon the Athenians burst out laughing, rose to their feet, and broke up the assembly.)

[8] But on the present occasion, Cleon had good luck, and with Demosthenes as his co-commander managed the campaign so well that within the stated time he took as prisoners of war, their weapons surrendered, all the Spartans who had not fallen in battle.[14] And this reflected great discredit upon Nicias. For he was thought not to have thrown away his shield, but to have done something worse and more disgraceful in voluntarily relinquishing his command out of cowardice, and giving his enemy the opportunity to achieve such a success, since he had actually voted himself out of office. . . . And indeed, Nicias did the city no little harm by letting Cleon attain so much renown and influence, by means of which the man wallowed in oppressive arrogance and ungovernable rashness and inflicted other misfortunes on the city, of which he, as much as anyone, bore the brunt. Violating the propriety of the dais, Cleon was the first to raise his voice when addressing the people, the first to pull off his cloak and strike his thigh and dash about while speaking. And he thus implanted in those who managed the government an indifference to baseness and a contempt for what was proper that soon confounded the whole city.

[9] By now Alcibiades[15] was becoming a force in Athens, and as a popular leader was not quite as intemperate as Cleon. But just as the land of Egypt, in its fertility, is said to bring forth

---

14. There were 292 surviving prisoners, of whom 120 were Spartan citizens. Brought back to Athens, they became a major bargaining chip that allowed Athens to conclude a peace treaty on favorable terms.

15. A handsome, wealthy, ambitious young man who had grown up as Pericles' ward; see *Alcibiades* in this volume.

Medicinal herbs, many of them healing, and many harmful,[16]

so the nature of Alcibiades, inclining strongly in both directions, gave rise to serious upheavals. That was why Nicias, though rid of Cleon, had no opportunity to soothe and calm all the city's troubles: once he had set its affairs on a path to safety, he lost his influence, and through the power and vehemence of Alcibiades' ambition was again embroiled in war.

This came about in the following way. The men most at war with the peace of Greece were Cleon and Brasidas,[17] since war concealed the baseness of the one, and adorned the prowess of the other. When these men both fell in the same battle at Amphipolis,[18] Nicias immediately learned that the Spartans had long been yearning for peace, that the Athenians had lost heart for the war, and that both sides were unstrung, as it were, and willing to drop their arms. He therefore took steps to ally the two cities, free the other Greek states from their troubles, and give them a respite, thereby ensuring for all time his renown as a successful statesman. The affluent, the elderly, and most of the farmers were immediately in favor of peace; and by meeting with many of the other citizens and instructing them in private, Nicias blunted their keenness for the war. Then, offering hope to the Spartans, he invited and urged them to embrace peace. They were inclined to trust him both because of his reasonableness on other occasions, and because, having charge of the men who had been captured at Pylos and imprisoned, he was treating them humanely and lightening their misfortune. . . .

[10] Meanwhile Alcibiades, who was not naturally disposed to remain quiet, was vexed with the Spartans because they ignored and disdained *him*, while heeding and embracing Nicias. At first, though he did what he could to oppose and resist the peace, he accomplished nothing. But shortly thereafter, seeing that the Athenians were no

16. A quotation from Homer's *Odyssey* 4.229.

17. "The peace of Greece" refers to the attempts by Sparta and Athens to conclude a treaty, following the Athenian seizure of the Spartans on Sphacteria. Brasidas, an ambitious Spartan general, was unwilling to surrender the advantageous position he had achieved and the gains he had made in order to secure a treaty.

18. In 422 BCE. Peace efforts immediately went forward after the deaths of these two men, and a treaty was concluded that brought a temporary halt to the Peloponnesian War. Nicias was the principal Athenian negotiator, with the result that the treaty is generally known today as the Peace of Nicias.

longer so pleased with the Spartans (they supposed themselves wronged when the latter made an alliance with the Boeotians and failed to hand over Panactum with its fortifications restored, or Amphipolis at all),[19] he harped on these grievances and sharpened the people's indignation at every slight. Finally, sending for envoys from Argos, he tried to forge an alliance between the two cities.[20] When ambassadors had arrived from Sparta with full powers, and after their first meeting with the council seemed to have come with perfectly fair proposals, Alcibiades, fearing that the assembly might be swayed by the same arguments, circumvented the ambassadors by a trick.[21] He promised under oath that he would cooperate with them in everything if they would not claim or admit that they had come with full powers. He declared that if they heeded him in this they would certainly obtain what they desired. When they had been persuaded, and had transferred their allegiance from Nicias to *him*, he introduced them in the assembly and immediately asked whether they had come with full powers to negotiate about all issues. When they said no, he reversed course, contrary to their expectations, and called upon the members of the council to bear witness to what the embassy had told *them*, and urged the people not to heed or trust men who were so obviously lying and saying now one thing, now its opposite. The ambassadors, naturally enough, were confused, and Nicias was unable to say anything, as he was overcome with dismay and astonishment. But though the people were eager to summon the Argives at once and make them allies, an earthquake came to Nicias' aid and broke up the assembly. On the following day, when the people again assembled, Nicias, by assiduous activity and oratory succeeded, with difficulty, in persuading them to suspend their overtures to the Argives and to send him to the Spartans, promising them that all would be well.

On reaching Sparta, though in other respects he was honored as a good and diligent man, Nicias accomplished nothing. Instead,

19. The Peace of Nicias called on both Athens and Sparta not to alter the existing balance of power by making new alliances with states hostile to the other, and demanded restoration by both sides of certain territories taken during the war. Athens was also required to return the prisoners it had captured on Sphacteria.

20. Since Argos had thus far been neutral in the war, the attempted alliance did not violate the terms of the Peace of Nicias.

21. See *Alcibiades* 14.

after being overruled by those who sided with the Boeotians, he returned home, not only discredited and maligned, but also fearful of the Athenians, who were grieved and vexed that they had been persuaded by him to restore so many distinguished prisoners of war. (For the captives brought from Pylos came from the foremost families of Sparta and had powerful friends and kinsmen.) Though the people did nothing harsher in their anger at Nicias, they chose Alcibiades as general, formed an alliance with the Mantineans and Elians (who had revolted from the Spartans) along with the Argives, sent marauders to Pylos to plunder Laconia, and thus again embroiled themselves in war.

[11] At the height of Alcibiades' quarrel with Nicias an ostracism was held. By this procedure, which the people were accustomed to perform every few years,[22] one of those persons who were viewed with suspicion because of their high renown or envied because of their wealth was forced to emigrate for ten years. Alcibiades and Nicias now found themselves beset and menaced by a great uproar, since it was assumed that one of the two would surely be subjected to the ostracism. For the people felt a loathing for Alcibiades' way of life and feared his boldness, as has been brought to light in greater detail in my account of his career,[23] while Nicias had incurred ill will partly because of his wealth, but especially because his way of life, which was not genial or affable but unsociable and oligarchical, struck people as strange. And since by then he had often opposed the people's desires and forced them, contrary to their judgment, to do what was in their interest, he was felt to be oppressive. But to put it simply, the ostracism represented a contest between the warmongering young and their peacemaking elders,[24] the former aiming the ostracism at Nicias, the latter at Alcibiades.

"In time of strife even villains win a portion of honor," and likewise in this instance, the common people, by dividing into two factions, made room for the boldest and basest men, among whom was Hyperbolus, from the deme of Perithoedae, a man who ventured

22. An exaggeration; though ostracisms had been called rather frequently in the first half of the fifth century BCE, the procedure had by this time become rare.

23. That is, in *Alcibiades*.

24. The idea of a generational split at Athens, pitting hawkish youth against more conservative, less aggressive elders, seems to be derived from Thucydides (e.g., 6.12–13).

though he lacked power, but was gaining power merely by venturing, and by means of the renown he was acquiring in the city was giving the city a bad name. At the time, Hyperbolus considered himself beyond the reach of the ostracism, since he was a more appropriate candidate for the pillory. But as he expected that when one of his two rivals had been banished he would himself become a rival to the man who remained in the city, it was clear that he was delighted by their quarrel and was inciting the common people against both men. But Nicias and Alcibiades, on becoming aware of Hyperbolus' rascality, consulted one another in secret and brought their factions together. Having united to form one party, they carried the day, and thus, instead of either of *them*, Hyperbolus was ostracized. In the immediate aftermath, this afforded the common people delight and amusement; but later they were vexed, thinking that the practice had been abused by being applied to an unworthy man. For there was actually a hierarchy of punishment, and they considered the ostracism a form of punishment more suited to a Thucydides or an Aristides and their like, whereas for Hyperbolus it was an honor and a pretext for boasting, since by his rascality he had suffered the same punishment as the best men.

[12] When the embassies from Segesta and Leontini arrived and persuaded the Athenians to wage war on Sicily,[25] Nicias stood up to oppose the idea but was defeated by the ambitious counsel of Alcibiades. For even before the assembly convened, Alcibiades had gained control of the majority, whose judgment had already been perverted by hopes and stories, so that the young men in their wrestling-schools and the old men in their workshops would sit in semicircles sketching maps of Sicily, charts of the sea around it, and plans of the harbors and positions on the island's coast facing Libya. For they did not regard Sicily as a prize of the war but as a base of operations from which they would contend against the Carthaginians and gain control of Africa and the sea inside the Pillars of Heracles.

Their eagerness was such that Nicias, though he opposed them, had few influential allies. For the affluent citizens, afraid they might appear to be avoiding their civic obligations, which included the fitting out of triremes, kept quiet against their better judgment. But Nicias, never flagging, would not give up; even after the Athenians

---

25. These embassies occurred in the years before 415 BCE (see Thucydides 6.6). Segesta and Leontini were small Sicilian cities, allied with Athens, that felt themselves threatened by the regional superpower, Syracuse.

had voted for the war and elected him general first, and after him Alcibiades and Lamachus, he stood up at the second assembly and tried to dissuade the people and to argue against the expedition, and ended by slandering Alcibiades, asserting that for the sake of private gain and ambition he was driving the city into a difficult and dangerous action overseas. But he accomplished nothing more; on the contrary, since the Athenians regarded his experience as highly useful and thought they would enjoy security against the rashness of Alcibiades and the harshness of Lamachus if these were tempered by Nicias' caution, he succeeded only in confirming their resolution.

[13] Yet it is said that the expedition met with considerable opposition, even from the priests. But Alcibiades, who consulted different seers, cited a number of ancient oracles declaring that the Athenians would win great renown in Sicily. . . . No signs, not even those that were clear and conspicuous, could deter the Athenians, as for example the mutilation of the Herms.[26]

[14] Lamachus moved that they should sail at once against Syracuse and fight a battle right near the city, and Alcibiades that they should incite the cities allied to Syracuse to revolt and then go after the Syracusans themselves.[27] But Nicias espoused the opposite course. And by urging them to proceed quietly along the Sicilian coast, circumnavigate the island, display their weapons and triremes, and then sail back to Athens after detaching a small force to aid the Segestans, he soon dampened his men's spirits and sapped their resolution.

Shortly thereafter, the Athenians sent orders for Alcibiades to return and stand trial.[28] Though a replacement commander was named, Nicias actually assumed sole command.

[15] Nicias was constantly delaying and exercising caution. First, by cruising around Sicily as far from the coast as possible, he heartened the enemy; and then, attacking the small town of Hybla and departing before capturing it, he elicited utter contempt. Finally,

---

26. The episode is described more fully in *Alcibiades* 18. Just before the ships were to sail for Sicily, vandals defaced a number of religious monuments called Herms in the streets of Athens. Alcibiades was blamed for the sacrilege, perhaps unfairly.

27. These deliberations occurred after the fleet had already reached Sicily, in the summer of 415 BCE. Plutarch has skipped over the magnificent departure of the fleet, memorably recorded by Thucydides (6.30–31).

28. The recall of Alcibiades, and his defection to the Spartans, are described more fully in *Alcibiades* 18–24.

he left for Catana,[29] having achieved nothing beside the conquest of Hyccara, a barbarian fortress.

[16] The summer had passed when Nicias learned that the Syracusans, who had gained confidence, intended to make the first move and come out against them. . . . Nicias embarked, though reluctantly, on a campaign against Syracuse. Since he wanted to encamp the army safely and easily, he secretly sent a man from Catana who told the Syracusans that if they wished to seize the deserted camp and get possession of the Athenians' weapons they should approach Catana on a given date with their entire army. Since the Athenians, he explained, spent most of their time in the city, the Syracusans' friends had planned, as soon as they noticed them approaching, to seize the gates and set fire to the dockyard; he assured them that many conspirators were already awaiting their arrival.

This was Nicias' finest stroke of generalship in Sicily. For after drawing the enemy and their entire army out of the city, and practically emptying it of men, he himself set sail from Catana, got possession of the enemy's harbors, and seized a spot for his camp where he expected to incur the least harm from that branch of his enemy's forces in which he was inferior, namely the cavalry, and wage war without hindrance, deploying the branches of his own army in which he had confidence. When the Syracusans, having turned back from Catana, drew themselves up in battle array before the city, Nicias quickly led the Athenians against them and won a victory. . . .

But he took no advantage of his famous victory. When a few days had elapsed Nicias withdrew again, to Naxos.[30] . . . And consequently the Syracusans, again taking heart, rode out to Catana, ravaged the countryside, and burned down the Athenians' camp. Everyone held Nicias to blame for this, since by pondering, delaying, and exercising caution he missed the critical moment for taking action. For no one could find fault with the man in the course of an action, since once he had begun he was energetic and effective; but he procrastinated and hesitated to engage.

29. This city to the north of Syracuse had agreed to become an Athenian ally.
30. Thucydides explains at 6.71 that Nicias felt he needed to raise more forces, in particular the cavalry forces in which he was outclassed by the Syracusans, before making a further assault; and the onset of foul weather required, he felt, a more secure winter camp.

[17] When he moved the army back to Syracuse,[31] he managed his command so cleverly and his approach so unerringly that he reached Thapsus with his ships and disembarked without being observed, getting possession of Epipolae[32] before anyone could stop him. . . . But what especially astonished the Sicilians and struck the Greeks as incredible was how quickly he threw a wall around Syracuse,[33] a city no smaller than Athens, though the unevenness of the surrounding terrain and the proximity of the sea and marshes made it that much harder to construct such a wall. But he came within an ace of completing the task—a man who was not even enjoying good health while engaged in such demanding efforts, but was suffering from a kidney disease, to which one may fairly attribute his failure to complete the work. In what they did succeed in accomplishing I marvel at the diligence of the general and the fortitude of his soldiers.

[18] Though ailing, Nicias was present at most of their actions. But once, during a severe bout of illness, he was lying in bed within the walls, attended by a few servants, while Lamachus led the army in an attack on the Syracusans who were extending a wall from their city to the one the Athenians were building, to intercept and hinder its completion. When the Athenians, having prevailed in battle, were engaged in a disorderly pursuit, Lamachus, left alone, stood his ground against the Syracusan horsemen who charged at him. The first of these was Callicrates, a skillful and spirited warrior. When challenged, Lamachus engaged him in single combat; receiving the first blow, he gave one back, fell, and died. . . .

Nicias was now the sole surviving commander, and his hopes were high. For cities changed their allegiance, and vessels filled with grain came to the camp from all directions, since everyone sides with those who are prospering. And proposals for a truce were already reaching him from the Syracusans who despaired of defending their city. When Gylippus, sailing to their rescue from Sparta,[34] heard on his voyage of the wall surrounding them, and

31. The following spring, early 414 BCE.
32. An area of high ground overlooking the city of Syracuse, and therefore a strategically vital position for an attacker.
33. Completion of this wall would have cut off Syracuse from supply and allowed Athens to starve the city into surrender.
34. Gylippus was a Spartan general, sent by the Spartans to supervise operations of the Syracusans against Athens. Plutarch explains the entry

of their troubles, he pressed on in the belief that Sicily was already occupied, and that he could only save the Greek cities on the Italian mainland, if that were still possible. For the report was spreading far and wide that the Athenians were in complete control and possessed a commander whose good fortune and sagacity made him invincible.

Nicias himself was uncharacteristically heartened by his present strength and luck, and especially by the persons sent from Syracuse to consult with him in secret,[35] since he thought that the city was just about to surrender under treaty. He therefore attached no importance to the fact that Gylippus was sailing against him, nor did he even post a proper guard. And consequently Gylippus, finding himself utterly ignored and despised, sailed through the strait unnoticed, and having landed at a point far distant from Syracuse, mustered a large army. The Syracusans remained unaware and were not even expecting him. That was why they summoned an assembly to discuss the terms of a peace with Nicias. Some were already on their way to it, as they supposed that a peace settlement should be made before the city was completely walled in. For only a very small part of the work remained to be done, and along that interval all the materials for wall-building had been conveniently scattered.

[19] At that point—at the critical moment of their danger— Gongylus arrived from Corinth[36] with one trireme. And when all the Syracusans, as may be imagined, flocked to meet him, he said that Gylippus would soon be arriving and that other ships were sailing to their aid. Though they were not yet sure they should believe Gongylus, a messenger arrived from Gylippus urging them to come out and meet him. Taking courage, they armed themselves; and straight from his journey, Gylippus led them, arrayed for battle, against the Athenians. When Nicias had ranged his men opposite them, Gylippus halted his armed force in front of the Athenians and sent a herald to say that he was offering them safe conduct if

---

of the Spartans into the war for Sicily at *Alcibiades* 23. After deserting the Athenian-led army, Alcibiades had landed in Sparta and convinced the leadership there that Sparta had a vital interest in stopping the Athenian effort in Sicily.

35. The pro-Athenian party inside Syracuse had secret communications with Nicias during this period, hoping to betray the city to him and force it into an alliance with Athens.

36. The Corinthians, allies of the Spartans, had sent a fleet to aid the Syracusan resistance, and Gongylus was commander of the first ship to reach Sicily.

they left Sicily. Nicias did not think fit to respond, and some of his soldiers laughingly asked whether by the arrival of one threadbare cloak and staff[37] the position of the Syracusans had suddenly become so formidable that they despised the Athenians. . . .

   In the first battle, the Athenians prevailed and killed a few of the Syracusans along with Gongylus the Corinthian; but on the next day Gylippus showed why experience counts. For he used the same arms, the same horses, and the same battleground, but not in the same way; and having changed his tactics, defeated the Athenians. And as the latter were fleeing to their camp, he halted his Syracusans, and with the very stones and wood the Athenians had brought together for their own use, built a fortification that extended all the way to the besiegers' wall, so that they derived no advantage from their success in the field.[38]

   The Syracusans now regained confidence and manned their ships. Riding about with their own cavalry and that of their allies, they took many prisoners. Gylippus, meanwhile, approached the cities in person and roused them all to unite, follow his orders, and give him their vigorous support. And consequently Nicias, again reverting to his original arguments and acknowledging their reverses, grew disheartened and wrote to the Athenians, urging them either to send out another army or to recall this one from Sicily, and requesting in any case that they relieve him of command because of his illness.[39]

   [20] Even before this the Athenians had been intending to send a second force to Sicily, but envy of Nicias' early successes had occasioned many delays. Now, however, they were eager to hasten in aid. Demosthenes was planning to sail with a large force in early spring. . . . But at that point Nicias was suddenly attacked by both land and sea. Though defeated at first, he nevertheless managed, with his naval force, to drive out and disable many enemy ships. But he did not arrive in time to aid the infantry. Gylippus, attacking unexpectedly, captured Plemmyrium,[40] where he got possession of all the naval

37. A jest at the famous poverty and asceticism of Spartan society.

38. The Syracusan counterwall cut off the Athenian wall so that it could not be completed, and secured control of part of Epipolae for Syracuse. The Athenians' position was very much undermined by this wall, which effectively made them the besieged instead of the besiegers.

39. Thucydides preserves a version of the letter (7.11–14). It was sent at the end of the 414 BCE campaigning season.

40. A headland south of Syracuse where Nicias had established his base camp.

equipment and large deposits of money, slaughtered many men, and took many alive. But most important of all, he deprived Nicias of easy access to a market. For the conveying of supplies past Plemmyrium had been managed safely and quickly while the Athenians were in control; but once they had been expelled, provisioning became difficult and entailed fighting with the enemy forces lying in wait for them there.

[21] At that point Demosthenes, resplendent in military gear that utterly disconcerted the enemy, came into view outside the harbors, leading five thousand hoplites on twenty-three ships, and no fewer than three thousand javelin-men, archers, and slingers. By the good order of his weapons, the ensigns of his triremes, and the dense mass of signalmen and flute-players spectacularly arrayed, he astonished the enemy. And thus the Syracusans, as was to be expected, were again overcome with dread. Without hope of any ultimate release, they saw themselves toiling futilely and perishing in vain. . . .

Demosthenes took the infantry and attacked Epipolae[41] at night. He caught some of the enemy by surprise and killed them; the rest, though they defended themselves, he put to flight. Though victorious he did not remain where he was, but marched ahead until he encountered the Boeotians,[42] who had already drawn themselves up in close formation. Running en masse against the Athenians with their spears couched, the Boeotians sent up a shout and thrust the Athenians back, killing many of them there. Terror and confusion overwhelmed the entire army. The part that was prevailing was now mixed up with the part that was fleeing, and the part that was advancing to attack was driven back by panic-stricken men and fell foul of itself, the men thinking the fugitives were pursuers, and thus treating their friends as foes. The disorderly scramble, the combination of fear and ignorance, and the untrustworthiness of their vision plunged the Athenians into terrible perplexities and reversals. For the night was not pitch dark, but neither was the light steady. The moon, hanging low on the horizon, was obscured by masses of weapons and bodies in motion, and the inability to discern shapes distinctly, coupled with fear of the enemy, led friendly forces to suspect one another. Furthermore, it somehow happened that the Athenians had the moon

41. The focus of this battle was the point at which the Syracusan counterwall cut off the Athenian wall. If Athens could regain control of this position, it could safely complete its wall.
42. The Boeotians (Thebans and others), allies of Sparta, had sent troops to aid the Syracusan resistance.

at their backs, so that they cast shadows on one another and thus concealed the number and brightness of their weapons, whereas the reflection of the moonlight on the enemy's shields made *them* appear brighter and much more numerous.

Finally, when the Athenians gave ground and the enemy attacked them from all sides, they fled, some of them perishing at the enemy's hands, others at one another's hands, and still others when they fell from the cliffs. The Athenians who dispersed and wandered away were overtaken by horsemen the next day and put to death. The corpses numbered two thousand; and of the survivors, few got away safe with their armor.

[22] Stricken though not surprised by the defeat, Nicias blamed Demosthenes for his headlong haste. Demosthenes defended his conduct and urged that they sail away as soon as possible. . . . Nicias was dismayed to hear talk of fleeing and sailing away, not because he did not fear the Syracusans, but because he had an even greater fear of the Athenians and their lawsuits and dishonest prosecutions. He maintained that nothing dreadful was to be expected, and even if the worst should happen he would choose death at the hands of the enemy rather than at the hands of his fellow citizens. . . . But when a fresh army came to aid the Syracusans, and more of the Athenians were being infected by disease, even Nicias finally considered it advisable to change their position, and sent word to the soldiers to prepare to sail away.

[23] When all their preparations had been made and none of the enemy was keeping close watch, since they expected no such move, there occurred an eclipse of the moon at night, which terrified Nicias. . . . Nicias persuaded the people to wait until another lunar cycle had been completed.

[24] Abandoning almost everything else, Nicias sat sacrificing and taking omens until the enemy attacked, besieged the Athenians' walls and camp with their infantry, and surrounded their ships in the harbor. Not only the men of Syracuse in their triremes, but boys in fishing boats and skiffs sailed from all sides against the Athenians, called them out to fight, and showered them with reproaches. When one of these boys, Heracleides, the son of distinguished parents, drove his boat out ahead of the others, an Attic ship pursued and tried to capture him. Fearing for Heracleides, his uncle Pollichus sailed in pursuit with the ten triremes under his command, and then the others, fearing for Pollichus, likewise put out after them. In the fierce naval battle that took place, the Syracusans won a victory and slaughtered Eurymedon along with many others.

The Athenians, accordingly, could no longer bear to remain where they were but railed against their commanders and urged them to withdraw by land. For as soon as the Syracusans had prevailed at sea, they blocked up their harbor and barred its entrance. But Nicias and his officers would not comply, saying it would be terrible to abandon so many merchant ships and nearly two hundred triremes. Embarking the best of their infantry and the bravest of their javelin-men, they manned 110 triremes; the rest lacked oars.[43] Nicias stationed the remaining throng along the shore.

[25] The sea battle proved by far the greatest and most desperate. It dismayed and distressed those who witnessed it no less than the combatants, since the entire engagement, encompassing a great variety of unexpected reverses within a brief time, was unfolding in plain sight; and the Athenians found themselves disabled by their own equipment no less than by that of the enemy. For with their heavy ships[44] crowded together they were fighting against light vessels attacking from all directions. Assailed from all sides by stones, which generally hit their mark, the Athenians were firing back with javelins and arrows, whose aim was disturbed by the motion of the water. But the Syracusans had been trained to fight under these conditions by the Corinthian pilot Ariston. Though he fought throughout the battle itself, Ariston fell just as the Spartans were prevailing.

The rout and slaughter were tremendous, and the Athenians found their route of escape by sea cut off. Observing that their deliverance by land would be difficult, they made no effort to hinder the enemy soldiers who were still nearby, towing away their ships, nor did they request permission to retrieve their dead, whose lack of burial seemed less pitiable now that they had to face the abandonment of their sick and wounded.[45] And they considered themselves worse off than the corpses, since after suffering further misfortunes they would meet with the very same end.

43. A lot of Athenian naval gear had been lost when Gylippus and the Syracusans took Plemmyrium. Nicias had become caught in what today might be called a negative feedback loop, in which every setback led to a further setback.

44. As Thucydides makes clear, the Athenians, lacking a secure harbor, had been unable to properly dry out and re-tar their ships, which as a result had become waterlogged.

45. Those not fit to travel with the retreating forces had to be left behind to the mercy of the Syracusans, a scene Thucydides records in harrowing detail (7.75).

[26] The Athenians were eager to set out that night. And Gylippus and his men, seeing the Syracusans occupied in sacrifices and carousals in honor of their victory and festival, had no thought of persuading or compelling them to rise up and attack the departing enemy. But Hermocrates,[46] acting on his own initiative, hatched a plot against Nicias and sent him certain friends who pretended they came from those who had often held secret talks with him. They advised him not to travel during the night, since the Syracusans had set ambushes for them and were in possession of the roads. Outwitted by this, Nicias stayed where he was, only to actually suffer at his enemy's hands what he had mistakenly feared. For the Syracusans, going forth at daybreak, got possession of the rough patches of their roads, fortified the fords of the rivers, cut off the bridges, and stationed their horsemen in the smooth and level areas, leaving no spot where the Athenians could advance without fighting.

Remaining where they were both that day and another night, they marched forth weeping and lamenting (as if they were being forced to leave their native land rather than that of their enemy), both on account of their utter lack of necessities and because they were abandoning their disabled friends and intimates. And yet they imagined that their present ills were easier to bear than those they had to look forward to. But of the many dreadful sights in the army, none was more pitiable than that of Nicias himself, afflicted by illness and reduced undeservedly to a subsistence diet and the most meager share of the many provisions he needed because of his illness. Though weak, he persevered under conditions that many of the strong could barely tolerate, and it was clear to all that he bore these hardships not for his own sake or from any love of life; it was for his men's sake that he would not give up hope. The others wept and lamented from fear and pain; but whenever Nicias was compelled to do so, it was plainly because he was comparing his expedition's disgrace and ignominy with the stature and renown he had hoped to achieve.

And it was not only the sight of his person, but also the memory of the arguments and addresses with which he had tried to prevent the expedition, that sharpened their awareness of how undeserved his sufferings were. They also lost heart about their prospects for divine aid when they reflected that a highly favored man, who had distinguished himself by many important services to the gods, now

46. A Syracusan politician who had rallied the city to resist Athens.

met with a fortune no more seemly than the basest and meanest in his army.

[27] Yet Nicias strove, in his tone, his countenance, and his manner, to show himself superior to his dreadful plight. And throughout the entire eight-day march, though his men were being assailed and wounded by the enemy, he kept his force unconquered until Demosthenes and *his* force were captured. Left behind, they had joined battle when surrounded near the country house of Polyzelus. Demosthenes drew his sword and stabbed but did not kill himself, at which point the enemy surrounded and seized him.[47]

When the Syracusans rode up to inform Nicias, he sent horsemen to make certain that Demosthenes' force had been captured. He then sought to make a treaty with Gylippus, according to which the Athenians would be released from Sicily after giving hostages for all the money the Syracusans had spent on the war. But the enemy, paying no heed, assailed him with insolent threats and angry abuse, though he was now destitute of all necessities. Yet Nicias endured through the night, and on the next day advanced under fire to the river Asinarus. Meeting the Athenians there, the enemy thrust some of them into the stream, while others, driven by thirst, plunged in headlong. And it was there, in the river, that the heaviest and most savage slaughter took place, with men being slain as they drank, until Nicias fell at Gylippus' feet and said, "Have pity in victory, Gylippus, not on me, who over the course of a varied and fortunate career won fame and glory, but on the Athenians, and remember that the fortunes of war are apportioned impartially, and that the Athenians, when they were prospering, treated you fairly and gently."

As Nicias was speaking, Gylippus was moved both by his appearance and his words, since he knew that the Spartans had been treated well by Nicias when the peace was made.[48] Gylippus also felt that his own renown would be enhanced if he brought his enemies home alive. He therefore raised Nicias up and urged him to take heart, and gave orders that his men were to be taken prisoner. But as these orders traveled slowly across the battlefield, the slain far outnumbered those who were spared, though many were stolen away and concealed by the soldiers.

47. A rare case in this *Life* where Plutarch uses material not found in Thucydides. The account of Demosthenes' surrender in Thucydides (7.81–82) makes no mention of Polyzelus nor of Demosthenes' attempt at suicide.
48. That is, the Peace of Nicias, concluded eight years earlier.

After gathering together those who had been captured openly, they hung their prisoners' armor from the tallest and finest trees near the river, crowned themselves with garlands, adorned their horses splendidly, cut the hair of the enemy's horses, and rode into the city, having contended in the most brilliant combat of Greeks against Greeks, and having won the most perfect of victories with the strongest force and the utmost display of zeal and valor.

[28] At an assembly of the entire citizen body of Syracuse and its allies, the popular leader Eurycles moved first that the day on which they had captured Nicias be a holiday, on which they would offer sacrifices and abstain from work, and that the festival be called the Asinaria, after the river Asinarus (the Asinaria fell on the twenty-sixth of the month of Carneius, which the Athenians call Metageitnion); and second, that the Athenians' servants and their other allies be sold into slavery, and that the Athenians themselves and the Sicilian Greeks who had protected them be thrown into the quarries—all except for their generals, who should be put to death.

These resolutions were accepted by the Syracusans, whereupon Hermocrates, protesting that the noble use of victory was better than victory itself, was met with no small furor. And when Gylippus demanded the Athenian generals, so he might escort them to the Spartans, the Syracusans, now made insolent by their good fortune, rebuked him, especially since throughout the war they had found it hard to bear his harshness and the Laconic manner with which he wielded authority. . . . Timaeus denies that Demosthenes and Nicias were put to death at the Syracusans' order, as Philistus and Thucydides have written; instead, he says that Hermocrates sent word to them while the assembly was still in session, and with the help of one of their guards they did away with themselves. Their bodies, however, were cast out by the entrance, and lay in plain sight for those who wished to set eyes on them. I hear that to this day, in a temple at Syracuse, they point out a shield that is said to have belonged to Nicias. Its gold and purple web is welded together with great skill.

Alcibiades

With his flamboyance, beauty, and boundless political ambition, Alcibiades (c. 450–404 BCE) cuts one of the most vivid figures in all of Greek history. Plutarch's Alcibiades has been excerpted here at greater length than the other Lives. The Alcibiades is compelling as both a personal drama and a morality tale about the perils of self-pride. Alcibiades had the natural talent of a Julius Caesar or an Alexander the Great, and perhaps could have rivaled these leaders by making himself sole ruler of Athens and making Athens the supreme power of Greece. But his need to promote himself, to trumpet and display his achievements, made many in Athens mistrust him. Always resentful of those better than themselves, the Athenian people became positively outraged when someone flaunted their betterness.

Short though it was, Alcibiades' political career was highly eventful and filled with dramatic ups and downs. It coincided with the great war between Athens and Sparta that has come to be known as the Peloponnesian War, in the last third of the fifth century BCE. Alcibiades played the most consequential role of any individual in that war, with his contemporary Lysander—a man every bit Alcibiades' equal in cunning, ambition, and military brilliance—running a close second. (Plutarch contrasts the natures of the two men at Lysander *19, a passage not included in this volume, when he says that Alcibiades alienated people with his arrogance and willfulness, Lysander with his cruel streak.)*

[1] Alcibiades' family is thought to trace its descent back to Eurysaces, son of Ajax; and on his mother's side he was an Alcmaeonid,[1] being the son of Deinomache, daughter of Megacles. Alcibiades' father Clinias fought with distinction at Artemisium[2] in a trireme fitted out at his own expense, and was afterward slain at Coroneia, fighting the Boeotians.[3] Pericles and Ariphron, the sons of Xanthippus, became Alcibiades' guardians, as they were his kinsmen.[4] . . .

---

1. That is, a descendant of the wealthy Alcmaeon, an Athenian of the sixth century BCE, whose family had long been prominent in politics (its members included Megacles, Cleisthenes, and Pericles).

2. In 480 BCE. See *Themistocles* 7–8.

3. In 447 BCE, when Alcibiades was three or four years old.

4. The familial relationship between Pericles and Alcibiades is unclear; two ancient sources say they were uncle and nephew.

Now it may be unnecessary to say anything about Alcibiades' beauty[5] except that it blossomed forth at every stage of his physical growth—in childhood, youth, and manhood—and made him charming and desirable. For it is not true in all instances that "the autumn of beauty is also beautiful," as Euripides says, but it was true in the case of Alcibiades, and a few others, because of his excellent constitution and superb physique.

[2] Alcibiades' character eventually displayed many inconsistencies and variations, as was natural over the course of a momentous career and its shifting fortunes. Though he was endowed by nature with many powerful passions, the strongest among them were his love of competition and his eagerness to be first, as is clear from the accounts of his childhood.

He was once pressed hard while wrestling, and in order not to fall set his teeth in his opponent's hands where they gripped him, as though he meant to devour them. Relaxing his hold, his opponent said, "You bite, Alcibiades, just like a woman." "No," replied Alcibiades, "but like a lion."

[4] Before long, many well-born men were swarming around Alcibiades and seeking his company. Most of them, plainly captivated by the brilliance of his youthful bloom, paid court to him;[6] but Socrates' love was great proof of the boy's merit and good disposition. Discerning these qualities behind and through Alcibiades' personal beauty, and fearing that the lad would be overpowered by wealth and rank and that the throng of citizens, foreigners, and allies would enthrall him with flattery and favors, Socrates was of a mind to guard against and prevent this, just as one would prevent a plant in flower from losing its fruit or letting the fruit spoil. For no man is so insulated and hemmed in by the so-called good things of life that he cannot be touched by philosophy or reached by frank and incisive discourse. And so it was that Alcibiades, though indulged right from the start, and prevented by his pleasure-seeking companions from listening to one who would admonish and educate him, nevertheless, through his innate integrity, became acquainted with Socrates, embraced him, and kept his wealthy and distinguished admirers at a distance.

5. The physical attractiveness of Alcibiades was legendary, as attested by Plato's *Symposium*.

6. In the normal pattern of male homosexual relationships at Athens, young men, in their early adolescence, would be wooed, sometimes quite competitively, by men a generation or more older.

And soon, having made Socrates an intimate, and hearing the words not of a lover hunting down an unmanly pleasure, nor one importuning him for kisses and caresses, but one who made him ashamed of the rottenness of his soul and chided him for his empty and foolish vanity, "he crouched, though a fighting cock, like a slave, and folded his wings."[7] He believed that Socrates really had a divine mission to look after and safeguard the young. Despising himself, admiring *him*, welcoming his affection, but put to shame by his goodness, Alcibiades acquired, without realizing it, what Plato calls "that counterlove which is the image of love," with the result that everyone marveled to see him taking his meals with Socrates, wrestling and sharing a tent with him, and treating his other lovers harshly and implacably.[8]

[7] Wanting to see Pericles, Alcibiades came to his door. Informed that Pericles was not at leisure, but was considering how to render an account to the Athenians, Alcibiades departed, saying, "Wouldn't it be better for him to consider how *not* to render an account to the Athenians?"

When he was still a lad he went on the campaign to Potidaea, where he had Socrates as a tentmate and comrade-in-arms.[9] When a fierce engagement took place, both of them distinguished themselves; and when Alcibiades was wounded and fell, Socrates stood over him, defended him, and quite plainly saved him along with his weapons. Accordingly, by the fairest calculation the prize of valor belonged to Socrates. But when the generals were clearly anxious, because of Alcibiades' rank, to award *him* the honor, Socrates, wishing to foster Alcibiades' honorable ambition, was the first to give evidence, and urged them to crown Alcibiades and give him the suit of armor.

[11] Alcibiades' horse-breeding and large collection of chariots were famous. For no one else, whether private citizen or king, ever

7. The meter of this line suggests it came from a tragedy, but the source is not known.

8. Plutarch here relies on Plato's portrait of Alcibiades' relationship with Socrates, as drawn in the *Symposium* and reinforced by the pseudo-Platonic dialogue *Alcibiades*. According to Plato, Alcibiades was totally smitten with Socrates' virtues and spiritual qualities, and wished to become his lover, but Socrates showed him that a love based on shared philosophic pursuit was far superior to one based on sexual passion.

9. This story, too, is borrowed from Plato, *Symposium* 220d ff. The battle took place in the opening phase of the Peloponnesian War, when Alcibiades was about twenty and Socrates forty (in 431 BCE).

entered seven chariots in the Olympic Games; he alone enjoyed that distinction. And his having won first, second, and fourth place, according to Thucydides[10]—third, according to Euripides—surpasses in brilliance and renown every ambition in that sphere.

[13] As soon as he entered public life, though still very young, Alcibiades humbled all the other popular leaders except Phaeax, son of Erasistratus, and Nicias, son of Niceratus,[11] with whom he had to contend. Nicias, already a mature man, was considered an excellent general, while Phaeax, like Alcibiades, was then beginning to gain influence. He was of a well-known family, but inferior to Alcibiades in other respects, particularly as a speaker. He was more affable and persuasive in private conversation than in public debates. For he was, as Eupolis says, "Great at chattering, but utterly incapable of speaking." A speech has survived, "Against Alcibiades," written by Phaeax, in which he mentions, among other matters, that when the city had acquired many gold and silver ceremonial vessels, Alcibiades made use of them at his own table, as if they had been his own.

There was a certain Hyperbolus, from the deme of Perithoedae, whom Thucydides mentions as a mediocre fellow, and who furnished all the comic writers with material, as he was forever being made fun of in their shows. But he was unaffected by being maligned, and impervious to it because of his contempt for public opinion. (Though some call this feeling courage and valor, it is really just shamelessness and inanity.) Nobody liked him, yet the common people often made use of him when they were eager to disgrace or slander men of rank. Now at a certain point, persuaded by Hyperbolus, they were about to conduct an ostracism, a procedure by which they periodically banished a citizen whose renown and influence were preeminent, thereby assuaging their envy rather than their fear. When it was clear that the ostracism would remove one of three men, Alcibiades conferred with Nicias, united their two parties into one, and turned the ostracism against Hyperbolus.[12]

[14] It vexed Alcibiades that Nicias was just as admired by Athens' enemies as by fellow citizens. For Alcibiades was serving as resident consul for the Spartans at Athens and had ministered

10. See Thucydides, *The Peloponnesian War* 6.16, where Alcibiades makes his chariot victories a principal reason why Athenians should regard him as their best leader.

11. See *Nicias* in this volume.

12. See *Nicias* 11. The ostracism of Hyperbolus took place around 415 BCE.

carefully to their soldiers who had been captured at Pylos.[13] But since it was primarily through Nicias that the Spartans obtained peace and recovered their men,[14] they were exceedingly devoted to him. Among the Greeks it was commonly said that Pericles had engaged them in war, but Nicias had disengaged them, and most people referred to the peace as the Peace of Nicias. Galled by this, and nursing a grudge, Alcibiades laid plans to violate the treaty. First, observing that the Argives, in their hatred and fear of the Spartans, were seeking to be rid of them, he secretly fanned their hopes of an alliance with Athens, and encouraged them, by conferring with the chiefs of the people's party, not to fear or yield to the Spartans, but to turn to the Athenians and await their action, since they had all but repented and were eager to abandon the peace treaty. When the Spartans formed an alliance with the Boeotians and surrendered Panactum to Athens, not intact, as it should have been, but in shambles,[15] Alcibiades sought to exacerbate the Athenians' anger. Pressing slanderous (though plausible) charges, he raised an outcry against Nicias. He said that Nicias, as acting general, had been unwilling to capture the enemy troops cut off on Sphacteria;[16] and when others had captured them he had released and returned them to the Spartans, whom he sought to gratify; after which he had not dissuaded the Spartans, with whom he was so friendly, from forming an alliance with the Boeotians or the Corinthians, though he *had* deterred any of the Greek states who wished to be a friend and ally of Athens, unless the Spartans approved.

Nicias was taking this hard, when, as if by a stroke of good luck, ambassadors from Sparta arrived with patently reasonable proposals, claiming that they had come with full powers to arrange a wholly conciliatory and fair agreement.[17] When the council had received the ambassadors favorably, and the assembly was scheduled to con-

13. On the capture of the Pylos prisoners, see *Nicias* 7–8. They resided in Athens for more than three years.

14. The treaty that brought a temporary halt to the Peloponnesian War was known (as Plutarch goes on to say) as the Peace of Nicias, because Nicias played such a large role in negotiations.

15. See Thucydides 5.39. Sparta was supposed to give back Panactum by the terms of the Peace of Nicias, but the Boeotians destroyed it first.

16. Nicias had transferred his command to Cleon when pressed to bring the confrontation at Sphacteria to a head. See *Nicias* 7.

17. The same anecdote is related at *Nicias* 9. See also Thucydides 5.45–46.

vene the next day, Alcibiades grew alarmed and arranged for the ambassadors to meet and talk with him. When they had assembled, he said, "What ails you, men of Sparta? How has it escaped your notice that the council is always reasonable and generous to anyone it encounters, whereas the assembly is presumptuous and grasping? If you claim to have come with full powers, the assembly will treat you unfairly, order you about, and force you to accept their terms. Come now, give up this foolishness! If you wish to be dealt with reasonably by the Athenians and not be forced to accept terms you dislike, present what you would regard as fair terms on the understanding that you do *not* possess full powers. I shall assist you, out of regard for the Spartans." So saying, he gave them his oath and detached them from Nicias. The ambassadors trusted him completely and admired his cleverness and sagacity, thinking it surpassed that of the average man.

The assembly met the next day, and the ambassadors came forward. When with great courtesy Alcibiades asked them why they had come, they stated that they had not come with full powers. Alcibiades immediately assailed them with an angry shout, as if *he*, and not they, were the injured party, calling them unreliable and untrustworthy men who had come neither to say nor do anything sound. The council was indignant, and the assembly furious, and Nicias was racked with dismay and sorrow at the ambassadors' change of heart, ignorant as he was of the deceit and subterfuge.

[15] When the Spartans had thus come away empty-handed, Alcibiades, appointed general, immediately made the Argives, Mantineans, and Elians allies of Athens.[18] No one praised the manner in which this was done, but its effect was enormous, since it divided and agitated almost the entire Peloponnese; arrayed an extraordinary number of shields against the Spartans on a single day at Mantinea;[19] and set the battle and the danger to Athens at the farthest distance from the city, where the victory of the Spartans did not yield them any great return, but where, had they faltered, Sparta's very survival would have been in jeopardy.

After the battle, the Thousand[20] immediately tried to topple the popular party in Argos and make the city submissive, and when the Spartans arrived they deposed the democracy. But the people again took up arms and prevailed. Then Alcibiades arrived and strength-

---

18. See Thucydides 5.61.
19. See Thucydides 5.70–4. The battle of Mantinea took place in 418 BCE.
20. An elite corps of handpicked Argive troops.

ened the people's victory. He persuaded the Argives to build long walls connecting their city to the sea,[21] and to associate themselves in every way with the power of Athens. He brought carpenters and masons from Athens,[22] and displayed a whole-hearted zeal, acquiring favor and power no less for himself than for his city. He likewise persuaded the citizens of Patrae to link their city to the sea by means of long walls. When someone remarked to the citizens that "the Athenians will swallow you whole," Alcibiades replied, "Perhaps, little by little and feet first; but the Spartans would start with the head and swallow you down in one gulp."

[16] But all this statesmanship, eloquence, high purpose, and sagacity were conjoined with an exceedingly luxurious way of life, insolent behavior associated with carousals and carnal desires, the effeminacy of purple garments being trailed across the marketplace, haughty extravagance, the removal of the decks in his triremes (that he might sleep more comfortably, his bedclothes spread not on planks but on corded bedsteads), and the making of a shield of pure gold, emblazoned not with an ancestral device, but with Eros wielding the thunderbolt.[23] Respectable men viewed these things with irritation and disgust, and feared Alcibiades' contempt for duty and decency, thinking it tyrannical and monstrous. In an apt description of the people's attitude toward Alcibiades, Aristophanes has said,

> They long for him, they loathe him, they want him back;

and implying something stronger with his metaphor:

> Take care not to rear a lion in the city;
> But if one is raised, humor its ways.[24]

---

21. The building of "long walls" was a way of ensuring communication with the sea and therefore with the naval power of Athens. Sparta opposed all such walls, which diminished the effectiveness of its own land-based power.

22. For the purpose of building the long walls.

23. This fascinating list of affectations attests to Alcibiades' wealth and flamboyance. Like some modern celebrities, Alcibiades chose to push the envelope of socially sanctioned behavior, knowing this would alienate some of his contemporaries but win the adoration of others.

24. Both quotes are from *Frogs* (1425 and 1431–32), a play put on after Athens had exiled Alcibiades a second time (see chapter 36). The context of the quotes is a discussion in the underworld, between the ghosts of Aeschylus and Sophocles, about how Athens could redeem its waning fortunes in the war against Sparta.

And in fact, Alcibiades' voluntary contributions to the state, his support of public performances, his surpassingly lavish generosity to the city, the renown of his ancestors, the force of his eloquence, and the beauty and power of his physique, together with his experience and prowess in war, rendered the Athenians lenient and tolerant of everything he did. They always used the mildest of terms when referring to his faults, chalking them up to "youthful spirits" and "ambition."

Having chosen a Melian woman from among the prisoners of war,[25] he lived with her and raised the child she bore him. The people actually called that an instance of his generosity, though Alcibiades bore the greatest responsibility for the slaughter of the adult male population of Melos, since he had supported the decree.

Timon the misanthrope[26]—when Alcibiades had carried the day and was being escorted from the assembly—did not walk past or avoid him, as was his habit with everyone else, but accosted him, clasped his hand, and said, "It's a good thing your star's on the rise, my boy. For you'll be the undoing of all these people."[27] Some laughed at his remark, and some scorned it, but some were deeply impressed by what he had said. So equivocal was Alcibiades' reputation, in light of his mercurial nature.

[17] The Athenians, during Pericles' lifetime, had set their hearts on Sicily, and after he died they applied themselves to her conquest. On every occasion they sent the so-called auxiliary forces and allies to those who were being injured by Syracuse,[28] thereby laying the groundwork for the larger expedition. And Alcibiades was the man who in every way inflamed their desire and persuaded them not to try to satisfy it piecemeal or little by little, but to sail with a great force, attack, and subjugate the island. It was Alcibiades who persuaded the common people to expect great things, while he himself was grasping for a great deal more. For his hopes were such that

25. Athens had overwhelmed Melos and enslaved much of its population in 416 BCE, the setting for the famous Melian dialogue in Thucydides 5.

26. A famous Athenian curmudgeon, later immortalized by Lucian and Shakespeare.

27. The anecdote seems to have inspired much of Act IV, Scene 3 of Shakespeare's *Timon of Athens*, which features an encounter between Timon and Alcibiades.

28. Syracuse was at this time the regional superpower of Sicily and often injured smaller Sicilian states by its exercise of hegemony. Some of these states called on Athens for support, giving the Athenians a pretext to begin projecting power in that direction.

he regarded Sicily not as an end of the expedition, as others did, but as a beginning. And while Nicias was trying to dissuade the people from conquering Syracuse, arguing that it would be a formidable undertaking, Alcibiades, dreaming of Carthage and Libya (and once these had been acquired, of encompassing Italy and the Peloponnese), practically regarded Sicily as the ways and means of the war. And once he had elated the young men with these hopes, and they heard their elders relating many marvelous things about the proposed expedition, many of them would sit in the wrestling-schools and meeting places tracing the shape of the island and the position of Libya and Carthage.[29]

But the philosopher Socrates and the astronomer Meton are said to have expected no good to come to the city from this expedition, the former apparently because his familiar divine sign[30] manifested itself and forewarned him. Meton, on the other hand, dreaded what lay ahead (either on rational grounds or because he had employed some method of prophecy) and pretended to be mad, snatched a lighted torch, and behaved as though he meant to set fire to his own house.[31]

[18] Nicias was appointed general against his will. He shunned the office, not least because of his fellow commander. The Athenians imagined that the war would be better conducted if Alcibiades were sent forth with a tempering influence, his boldness blended with Nicias' forethought. For the third general, Lamachus, though advanced in years, seemed no less fiery and venturesome in battle than Alcibiades. When they were deliberating about the size and character of their armament, Nicias again attempted to resist and stop the war. But when Alcibiades voiced the opposing view and won the day, the orator Demostratus proposed that the generals be invested with absolute authority over the preparations and the management of the entire war.[32]

29. Thucydides shows Alcibiades vowing aloud that conquest of Sicily would be followed by that of Carthage (6.90), but the image of average Athenians getting so caught up in this imperialist dream as to draw maps in the sand is exclusive to Plutarch.

30. The *daimonion* of Socrates, according to Plato, warned him whenever he was about to do something ill-advised or morally wrong.

31. An early example of draft-dodging.

32. That is, the three *stratēgoi* in charge of the expedition had power to make decisions on their own, without consulting the assembly.

When the people ratified the motion and the expedition was ready to set sail, there were a number of unfavorable signs, some of them associated with the festival. The Adonia was in progress at the time, and images resembling corpses laid out for burial had been placed everywhere by the women, who mimicked funeral rites, beat their breasts, and chanted dirges.[33] But the mutilation of the Herms—on one night the phalluses of most of them were lopped off[34]—disturbed many, even among those who tended to overlook such things. It was said that the Corinthians had perpetrated the deed (since the Syracusans had come from Corinth originally)[35] in the hope that bad omens would delay or stop the war. But most were not moved by that explanation, nor by that of people who supposed that the incident portended nothing terrible, but merely reflected the usual effects of unmixed wine[36] on unbridled youths, who in a joking spirit are led on to acts of violence. They regarded the incident with anger and fear, assuming it betokened a serious conspiracy. They therefore subjected every conjecture to rigorous testing, the boulē[37] and the assembly convening frequently for that purpose over the course of a few days.

[19] At that point, the popular leader Androcles brought forward some slaves and resident aliens who accused Alcibiades and his friends of mutilating other statues of the gods, and of parodying the Mysteries[38] while under the influence of wine. They reported that a certain Theodorus had played the role of the herald, Pulytion that of the torch-bearer, and Alcibiades that of the high priest, and that the

33. The Adonia was a religious observance recalling the death of Adonis, a beautiful youth. The women of Athens made up dummy corpses of Adonis and mourned his death.

34. Strange as it may seem to modern sensibilities, the ancient Herm, a pillarlike statue set up to invite good fortune, bore an image of an erect phallus—a symbol of fertility and therefore prosperity—near its base.

35. Syracuse was the leading city of Greek Sicily and therefore the principal target of the Athenian expedition.

36. Greeks normally mixed their wine with water and regarded unmixed wine as dangerous to the sanity of the drinker.

37. The boulē was a council of five hundred serving as a steering committee for the public business of the assembly.

38. The Mysteries were rites associated with Demeter and Persephone, said to ensure a happy afterlife for those who went through them. They were kept strictly secret from outsiders, hence the meaning of the modern English word.

rest of his companions, who were there in the role of initiates, had been referred to as mystae.[39] These were the items included in the indictment that Thessalus, son of Cimon, presented in the assembly when he charged Alcibiades with impious mockery of the goddesses. The people were outraged. They harbored bitter feelings for Alcibiades, and Androcles, one of his worst enemies, spurred them on. At first Alcibiades and his friends were distressed. But when they perceived that all the sailors and soldiers who were about to sail to Sicily were well-disposed to them, and when the Argives and Mantinean hoplites, who numbered a thousand, were heard to say openly that it was because of Alcibiades that they were serving in a great expedition overseas, and that if anyone treated him unfairly they would immediately withdraw, Alcibiades regained confidence and secured the opportunity to defend himself in the assembly. His enemies in turn lost heart, fearing that the people would prosecute Alcibiades less vigorously because he was so useful to them.

So they arranged for some of the orators who were not thought to be his enemies, but who hated him no less than those who admitted their hatred, to stand up in the assembly and say that it was absurd, when a general with full powers had been appointed over such a force, and when their allies had mustered an army, to undermine his opportunity by enrolling a jury and measuring out time for his trial. "Let him sail now, and good luck to him. And when the war has been fought, let him return and present his defense in accordance with the same laws." The ill will behind the delay did not escape Alcibiades. Coming forward, he said it was a terrible thing to be sent off in command of so great a force with his case still in suspense, leaving behind an accusation and slanders against himself.[40] For he ought to be put to death if he could not refute the charges, whereas if he succeeded in refuting them and clearing himself he should proceed against their enemies without fear of informers.

[20] When he failed to persuade them, and they ordered him to sail, he set out with his co-commanders and nearly 140 triremes, 5,100 hoplites, about 1,300 archers, slingers, and light-armed troops, and all the corresponding provisions. After reaching Italy and seizing

39. These roles mimic or parody those of the actual Mysteries rites, the exact structure of which is not known. "Mystae" was the term used for those undergoing initiation into the Mysteries.
40. In other words Alcibiades wanted the trial held then and there, so a verdict could be obtained before the start of the expedition.

Rhegium,[41] he presented his views on how the war should be conducted. When his plan was opposed by Nicias, but approved by Lamachus, Alcibiades sailed to Sicily and brought Catana over to their side. But he accomplished nothing more, since he was soon summoned by the Athenians to stand trial.[42]

At first, as has been mentioned, certain vague suspicions and slanders had been advanced against Alcibiades by slaves and resident aliens. Then, in his absence, his enemies attacked him more vehemently and associated the violence done to the Herms with the mimicking of the Mysteries. On the assumption that a single revolutionary conspiracy had prompted these outrages, they were imprisoning without trial those who were held in any way to blame. The people were vexed that they had not voted at the time to try and convict Alcibiades on such charges, and anyone they connected with their anger at him, whether relative or friend or intimate, met with very harsh treatment at their hands.

[21] Yet the people's anger was not wholly appeased, and once they were done with the mutilators of the Herms, they seized the opportunity to vent their full fury on Alcibiades. In the end they dispatched the *Salaminia*[43] for him, prudently giving its officers express orders not to use violence or seize his person, but to address him mildly and urge him to follow them home to await his trial and exonerate himself before the people. For they feared that mutinies and dissension, which Alcibiades could have excited had he so desired, might engulf the army in enemy territory. And the men were indeed disheartened by his absence, and expected that under Nicias' command the war would be conducted sluggishly, and thus prolonged, now that the gadfly for their actions had been removed. For Lamachus was warlike and courageous, but he lacked prestige and dignity because he was poor.

[22] Sailing away at once,[44] Alcibiades robbed the Athenians of Messana. There was a party there that intended to betray the

41. A rare instance where Plutarch departs from Thucydides' account, in which the Athenians merely camp outside Rhegium without seizing the city (6.44).

42. For the account of what became of the Sicilian expedition after Alcibiades' departure, see *Nicias* 18–28.

43. A special warship reserved for important state missions.

44. Plutarch speaks somewhat vaguely, trusting that his audience knows the basic story. What he means by "sailing away" is that Alcibiades escaped by ship from those sent to arrest him and deserted the army.

city.[45] Alcibiades knew them, furnished the friends of Syracuse with the clearest information about them, and thereby foiled the plot. Reaching Thurii[46] and disembarking from his trireme, he concealed himself and eluded those who were searching for him. When someone recognized him and said, "Don't you trust your country, Alcibiades?" he replied, "In everything else, I do. But where my life is at stake I wouldn't trust my own mother, lest she mistake black for white when casting her vote."[47] And later on, when he heard that the city had sentenced him to death, he said, "Well, I'll show them that I'm alive." . . . The Athenians sentenced him in absentia and confiscated his property, and also decreed that all the priests and priestesses were to call down curses on him.

[23] When these grave decrees and sentences were passed upon him, Alcibiades was living in Argos, having crossed over to the Peloponnese after fleeing from Thurii. Fearing his enemies, he renounced his country outright and sent word to Sparta, requesting immunity and safe conduct, and promising that he would render the Spartans services and benefits greater than the harm he had done them earlier when fighting on the other side. When the Spartans had granted his request and received him, he zealously applied himself, as soon as he arrived, to achieving one goal. Though the Spartans were delaying and postponing aid to Syracuse, Alcibiades roused and incited them to send Gylippus to Syracuse as commander,[48] and to crush the Athenian forces there. Then he urged them to make war on the Athenians at home. But his third recommendation was the most important: he advised the Spartans to fortify Decelea[49]—a measure that, more than any other, inflicted ruin and destruction on Athens.

Esteemed in public, and admired no less in private, Alcibiades captivated and charmed the multitude by adopting the Spartan way of life. When they saw him growing his hair, bathing in cold water,

45. That is, to open the gates to the Athenians at a prearranged time.
46. In southern Italy.
47. For certain kinds of votes in the assembly, citizens placed a black pebble into an urn to signify a vote for conviction, a white pebble for acquittal.
48. The sending of Gylippus proved to be a turning point in the struggle for Sicily, as related in *Nicias* 19.
49. A region of high ground on the outskirts of Attica, commanding the routes toward Boeotia and Euboea. By building a fort in this place and occupying it year round, the Spartans gave themselves a secure base of operations in Athens' home territory and deprived the Athenians of much of their freedom of movement.

delighting in barley cake, and dining on black broth,[50] they could scarcely believe that this man had ever had a chef at home, or set eyes on a perfumer, or consented to touch a Milesian cloak. For among his many talents, he is said to have had one supreme gift, one means of captivating his fellow mortals: he had a genius for assimilating and affecting their pursuits and way of life, thereby transforming himself more quickly than the chameleon. (Though that creature, it is said, is quite unable to turn itself one color, namely white.) But since Alcibiades mingled with the noble and the base alike, there was nothing he could not imitate or emulate. . . .

He so corrupted Timaea, Agis' wife,[51] while her husband was away on campaign, that she was pregnant by Alcibiades and did not deny it. And when she gave birth to a boy, he was called Leotychides in public, though in private the mother whispered to her friends and attendants that his name was Alcibiades, so powerful was the passion that possessed her. Exulting over this, Alcibiades used to say that he had not been driven by hubris, nor overmastered by pleasure; he had merely sought to ensure that his descendants might be Spartan kings. This being the state of affairs, many persons accused him to Agis. Now Agis relied chiefly on the matter of timing. For during an earthquake he had run in terror from his wife's bedroom, and in the succeeding ten months had not had intercourse with her. Thereafter, when Leotychides was born, Agis denied that the child was his. And that was why Leotychides was later barred from the royal succession.[52]

[24] After the Athenian disaster in Sicily,[53] the Chians, Lesbians, and Cyzicenians sent embassies to Sparta to discuss a revolt from Athens.[54] But though the Boeotians were active on behalf of the Lesbians, and Pharnabazus[55] supported the Cyzicenians, the

50. See *Lycurgus* 10–18 for the basic elements of Spartan military life.

51. Agis was one of the two Spartan kings reigning at this time.

52. See *Agesilaus* 3. The suspicions about Leotychides' paternity resulted in Agesilaus taking the throne.

53. Narrated in full in *Nicias* and in books 6–7 of Thucydides.

54. Thucydides says only that the Chians sent an embassy (8.5), and that the Chians later aided the Mytileneans on Lesbos to revolt (8.22). The revolt of Cyzicus is referred to at 8.107, but without many specifics. All three states were linchpins of Athens' Aegean empire.

55. One of the Persian satraps in Asia Minor. The Persians had by this time gotten involved in the Athens–Sparta conflict by giving funds to one side or the other.

Spartans, persuaded by Alcibiades, chose to help the Chians first. Sailing out himself, Alcibiades incited almost all of Ionia to revolt. Through his many contacts with the Spartan commanders, he inflicted harm on the Athenians. But Agis was hostile to him because of the affair with his wife, and found Alcibiades' renown irritating, since it was commonly said that most of the Spartan successes had been due to Alcibiades. As for the other Spartans, the most powerful and ambitious among them, never well-disposed to Alcibiades, were by now sick and tired of him. They therefore prevailed on the magistrates at home to send him to Ionia, where they might do away with him.[56]

Stealthily learning of this, Alcibiades grew alarmed, and while he participated in all the Spartans' exploits he took care not to fall into their hands. And when, for safety's sake, he offered his services to Tissaphernes, the Great King's satrap,[57] Alcibiades' high rank and importance were acknowledged at once. Though Tissaphernes was insincere, malicious, and inclined to befriend worthless men, the barbarian admired Alcibiades' versatility and his remarkable cleverness. And indeed no disposition or nature could resist the charm of living and associating with Alcibiades on a daily basis. Even those who feared and envied him felt pleasure and affection when they caught sight of the man and consorted with him. And thus Tissaphernes, who in all other instances was the Persian most hostile to the Greeks, so lent himself to being flattered by Alcibiades that he outdid the man when it was *his* turn to flatter. Of the parks in his possession he bestowed the name Alcibiades on the park[58] that, because of its waters and fertile meadows, its exquisite haunts and royally appointed refuges, was the most beautiful of all. And everyone always called it by that name.

[25] Alcibiades now renounced the cause of the Spartans. And since he distrusted them and feared Agis, he abused and slandered the Spartans to Tissaphernes, advising him not to offer them generous assistance or even to depose the Athenians, but to spend

56. Thucydides' account of Alcibiades' departure (8.12) does not indicate that the Spartans then wished, or planned, to get rid of him; Thucydides believed they began to hate him only later, after reverses at Miletus (8.45).

57. As always in Greek, "Great King" refers to the ruler of the Persian empire (as does "King"). Tissaphernes was satrap, or provincial governor, of Lydia.

58. The Persian ruling class was extremely fond of game parks, to which they gave the name *pardeiza*, the root of our word "paradise."

modest sums squeezing and gradually wearing out both sides and making them weary of one another and governable by the King.[59] Tissaphernes was easily persuaded and it was clear to everyone that he loved and admired his guest, and consequently the Greeks on both sides paid close attention to Alcibiades, and the Athenians, who were faring poorly, regretted the sentence they had passed upon him. Alcibiades himself was now oppressed by the fear that if Athens were utterly ruined he might find himself in the hands of the Spartans, who hated him.

Almost all the Athenian forces were then at Samos. Making the island their base, they were deploying their fleet to recover some of the allies that had revolted, and to keep watch on others. Though they somehow managed to remain a match for their enemies at sea, they feared Tissaphernes and the fleet of Phoenician triremes,[60] 150 in number, that was reportedly due to arrive at any moment. If it *did* arrive, no hope of deliverance was left for their city. Knowing this, Alcibiades sent word in secret to the influential Athenians at Samos, encouraging them to hope that he might make Tissaphernes their friend. He said he had no interest in pleasing the multitude, whom he did not even trust; instead, he assured them, he placed his trust in the aristocrats, confident that if they should venture to be brave, and put a stop to the people's insolence, they would, by their own efforts, save both their cause and their city.

[26] When Alcibiades' friends had gotten the upper hand at Samos, they sent Peisander to Athens to change its form of government and to encourage the leading men to take charge of the state and depose the democracy, since these were the terms on which Alcibiades would make Tissaphernes their friend and ally.[61] For this was the excuse, the professed motive, of those who established the oligarchy. Once the so-called Five Thousand (they were actually four

59. This policy (which must have been obvious enough to Tissaphernes without Alcibiades suggesting it) was in fact what the Persians did for the rest of the fifth century BCE and long thereafter: offering subsidies to whatever Greek city was in second position of power, encouraging it to fight against the first.

60. The Persians employed Phoenician ships as their principal naval contingents.

61. See Thucydides 8.53. In most texts of Thucydides the name of the envoy is spelled Pisander.

hundred)[62] prevailed and got control of the government, they paid very little attention to Alcibiades, and prosecuted the war less vigorously, partly because they distrusted the citizens, who were still wary of the new form of government, and partly because they thought that the Spartans, who had always been favorably disposed to oligarchy, would be more lenient to them. The people in the city kept quiet reluctantly, out of fear, since no small number of those who openly opposed the Four Hundred were put to death by them. But when the crews in Samos learned of these developments, they were indignant; and in their eagerness to sail straight to the Piraeus, they summoned Alcibiades, appointed him general, and urged him to take command and depose the tyrants.[63]

A different sort of man, raised suddenly to a position of power through the favor of the multitude, would have been submissive and indulgent, thinking he should immediately gratify them in every way and not contradict those who had appointed him, after his wandering and exile, as leader and commander of so large a fleet, so strong an army, and so great a power. But Alcibiades chose to act in a manner befitting a great ruler who opposes those who are swept along by anger, and prevents them from committing a grave error. On that occasion, at any rate, Alcibiades' noble conduct saved the city. For had their fleet sailed home, it would have been possible for their enemies to gain immediate possession, without a battle, of all of Ionia, the Hellespont, and the islands, while Athenians were fighting with Athenians and making their own city the battleground of a civil war. Alcibiades alone prevented this, not only by persuading and instructing the multitude, but by speaking privately with individuals—entreating some, haranguing others. Thrasybulus of

62. The new government instituted at Athens in 411 BCE was composed of four hundred men who were instructed to draft a new constitution that would allow the five thousand wealthiest citizens to participate. But the Four Hundred took their time doing this, raising suspicions that they did not want to cede power.

63. This paragraph summarizes a bewilderingly complex series of events in 411–410 BCE. The new oligarchic government at Athens, the Four Hundred, became so harsh and autocratic as to alienate the navy at Samos, the very force that had helped put it in power. The navy now reverted to its former democratic leanings and threatened to invade its own home city (by sailing into the Piraeus) to depose the Four Hundred. Alcibiades, who had formerly backed the change to an oligarchic government, now became the leader of the democratic opposition.

Steirus acted as his assistant, accompanying him and shouting at the top of his voice. For it is said that among the Athenians Thrasybulus possessed the loudest voice.[64]

[27] Thereafter the Four Hundred were deposed,[65] Alcibiades' friends eagerly assisting the party of the people. When the citizens desired and commanded Alcibiades to return from exile, he himself thought he should not return empty-handed and unsuccessful, through the pity and favor of the people, but rather in triumph. So first, on setting out with a few ships from Samos, he cruised about near Cnidus and Cos. When he heard there that Mindarus the Spartan[66] was sailing up to the Hellespont with his entire fleet and that the Athenians were following him, he hastened to aid the Athenian commanders. And by luck he arrived with eighteen triremes at the very moment when both sides, encountering one another with all their ships and joining battle near Abydos, engaged in a great struggle, the advantage passing back and forth between them until evening. Alcibiades' arrival raised false expectations on both sides: the enemy took heart, and the Athenians were thrown into confusion. Alcibiades quickly hoisted the Athenian ensign on his flagship and hastened straight against the victorious and pursuing Peloponnesians. Putting them to flight, he thrust them to land, ramming and disabling their ships. The crews swam ashore, and Pharnabazus, coming to their aid with his infantry, fought along the beach in defense of their ships. Finally, the Athenians seized thirty of them, saved their own men, and erected a trophy.[67]

After winning so brilliant a victory, Alcibiades was eager to display himself at once to Tissaphernes, and after preparing gifts of hospitality and friendship went to visit him with an entourage worthy of a commander. But he met with an unexpected reception. For Tissaphernes, who had long been maligned by the Spartans, and was afraid of being called to account by the King, concluded that Alcibiades had arrived in the nick of time. He arrested and

---

64. See Thucydides 8.86. Thrasybulus, who first comes to political prominence here, was destined for an eventful career in the aftermath of the war; see *Lysander* 29 with n. 45, and *Pelopidas* 7.

65. That is, full democracy was reinstated.

66. Occupant of the office of navarch, or chief admiral, shortly before the appointment of Lysander.

67. The first episode of Xenophon's *Hellenica*, the historical narrative that quite deliberately picks up where Thucydides leaves off.

imprisoned him in Sardis, hoping that by this act of injustice he would dispel the Spartans' insinuations.

[28] Thirty days later, Alcibiades somehow got hold of a horse, eluded his guards, and escaped to Clazomenae, where he brought Tissaphernes into even greater disfavor by claiming that the Persian had freed him. Sailing straight to the camp of the Athenians and learning that Mindarus was in Cyzicus with Pharnabazus, Alcibiades roused the soldiers, declaring that they must engage in land battles, sea fights, and even, by Zeus, siege warfare, since unless they prevailed in every instance they would have no money. When he had manned the ships and landed at Proconnesus, he issued orders for all light vessels[68] to be seized and guarded, so that the enemy would not, from any quarter, be forewarned of his approach.

It happened that a sudden downpour of rain, accompanied by thunder and darkness, helped to conceal his preparations. For not only did he escape the enemy's notice, but even the Athenians had given up hope of fighting, when he suddenly ordered them to embark and put out to sea. Before very long the darkness lifted, and the ships of the Peloponnesians were seen bobbing in front of the harbor of Cyzicus. Fearing that if they saw the full extent of his array they might flee ashore, Alcibiades ordered the commanders to advance slowly and remain in the rear, while he himself appeared with forty ships and challenged the enemy. Since the Peloponnesians were utterly deceived, and viewed Alcibiades' numbers with contempt, they sailed out against them and were immediately grappled and taken in tow. And when the rest of the fleet attacked the force already fighting, the astonished Peloponnesians fled.

Upon breaking through the enemy line with twenty ships, putting ashore, and disembarking, Alcibiades attacked and slaughtered many of the sailors who were running from their ships. Getting the better of Mindarus and Pharnabazus, who were hastening in aid, he killed Mindarus, who fought valiantly; Pharnabazus managed to escape. Getting possession of many corpses and weapons, the Athenians seized all the enemy ships. And once they had subdued Cyzicus, which Pharnabazus had abandoned, and slaughtered its Peloponnesian garrison, they not only held the Hellespont securely, but ousted the Spartans from the rest of the sea. A letter was found, describing to the ephors, in laconic style, the misfortune that had occurred: "The ships are destroyed; Mindarus has perished; the men are starving; we are at a loss what to do."

68. That is, ships belonging to local fishermen and traders.

After leading the Athenians to further naval victories, Alcibiades finally felt ready, in 407 BCE, to return to Athens, though he was technically still under a death sentence there.

[32] Longing now to see his home, and wanting even more to be seen by his fellow citizens, having defeated their enemies on so many occasions, Alcibiades set sail, his Attic triremes adorned with many shields and other spoils. Many ships captured in war were being towed, and even more numerous were the figureheads of the ships he had overpowered and destroyed, since these numbered no fewer than two hundred all together. . . . He returned in dread;[69] and on landing did not leave his trireme until, from the deck, he caught sight of his cousin Euryptolemus and many of his other friends and relations welcoming and encouraging him. And when he stepped ashore, people disdained even to look at the other generals they encountered, but ran roaring up to Alcibiades, embracing and escorting him, approaching and crowning him with wreaths, while those who could not come near looked on from a distance, the elders pointing him out to the young. Many a tear accompanied the city's rejoicing, as the memory of their former misfortunes mingled with people's joy in their present success, and they reflected that they would not have failed to acquire Sicily, nor would any of their expected successes have eluded them, had they left Alcibiades in charge of their affairs.

[33] The vote authorizing his recall had been ratified earlier. . . . When the people were summoned to the assembly, Alcibiades came forward. Lamenting and bewailing his own misfortunes, and charging the people with minor or moderate errors, he ascribed his entire misfortune to wretched luck and an envious deity. He discoursed at length about their enemies' hopes, and sought to encourage and rouse the people. Finally, the people crowned him with golden crowns and elected him general with full powers by land and sea.

[34] Everything turned out as Alcibiades wished, and one hundred triremes were manned, with which he expected to sail out again. But meanwhile he was possessed by a great and admirable ambition, which detained him until the celebration of the Mysteries.

Ever since Decelea had been fortified, and the enemy, now present in the neighborhood, had got control of the approaches to Eleusis,

69. Alcibiades still had a cloud of disfavor hanging over him for the alleged profanation of the Mysteries and mutilation of the Herms.

the procession, which was sent by sea,[70] had lacked splendor. And the sacrifices, and dances, and many of the sacred rites that are performed along the way . . . had necessarily been suspended. Alcibiades, accordingly, thought it would be a fine gesture, which would honor the gods and win him esteem among men, to restore the rites to their ancestral form.[71] He would send his infantry along to escort the procession and keep watch as it advanced past the enemy, and would thereby either utterly degrade and humiliate Agis (if the king kept quiet) or fight a holy war, one that the gods approved, in defense of the most sacred and solemn of ceremonies, in sight of his native city, and with all the citizens present as witnesses of his courage.

When he had laid these plans and given advance notice to the Eumolpidae and Heralds, he stationed lookouts on the heights and sent some scouts ahead at dawn. Taking along the priests, mystae, and mystagogues,[72] whom he surrounded with men-at-arms, he led them decorously and in silence. So noble, so fit for a god was the spectacle he displayed as general, that he was called high priest and mystagogue by those who did not begrudge him those titles. Since no enemy soldier dared to attack him, Alcibiades led the procession safely back to the city. He himself was exalted in spirit, and he exalted the soldiers, who felt themselves invincible and unconquerable under his command. And he so entranced the common people and the poor with his leadership that they felt an amazing desire to have him as their sole ruler.[73] Some of them approached him and broached the matter, urging him to become proof against envy, and to get rid of votes and laws and the people who were ruining the city, that he might act freely and conduct state affairs without fear of informers.

70. The rites of the Mysteries included a festal procession from Athens to Eleusis, in which all the new initiates marched for several days. The Spartan occupation of Decelea made such an overland journey unsafe, so the initiates had been conducted to Eleusis by ship instead, bypassing many of the sacred sites associated with the cult.

71. This gesture has important political point, since it was alleged disrespect of the Mysteries that had led to Alcibiades' condemnation and exile.

72. The title of the officials who led the procession to Eleusis.

73. The Greek says "to be tyranted by him," but the political notions that stand behind the Greek word *tyrannos* do not translate easily. A *tyrannos* was simply a nonconstitutional ruler holding sole power; he might be benevolent, as the Athenians clearly hoped in this case, or cruel and despotic. The English words "tyrant," "autocrat," and "dictator" all carry too negative a valence to serve as equivalents.

[35] Alcibiades' own views about sole rule are unknown. But the most influential citizens, taking fright, urged him to sail away with all possible speed, having voted him, in addition to everything else, the co-commanders he desired. Sailing out with one hundred ships, he attacked Andros and overpowered the islanders in battle, as well as all the Spartans who were there. But he did not capture the city, and this was the first of the new charges brought against him by his enemies.

It would seem that if anyone was brought down by his own reputation, it was Alcibiades. For his renown was so great, based as it was on the daring and intelligence that had ensured his success, that if he failed in anything, his zeal was questioned. People did not credit the notion of his fallibility. It was felt that nothing he earnestly desired could elude him. The Athenians therefore expected to hear that Chios had been captured along with the rest of Ionia, and they were accordingly annoyed when they learned that everything had not been accomplished quickly and immediately, as they had wished. They did not take into account his lack of money, which often compelled him, while making war against men whose expenses were defrayed by the Great King, to leave his camp and sail off to procure money for wages and provisions.[74] And in fact the final charge against him was occasioned by this necessity.

For when Lysander[75] was dispatched as admiral by the Spartans, and was paying his sailors four obols a day (instead of three) from the money he had received from Cyrus,[76] Alcibiades, already finding it difficult to provide even three obols, departed to levy funds in Caria. Antiochus, the man left behind in charge of the fleet, was an excellent pilot, but otherwise unintelligent and boorish. Though he was under orders from Alcibiades not to engage in a sea battle even if their enemies sailed against them, he was so insolent and contemptuous that on manning his own trireme and one of the others, he sailed to Ephesus and rowed past the prows of the enemy ships, doing and saying much that was intemperate and vulgar. At first Lysander put out to sea with a few ships and pursued Antiochus. But when the

74. Greek generals could neither sell bonds nor write checks. If the heaps of coin they carried with them ran out, and their men could not be paid, they had to drop whatever they were doing and raise more cash.

75. The principal new commander of Sparta's forces, especially its navy; see *Lysander*.

76. See *Lysander* 4.

Athenians rushed to Antiochus' aid, Lysander put out with all his
ships, and after prevailing in battle, slew Antiochus, captured many
ships and men, and erected a trophy. On hearing of this, Alcibiades
returned to Samos, sailed out with his entire fleet, and challenged
Lysander. But Lysander, content with his victory, did not put out
to sea.

[36] Of those in the army who hated Alcibiades, Thrasybulus,
son of Thraso,[77] a personal enemy, sailed off to Athens to bring
charges against him. Rousing the Athenians' anger, he told the people
that Alcibiades had ruined their cause and lost their ships. Leading a
life of luxury in office, he had handed over the command to men who
had won his favor by carousals and sailors' gossip, so that he might
sail about in safety, making money, overindulging in drink, and con-
sorting with Abydenian and Ionian prostitutes while the enemy was
moored only a short distance away. Alcibiades' enemies also charged
him with having built a fortress in Thrace near Bisanthe, presumably as a refuge for himself should he be unable or unwilling to live
in his own country.[78] The Athenians were persuaded, and showed
their anger and ill will toward Alcibiades by choosing other generals.
Informed of this, Alcibiades grew fearful and abandoned the army
entirely. Assembling mercenary troops, he conducted private operations against the kingless Thracians.[79] He amassed a great deal of
money from his captives, and at the same time protected the neighboring Greeks from barbarian attacks.

*Plutarch skips over two and a half years during which Alcibiades lived in
Thrace and played little part in Athenian politics. When the story resumes, it
is late 405 BCE and Athens has had very mixed success in the war with Sparta
since Alcibiades' departure. Their navy, now consisting of 180 ships, has gone
to the Hellespont to counter the Spartan fleet led by Lysander. The two fleets
have taken up positions on opposite sides of the strait, and the Athenian camp
happens to be within view of the castle where Alcibiades now lives in exile.*

77. A different man than the Thrasybulus mentioned in chapter 26, who is
clearly one of Alcibiades' close allies.
78. Alcibiades could hardly have been blamed for not trusting his fate to
the Athenians, given all that had happened.
79. The Thracians, a non-Greek people, were at this time organized into
a loose network of tribes. Aristotle observed that their warlike spirit would
have made them a formidable nation, but they had no political unity.

When the generals . . . who were keeping all the Athenian ships together at Aegospotami got in the habit of sailing out against Lysander, who lay near Lampsacus, and challenging him at daybreak, and then turning back and passing the day carelessly and without order, out of contempt for the enemy, Alcibiades, who was nearby, could not overlook or ignore their danger, but rode to the generals on horseback and pointed out to them that they had chosen a poor anchorage, where there was no harbor or town; that they were obtaining their supplies from Sestos, a long way off; and that they were allowing their crews, whenever they were on land, to wander and scatter wherever they liked, while a force lay at anchor against them—a force trained to do everything silently at the command of a single general.

[37] Despite what Alcibiades said—he also advised them to move the fleet to Sestos—the generals paid him no heed. . . . Suspecting that there was some treachery afoot among them, Alcibiades departed and told the acquaintances who escorted him from the camp that had he not been so poorly treated by the generals he would within a few days have forced the reluctant Spartans either to engage them at sea or lose their ships. Some thought that this was mere boasting; but others that his claims were credible, since he might have brought in many Thracian javelin-men and horsemen by land to assault and confound the enemy's camp.[80]

But events soon proved that he had accurately gauged the Athenians' missteps. For when Lysander suddenly and unexpectedly assaulted them, only eight Athenian triremes escaped with Conon, while the rest, just short of two hundred, were captured and taken away, along with three thousand men, whom Lysander put to death. And before long he also seized Athens, burned her ships, and destroyed her long walls.[81]

Afraid of the Spartans, who now held sway on land and sea, Alcibiades moved to Bithynia, taking with him a great deal of money and plunder, though even more was left behind in the fortress where he had been living. In Bithynia, where he again lost much of his

---

80. See *Lysander* 10 for a shorter version of this story. In the last sentence above, Plutarch seems to tip his hat to the very different version recorded by Diodorus (*Library of History* 13.105): Alcibiades offered to take over the Athenian forces and lead them to certain victory, using his new Thracian allies as reserves.

81. See *Lysander* 11–15.

wealth when robbed by the local Thracians, he decided to go to the court of Artaxerxes,[82] thinking he would appear no less a man than Themistocles, should the King put him to the test.[83] For it would not be in opposition to his fellow citizens, as had been the case with Themistocles, but on behalf of his country that he would assist the King and request a force with which to resist their common enemy. And thinking that Pharnabazus, more than anyone, would most readily provide him with a safe conduct, Alcibiades visited him in Phrygia and took up residence there, paying court to him and being treated as an honored guest.

[38] Deprived of their hegemony, the Athenians were disheartened, and when Lysander also deprived them of their freedom and handed the city over to thirty men,[84] they recognized, now that their cause was lost, the course they had failed to take when salvation was still possible. Lamenting their lot, they recounted their errors and failures of judgment, the greatest of which they acknowledged to be their second outburst of rage against Alcibiades. For he had been rejected through no fault of his own; instead, they themselves, incensed at his subordinate, who had shamefully lost a few ships, had much more shamefully deprived the city of its strongest, most accomplished general. But despite their present predicament, they were buoyed up by some faint hope that all was not lost for the Athenians while Alcibiades lived. For he had never been content to lead an idle or quiet life in exile; nor would he now disregard, if his means were sufficient, the insolence of the Spartans or the Thirty's atrocities.

And it was not unreasonable on the people's part to harbor such dreams, since it occurred even to the Thirty to take thought for Alcibiades, to inquire about him, and to pay close attention to what he was doing and planning. Finally, Critias informed Lysander that while Athens was governed by a democracy the Spartans could not rule Greece securely. For even if the Athenians were mild and well-disposed to an oligarchy, Alcibiades, while he lived, would not

82. Artaxerxes II, the Great King of the Persian empire.

83. In the aftermath of the Persian wars, after being indicted and exiled by Athens, Themistocles sought refuge with Xerxes, the Great King of that day. Xerxes took him in and made him a satrap in his empire. See *Themistocles* 28, 31.

84. Lysander established a ruling board of thirty handpicked men ("the Thirty") to govern Athens as Spartan puppets. Led by the cruel and despotic Critias, they quickly embarked on a reign of terror over their opponents.

allow them to resign themselves to their present circumstances. But Lysander was not convinced of this until a message arrived from the authorities at home ordering him to put Alcibiades out of the way, either because they too feared the man's cleverness and daring, or because they wished to please Agis.[85]

[39] Lysander accordingly sent word to Pharnabazus, commanding him to execute the order, whereupon Pharnabazus directed his brother Magaeus and his uncle Susamithres to perform the deed. At that time Alcibiades was living with the courtesan Timandra in a village in Phrygia. . . . The men who were sent to him did not dare to enter his house, but stood in a circle around it and set it on fire. When Alcibiades realized what was happening, he collected most of his cloaks and bedclothes and threw them on the fire. Donning his own cloak with his left hand, and with his right drawing his dagger, he came out unscathed, before his garments had caught fire, and scattered the barbarians as soon as they caught sight of him. For none of them stood their ground or came to blows with him, but everyone stood at a distance and shot at him with javelins and arrows. And when he had fallen, and the barbarians had departed, Timandra took up his corpse, shrouding it with her own garments. She buried him as splendidly and lavishly as circumstances permitted.

85. The Spartan king still hated Alcibiades for having seduced his wife.

Lysander

Plutarch's Life of Lysander *the Spartan (before 440–395 BCE) has almost no information about Lysander's early life, and as a result, very little is known, other than that Lysander's family was poor and not of high stature. When Lysander appears on the stage of history here, in 407 BCE, already an admiral commanding a Spartan fleet, he seems to have pulled himself up from nowhere. In* Agesilaus *2, by contrast, we learn that Lysander had advanced his fortunes by becoming the* erastēs, *the older male lover, of a son of one of Sparta's two kings.*

Lysander *should be compared closely with* Alcibiades *as two Plutarchan variations on a theme: the high cost of personal ambition, when its excesses roil the tightly connected community of the city-state. It should also be noted that Lysander and Alcibiades were close contemporaries who were evenly matched in military talent, as demonstrated in the naval warfare of the last phase of the Peloponnesian War, when they faced one another in combat.*

[3] The Peloponnesian War had been carried on for a long time, and it was assumed that the Athenians, after their misadventure in Sicily,[1] would immediately lose their supremacy at sea and give way on every front. But Alcibiades, when he returned from exile,[2] took charge of affairs and effected a great change, making the Athenians a match for their enemies at sea. The Spartans, accordingly, again took fright and renewed their zeal for the war; and in the belief that a formidable commander was needed and a stronger armament, they sent Lysander out to assume command at sea. On reaching Ephesus, he found the city well-disposed to him and full of zeal for Sparta's cause, but faring poorly and in danger of becoming quite barbarous through contact with Persian customs. For the city was surrounded by Lydia,[3] and the generals of the King[4] were spending a good deal of their time there. After setting up camp, Lysander gave orders for all the vessels thereabout to haul their merchandise to Ephesus; and by having ships built there he revived the Ephesians' harbors for

---

1. See *Nicias* 15–28 and *Alcibiades* 17–23.

2. See *Alcibiades* 32. The date of this event is 407 BCE.

3. The non-Greek (though partly Hellenized) region surrounding Ephesus.

4. As always in this volume, "King" when capitalized refers to the Great King of Persia, at this time Darius II.

trading, and their marketplace for commerce. He filled their houses and workshops with profits, so that from then on, through Lysander's efforts, the city had hopes of attaining the importance and stature it enjoys today.[5]

[4] Upon learning that Cyrus,[6] the King's son, had reached Sardis, Lysander journeyed there to consult with him and to accuse Tissaphernes,[7] who, though he was under orders to assist the Spartans and drive the Athenians from the sea, seemed to have lowered his tone under Alcibiades' influence; he showed a lack of zeal, and appeared to be weakening the naval force by barely furnishing it with supplies. And Cyrus was glad to find that Tissaphernes was being accused and maligned, since the man was base and apt to quarrel with him in private. From these circumstances and his behavior in general, Lysander endeared himself to Cyrus, particularly by the deference he showed in conversation. He captivated the young man and incited him to prosecute the war. And when Lysander wished to depart, Cyrus entertained him at a banquet and urged him not to reject his kindness, but to ask for whatever he desired, since nothing would be refused him. In reply Lysander said, "Well then, Cyrus, since you are so eager, I beg and entreat you to add an obol to the sailors' wages, so that they may earn four a day instead of three."[8] Delighted with the man's public spiritedness, Cyrus gave him 10,000 darics,[9] from which Lysander gave the sailors an additional obol; and by thus gaining renown, he soon emptied the enemy's ships of their men. For most of the crews went over to those who were offering better pay, while the sailors who remained behind became listless and quarrelsome and gave daily trouble to their commanders. Yet though he had stripped his enemies bare and was injuring them, he shrank from fighting at sea; for he dreaded Alcibiades, who was energetic, had more ships, and remained unconquered in all the battles on land and sea in which he had contended up to that time.

5.   Like many Greek cities of western Asia, Ephesus had fared far better in the post-classical Greek world, when Greek trade and commerce extended much farther east, than during the fifth century BCE.

6.   Cyrus the Younger, who later (401 BCE) hired the army of ten thousand mercenaries that became the subject of Xenophon's famous *Anabasis*.

7.   Tissaphernes was the satrap, or governor, of Persian-occupied Lydia.

8.   An obol was an Athenian unit of currency, one-sixth of a drachma; but since Athens had long dominated all Aegean trade and shipping, Athenian coins had become a kind of de facto common currency for Greece.

9.   The daric is a Persian coin.

[5] Lysander, summoning from their cities to Ephesus men whom he perceived to be surpassingly bold and intrepid, secretly sowed the seeds of his decarchies[10] and the revolutionary movement he instituted later on, urging and inciting them to form political clubs and apply themselves to public affairs so that as soon as the Athenians had been overthrown they could get rid of their democracies and wield power in their various countries.

Lysander was replaced for a time by a new Spartan admiral, Callicratidas, who proved much less adept at winning the affections of his crews or getting handouts from the Persians. Lysander also did his best to undermine Callicratidas' position. After the new admiral lost a sea battle against the Athenians at Arginusae, his term of service was over.

[7] As their cause was not prospering, the allies sent an embassy to Sparta requesting that Lysander be appointed as admiral, declaring that they would deal with their plight much more energetically if he were in command. Cyrus also wrote a letter making the same request. Now Spartan law did not allow the same man to serve twice as admiral; but since the Spartans wished to gratify their allies, they gave the title of admiral to a certain Aracus, and sent Lysander out, officially as vice-admiral, though in fact he held supreme authority. So out he came, as most men who were active in their governments and exerted influence in their cities had long desired; for they were hoping to become even more powerful with his help when the democracies were completely overthrown. But for those who appreciated the sincere and noble character of their leaders, Lysander, when compared with Callicratidas, was thought to be a rogue and a sophist, who prettified with deceits much that occurred during the war, and who extolled justice when it served his advantage, but when it did not, embraced what was advantageous on the grounds that it was noble. And as he regarded the truth as not intrinsically superior to falsehood, he defined the value of each according to its usefulness. He would deride those who asserted that the descendants of Heracles[11] should not resort to trickery when making war, saying, "Where the lion's skin does not reach, it must be patched with the skin of

10. The decarchies were boards of ten, selected by Lysander from the oligarchic and pro-Spartan elements in the Asian Greek cities, who were installed in those cities as puppet governments after the defeat of Athens in 404 BCE.

11. Many Spartans traced their ancestry back to the god Heracles.

a fox." . . . Androcleides relates a saying of Lysander's which proves that the man had an extremely careless attitude about oaths. For he says that Lysander used to recommend that one deceive children with dice, and adults with oaths.

Finding the Hellespont undefended, Lysander attacked Lampsacus from the sea with his ships, while Thorax, cooperating with the land army, assaulted its walls. Taking the city by storm, he gave it to his soldiers to plunder. But as soon as the Athenian force, which consisted of 180 triremes,[12] landed at Elaeus in the Chersonese and learned that Lampsacus had been lost, it immediately put ashore at Sestos. And from there, after supplying themselves with provisions, the Athenians sailed around to Aegospotami,[13] which lay opposite[14] the enemy ships still stationed near Lampsacus. One of the many Athenian commanders was Philocles, who had recently persuaded the people[15] to pass a decree to cut off the right thumbs of their prisoners of war, leaving them unable to carry a spear or ply an oar.

[10] At that point everyone rested, expecting to fight at sea the next day. But Lysander had other plans, and ordered his seamen and pilots to board their triremes near dawn, as if there would be a contest at daybreak, and to sit in orderly silence and await the word of command. He likewise ordered the infantry to remain calm and in formation by the sea. But when the sun rose, and the Athenians, with all their ships forming a close front, sailed forward and challenged them, Lysander did not put out to sea, though he kept his ships with their prows facing forward, having manned them when it was still night; and sending tenders to the front rank of his ships, he ordered

---

12. A trireme is a standard Greek warship of the Classical Age, shipping a crew of about two hundred. The Athenian navy consisted almost entirely of triremes. Many had been lost in the disaster at Sicily, but the Athenians had gradually rebuilt their navy since that time. The number present at this engagement, 180, represented almost their entire force.

13. The name of this town, "Goat's Rivers" in Greek, has also become the name of the battle described in what follows. The battle of Aegospotami was fought—if that verb can even be used in this case—in 405 BCE. See *Alcibiades* 36–37.

14. "Opposite" here means across the strait of Dardanelles, the narrow waterway the Greeks called Hellespont. Control of the straits was vital for Athens since much of the city's food supply was imported from the Black Sea and had to move through them.

15. The *ekklēsia* or assembly at Athens is often referred to simply as "the people."

them to keep still and remain in formation, and not get into confusion or sail out against the enemy. When the Athenians sailed back in the early afternoon, Lysander did not release his men from their ships until two or three triremes, which he had sent to reconnoiter, came back after seeing that the enemy had disembarked.[16] This happened again the next day, and on the third and the fourth, with the result that the Athenians grew quite confident and contemptuous, thinking that the enemy was cowering in fear.

[11] On the fifth day, when the Athenians had sailed out against the Spartans and then sailed back, as was now their habit, very carelessly and contemptuously, Lysander sent out his lookout vessels and commanded their captains to turn back and advance at full speed as soon as they saw that the Athenians had disembarked, and to raise a bronze shield from the prow when they had reached the middle of the strait, as a signal for the attack. He himself, sailing to the helmsmen and captains, encouraged and urged each of them to keep their full crews—oarsmen and marines alike—at their posts, and as soon as the signal was given, to row with all their zeal and strength against the enemy. And when the shield was held up from the lookout ships, and Lysander had the war-trumpet sound the signal for putting out to sea, the ships sailed forward and the infantry hastened down the length of the beach toward the promontory. The continents, at that point, lie roughly two miles apart, an interval that was rapidly traversed thanks to the oarsmen's eagerness and zeal. Conon,[17] the first Athenian commander on shore to catch sight of the enemy fleet sailing up, instantly shouted orders to embark; deeply dismayed at their plight, he summoned some of his men, begged others, and forced still others to man the triremes. But his eager efforts had no effect, since the men had dispersed. For as soon as they had disembarked, expecting no trouble, they were in the marketplace, wandering about the country, sleeping in their tents, getting their breakfast—as far removed as possible from what lay ahead, thanks to the inexperience of their generals. And then, in the roar and surge of enemy troops attacking, Conon secretly sailed away with eight ships. . . . But when the Peloponnesians fell upon the rest of the ships, they

16. When triremes were not in active use, they were hauled up on shore so their crews could get onto dry land. The cramped quarters of the rowing decks did not allow them to prepare food, or even move about, while at sea.

17. Later a top commander in the naval power struggles of the fourth century BCE; see, for example, *Agesilaus 23*.

seized some quite empty, and disabled others while the sailors were
still coming aboard. And when the unarmed and scattered men ran
up to help, some were killed near the ships, and those who fled by
land were killed when the enemy disembarked. Lysander took three
thousand prisoners of war, along with their generals, and seized the
entire Athenian fleet except for the *Paralus*[18] and the ships that had
escaped with Conon. After taking the ships in tow and plundering
the Athenian camp, he sailed up to Lampsacus to the sound of flute-
music and paeans, having achieved the greatest result with the least
effort, and having brought to a close in a single hour a war that, in
its length and in the incredible variety of its misfortunes and disas-
ters, had surpassed all previous wars. This war, which had assumed
innumerable changes of shape, both in battles and regimes, and had
destroyed more generals than had served in all previous Greek wars
combined, had now been brought to an end through the sound judgment and cleverness of one man. Some, therefore, attributed the
result to divine intervention.[19]

[13] When the three thousand Athenians Lysander had captured
had been sentenced to death by the commissioners, Lysander summoned their general, Philocles, and asked him what penalty should
be imposed on him for having given his fellow citizens such advice
about Greeks. But Philocles, far from bowing to his misfortune, told
Lysander not to make accusations in the absence of a judge, but to
inflict, as conqueror, whatever penalty he would have undergone had
he been conquered. Then, after bathing and taking up a bright cloak,
Philocles led his fellow citizens to their execution, as Theophrastus
reports.[20]

Thereafter, when Lysander sailed out against the Athenian-held
cities, he told all the Athenians he encountered to return to Athens,
since he would spare no one, but would slaughter anyone he seized

18. One of two Athenian triremes reserved for religious missions and other
special needs.
19. Modern historians, with their more skeptical outlook, are more inclined
to see internal treachery or bribery behind the massive Athenian defeat.
Note that in *Alcibiades* 37, Alcibiades suspected treachery when he saw how
sloppily the Athenian admirals were conducting their operations. Some
Athenians no doubt wanted the war to end, even at the cost of total defeat,
after nearly three decades of struggle.
20. Theophrastus, a student of Aristotle, was a philosopher and scientist of
the fourth century BCE. Many of his works survive, but the source of the
anecdote given here is not known.

outside the city. He pursued this course and drove everyone into the city together because he wanted to cause an immediate famine and scarcity there,[21] lest the Athenians give him trouble by withstanding the siege with abundant provisions. Deposing the democratic governments and all other polities, he left one Spartan governor behind in each city and ten magistrates[22] from the political clubs he had organized in the various towns. Doing so in the cities of enemies and allies alike, he sailed about in a leisurely manner, in some sense establishing for himself the supremacy of Greece.

[14] After he had devoted some time to these matters and sent messengers to Sparta to report that he was sailing there with two hundred ships, he joined forces near Attica with Agis and Pausanias, believing that he would soon capture the city. But since the Athenians were standing their ground, he took his ships and again crossed to Asia. There he deposed the governments of all the cities in like manner and established decarchies. . . .

When he had learned that the inhabitants of Athens were badly afflicted by famine, he sailed into the Piraeus and vanquished the city, which was compelled to make peace on his terms. . . . The ephors' decree ran thus: "The Spartan authorities have decreed: tear down the Piraeus and your long walls;[23] depart from all the cities and keep to your own land; if you do so and restore your exiles, you may have peace if you so desire. As for the numbers of your ships, do whatever shall be decided there." The Athenians accepted this dispatch on the advice of Theramenes son of Hagnon.

[15] As soon as Lysander had taken possession of the walls of Athens and all but twelve of her ships on the sixteenth day of the month of Munichion (on which date the Greeks had defeated the barbarian at the battle of Salamis),[24] he took steps to alter the city's form of government. When the Athenians stubbornly resisted, he

21. Since Sparta now decisively controlled the sea, it could interdict food shipments headed for Athens and starve the city into submission. Even after the disastrous loss at Aegospotami, as Lysander knew, the Athenians were not willing to surrender.

22. The so-called decarchies; see chapter 5 and note 10.

23. The instruction to "tear down the Piraeus" meant to demolish the fortifications around the harbor. These, together with the long walls (which connected the Piraeus to Athens), were the bulwarks of Athenian naval power.

24. The coincidence of the date is sharply pointed, since the battle of Salamis in 480 BCE had marked the first great triumph of Athenian naval strategy (see *Themistocles* 11–16 and *Aristides* 8–10).

sent word to the people that the city had been found to have violated her oath; for her walls were standing, though the time during which they should have been taken down had elapsed; he should therefore lodge a new motion against them, since they had violated their agreements. Some say that among the allies a motion was actually made to sell the Athenians into slavery, and it was then that the Theban Erianthus introduced a motion to raze the town and let the countryside be grazed by sheep. But later, when the commanders held a drinking party, and a certain Phocian sang the first chorus from Euripides' *Electra*, which begins,

> O daughter of Agamemnon,
> I have come, Electra, to your rustic hall,

everyone was overcome with pity, and declared it a cruel thing to demolish and destroy a city of such renown, which had produced such men.

After the Athenians had yielded on all fronts, Lysander sent for several flute-girls from the town, assembled all who were in the camp, and razed the walls and burned the triremes to the sound of the flute, while the allies, wearing garlands, disported themselves, thinking that that day marked the beginning of their freedom. Lysander also proceeded at once to alter the government, installing thirty magistrates in the city and ten in the Piraeus, stationing a garrison on the Acropolis, and appointing Callibius, a Spartan, as governor.

[16] When Lysander had settled these matters, he himself sailed away to Thrace. But the remainder of the public funds and all the crowns he had received as gifts—many persons, as was to be expected, gave gifts to a man of surpassing power, who in some sense held supreme authority in Greece—he sent off to Sparta in the care of Gylippus, who had served as general in Sicily.

[18] From the spoils Lysander cast bronze statues of himself and each of the admirals and set them up at Delphi, and also cast gold stars in honor of the Dioscuri.[25] (The latter disappeared before the battle of Leuctra.)[26] . . . Lysander was at that time thought to enjoy more power than any previous Greek, and to harbor a pride and a self-importance that exceeded his power. For Duris reports that

---

25. The Dioscuri, Castor and Pollux, were divine twins, the offspring of Leda (later called Gemini in Latin). Their favor was particularly thought to benefit sailors at sea.

26. In 371 BCE; see *Pelopidas* 23ff.

Lysander was the first Greek to whom the cities dedicated altars and performed sacrifices as to a god,[27] and the first to whom hymns of worship were sung, the opening of one of which is remembered as follows:

> The general of divine Greece,
> From spacious Sparta,
> Will we praise, *O! Io! Paean!*

[19] To the foremost citizens, and to his equals, Lysander's ambition was merely annoying. But since, as a result of being courted, great arrogance and harshness developed in his character, along with ambition, he lacked the moderation of a man of the people when it came to rewards and punishments. His rewards for friendship and hospitality were irresponsible sovereignties over cities, and tyrannies not subject to scrutiny, while his anger could be satisfied only by the death of his enemy; even banishment would not suffice. Indeed, at a later period, when he feared that the popular leaders of Miletus might flee, and wanted to bring into the open those who had gone into hiding, he swore that he would not injure them; but when they trusted him and came forward he handed them over to the oligarchs to slay—no fewer than eight hundred men of both parties.[28] There were also countless murders of other popular leaders, since he killed not only for private reasons, but sought in many instances to gratify the enmity and avarice of his friends everywhere by abetting their wrongdoing. That was why Eteocles the Spartan won renown when he said that Greece could not have borne two Lysanders.

The Spartans paid very little heed to Lysander's other accusers, but when Pharnabazus, who was injured when Lysander swept his country of all its plunder, dispatched accusers to Sparta, the ephors were vexed. . . . They sent a *skytalē* to Lysander, ordering him home.

The *skytalē* merits a description. Whenever the ephors send out an admiral or a general, they make two wooden cylinders exactly

---

27. No human being had yet been worshiped as a god in the Greek world during his or her lifetime, though the advent of that kind of idolatry was not far off. The Spartan general Brasidas, killed in 424 BCE, was given rites of cult worship after his death, according to Thucydides (*The Peloponnesian War* 5.11).

28. See chapter 7 for Lysander's cynical comment about oaths. Thucydides recounts other cases in the Peloponnesian War when promises of safe passage were suddenly revoked, but he characterizes these episodes as moral outrages.

equal in length and thickness, so that their dimensions are identical. They keep one and give the other to the officer being sent out. They call these wooden cylinders *skytalēs*. Whenever they want to communicate some important secret matter, they cut a piece of parchment, making it long and narrow like a thong, and wind it around their *skytalē*, leaving no empty space, but covering its entire rounded surface. On doing so, they write whatever they want on the parchment as it lies in place around the *skytalē*; and when they have finished writing, they remove the parchment and send it off to the general without the wooden cylinder. When he receives it he is utterly unable to read it, as the letters have no connection, but are scrambled. But when he takes the strip of parchment and stretches it around his own *skytalē*, so that the spiral is restored to its original order (the words added later connecting with those set down first), he reads around the cylinder and discovers the continuity. The parchment, like the cylinder, is called a *skytalē*, since the thing measured is given the name of the measure.

[20] When the *skytalē* reached Lysander at the Hellespont, he was dismayed. And as he particularly feared the accusations of Pharnabazus, he hastened to enter into discussions with him, intending to patch up their quarrel. At their meeting, Lysander asked Pharnabazus to write the magistrates a second letter about him in which he stated that he had not been wronged and was not accusing Lysander. But in "playing the Cretan with a Cretan,"[29] as the saying goes, Lysander misjudged Pharnabazus. For the latter, promising to do everything he was asked, apparently wrote a letter of the kind Lysander expected, but secretly kept handy another that had been written earlier. And when Pharnabazus came to seal the letter, he exchanged the two (which looked identical), and gave Lysander the one that had been written in secret. When Lysander reached Sparta and went, as the custom is, to the town hall, he gave the ephors Pharnabazus' letter, convinced that he had removed the weightiest of the accusations against him. For Pharnabazus was beloved by the Spartans, having proved, during the war, the most zealous of the King's commanders. When the ephors, having read the letter, showed it to Lysander, he realized that

Odysseus is not the only wily one,[30]

at which point he departed in great distress.

29. Cretans were famous in the Greek world for lying.
30. The source of this quote, probably a tragedy, is unknown.

[21] After he had with great difficulty won his release from the ephors, he sailed away. When he had gone abroad and the kings realized that by gaining control of the cities through his political clubs Lysander had achieved absolute sway and was master of Greece, they took steps to expel his friends and to restore control of their affairs to the people. But when a fresh uproar broke out in response to these changes, and the Athenians from Phyle attacked the Thirty and overpowered them,[31] Lysander promptly returned and persuaded the Spartans to aid the oligarchies and curtail the democracies. Accordingly, to the Thirty, first of all, they sent one hundred talents for the war, and Lysander himself as general. But the Spartan kings, who were jealous of Lysander and feared that he might capture Athens a second time, decided that one of them should go out. Pausanias did so, ostensibly on behalf of the tyrants against the people, but actually with the intention of ending the war, in order that Lysander might not, through his friends, again become master of Athens. Pausanias managed this easily, and by reconciling the Athenians and ending their strife, he thwarted Lysander's aspirations.[32]

[22] When King Agis died, leaving a brother, Agesilaus,[33] and a suppositious son, Leotychides, Lysander, who had become a lover of Agesilaus, persuaded him to lay claim to the kingdom on the grounds that he was a legitimate descendant of Heracles.[34]

[23] Lysander at once spurred Agesilaus on and persuaded him to make an expedition into Asia, encouraging him to hope that he would depose the Persians and become supremely powerful.[35]

[24] Lysander was then sent as an ambassador to the Hellespont; and though angry with Agesilaus, he did not neglect his duty. He induced Spithridates the Persian, an honorable man who possessed an army, to revolt from Pharnabazus, with whom he had clashed,

---

31. In 403 BCE a democratic insurgency at Athens overthrew the regime of the Thirty installed by Lysander. They began their campaign by seizing a fort at Phyle, on the border between Attica and Boeotia.

32. Plutarch's account here seems to follow that of Xenophon (*Hellenica* 2.4.29–43), which attributes the end of Spartan-supported rule at Athens to the rivalry between Pausanias and Lysander.

33. See *Agesilaus*, including much further information on the relationship between this young king and the older, craftier Lysander.

34. See *Agesilaus* 3. Leotychides was apparently fathered by Alcibiades, who was having an affair with Agis' wife (see *Alcibiades* 23).

35. The full account of this expedition is given in *Agesilaus* 7–15.

and brought him to Agesilaus. But the king made no further use of Lysander in the war, and when his time had elapsed he sailed, without honor, back to Sparta. Angry with Agesilaus, and detesting the entire system of government even more than before, he resolved to put into effect, without delay, the plans for a revolutionary change that he is thought to have framed and devised some time earlier.

The plan was as follows. Of the Heraclids[36] who joined with the Dorians and migrated south into the Peloponnese, there was a numerous and brilliant stock flourishing in Sparta, though the royal succession was not open to everyone. The Spartans were ruled by two families only: the Eurypontids and the Agiads; the others had no privileges in the government because of their noble birth, though the powerful were eligible for the honors awarded on the basis of merit. Into the latter class Lysander had been born, and when elevated by his exploits to a position of high renown he was vexed to see the city growing in size by his efforts, but ruled by others whose birth was no nobler than his own. He therefore planned to wrest the sovereignty from the two houses and restore it to all the Heraclids in common, though some say it was to be given not to the Heraclids but to the Spartans in general, so that it might belong not to anyone who happened to be a descendant of Heracles, but only to those who like Heracles were awarded the privilege for merit, since it was this that had raised Heracles to divine honors. Lysander hoped that if the sovereignty was awarded in this manner, no Spartan would be chosen in preference to himself.

[25] So he set to work preparing to persuade the citizens by his own efforts, and for that purpose rehearsed a speech written by Cleon of Halicarnassus.[37] Then, seeing that the strangeness and magnitude of his proposed innovation required a more urgent support, he resorted, as they do in tragedy, to affecting the citizens by means of a deus ex machina.[38] He collected and arranged prophecies

36. The Heraclids were, according to legend, the children of Heracles and the ancestors of many Spartans, among whom Lysander counted himself.

37. Plutarch reports, in a passage not presented here, that the speech advocating an elective monarchy was found among Lysander's papers after his death and suppressed by the Spartan high command, who feared its arguments were too persuasive.

38. Apparently the phrase describing a technique of drama, to wrap up the plot by dropping a god onto the stage "from the machine," had already become proverbial in Plutarch's time to refer to an artificial or contrived resolution.

and Pythian[39] oracles, thinking he would derive no benefit from Cleon's clever oratory unless he first struck the fear of god into the people, cowed them with superstitious dread, and *then* won them over to his proposal. Ephorus says that after Lysander had tried to corrupt the Pythian priestess and had again failed to persuade the priestesses of Dodona[40] through Pherecles, he journeyed to the temple of Ammon[41] and conferred with the prophets, offering them considerable sums. But they took offense and dispatched representatives to Sparta to denounce Lysander. When he was acquitted, the Libyans, as they departed, remarked, "Well, we, at any rate, shall judge better, Spartans, when you come to us in hopes of settling in Libya," since there was actually an ancient prophecy that the Spartans would settle in Libya.

[26] There was a woman in Pontus[42] who claimed that she was with child by Apollo, which many, as was natural, disbelieved, but many also credited, so that when she gave birth to a male child its rearing and care were eagerly undertaken by many distinguished persons. The child was for some reason named Silenus.[43] Taking this as his point of departure, Lysander wove the rest of his cunning web himself, making use of several by no means insignificant champions of his story, who lent credence to the report about the boy's birth without arousing suspicion. They also brought back another response from Delphi, which they circulated in Sparta, to the effect that certain very ancient prophecies were kept in secret documents by the priests there, and that it was not possible to obtain them, nor even lawful to read them, unless someone born of Apollo should come after a long period of time, furnish the keepers with an intelligible token of his birth, and take away the tablets on which the prophecies had been recorded. With this groundwork laid, it was necessary that Silenus visit and ask for the prophecies, on the grounds that he was Apollo's son; that priests who had been enlisted in the

---

39. The term "Pythian" here means derived from the oracle of Apollo at Delphi.

40. Dodona, in northern Greece, was the site of a famous oracle of Zeus.

41. Ammon, an Egyptian god roughly equated by the Greeks with Zeus, had an oracular shrine in the desert west of Egypt, in the region the Greeks called Libya (modern North Africa).

42. The Black Sea region.

43. Silenus was the name of a leading satyr in Greek mythology who also had a gift of prophecy.

scheme make a precise and detailed inquiry about his birth; that finally, persuaded that he was indeed the son of Apollo, they show him the letters; and that he read aloud, with many people present, a number of other prophecies as well as the one for the sake of which everything else had been contrived, namely the prophecy about the sovereignty, which declared that it was better and more desirable for the Spartans to choose their kings from among their best citizens.

But when Silenus had reached young manhood and was ready to play his part in the affair, Lysander's drama miscarried because of the cowardice of one of his actor–accomplices, who, when it came to the point, flinched and drew back.[44] None of this, however, was discovered during Lysander's lifetime; it came out only after his death.

[28] And since Lysander was now altogether harsh of temper, owing to the melancholy that persisted into his old age, he stirred up the ephors and persuaded them to order an expedition against the Thebans. Assuming the command, he marched forth. Afterward the ephors also sent King Pausanias out with an army. Now Pausanias, taking the route that skirted Mount Cithaeron, was to invade Boeotia, while Lysander advanced with a large force through Phocis to meet him. After seizing the city of Orchomenus, which came over to him of its own accord, Lysander attacked and plundered Lebadeia. He then wrote to Pausanias, urging him to march from Plataea and join forces with him in Haliartus, since he would himself reach the walls of Haliartus at daybreak. But this letter was brought to Thebes when its bearer was waylaid by some scouts. When the Athenians came to their aid, the Thebans entrusted them with the city, while they themselves, setting out early that night, reached Haliartus shortly before Lysander, and a detachment of them entered the city. At first Lysander decided to post his army on a ridge and wait for Pausanias; but later, as the day advanced, finding it impossible to remain inactive, he seized his weapons, urged the allies on, and led the phalanx in column along the road to the fortress. The Thebans who had remained outside kept the city on their left and advanced to the enemy's rear at the spring known as Cissusa.

The Thebans inside the city, who had been drawn up in array with the inhabitants of Haliartus, kept still for some time. But when

44. After giving such intricate details about the plot, Plutarch is maddeningly vague as to how it unraveled. It appears that Lysander was incubating his scheme for more than a decade. There are no other ancient sources for this episode.

they saw Lysander approaching the wall with his foremost men, they suddenly threw open the gates and attacked, killing Lysander and the seer who was with him, but only a few of the others, since the greater part quickly fled back to the phalanx.

[29] The calamity was reported to Pausanias as he was marching along the road from Plataea to Thespiae. Drawing his men up in battle array, he reached Haliartus. Thrasybulus[45] had also arrived from Thebes, leading the Athenians. When Pausanias was planning to request the bodies of the dead under a truce, the Spartan elders were dismayed and expressed their annoyance among themselves. Approaching the king, they protested that Lysander should not be retrieved under a truce, but by force of arms;[46] and that if they prevailed they would bury him, but if they were defeated it would be honorable to lie dead with their commander. So said the elders; but Pausanias saw that it would take a great effort to prevail in battle over the recently victorious Thebans; and since Lysander's body was lying near the wall, it would be hard to retrieve it without a truce, even if they were victorious. He therefore sent a herald, and after making a truce, led his forces away. As soon as they had carried Lysander past the border of Boeotia they buried him in the friendly soil of their allies the Panopeans, where his memorial stands today beside the road leading from Delphi to Chaeronea.

45. This long-serving Athenian general has been encountered earlier (see *Alcibiades* 26) as the strong-voiced supporter of Alcibiades in 411 BCE. In the intervening quarter century he had played many leading roles in the events of his times, including the overthrow of the Thirty at Athens in 403 (see *Pelopidas* 13).
46. To retrieve corpses under a negotiated truce, a Greek general had to formally admit defeat.

Agesilaus

Agesilaus (444–360 BCE) was king at Sparta for more than forty years in the post–Peloponnesian War period, from about 400 to 360. His exceptionally long reign, his strong and assertive nature, and his veering fortunes fascinated not only Plutarch but also Xenophon, who wrote an admiring study of his life, known as Agesilaus, in the fourth century BCE. Agesilaus' political career coincided closely with that of Pelopidas, and the Plutarchan Lives of those two leaders overlap at many points. Both examine, from different perspectives, the decline of Spartan power in the first half of the fourth century and the rise of Thebes.

[1] Archidamus, son of Zeuxidamus, after reigning illustriously as king of the Spartans, left behind a son Agis by his honored wife Lampido, and a much younger son Agesilaus by Eupolia, daughter of Melesippidas. Since by law the throne belonged to Agis, and Agesilaus assumed he would live as a private citizen, he was given the traditional Spartan training, which required young men to lead an austere and laborious life and learn to be ruled.[1] . . . According to Spartan law, boys raised for the monarchy were not required to undergo this training. Agesilaus was thus unique among Sparta's kings in that he brought to the task of ruling the training associated with being ruled.

[2] In the "companies" of boys being reared together, he became the beloved of Lysander,[2] who was especially struck by Agesilaus' innate decency. For though he was intensely competitive, unequalled among the young men for courage, eager to excel, and in possession of an impetuosity and fury that were invincible and irresistible, yet, on the other hand, he was so courteous and amenable that he obeyed orders not from any sense of fear, but from a sense of honor, since

---

1. The rigorous demands of Spartan military education are described in *Lycurgus* 16–18.

2. The relationship between Lysander and Agesilaus seems to have begun as a love match but soon developed political dimensions, as detailed both in *Agesilaus* and *Lysander*. By the term "beloved" (Greek *erōmenos*), Plutarch indicates that the relationship began when Agesilaus was in early adolescence and Lysander somewhat older (the date of Lysander's birth is not known). Such homosexual relationships were considered normal and natural in much of the Greek world, though it is unclear how they were regarded at Sparta (see *Lycurgus*, n. 27).

he was more pained by reproaches than oppressed by hardships. The deformity of his leg[3] was overshadowed by the beauty of his blooming physique; and the fact that he bore such a disability easily and cheerfully—he was the first to jest about it and make fun of himself—did much to compensate for the defect. It also made his ambition more conspicuous, since he declined no effort or undertaking because of his lameness.

[3] Agis was reigning when Alcibiades arrived in Sparta as a fugitive from Sicily; and he had not been long in the city before he was suspected of an illicit affair with the king's wife Timaea.[4] Agis refused to recognize the child she bore, claiming that it had been sired by Alcibiades. According to Duris, Timaea was not at all disconsolate; on the contrary, when whispering at home to her helot maids, she would call the child Alcibiades, not Leotychides; furthermore, Alcibiades himself even claimed that he had consorted with Timaea not out of unbridled passion, but because he was ambitious to have the Spartans ruled by men descended from himself. And thus, in fear of Agis, Alcibiades stole out of Sparta, and the boy was always suspected by Agis and not honored by him as legitimate. But when Agis became ill, the boy fell weeping at his feet and persuaded him to declare him his son in the presence of many witnesses.

But after Agis died, Lysander, who had by then defeated the Athenians at sea[5] and was highly influential in Sparta, sought to advance Agesilaus to the throne on the grounds that it did not belong to Leotychides, since he was a bastard.[6] And many of the other citizens, because of Agesilaus' excellence and the fact that he had been reared and educated with them, shared Lysander's zeal and supported his efforts.

[4] And thus Agesilaus, as soon as he was proclaimed king, came into possession of Agis' fortune as well, once he had expelled the bastard Leotychides.

---

3. Agesilaus was lame from a birth defect, a deformity that complicated both his accession to the throne and his participation in military life.

4. These events, dating to 414–412 BCE, are narrated in more detail in *Alcibiades* 23.

5. Especially at the battle of Aegospotami; see *Lysander* 10–11.

6. That is, since he was presumed to be the son of Alcibiades. The year of this accession drama is 401 BCE. Lysander took the side of Agesilaus presumably because he assumed he would gain in political influence if his beloved became king.

[6] Soon after Agesilaus had succeeded to the throne, word came from Asia that the King[7] of the Persians was readying a large force with which he intended to drive the Spartans from the sea.[8] Lysander wished to be sent back to Asia to help his friends.[9] These men, whom he had left as rulers and masters of its cities, were being banished by the citizens, and even put to death, for their base and violent conduct. He therefore persuaded Agesilaus to devote himself to the campaign and make war on behalf of Greece, crossing the sea to its farthest shore[10] and thus anticipating the barbarian's preparations. At the same time Lysander wrote to his friends in Asia, instructing them to send messengers to Sparta requesting that Agesilaus be appointed as their commander. Agesilaus then came before the people and agreed to undertake the war provided they gave him thirty Spartans as commanders and counselors, two thousand selected men who were newly enrolled,[11] and an allied force numbering up to six thousand. And because Lysander was participating, they readily voted for everything and sent Agesilaus off at once with the thirty Spartans. Of these Lysander was the foremost, not only because of his reputation and influence, but also because of his friendship with Agesilaus, who regarded Lysander's procuring him that command as a greater blessing than his promoting him for the sovereignty.

In the spring of 396 BCE Agesilaus brought his invasion force into Asia, crossing by ship from the coast of Euboea to western Anatolia. This was the

---

7. As always in this volume, "King" when capitalized refers to the Great King of Persia.

8. The Persians had aided Sparta in the last phase of the Peloponnesian War, principally by giving them money to build and man a navy. In this way the Persians hoped to make Sparta a counterweight to the naval power of Athens. But once the Spartans had triumphed and become a naval power in their own right, it was they, rather than the Athenians, who posed the greatest threat to the Persians.

9. At the end of the Peloponnesian War Lysander had installed decarchies, boards of ten, to govern the Greek cities of Asia Minor in a way congenial to Sparta's interests (see *Lysander* 14). Like the Thirty whom he installed at Athens, these political cronies often took great license with their newfound power.

10. That is, crossing the Aegean to Asia Minor, where much of the coast was now controlled by Persia ("the barbarian").

11. The "newly enrolled" (*neodamōdeis*) represent some kind of noncitizen draftee, but just who they were is obscure.

same route followed, according to legend, by Agamemnon's forces in the Trojan War, and Agesilaus made ritual gestures before embarking designed to evoke parallels with that mythic campaign. The motives for the invasion are complex and unclear; Sparta was not in the habit of projecting power across the Hellespont, into Asia. Indeed, the Spartans had declined just such an extension of power in 479, leaving the Athenians a free hand in Asia Minor. Perhaps Plutarch is at least partly right, that Lysander, a very un-Spartan Spartan, was the driving force behind the invasion of 396, using Agesilaus as his vehicle to attain ever greater power and wealth.

[7] From the moment he arrived in Ephesus, Agesilaus found Lysander's great prestige and power onerous and irksome. There was invariably a crowd at Lysander's door, and everyone dogged his steps and courted him; for in name and outward show Agesilaus held the command, as this was the custom, but in fact Lysander held sway over everyone and wielded absolute power. For none of the generals sent to Asia had been cleverer or more fearsome than he; nor did anyone else do more to benefit his friends or inflict great injuries on his enemies. As there were recent instances of this, people were mindful of them; and seeing that Agesilaus was plain, simple, and affable in company, whereas Lysander retained the same vehemence and severity and curtness as before, they utterly fawned on the latter and paid heed only to him. As a result, all the other Spartans were vexed at finding themselves attendants of Lysander rather than advisers of the king. Thereupon Agesilaus, though he was not envious or vexed when others were honored, but highly ambitious and competitive himself, feared that even if his undertakings were successful they would be attributed to Lysander, owing to his renown. He therefore adopted the following course of action.

First, he resisted Lysander's counsels and neglected or ignored the exploits the man was particularly earnest about, pursuing others instead; then, of those who came to ask him a favor, he sent away unsatisfied any whom he knew to be especially loyal to Lysander. He did the same when it came to lawsuits: men whom Lysander insolently opposed were bound to obtain an advantageous judgment; and conversely, those whom Lysander was manifestly eager to help found it hard even to avoid being fined. As these outcomes were not fortuitous but intentional and predictable, Lysander, who was aware of the cause, did not hide it from his friends, but said that it was on *his* account that they were suffering dishonor, and advised them to go and pay court to the King and to those more powerful than himself.

[8] Since by word and deed Lysander seemed to be making the King an object of ill will, Agesilaus took further steps to chastise him, appointing him meat-carver[12] and remarking to him, it is said, in the presence of many, "Let them now go and pay court to my carver." Distressed, Lysander said, "You clearly know, Agesilaus, how to diminish your friends." "I do indeed, by Zeus," Agesilaus answered, "when they wish to be more powerful than I am." To which Lysander replied, "Well, perhaps your words are nobler than my deeds. But give me some post or territory where I'll be useful without offending you." Thereafter, when he was sent to the Hellespont, Lysander brought over to Agesilaus a Persian, Spithridates, from the region held by Pharnabazus, with an enormous amount of money and two hundred horsemen. But Lysander's anger was not appeased; and from then on, nursing his resentment, he gave thought to how he could remove the kingship from the two royal families and restore it to the Spartans, making all of them eligible for the office.[13] And it was thought that he might have effected an important change as a result of that quarrel had he not died on an expedition to Boeotia.[14]

[9] Tissaphernes,[15] who was afraid of Agesilaus at first, made a treaty in which he promised to make the Greek cities independent of the King; but later, convinced that he had sufficient power, he declared war—a war that Agesilaus gladly accepted. For the Spartans had high hopes for the campaign; and Agesilaus thought it would be a terrible thing if the Ten Thousand with Xenophon had reached the sea and defeated the King as many times as they liked,[16] but the commander of the Spartans, who held supremacy on land and sea, did not present the Greeks with a memorable exploit. He at once requited

12. A minor public official responsible for distributing meat after a sacrifice.

13. The plot is discussed in more detail in *Lysander* 24–25.

14. See the final chapters of *Lysander.*

15. Tissaphernes was the Persian satrap, or provincial governor, in command of Lydia, the sector of Asia Minor that Agesilaus' army now threatened. His capital and principal stronghold was the city of Sardis. See *Alcibiades* 24.

16. In 401 BCE a band of some ten thousand Greek mercenaries had been hired to support a coup attempt by a Persian royal. They were victorious in a battle near Babylon, but the usurper who had hired them was killed, leaving them cut off without support or political protection. With the help of Xenophon's deft leadership, the men fought their way north and west to the Black Sea, where they got sea passage back to Europe. Their ordeal was immortalized by Xenophon in his eyewitness narrative, the *Anabasis.*

Tissaphernes' perjury with a justifiable deception, proclaiming that he would lead his force onward to Caria; but when the barbarian had mustered his force there, Agesilaus marched out and invaded Phrygia. He seized many cities and got possession of boundless treasure, telling his friends that to violate an oath is to show contempt for the gods, but in deceiving one's enemy there is not only justice, but also great glory, in addition to profit and pleasure. But since his cavalry was inferior in size and the sacrificial victims were shown to lack lobes, he withdrew to Ephesus and enlisted horsemen, commanding the affluent, if they preferred not to serve, to provide, each of them, a horse and rider. There were many such, and Agesilaus soon found himself in possession of many warlike horsemen instead of faint-hearted hoplites.

[10] When it again came time to invade enemy territory,[17] he let it be known that he would lead his forces to Lydia. Agesilaus was no longer trying to deceive Tissaphernes, but the latter deceived himself: distrusting Agesilaus because of his previous trick, Tissaphernes thought that now, at any rate, Agesilaus would attack Caria, since it was unfit for horses,[18] and Agesilaus' cavalry was far inferior to his own. Thus when Agesilaus, proving good to his word, marched into the plain near Sardis, Tissaphernes was forced to hasten there from Caria to lend aid; and as he rode through with his cavalry, he slaughtered many of the enemy who were out of formation and plundering the plain. Agesilaus, reflecting that the enemy's infantry had not yet arrived, whereas none of his own forces were absent, was eager to join battle. After mixing his light-armed troops with his horsemen, he ordered them to charge at full speed and attack the enemy, while he himself immediately advanced his hoplites. When the barbarians were put to flight, the Greeks, following on their heels, seized their camp and killed many men. After that battle they were able not only to plunder the king's territory with impunity, but also to see Tissaphernes, a villainous man and the Greeks' most hated enemy, suffer punishment. For the Great King immediately dispatched Tithraustes,[19] who cut off Tissaphernes' head and asked Agesilaus

17. In the spring of 395 BCE. The normal pattern for Greek armies was to campaign only during seasonable months, and to disperse or remain in camp during inclement winters.

18. That is, lacking in level plains on which cavalry operations were most effective.

19. A new satrap of Lydia to replace the old, Tissaphernes having obviously failed.

to make terms and sail home; Tithraustes even offered Agesilaus money,[20] which was brought to him by envoys. But Agesilaus replied that his city was responsible for making peace, and that for his own part, he delighted more in enriching his soldiers than in becoming rich himself; he also said that the Greeks did not think it honorable to receive gifts, rather than spoils, from their enemies. Nevertheless, as he wished to gratify Tithraustes, who had punished their common enemy Tissaphernes, he led his army away to Phrygia,[21] accepting supplies and provisions worth thirty talents.

While on the road, Agesilaus received a *skytalē*[22] from the magistrates at home ordering him to command the fleet as well as the army. This was an honor accorded to no one but Agesilaus.[23] And he was admittedly the greatest and most distinguished man of his day, as even Theopompus has somewhere said, though he prided himself more on his rectitude than on his supreme command.

The arrival of Agesilaus' army in Phrygia alarmed Pharnabazus, the satrap there, prompting him to arrange the following memorable parley:

[12] Pharnabazus wished to hold talks with Agesilaus; and Apollophanes of Cyzicus, who was a guest-friend of both men, brought the two together. Agesilaus, who reached the place first with his friends, threw himself down in the shade of some high grass and waited for Pharnabazus. When the latter arrived, and soft fleeces and embroidered carpets were spread for him, Pharnabazus was ashamed to find Agesilaus lying as he was, and reclined likewise, in a casual manner, on the grass, though he was dressed in dyed garments of marvelous delicacy.

20. That is, a bribe in exchange for retreat, a standard ploy in warfare of this time.

21. Phrygia was under the command of a different Persian satrap, Pharnabazus; by getting the Greeks to move there, Tithraustes protected his own territory, even though the Persian empire as a whole was still just as much under threat.

22. Plutarch's own explanation of the *skytalē* or coded message stick used by the Spartans is our best evidence for how it functioned; see *Lysander* 19.

23. Formerly Spartans had divided command of land and sea forces, but in the Asia Minor campaign it was obviously of great benefit to have them unified under a single leader.

By such displays of contempt for wealth and adherence to traditional Spartan ways, Agesilaus won great renown throughout the Greek-settled parts of Asia Minor. By 394 BCE, after two years in the field, he had established control of Asia Minor and was preparing to move into the Persian-held interior.

[15] When Asia Minor was stirred up and in many places inclined to revolt, Agesilaus brought harmony to her cities and restored their governments' proper form without recourse to murders and banishments. He then decided to go farther afield, to move the war away from the Greek sea,[24] to fight for the person of the King and the wealth of Ecbatana and Susa, and above all to deprive the monarch of the power to sit idly on his throne, playing umpire in the wars of the Greeks and corrupting their politicians.[25] But at that point Epicydidas the Spartan came to him to report that a great Greek war was enveloping Sparta,[26] and that the ephors were summoning and exhorting him to help those at home.

"O barbarous ills contrived by Greeks!" How else could one speak of that jealousy or that mustering and arraying of the Greeks against one another? They arrested Fortune in her flight and turned the weapons that threatened the barbarians, as well as the war that had been banished from Greece, against themselves yet again. For my part, at any rate, I cannot agree with the Corinthian Demaratus, who said that those Greeks had been deprived of a great pleasure who had not seen Alexander seated on the throne of Darius; instead, I think those Greeks would probably have wept when they saw that that "great pleasure" was being bequeathed to Alexander and the Macedonians by those who now squandered the lives of Greek generals at Leuctra, Coroneia, Corinth, and Arcadia.

24. The Aegean.

25. The Persians were widely resented in Greece for their ability to bribe Greek politicians, using their enormous hoard of gold and silver to achieve what their military forces could not. Plutarch's own anguished comment just following attests to that resentment.

26. Plutarch leaves the nature of this "great Greek war" unexplained. In Agesilaus' absence, Sparta's many rivals and enemies, including Athens, Thebes, and Corinth, had been combining forces and preparing for an attack, prompted in some cases by the Persian bribes mentioned in note 25. By 395 BCE they were massing at Corinth for an invasion, the start of the so-called Corinthian War. The looming threat prompted the Spartan government to recall Agesilaus and end his thus far successful invasion effort.

Plutarch

Nevertheless, no deed performed by Agesilaus was nobler or greater than that return home, nor has there ever been a nobler example of just obedience to command. . . . Alexander even jested when he learned of Antipater's war with Agis, saying, "It seems, gentlemen, that while *we* were conquering Darius *here*, a battle of mice was taking place in Arcadia."[27] So how could one not consider Sparta blessed in the honor Agesilaus showed her and in his reverence for her laws? For as soon as the dispatch arrived he renounced his present success, power, and high hopes, and immediately sailed home "with his task unaccomplished," leaving behind a great longing for him among his allies. . . . Persian coins bore the impress of an archer, and Agesilaus, when breaking up camp, remarked that he was being driven from Asia by the King with ten thousand archers; for when that amount of money had been sent to Athens and Thebes and distributed among the politicians, their peoples were roused to make war on the Spartans.

[16] When Agesilaus had crossed the Hellespont and was marching through Thrace, he requested nothing of any of the barbarians; he merely sent word to each tribe, inquiring whether he should travel through their country as a friend or as an enemy. All the others welcomed him as a friend, and each tribe that was able to do so escorted him. But the tribe known as the Trallians, to whom even Xerxes reportedly gave gifts, demanded of Agesilaus one hundred talents of silver and an equal number of women as a fee for his passage. On replying ironically, "Why didn't they come at once to accept their fee?" he led his men forward; and finding the Trallians drawn up in battle array, he engaged and routed them, slaughtering many. He sent the king of the Macedonians the same question, and when the man replied that he would consider the matter, Agesilaus said, "Well, let *him* consider, but *we* are marching on." Astonished at his daring, and taking fright, the king urged Agesilaus to lead his men forward as a friend.

27. While Alexander the Great was making deep inroads into the Persian empire, in 331 BCE, his adversary Darius III tried to draw him back to Europe by fomenting a Spartan-led war against Macedonian hegemony there. Alexander managed to send his deputy, Antipater, just enough force and money to quell the Spartans on his own. Plutarch regards Agesilaus as the more noble commander because he turned back to aid his homeland rather than risking its destruction in order to press on, as Alexander had done.

[17] He was met [in Pharsalus] by Diphridas, an ephor[28] from home, who ordered him to invade Boeotia at once.

[18] When Agesilaus had advanced as far as Coroneia[29] and was within sight of the enemy, he arrayed his forces, giving the Orchomenians the left wing, while he himself led the right. On the other side, the Thebans held the right wing themselves, the Argives the left. Xenophon says that this battle was like none that had ever been fought;[30] and he himself was present, contending with Agesilaus after crossing from Asia. The first clash did not involve much thrusting or close combat, though the Thebans swiftly routed the Orchomenians, as Agesilaus did the Argives; but when both parties heard that their left wings, pressed hard, were taking to flight, they turned back. At that point Agesilaus might have enjoyed a victory without incurring danger, had he been willing to give up fighting the Thebans head on and simply followed and assaulted them as they rushed past. But anger and a lust for victory moved him to advance with his men head on, as he wished to repulse the enemy with all his might. Yet the Thebans met his attack no less stoutly, and though the fighting was fierce throughout the army, it was fiercest where Agesilaus himself was posted with his fifty volunteers, whose zeal at the critical moment appears to have saved the king's life. For though they were fighting bravely and risking their lives on his behalf, they could not keep him from being wounded, and snatched him up barely alive when he had sustained many blows from spears and swords that had pierced his armor and entered his body. After closing ranks around him, they slaughtered many, though many of their own men fell. When a great effort was made to thrust the Thebans headlong, the Spartans were compelled to do what from the start they had been reluctant to do. For they stood at intervals, separating their phalanx; and then, when the enemy had passed through and were already marching in looser array, the Spartans followed and smote them from the side while running past their flank. Yet they did not

28. One of a board of five Spartan officials who oversaw much of state policy.

29. In Boeotia.

30. At *Hellenica* 4.3.16 Xenophon does indeed say that this battle was "quite unlike any other in our era," though he does not say why it was unique, and neither his description nor Plutarch's makes this clear. Xenophon does not say in his description that he fought in the battle, but his presence there can be inferred from statements he makes elsewhere.

manage to rout them, and the Thebans withdrew to Helicon, glorying in the battle, since their own contingent had proved invincible.

[19] At daybreak, as Agesilaus wished to test the Thebans and see whether they would fight, he ordered his soldiers to don wreaths and his flute-players to play their flutes, while a trophy in honor of their victory was set up and adorned. When the enemy requested permission to retrieve their corpses, he concluded a treaty.[31]

[22] While he was spending time in Corinthian territory, and after seizing the Heraeum[32] was watching his soldiers plundering enemy property, envoys arrived from Thebes to discuss an alliance. As he had always hated the city and thought this would be an opportune moment to insult it, he pretended neither to see nor hear its ambassadors when they met with him. But he incurred retribution; for before the Thebans had departed, men arrived to report that his detachment had been cut down by Iphicrates.[33] This was the greatest calamity to befall them in a long time; for they lost many brave men—Spartan hoplites overwhelmed by light troops and mercenaries.

Agesilaus at once leaped up to lend aid; but when he learned that the unit had been defeated, he went again to the Heraeum; and after ordering the Boeotians to approach him there, he held an audience. When they insulted him in turn by making no mention of the peace, but asked to be allowed to enter Corinth, Agesilaus angrily replied, "If you wish to see your friends, who are exulting at their successes, you will be able to do so safely tomorrow."[34] Taking them

31. The Spartans were "victors" in the sense that they retained possession of the battlefield and got to grant permission for retrieval of the Theban dead. Nonetheless, they had been stymied in the fighting and denied their objectives.

32. A shrine to the goddess Hera.

33. Plutarch makes only a brief, shorthand reference to an episode described fully by Xenophon (*Hellenica* 4.5.11–18). A Spartan contingent had been making its way homeward from Corinth, fearlessly exposing itself since it believed no enemy would dare attack it. Iphicrates, an Athenian general, made ingenious use of his light-armed troops and did enormous damage to this corps, killing around 250. It was an early instance of the asymmetrical warfare that would become increasingly common in the fourth century.

34. With his boastful irony, Agesilaus tries to counter the insult delivered by the Theban ambassadors, who had changed the nature of their request after learning of the Spartan disaster. To "see your friends safely tomorrow" implies that Agesilaus will by then have forced an entry into Corinth.

with him the next day, he devastated the Corinthian countryside and approached the city itself. And when he had proved that the Corinthians did not dare to defend themselves, he dismissed the embassy. He himself, taking up the detachment's survivors, led them back to Sparta, breaking camp before daybreak and again encamping during the night, so that the Arcadians who hated and envied them might not rejoice.

[23] When Conon and Pharnabazus,[35] holding supremacy at sea with the King's fleet, were plundering the coasts of Laconia, and the walls of Athens had been rebuilt with the money furnished by Pharnabazus,[36] the Spartans decided to make peace with the King. They sent Antalcidas to Tiribazus[37] and thereby ceded to the King, in the most shameful and lawless fashion, the Greeks who had settled in Asia,[38] on whose behalf Agesilaus had made war. Agesilaus, accordingly, had no part in this infamy. For Antalcidas, who was his enemy, was doing all he could to make peace, since the war was enhancing Agesilaus' prestige and increasing his power. Nevertheless, to someone who said that the Spartans were siding with the Medes, Agesilaus replied that it was more the case that the Medes were siding with the Spartans.[39] And by threatening with war those Greeks who were reluctant to accept the peace, he compelled everyone to abide by the terms the Persian favored, principally with regard to the Thebans,

35. A seemingly unlikely pair, Conon being an Athenian admiral and Pharnabazus a Persian satrap. But Persia had opted to rebuild the Athenian navy as a counterweight to Spartan power, only one generation after making it possible for the Spartans to destroy the same navy.

36. The reference is to the long walls that connected Athens with its harbor, the Piraeus. A portion had been pulled down by the terms of the treaty that ended the Peloponnesian War, a simple way of ensuring that Athens would relinquish its naval empire.

37. Antalcidas was a Spartan envoy who negotiated the agreement with Persia that, as a result, bears his name: the Peace of Antalcidas (387 BCE). Tiribazus was one of Persia's satraps in Asia Minor.

38. The Greek cities on the coast of Asia Minor had been liberated by the Greek victories over the Persians in 480 and 479 BCE. A subsequent treaty forced the Great King to keep Persian forces a safe distance from the coast. The ease with which Sparta now undid all these gains, ceding control of the liberated Greek cities back to the Persians, strikes Plutarch (and many modern historians) as outrageous.

39. Implying that his own recent invasion had pressured the Persians into making a treaty.

who would be weakened if Boeotia were left independent of Thebes.[40] This became clear from his subsequent actions. For when Phoebidas flagrantly violated the peace treaty and seized the Cadmeia,[41] and all the Greeks were indignant and the Spartans displeased, and when those who were especially at odds with Agesilaus angrily asked Phoebidas at whose command he had acted, thereby directing suspicion at Agesilaus, the latter did not scruple to help Phoebidas, declaring openly that one should consider whether or not the action itself was useful; for anything that benefited Sparta should be done independently, even if no one had ordered it. Yet in conversation he was always claiming that justice held first place among the virtues; for valor was of no use without justice, and if everyone became just, there would be no need for valor. . . . Yet in his actions he no longer adhered to that view, but was often carried away by ambition and rivalry; and especially in this instance at Thebes, he not only saved Phoebidas,[42] but persuaded Sparta to assume responsibility for his crime and occupy the Cadmeia on its own account, besides placing the government of Thebes in the hands of Archias and Leontidas,[43] with whose help Phoebidas had entered and seized the citadel.

[24] This aroused an immediate suspicion that though Phoebidas had carried out the action, Agesilaus had recommended it—a view that was reinforced by his later actions. For when the Thebans expelled the garrison and freed the city,[44] Agesilaus charged them with having killed Archias and Leontidas . . . and declared war on

40. The terms of the peace required the dissolution of all leagues and regional power structures, of which the Boeotian League, headed by Thebes, was the most prominent. It therefore had the effect of greatly weakening Thebes. There were to be several diplomatic clashes in the decade following over Theban adherence to this treaty (see chapter 28).

41. This refers to an unprovoked Spartan seizure of the Cadmeia, the citadel that dominated Thebes, in 382 BCE. With the Cadmeia under control of its troops, Sparta could effectively run Thebes by way of a puppet government (the regime of Archias and Leontidas, mentioned below). See *Pelopidas* 5 for a fuller account.

42. In *Pelopidas* Plutarch reports that Phoebidas was fined the huge sum of 100,000 drachmas for his unauthorized action, but some historians speculate that Agesilaus paid part or all of the fine for him.

43. Members of the pro-Spartan faction at Thebes, in opposition to the liberal wing that included Pelopidas and Epaminondas.

44. The coup that, in Plutarch's account, was engineered by Pelopidas (see *Pelopidas* 7–13).

Sparta. Thereupon Cleombrotus, who had been reigning since the death of Agesipolis, was sent with a force to Boeotia, while Agesilaus, who by then had borne arms for forty years and was exempt by law from service, avoided that command. For he was ashamed, having only recently made war on the Phliasians on behalf of their exiles,[45] to be again seen injuring the Thebans on behalf of their tyrants.

There was a Spartan named Sphodrias,[46] from the party opposed to Agesilaus, who had been appointed governor in Thespiae. Neither timid nor without ambition, he was always full of hopes rather than sound judgment. This man, desiring great renown, and thinking that Phoebidas had won fame and glory by his daring deed at Thebes, was convinced that it would be far nobler and more brilliant if he seized the Piraeus on his own account and robbed the Athenians of the sea, attacking unexpectedly by land. They say that his scheme originated with the boeotarchs[47] Pelopidas and Melon. For they secretly sent men who, pretending to be Spartan sympathizers, praised and exalted Sphodrias as the only man worthy of such an exploit, and thus roused and incited him to undertake an action as unjust and unlawful as the seizure of the Cadmeia, though it was ventured without courage or good fortune. For daylight overtook Sphodrias in the Thriasian plain,[48] though he had hoped to assault the Piraeus at night; and they say that when his soldiers saw a light gleaming from certain shrines at Eleusis they shuddered in fear.[49] Sphodrias himself lost courage, since it was no longer possible to escape detection, and after engaging in some petty robbery withdrew in disgrace and ignominy

45. In 381 BCE; see Xenophon, *Hellenica* 5.3.20–24.

46. Plutarch here commences the story of one of ancient history's stranger episodes, dated to 378 BCE. At that time Athens had either refounded her naval empire as the Second Athenian League, or was contemplating doing so. The Spartan Sphodrias, perhaps prompted by Theban friends, took it upon himself to make a commando raid on the Piraeus, in an attempt to capture it. Doing so would have given Sparta total control over Athens, since the Athenians had to import food supplies by way of the harbor.

47. The boeotarchs, elected annually, formed a kind of executive board leading the military operations and foreign policy of the Boeotian League.

48. Apparently the ill-planned raid had simply gotten a late start; the raiders were still in the Thriasian plain, several miles from the Piraeus, when daylight revealed them.

49. Eleusis was a religious site and the center of the Athenian cult of the Mysteries. The lights seen there by Sphodrias were interpreted as signs of divine favor for Athens.

to Thespiae. After this, accusers were sent to Sparta from Athens, but found that the magistrates there had no need of an accusation against Sphodrias, since they had themselves indicted him on a capital charge. Sphodrias had decided not to face the charge, since he feared the anger of his fellow citizens, who were ashamed before the Athenians and wished to appear to have been injured along with them, lest they be thought to have abetted Sphodrias' wrongdoing.

[26] When Sphodrias was acquitted, and the Athenians, on learning of it, prepared for war, Agesilaus was severely maligned, as he was thought to have prevented a fair trial because of an absurd and childish desire, and to have made the city an accessory to serious transgressions against the Greeks. When he saw that Cleombrotus was not eager to make war on the Thebans, Agesilaus disregarded the law he had invoked previously with regard to the expedition, and he himself now invaded Boeotia, inflicting harm on the Thebans and suffering harm in turn, with the result that on one occasion, when Agesilaus was wounded, Antalcidas said to him, "You are certainly receiving handsome tuition fees from the Thebans, having taught them to fight despite their reluctance and ignorance." For it is reported that the Thebans had by then become outstandingly warlike, having acquired practice in their many campaigns against the Spartans. It was for this reason that the ancient Lycurgus, in his so-called *rhetras*, forbade the Spartans to fight frequently with the same men, lest the latter learn how to wage war.[50]

[27] In that period the Spartans suffered many defeats both on land and at sea, the most important being the defeat at Tegyra, where they were overpowered in a pitched battle for the first time and defeated by the Thebans. It therefore seemed best to everyone to conclude a general peace, and ambassadors from Greece convened in Sparta to arrange a settlement. One of the ambassadors was Epaminondas,[51] a man esteemed for his culture and philosophy, though he had not yet given proof of his generalship. He alone, when he saw all the others yielding to Agesilaus, expressed his opinion frankly and presented an argument not on behalf of Thebes but

50. See *Lycurgus* 13.

51. The first political role played by Epaminondas, the great Theban leader who was to dominate the stage of Greek history for the next decade, dates to 371 BCE. Though the Plutarchan *Life* of Epaminondas has been lost, that of his close associate Pelopidas, in this volume, gives much information about him.

of Greece as a whole: he declared that war, while exalting Sparta, brought wretched suffering to all the other cities, and he urged that the peace be based on equality and justice, since it would endure only if all parties to it were equals.

[28] Observing that the Greeks heeded Epaminondas and admired him enormously, Agesilaus asked him whether he thought it justice and equality for Boeotia to be independent.[52] When Epaminondas quickly and boldly asked in turn whether *he* thought it justice for Laconia to be independent, Agesilaus angrily ordered him to say clearly whether he would allow Boeotian autonomy. When Epaminondas, again answering with the same question, asked whether *he* would allow Laconian autonomy, Agesilaus became so enraged that he welcomed the pretext to erase the name of the Thebans from the peace treaty at once and declare war on them. . . .

At that time Cleombrotus happened to be in Phocis with an army. The ephors immediately sent him orders to lead his force against the Thebans. They also sent word ordering their allies to assemble. The allied cities, though unready and oppressed by the war, were not yet bold enough to contradict or disobey the Spartans. Though many ominous signs appeared, as has been mentioned in my *Life of Epaminondas*,[53] and Prothous the Laconian opposed the expedition, Agesilaus did not give up, but inaugurated the war in the expectation that with all of Greece on their side, and the Thebans in violation of the treaty, it was the right moment to exact a penalty from them. That it was considered "the right moment" proves that this expedition resulted more from anger than from calculation. For they concluded the treaty at Sparta on the fourteenth of Scirophorion, and on the fifth of Hecatombaeon they were defeated at Leuctra, twenty days having elapsed.[54] A thousand Spartans died along with

52. See chapter 23 and note 37. The Peace of Antalcidas of 387 BCE required that regional powers such as Thebes break up their "leagues" or hegemonies. Sparta was in a somewhat different position, dominating its region, Laconia, not through a formal league but either through armed occupation (in the case of Messenia) or intimidation and political manipulation. In the diplomatic exchange described here, Epaminondas attempted to equate Sparta's situation with that of Thebes and insisted that the treaty terms apply to both.

53. One of the lost *Lives*.

54. Plutarch here omits a description of the crucial battle of Leuctra (371 BCE), seeing that Agesilaus was not involved. See *Pelopidas* 23 for Plutarch's description, or, more fully, Xenophon's *Hellenica* 6.4.4–15.

Cleombrotus their king and his retinue, which included the strongest of the Spartans. Among them was Cleonymus, the beautiful son of Sphodrias, who they say fell three times in front of the king, rose as many times to his feet, and died fighting the Thebans.

[31] Thereafter Epaminondas arrived in Laconia[55] with his allies—a host that included no fewer than forty thousand hoplites. Many light-armed and unarmed troops, bent on plunder, accompanied the force, with the result that, all told, a throng of seventy thousand made an inroad together into Laconia. No fewer than six hundred years had elapsed since the Dorians had settled in Sparta, yet this was the first time an enemy was seen in the country; in all that time, none had dared to enter. Invading a country that had never been ravaged or touched, they plundered and burned it as far as the river and the city, since no one came out to oppose them. For Agesilaus would not allow the Spartans to face so large "a stream and surge of war," as Theopompus[56] phrases it. Instead, after concentrating his troops in the central and most commanding parts of the city, he endured the threats and boasts of the Thebans, who were challenging him by name and urging him to fight for his country, since he, by sparking the war, was responsible for its plight. Agesilaus was equally harassed by the tumult and shouting within the city and the running to and fro of the elderly men, who were greatly vexed at what was happening, and the women who were unable to keep still but were altogether beside themselves when they heard the shouts and saw the fires of the enemy.[57] He was also worried about his reputation; having assumed authority over the city when she was at the peak of her power, he was witnessing her loss of prestige and the disproving of the boast he himself had often made, that no Spartan woman had ever seen the smoke of an enemy's fire.

[32] Yet they say it was then that Antalcidas, who was an ephor, became so fearful that he secretly sent his children to Cythera. But Agesilaus, when the enemy tried to cross the river and force its way to

---

55. Epaminondas, the great Theban general who had won at Leuctra, followed up his victory by leading a bold invasion of the Peloponnese and a direct attack on Sparta, the first ever in its long history. See *Pelopidas* 24 for a description of this same invasion from the Theban perspective.

56. A fourth century BCE historian whose work is now lost.

57. Sparta, unlike other Greek cities, was unwalled, having never before had need of fortifications. Hence the population had a full view of the enemy's approach.

the city, abandoned her other neighborhoods and arrayed his forces in front of her central heights. The Eurotas was then flowing at its fullest and widest, as snow had fallen, though the Thebans who tried to ford it were troubled less by its turbulence than by its icy coldness. When Epaminondas was crossing it at the head of his phalanx, he was pointed out to Agesilaus; and he, as we are told, after gazing at Epaminondas and watching him for a long time, said only: "A mover of mountains!"

Epaminondas was eager to join battle in the city and erect a trophy there; but when he was unable to draw or tempt Agesilaus out, he retired and set about plundering the countryside.[58] Meanwhile, some two hundred of the Spartans who had long been discontented and disloyal banded together and seized the Issorium, where the shrine of Artemis lies—a position well-fortified and hard to overpower. The Spartans wished to assault them at once, but Agesilaus, afraid of their sedition, ordered the others to keep still while he himself, wearing a cloak and attended by one servant, approached the shrine and shouted to the men that they had misheard his order; he said he had not commanded them to gather there or in a mass, but some *there* (pointing to a different place) and the rest at another part of the city. Those who heard him were pleased, thinking they had escaped detection, whereupon they separated and went to the posts he ordered them to occupy. Sending at once for other men, Agesilaus seized the Issorium, and when he had arrested some fifteen of the conspirators he had them put them to death overnight. But then he was informed of a second and larger conspiracy of Spartans who held meetings in a private house and were plotting a revolution. It was impracticable either to bring these men to trial in a time of such turmoil or to disregard their plots. After consulting the ephors, Agesilaus also put these men to death without trial, though no Spartan had ever before been summarily executed.[59] At that time many of the country folk and helots who had been enrolled in the army ran away from the city and joined the enemy, and this caused great despondency. Agesilaus therefore instructed his servants to go to the barracks every morning

58. Having come right up to the outskirts of Sparta, Epaminondas declined to plunder the city or attack its resident population. Thebes did not have the resources for a permanent occupation, and probably wanted Sparta to remain independent as a counterweight to Athens. Plutarch discusses other reasons at the end of this chapter.

59. A telling indication of the depth of the crisis and of Agesilaus' desperation.

and appropriate the weapons of deserters and hide them, so that their numbers might not be known.

As for why the Thebans withdrew from Laconia, most writers say that when the winter storms arrived the Arcadians began to depart and drift away in disorder; others say that after three whole months they had plundered most of the country; but Theopompus says that when the boeotarchs had already decided to depart, they were approached by Phrixus, a Spartan, who brought ten talents from Agesilaus as the reward for their withdrawal, with the result that they did what they had long decided to do and received traveling expenses from their enemy as well.

[33] I have no idea how all the other writers remained unaware of this story, but only Theopompus heard it. Yet everyone agrees that on that occasion Agesilaus earned the credit for Sparta's salvation by resisting his own innate tendencies—his contentiousness and ambition—and adhering to a policy of caution. He was unable, however, to recover the city's power and glory after her defeat, but as is true for a body that, though healthy, follows an excessively strict regimen at all times, it took only one critical error to undermine the city's well-being.

[34] When Messene was settled by Epaminondas,[60] her former citizens traveled there together from all sides. Though the Spartans did not dare to resist and could not prevent this, they nonetheless resented and were out of humor with Agesilaus because a land no smaller in area than Laconia and unsurpassed in Greece for fertility, whose possession and produce they had enjoyed for so long a time, had been lost to them during his reign. This was also why Agesilaus did not accept the peace offered by the Thebans. Unwilling to formally cede to them the territory they actually held, he persisted in his resistance, and consequently not only failed to recover Messenia, but nearly lost Sparta as well when he was outgeneraled.[61] For when

60. After threatening Sparta directly by his military incursion, Epaminondas struck a serious blow at the foundations of Spartan power by liberating Messenia (370 BCE), the region long enslaved by Sparta and exploited for agricultural produce. The helots who were formerly Spartan slaves were resettled into a city, Messene, and given the means to defend themselves against Spartan attack.

61. The context of the action here is unusually opaque. Plutarch has skipped ahead to 362 BCE, the time of a second invasion of the Peloponnese by Theban forces led by Epaminondas. After making a feint toward Mantinea and drawing Agesilaus' army there, Epaminondas changed course and

the Mantineans were again at odds with the Thebans and summoned the Spartans, Epaminondas, learning that Agesilaus had marched out with a force and was drawing near, broke up his camp without attracting the Mantineans' notice, led his army overnight from Tegea to Sparta itself, slipped past Agesilaus, and came very close to seizing the deserted city. But Euthynus of Thespiae, according to Callisthenes (or, according to Xenophon, a Cretan), brought word to Agesilaus, who quickly sent a horseman to alert the city; and shortly afterward he himself entered Sparta. A little while later, when the Thebans crossed the Eurotas and mounted an attack on the city, Agesilaus defended it vigorously and in a manner one would not have expected of a man his age. For he did not, as formerly, think that the crisis required safety and caution, but rather desperation and daring recklessness, in which at other times he never trusted or indulged; but on the present occasion it was by these alone that he thrust away the danger, snatched the city from the hands of Epaminondas, and erected a trophy.

[35] A few days later they fought near Mantinea,[62] and when Epaminondas had overpowered the front ranks and was still eagerly pursuing them, Anticrates the Laconian struck him with a spear, as Dioscurides has reported, though even today the Spartans call the descendants of Anticrates "Machaeriones," or swordsmen, on the grounds that he struck Epaminondas with a sword. For their dread of Epaminondas while he lived was so great that they admired and adored Anticrates, awarded him honors and gifts, and granted his family exemption from public burdens, which Callicrates, one of Anticrates' descendants, enjoys to this day.

After the battle and the death of Epaminondas, when the Greek cities had made peace with one another, Agesilaus and his associates tried to exclude the Messenians from the oath on the grounds that they had no city.[63] And when all the other Greeks welcomed the Messenians and accepted their oaths, the Spartans held aloof; they alone remained at war in the hope of recovering Messenia. Agesilaus was therefore thought to be violent, stubborn, and insatiable for wars; for he did everything he could to undermine and upset mutual

headed straight for Sparta, now undefended. Agesilaus had to work fast to save the city, as described below.
62. This battle of Mantinea (to be distinguished from an earlier battle of the same name; see *Alcibiades* 15) took place in 362 BCE.
63. A rejection of the liberation of the helots achieved by Epaminondas; see note 60.

reconciliations and was again compelled by lack of funds to burden his friends in the city and to borrow and receive contributions from them.

By 361 BCE Agesilaus was in his eighties and had reigned as Spartan king for four decades. He was still a vigorous leader both on and off the battlefield, though his reputation at Sparta was decidedly mixed. Partly out of a desire to escape his critics, and partly to satisfy his boundless appetite for military action, Agesilaus went to Egypt to serve as a mercenary captain—a most surprising role for a Spartan king, because it required giving preference to foreign interests over Spartan ones, and because it was paid work.

Egypt at this time had achieved freedom from Persian rule after many earlier failed attempts. Its pharaoh, Tachos, was engaged in battles against the Persians, for which he required Greek mercenary soldiers, and hired both Agesilaus and an Athenian general, Chabrias, to lead them. The political situation in Egypt then got very complicated and Agesilaus ended up working for a new pharaoh, Nectanebo II. These machinations have been omitted from the account below as they do not have any large impact on developments in the Greek world.

[36] Agesilaus was held in even greater contempt when he offered himself as general to Tachos the Egyptian. For people did not think that a man who had been judged the finest in Greece, and who had filled the world with his renown, should place his person, name, and fame at the disposal of a barbarian who had revolted from the King, and be paid to do the work of a mercenary and commander of mercenary troops. . . . But Agesilaus gave no thought to these considerations, nor did he think any performance of a public service unworthy; it was more unworthy of him, he thought, to live idly in the city and wait for death. For this reason, after assembling mercenaries and manning vessels with the money Tachos had sent him, he put to sea, taking along thirty Spartan counselors as before.

When he had landed in Egypt, the foremost of the king's governors and commanders came straight to his ship to pay their respects. The other Egyptians were also eager and expectant, owing to Agesilaus' name and reputation, and ran en masse to set eyes on him. But when they saw no splendid array, but an elderly man lying on the grass near the sea, his appearance plain, his stature small, and his cloak rough and common, they were moved to laugh and jest, remarking that this was a case of the proverbial mountain suffering the pains of labor only to give birth to a mouse.[64]

---

64. A colorful metaphor for the disparity between a grand, portentous prelude and a humble outcome.

[40] Thereafter the Egyptian's state affairs were flourishing and his security assured. And as he loved Agesilaus and wished to show his affection, he asked the Spartan to stay and spend the winter with him. But Agesilaus was agitated about the war at home, aware that the city was maintaining mercenary troops and needed money.[65] The Egyptian, accordingly, gave him a distinguished and splendid send-off. And in addition to other decorations and gifts, Agesilaus received money for the war amounting to 230 talents.[66] It being wintertime, he kept the fleet close to shore and sailed along the Libyan coast to a deserted spot they call the harbor of Menelaus. There Agesilaus died at the age of eighty-four, having reigned as king of Sparta for forty-one years. For more than thirty of those years he had proved the greatest and most powerful of all Sparta's kings, having been regarded as leader and king of almost all of Greece until the battle of Leuctra.

As it was a Spartan custom that, whereas any ordinary man who died in a foreign land had to be buried there and left behind, their kings' remains had to be brought home, the Spartans who were with Agesilaus poured melted beeswax over the corpse, since there was no honey,[67] and carried it back to Sparta.

65. "The war at home" probably refers to continuing Spartan attempts to recover Messenia. It is interesting to note that the Spartans had begun hiring mercenaries, a practice long accepted by other Greek states but regarded with contempt by Sparta. The population of full-fledged Spartan citizens had been declining for decades, and losses in the wars with Thebes had taken a big toll.

66. Enough to hire more than three thousand men for a year's service, calculating at the rate of one drachma per day (though much is uncertain about military pay in this period).

67. Honey was normally used as a preservative in cases in which a corpse had to be transported before cremation or burial.

Pelopidas

Pelopidas (c. 410–364 BCE) was one of only two Theban leaders Plutarch featured in the Lives; *the other was Epaminondas, close ally and contemporary of Pelopidas, but that* Life *has been lost. Hence* Pelopidas *gives us Plutarch's only focused treatment of the so-called Theban hegemony, the period in the 370s and 360s when Thebes became superpower of European Greece and inflicted two major defeats on the Spartans. The same period is dealt with more briefly in later chapters of Plutarch's* Agesilaus, *as well as in Xenophon's* Hellenica *(books 6 and 7) and Diodorus'* Library of History *(15.50–88).*

[3] The family of Pelopidas, son of Hippocles, was distinguished in Thebes, as was that of Epaminondas. Reared in affluence, and inheriting, while still a young man, a splendid house, Pelopidas hastened to assist worthy men in need, that he might truly be seen as a master of wealth, not a slave to it. For most wealthy men, as Aristotle says, either make no use of their wealth through stinginess, or misuse it through prodigality, and thus they are forever enslaved, the latter by their pleasures, the former by their busyness. Everyone else who profited by Pelopidas' liberality and generosity was grateful to him; Epaminondas was the only one of his friends he could not persuade to accept a share of his wealth. . . . Now Epaminondas made his poverty, which was habitual and hereditary, even more manageable and easy by studying philosophy and choosing from the start to lead a solitary life. Pelopidas, on the other hand, made a brilliant marriage and had a number of children; but by neglecting moneymaking none the less, and devoting himself to the city, he was constantly depleting his fortune.

[4] Both men were equally well-endowed by nature to excel in every sphere, though Pelopidas delighted more in physical exercise, Epaminondas in acquiring knowledge, the one devoting his leisure to wrestling and hunting, the other to lectures and philosophy. But among the many noble traits for which the two are esteemed, sensible men consider none so great as the unquestionable good will and friendship they maintained from beginning to end, through so many struggles, campaigns, and public services.[1] For if anyone examines

---

1. The varying success with which political leaders get along with one another is a recurring theme of the *Lives*. The partnership of Epaminondas and Pelopidas at Thebes can be contrasted with the highly contentious and adversarial relations of Athenian contemporaries, as Plutarch goes on to say.

the political careers of Aristides, Themistocles, Cimon, Pericles, Nicias, or Alcibiades, and sees how full they were of quarrels, jealousies, and mutual rivalry, and then considers the good will and respect Pelopidas felt for Epaminondas, he must admit that these two men are more rightly and fairly described as colleagues and comrades-in-arms than those who applied themselves more to contending against one another than against their enemies. . . .

Most people think that their firm friendship dated from the campaign in Mantinea,[2] where they fought alongside the Spartans, who were still their friends and allies and whom they were sent from Thebes to assist. For they were posted together among the hoplites and fought opposite the Arcadians; and when the Spartan wing to which they had been assigned gave way and most of its men were routed, they locked their shields together and warded off their attackers. And when Pelopidas, who sustained seven wounds in front, fell upon a heap of dead friends and enemies, Epaminondas, though he thought that Pelopidas was no longer alive, came and stood over his body and his arms, and braved great danger, one man against many, determined to die rather than leave Pelopidas lying there. And when he, too, was in a bad way, wounded in the chest by a spear and in the arm by a sword, Agesipolis, the Spartan king,[3] came to the rescue from the other wing and unexpectedly saved both men.

[5] Thereafter, though the Spartans ostensibly dealt with the Thebans as friends and allies, they in fact viewed Thebes' arrogance and power with suspicion. They especially hated the party of Ismenias and Androcleides, to which Pelopidas belonged, since it was thought to be liberal and democratic.[4] Accordingly, Archias, Leontidas, and Philip, wealthy oligarchs whose views were far from moderate, persuaded Phoebidas the Spartan to lead an army to Thebes, seize the

2. Thebes apparently participated in a Spartan attack on Mantinea in 385 BCE, though there is dispute about this, as some historians doubt Plutarch's statement that Thebes was still allied with Sparta at this time.

3. Agesipolis reigned at Sparta between 393 and 381 BCE, in tandem with the more dominant monarch Agesilaus.

4. Thebes had become split into two factions in the 390s, one leaning toward Sparta as an ally and political model, the other toward Athens. Ismenias and Androcleides led the pro-Athenian faction, which increasingly gained ascendancy over that of the pro-Spartans, led by Leontidas and Archias.

Cadmeia[5] without warning, expel those who thwarted them, and by installing an oligarchy make the Theban government subservient to the Spartans. Phoebidas was persuaded; and when he attacked the Thebans unexpectedly (they were holding their Thesmophoria)[6] and got control of the citadel, Ismenias was seized and carried off to Sparta, where he was soon put to death. But Pelopidas, Pherenicus, and Androcleidas fled with many others and were banished by proclamation. Epaminondas, however, remained at home, as he was not taken seriously; it was assumed he was a man whom philosophy rendered inactive and poverty powerless.

[6] When the Spartans had removed Phoebidas from power and fined him 100,000 drachmas,[7] but continued to occupy the Cadmeia with a garrison, all the other Greeks marveled at the absurdity of punishing the doer while esteeming the deed. As for the Thebans, they had lost their ancestral polity and been enslaved by Archias and Leontidas, nor could they even hope for any deliverance from the tyranny, which they saw was protected by the Spartan hegemony and would be impossible to overthrow until someone managed to bring Sparta's supremacy on land and sea to an end. Nevertheless, when Leontidas and his associates learned that the Theban exiles were living in Athens and were beloved by the people and honored by the nobility, they plotted against them in secret.

[7] But Pelopidas,[8] though he was among the youngest, was inciting each of the exiles in private, and at their meetings declared that it was neither noble nor honorable to allow their country to be enslaved and garrisoned, or to be content only to save themselves

5. The Cadmeia was an elevated and fortified sector of Thebes, a place from which the whole city could easily be controlled. The episode of Phoebidas' attack on the Cadmeia is also discussed in *Agesilaus* 23.

6. A religious festival celebrated by the Thebans in summer. Theban women used the Cadmeia for their rituals during the festival, making it all the easier for an invader to capture it. The Spartan attack occurred in 382 BCE.

7. The response of the Spartan government to Phoebidas' seizure of the Cadmeia, an act it had not authorized, is discussed in more detail in *Agesilaus* 23–24. Agesilaus mitigated Phoebidas' punishment and may even have paid his fine (which was enormous).

8. The scene has now shifted to Athens, where Pelopidas (and other prodemocracy leaders) have fled following the seizure of the Cadmeia. The time scale is unclear in Plutarch's narrative, but the exiles seem to have spent about three years in Athens.

and survive, relying on the decrees of the Athenians and forever
flattering and fawning on clever speakers to persuade the people.[9]
Instead they should be braving danger for the sake of an ideal and
adopting as a model the courage and prowess of Thrasybulus: just
as *he* had previously set out from Thebes and deposed the tyrants in
Athens,[10] so *they*, in turn, should march from Athens and liberate
Thebes. Persuaded by these arguments, they secretly sent word to the
friends they had left in Thebes, telling them what had been decided.
These men approved; and Charon, a man of great distinction, agreed
to offer them his house.

[8] When a day had been fixed for the undertaking,[11] the exiles
decided that Pherenicus should assemble the others and remain in
the Thriasian plain while a few of the youngest tried to enter the city;
and if these men came to grief at the hands of the enemy, all the rest
should see to it that neither their children nor their parents suffered
any want. Pelopidas was the first to undertake the exploit. . . . Twelve
men in all, they embraced those who remained behind, sent a messenger ahead to Charon, and marched forth wearing short cloaks,
accompanied by hunting dogs and carrying poles hung with nets,
so that they might be taken for hunters tramping about the country,
and not arouse suspicion in anyone who encountered them. When
their messenger reached Charon and said that they were on the way,
Charon himself did not change his mind despite the imminent danger, but kept his word and offered them his house.

[9] Pelopidas and his friends, after changing into farmers'
clothes, separated and stole into the city at various points while it
was still day. There was some wind and snow, as the weather was
beginning to change, which greatly assisted their concealment, since

9. That is, to try to win Athenian military support by political agitation.

10. The reference is to the fall of the Thirty at Athens in 403 BCE, engineered by Thrasybulus. This was another instance of an oligarchic government, supported by a Spartan garrison, being overthrown by the return of
prodemocracy exiles.

11. Plutarch's vivid account of the liberation of Thebes from Spartan control can be contrasted with that of Xenophon (*Hellenica* 5.4.2–12), in which
Pelopidas is not even mentioned (as an admirer and supporter of Sparta,
Xenophon was biased against Pelopidas and the Theban regime of the 370s
and 360s BCE). The events described in what follows occurred in late 379.
The generous space Plutarch gives to them is explained in his closing comment (chapter 13), that this was the beginning of almost two decades of
warfare between Thebes and Sparta.

most people were fleeing to their houses to avoid the storm. But those whose business it was to know what was happening received the men when they arrived and immediately brought them to Charon's house. They numbered forty-eight, including the exiles.

The tyrants' affairs stood thus. Phillidas the secretary was in sympathy with the exiles, collaborated with them in everything, and well in advance of that day had invited Archias and his friends to a carousal and a party that included some married women, his plan being that when they were completely relaxed by their pleasures and the wine, he would hand them over to the conspirators. But when the drinking had barely begun, some news reached them about the exiles, not false, but uncertain and very vague, to the effect that they were being concealed in the city. Phillidas tried to turn the conversation, but Archias sent one of his attendants to Charon, ordering him to come at once. It was evening, and Pelopidas and his friends in the house were preparing themselves, having already donned breastplates and taken up their swords. Suddenly there was a knock at the door. Someone ran to it, and after learning from the attendant that he had come from the polemarchs to summon Charon, returned in great confusion, bringing the news. It immediately occurred to everyone that their plot had been revealed and that they would perish before they had done anything worthy of their valor. Nevertheless, it was decided that Charon should obey and present himself to the magistrates to allay suspicion.

[10] When Charon had reached the door, Archias came out with Phillidas and said, "Charon, I have heard that certain men have entered the city and are concealing themselves, and that some of the citizens are collaborating with them." At first Charon was upset; but then, when he asked who had arrived and who was hiding them, he saw that Archias had no definite information; and suspecting that the report had not come from knowledgeable sources, he said, "Don't let yourself be disturbed by an empty rumor. Nevertheless, I shall look into the matter; for I suppose no rumor should be taken lightly." Phillidas, who was present, approved of this, and after leading Archias back, engaged him in a long bout of heavy drinking and diverted the party with his hopes of a visit from the women. But when Charon returned home and found the men there equipped not as if they were expecting victory or deliverance, but as if they were about to die gloriously after a great slaughter of their enemies, he told

Pelopidas the truth, but deceived the rest, pretending that Archias had talked to him about something else.[12]

[11] Now that the right moment for their venture seemed to have come, they set out in two bands: one with Pelopidas and Damocleidas against Leontidas and Hypates, who lived near one another, the other with Charon and Melon against Archias and Philip. The men in the latter band had thrown women's clothing over their breastplates and wore dense garlands of fir and pine that kept their faces in shadow, which was why, when they stood at the door of the drinking party, the company raised a rumpus and applauded, thinking that the women they had long been expecting had arrived. When the visitors, after looking around at the party and taking careful note of each of the reclining guests, drew their swords, rushed among the tables toward Archias and Philip, and revealed who they were, Phillidas persuaded a few of the company to keep still; the rest, who rose up together and sought to defend themselves with the polemarchs, were easily dispatched, since they were drunk.

The men with Pelopidas met with a more difficult task; for they were going after Leontidas, a sober and clever man, and found the door of his house barred, since he had already retired; and though they knocked for a long time, no one heard them. When Leontidas' servant finally heard the knocking, he came out and released the bolt from inside. As soon as the door yielded and gave way, they all burst in together, toppled the servant, and dashed toward the bedroom. Guessing from the din and the running what was afoot, Leontidas stood up from his bed and drew his dagger, but did not think to tip over the lamps and make the men fall against one another in the dark. Seen in full light, he met them at his bedroom door and struck and killed Cephisodorus, the first man to enter. When Cephisodorus had fallen and Leontidas came to blows with Pelopidas, their struggle was frustrated and hampered both by the narrowness of the doorway and the fact that it was now blocked by Cephisodorus' corpse. But Pelopidas prevailed, and after dispatching Leontidas led his men against Hypates. They stole into his house in the same way; and though he became aware at once and fled for protection to his neighbors, they pursued him closely, and caught and killed him.

12. It is not clear why Charon deceives all of the exiles except Pelopidas. Perhaps he thought their morale would be harmed if they thought Archias even suspected their presence in the city.

[13] Thereafter, elected boeotarch[13] with Melon and Charon, Pelopidas immediately blockaded the Acropolis and mounted attacks from all directions, since he was eager to oust the Spartans and liberate the Cadmeia before an army approached from Sparta. And he anticipated the Spartans by so small a margin that after releasing the men under a truce, they had only reached Megara when they were met by Cleombrotus marching against Thebes with a large force. Of the three Spartan governors in Thebes, the Spartans condemned and executed Herippas and Arcissus; the third, Lysanoris, was fined an enormous sum and emigrated from the Peloponnese.

This exploit, similar to that of Thrasybulus[14] with respect to the courage, dangers, and struggles of its participants, and likewise favored by good fortune, was declared by the Greeks to be a sister to it. For one cannot easily mention other instances where men so bereft of numbers and resources prevailed by daring and cleverness and gained credit for conferring such benefits on their countries. And the change it wrought in their political fortunes made the exploit particularly estimable. For the war that destroyed the prestige of Sparta and ended the Spartan supremacy on land and sea began on that night when Pelopidas, not by seizing a garrison or a wall or a citadel, but by entering a house with eleven others, shattered and severed—if one may employ a metaphor to express the truth—the bonds of the Spartan hegemony that were thought to be indissoluble and unbreakable.

A Spartan army, led by King Cleombrotus, invaded Boeotia in the aftermath of the coup of 379 BCE but failed to restore the Spartan garrison on the Cadmeia. King Agesilaus led a second invasion the following year, which resulted in the dramatic Theban victories described below.

[15] Both at Plataea and Thespiae the Spartans were defeated and put to flight. Phoebidas, who had seized the Cadmeia, died at Thespiae; he had also routed many Spartans at Tanagra, where he killed Panthoidas, the governor. But these clashes, though they instilled

13. The office of boeotarch combined the duties of military leader, diplomat, and foreign policy strategist. There were varying numbers of boeotarchs, sometimes eleven, at other times seven, elected for one-year terms. The office had been abolished after the Boeotian League was disbanded in 386 BCE, at Sparta's insistence; so the reestablishment of it here is clearly an effort to throw off all Spartan influence in the region.

14. See chapter 7 and note 10.

pride and confidence in the victors, did not altogether vanquish the spirit of the defeated. For it was not in pitched battles or engagements having any visible or proper order, but by making opportune charges, undertaking routs and pursuits, and fighting with the enemy at close quarters that the Thebans were enjoying success.

[16] But the engagement at Tegyra,[15] which in some sense turned out to be a preliminary contest before the battle of Leuctra, greatly exalted Pelopidas' reputation, since it left his co-commanders no basis on which to rival his success, and the enemy no excuse for their defeat. Against the city of Orchomenus, which had sided with the Spartans and received two of their detachments to provide security, he was constantly plotting and watching for an opportunity; and when he heard that its garrison had gone on a campaign to Locris, he marched to Orchomenus with the Sacred Band[16] and a small number of horsemen, expecting to find the city deserted. But when he approached the city and found that a relief force had arrived from Sparta, he led the expedition back through Tegyra, which afforded the only circuit along the foot of the mountains; for the country's entire plain is made impassable by the river Melas, whose waters are dispersed right from their source into navigable marshes and lakes.

[17] The Thebans, after leaving Orchomenus, entered Tegyra at the same time as the Spartans, who were returning from Locris—the two forces arriving from opposite directions. When the Spartans were first seen marching through the pass and someone ran up to Pelopidas and said, "We have fallen into our enemies' hands," he replied, "And why not they into ours?" He at once ordered his entire cavalry to ride up from the rear in order to charge, while he himself gathered his three hundred hoplites[17] into a compact array, expecting that wherever his phalanx charged it would cut through the enemy, who outnumbered them. There were two divisions of Spartans. (Ephorus says a division consisted of five hundred men, Callisthenes of seven hundred, and other writers, of whom Polybius is one, of nine hundred.) Full of confidence, the Spartan polemarchs, Gorgoleon and Theopompus, advanced against the Thebans. A forceful onslaught being made chiefly where the commanders from both sides were posted, the Spartan polemarchs, first of all, clashed with Pelopidas and fell; then, when those around them were being

15. A Theban victory over the invading Spartans; see *Agesilaus* 27.
16. An elite infantry unit; see chapter 18.
17. The Sacred Band, discussed in more detail in chapter 18.

struck and slain, their entire army was seized with fear and opened a lane for the Thebans in the belief that they wished to pass through and escape. But when Pelopidas used the opening to lead his men against the enemy soldiers who were still in array, and slew them as he went by, they all fled headlong. The pursuit was carried only a little way, however, since the Thebans feared the Orchomenians, who were nearby, as well as the relief force of the Spartans. But they had succeeded in defeating the enemy decisively and forcing their way through the entire defeated army. After setting up a trophy and stripping the corpses,[18] they headed homeward, exultant. For in all their previous wars with Greeks and barbarians, it seems that the Spartans, when superior in number, had never before been overpowered by an inferior force, nor, indeed, in a pitched battle against an enemy whose numbers equaled theirs.

[18] The Sacred Band, it is said, was first formed by Gorgidas[19] from three hundred handpicked men, for whom the city provided training and board and who encamped in the Cadmeia;[20] that was why they were also called the City Band; for in those days the citadels were appropriately called cities. Some say that this company was made up of lovers and beloveds.[21] . . . The corps bound together by the friendship of lovers is indissoluble and unbreakable, since lovers who love their beloveds, and beloveds who feel shame before their lovers, stand firm in danger for one another's sake. . . . Thus it was natural that the band be called sacred, since even Plato called the lover a divinely inspired friend.[22] It is said that the band remained

18. The erection of a trophy or monument on the field, and the stripping of armor from enemy dead, are both traditional signifiers of victory in battle.

19. A member of Pelopidas' political faction who took part in the overthrow of the Spartan occupation force.

20. State-supplied training and pay for the men of the Sacred Band essentially made them a professional army corps, a rare thing in the classical Greek world.

21. The terms "lover" and "beloved" translate the Greek terms *erastēs* and *erōmenos*, denoting, respectively, the older, pursuing member of a male homosexual couple and the younger, pursued member. The normal pattern for such relationships involved an older man and an adolescent, rather than two men close in age.

22. See Plato's *Phaedrus* 255b and *Symposium* 179a. The passage in the *Symposium* specifically mentions homosexual desire as a spur toward military bravery. Plato wrote that dialogue at about the same time that Gorgidas

undefeated until the battle of Chaeronea;[23] and when, after the battle, Philip was surveying the corpses and stopped at the place where the three hundred lay dead in their armor, having faced his phalanx's spears, he was astonished; and when he learned that this was the band of lovers and beloveds, he wept and said, "May they perish basely who suppose that these men did or suffered anything shameful."

[19] Gorgidas, by distributing the members of this Sacred Band into the front ranks and deploying them with the entire phalanx of hoplites, did not make the men's valor conspicuous, nor did he deploy the band on a venture of its own, since its members were distributed and dispersed throughout the large body of inferior troops. But Pelopidas, after their valor shone out at Tegyra, where they fought on their own and around his own person, stopped dividing or separating them, and deployed them, in his most important battles, as a single unit.[24]

[20] When the Spartans had made peace with all the other Greeks and launched a war solely against the Thebans,[25] and King Cleombrotus invaded with ten thousand hoplites and one thousand horsemen, the Thebans' danger was not what it had been formerly; they faced an outright threat and a proclamation calling for their removal, and fear possessed Boeotia as never before. . . . On proceeding to the camp and finding that the boeotarchs were not of one mind, Pelopidas was the first to support the judgment of Epaminondas, who voted to do battle with the enemy. (Pelopidas had not been appointed

---

formed the Sacred Band, but it is not clear whether either was aware of the other's ideas.

23. At Chaeronea in 338 BCE, the Macedonians under Philip and Alexander the Great defeated the combined armies of Athens and Thebes. Alexander personally oversaw the complete destruction of the Sacred Band (see *Alexander* 9).

24. Plutarch's brief note about the redeployment of the Sacred Band as a unit bespeaks a huge change in battlefield tactics during the fourth century BCE. Greek generals were beginning to think not in terms of maintaining consistent strength along a long battle line but rather of concentrating deadly force at a single point and using it to break the enemy's formation. Epaminondas (see chapter 23), and later Philip of Macedon and Alexander, were instrumental in developing this new approach.

25. The conflict referred to here resulted from the failure of the peace conference of 371 BCE, when Agesilaus and Epaminondas became embroiled in a dispute (see *Agesilaus* 28).

boeotarch;[26] but he served as leader of the Sacred Band and was rightly trusted as a man who had given his country signal proof that he was devoted to her freedom.)

[23] In the battle,[27] when Epaminondas drew the phalanx at an oblique angle toward the left wing so that the Spartans' right wing might be farthest from the other Greeks and he could thrust Cleombrotus back by attacking in flank with all his men at once, the enemy soldiers, on learning what was afoot, began to change their own formation, opening out their right wing and drawing it around so as to encircle and encompass Epaminondas with their superior numbers. At that point Pelopidas dashed forward and rallied his three hundred,[28] arriving on the run before Cleombrotus had time to expand his wing or gather it back to the same spot and close his ranks, and fell on the Spartans when they were out of formation and throwing one another into disarray. And yet the Spartans, who of all men are consummately skilled in the military arts, had trained and accustomed themselves above all else not to straggle or become distressed when their phalanx was disrupted, but to resume formation, with captains and hoplites all arrayed together, and to position themselves wherever the danger lay, remain united, and fight as well as ever. But on the present occasion, when Epaminondas' phalanx was aiming his charge only at the Spartans and ignoring the other Greeks, Pelopidas, displaying incredible speed and daring, so confounded their resolution and skill that he achieved a flight and slaughter of Spartans greater than any that had ever been seen before. For this reason, whereas Epaminondas was a boeotarch and Pelopidas was not, the latter, though he commanded only a small portion of the entire force, nevertheless shared equally in the glory of their victory and success.

[24] Both boeotarchs invaded the Peloponnese and won over most of its peoples, causing Elis, Argos, all of Arcadia, and most of Laconia itself to revolt from the Spartans. But since the winter solstice was upon them and only a few days remained of the last month of the year, it was necessary either that other commanders assume office at the start of the new year,[29] or that those who

26. For boeotarchs, see note 13. A new board of boeotarchs was chosen at the end of December, as related in chapter 24.

27. The battle of Leuctra in 371 BCE.

28. Again, the Sacred Band.

29. See note 26.

would not cede command be put to death. The other boeotarchs, dreading the law and wishing to avoid a winter campaign, were eager to lead the army home; but Pelopidas, who was the first to vote with Epaminondas, helped him hearten the citizens and led them to Sparta and across the Eurotas. He seized many of the enemy's cities and plundered the entire country as far as the sea, leading an expedition that included seventy thousand Greeks, less than a twelfth of whom were Thebans.[30] . . . In that campaign, they united all of Arcadia in one force, and on severing the Messenian territory from its Spartan masters, summoned and restored the old inhabitants of Messenia, with whom they settled Ithome.[31] Heading home through Cenchreae, they defeated the Athenians who tried to hinder their march by skirmishing with them at the passes.[32]

[25] In recognition of these achievements, all the other Greeks made much of their prowess and marveled at their good fortune; but the political jealousy of their fellow citizens, which increased with the men's glory, was preparing no appropriate or honorable reception for them. For both men, on their return, were prosecuted on a capital charge for violating the law stipulating that the office of boeotarch be surrendered to others in the first month of the year, which they call Bucation. Epaminondas and Pelopidas had retained authority for four additional months, during which time they had conducted their campaigns in Messenia, Arcadia, and Laconia. Pelopidas was brought to trial first and was therefore in greater danger, but both men were acquitted.[33]

---

30. This same invasion is recounted from the Spartan point of view in *Agesilaus* 31–33. The Thebans withdrew from Laconia before plundering the city of Sparta itself, for reasons about which Plutarch was unclear (see *Agesilaus* 32).

31. The Messenians, otherwise known as helots, had been enslaved by the Spartans for centuries. Their liberation by the Thebans was a blow aimed at the very heart of the Spartan system, by which helot agricultural labor freed Spartan citizens to train for war. Ithome was an easily defensible piece of high ground in central Messenia.

32. According to the peace conference arrangements of 371 BCE, the Athenians, as well as all other signatories, were obliged to support Sparta after it had come under attack by Thebes.

33. It is not surprising that Plutarch gives short shrift to this trial, since he reports elsewhere (*Moralia* 540d) that Pelopidas did himself no credit by weeping publicly and begging for mercy.

*The last years of Pelopidas' life, 368–364 BCE, saw several Theban incursions
into the northern regions of Thessaly and Macedonia. Traditionally these
regions were part of the Athenian sphere of influence, but Thebes, as its
power grew, began to assert itself as well, especially when called in by one
faction or another in the dynastic disputes there. One regional development
in particular troubled the progressive, democratic regime at Thebes: the rise
of a cruel and aggressive tyrant, Alexander of Pherae, who took power in
Thessaly thanks to the support of a large corps of mercenaries. Pelopidas felt
both an ideological and personal hatred of this man, and he devoted intense
efforts to controlling or removing him.*

[26] When Alexander of Pherae[34] was openly making war on most
of the Thessalians, but plotting against them all, their cities sent
an embassy to Thebes requesting a general and a force. Seeing that
Epaminondas was occupied in the Peloponnese, Pelopidas offered
and dedicated himself to the Thessalians, both because he could
not bear to let his own expertise and ability lie idle, and because he
thought that wherever Epaminondas was there was no need for a
second commander. When he had marched to Thessaly with a force
and immediately took Larissa, and Alexander arrived and pleaded for
a reconciliation, Pelopidas tried to transform him from a tyrant into
a man who would govern the Thessalians gently and according to
law. But since Alexander was incorrigible and brutal, and was much
denounced for his licentiousness and greed, Pelopidas grew exasperated and severe with him, whereupon Alexander departed, escaping by stealth with his guards. Pelopidas then left the Thessalians
in great security from the tyrant and in concord with one another,
and departed for Macedonia, since Ptolemy was making war on
Alexander, the king of the Macedonians,[35] and both parties were
summoning Pelopidas to be a mediator, judge, ally, and helper of
the party that appeared to be wronged. When he arrived and had
resolved their differences and restored the exiles, he took as hostages
the king's brother Philip and thirty other sons of the most promi-

34. Alexander of Pherae was a Thessalian Greek who had usurped the office
of *tagos*, the headship of the Thessalian League, and begun behaving cruelly
and despotically (see chapter 29). He is not to be confused with Alexander
the Great of Macedon, the subject of *Alexander* in this volume.

35. A dynastic dispute between Alexander II of Macedon (a different ruler
from either Alexander of Pherae or Alexander the Great) and his brother-
in-law Ptolemy (not the famous Ptolemy who served under Alexander the
Great).

nent men and established them in Thebes, showing the Greeks that Thebes' reputation for strength and fairness had made great strides. This was the Philip who later went to war to enslave the Greeks;[36] but at the time he was a boy, living in Thebes with Pammenes. Consequently, he was thought to have become a zealous admirer of Epaminondas, perhaps because he understood the man's effectiveness in wars and on campaigns, which was only a small part of his goodness; but in self-control, fairness, greatness of soul, and gentleness, by virtue of which Epaminondas was truly great, Philip had no share either by nature or as a result of imitation.

[27] After this, when the Thessalians again accused Alexander of Pherae of harassing their cities, Pelopidas was dispatched on an embassy with Ismenias; but since he arrived without a force from home, not having expected a war, he was forced to use the Thessalians themselves for the emergency. Meanwhile, Macedonian affairs were again in an uproar, since Ptolemy had killed the king[37] and seized power, and the friends of the dead man were calling for Pelopidas. Since he wished to intervene but had no soldiers of his own, Pelopidas hired some mercenaries on the spot and immediately marched with them against Ptolemy. When they were near one another, Ptolemy corrupted the mercenaries with bribes and persuaded them to come over to him; and because he feared Pelopidas' renown and his very name, he met the man as his superior. After greeting him and begging his indulgence, Ptolemy agreed to act as regent for the brothers of the dead king, and to have the same enemies and friends as the Thebans;[38] as proof of his good faith, he offered as hostages his son Philoxenus and fifty of his companions. After dispatching these men to Thebes, Pelopidas himself, who resented the treachery of his mercenaries and had learned that most of their money, children, and wives had been placed for safety in Pharsalus, sought to exact sufficient revenge for their effrontery by gaining possession of these. Enlisting some of the Thessalians, he marched to Pharsalus. But

---

36. Philip II of Macedon would, two decades after this time, defeat the combined armies of Thebes and Athens at the battle of Chaeronea, together with his son Alexander the Great. As Plutarch here points out, Philip had learned while living at Thebes how to train and lead a first-rate army, techniques he later brought back to Macedonia and put into practice.

37. Alexander II of Macedon.

38. "To have the same enemies and friends" is a standard Greek formula for alliance.

just as he arrived, the tyrant Alexander[39] appeared with his force.
Pelopidas and his party, thinking he had come to justify his conduct,
went to him themselves, aware that he was abominable and murder-
ous, but expecting that because of Thebes and their own prestige and
renown, they would suffer no harm. But when Alexander saw them
approaching alone and unarmed, he had them arrested at once, seized
Pharsalus, and struck horror and fear in all his subjects, who assumed
that after such recklessness and iniquity he would spare no one, but
would behave toward all men, and in all matters, as one who had now
utterly despaired of his life.

[28] The Thebans were displeased when they learned of this
and immediately sent out an army, though from some anger at
Epaminondas they appointed other commanders to lead it. When
the tyrant had brought Pelopidas back to Pherae, he at first allowed
anyone who wished to converse with him to do so, thinking Pelopidas
had become pitiful and humble as a result of his misfortune. But
when Pelopidas encouraged the downcast citizens of Pherae to take
heart, since now the tyrant would certainly suffer punishment, and
sent word to Alexander himself, saying it was strange that day after
day he tortured and murdered his wretched citizens, who had done
no wrong, but spared *him*, whom he certainly knew would avenge
him if he escaped. Marveling at the man's proud spirit and fearlessness, Alexander said, "Why is Pelopidas in a hurry to die?" to which
Pelopidas replied, "That you may perish the sooner, by becoming
more hateful to the gods than you are now." After this, Alexander
prevented outsiders from meeting with Pelopidas.

[29] When the Theban generals, on invading Thessaly, accomplished nothing, but either from inexperience or bad luck withdrew
disgracefully, the city fined each of them a thousand drachmas and
sent Epaminondas out with a force. There was at once a great stir
among the Thessalians, who were elated by the renown of their commander; and the tyrant's affairs were on the brink of destruction, so
great was the fear that assailed the commanders and friends in his
suite, and so great the desire of his subjects to revolt and their joy at
the prospect of seeing the tyrant suffer punishment. Nevertheless
Epaminondas, who considered his own glory less important than
Pelopidas' safety, and feared that Alexander, with his affairs in disarray, might in his desperation turn like a wild beast on Pelopidas, took

39. The Thessalian usurper, Alexander of Pherae, not Alexander II of
Macedon (now dead).

his time with the war. By going about and attending to his preparations and his threatened action, he kept the tyrant guessing, and thus
neither unleashed his boldness and audacity nor provoked his spite
and passion. For he had learned of the man's savagery and his contempt for honor and justice. He knew that Alexander sometimes buried men alive, and sometimes cloaked them in skins of wild boars and
bears, set his hunting dogs at them, and either tore them apart or shot
them down, treating this as a sport; and that at Meliboea and Scotusa,
friendly allied cities, when the people were holding assemblies, he
surrounded them with his guards and slaughtered their citizens from
the youth upward. . . . But this man, intimidated by the renown and
the name and the distinction of Epaminondas' expedition,

Crouched like a slave, a fighting cock with folded wing,[40]

and quickly sent along an embassy to justify his conduct. Epaminondas, however, could not bear to make such a man a friend and ally
of the Thebans; instead he agreed to a thirty-day truce, got custody
of Pelopidas and Ismenias, and withdrew.

[30] When the Thebans learned that embassies from Sparta and
Athens were on their way to the Great King to secure an alliance,[41]
they sent Pelopidas out—an excellent plan in light of his reputation.
For, in the first place, he traveled through the King's provinces as
a man well-known and celebrated, since the renown of his battles
with the Spartans had not traveled slowly or to any slight extent
across Asia; on the contrary, as soon as the report of the battle of
Leuctra spread abroad, it was constantly enhanced by the addition of
any new success, and reached the remotest regions; and then, when
Pelopidas was seen by the satraps, generals, and commanders at the
King's court, they spoke admiringly of him, saying that this was the
man who had expelled the Spartans from land and sea, and confined

40. For dramatic effect, Plutarch quotes a line from some lost Greek tragedy. It is a line he particularly liked, since he also quoted it to describe
Alcibiades humbled by his love of Socrates (see *Alcibiades* 4).

41. The Great King (Artaxerxes, ruler of the Achaemenid Persian empire)
had for a long time now been arbitrating Greek disputes and treaty arrangements. In 367 BCE the Spartans and Athenians enlisted his help for yet
another attempt at a general peace treaty to settle European Greek affairs.
Thebes, naturally, felt isolated by such a move and tried to insert itself into
the negotiations. The parley took place at Susa in what is now Iran. (As
always in this volume, "King" when capitalized refers to the Great King of
Persia.)

between Taygetus and the Eurotas that Sparta which only recently, under Agesilaus, had embarked on a war with the Great King and the Persians over Susa and Ecbatana.[42] This naturally delighted Artaxerxes, who esteemed the man for his renown and heaped him with honors, eager as he was to be revered and courted by the greatest men. And when he saw Pelopidas in person and considered his proposals, which were more reliable than those of the Athenians and simpler than those of the Spartans, he grew even fonder of him, and, in a manner befitting a king, did not conceal his regard for the man, nor did the other envoys fail to notice that the King accorded Pelopidas his highest honors. . . . He sent him the finest and most splendid of the customary presents and granted what he requested, namely that the Greeks be independent, that Messene be inhabited,[43] and that the Thebans be regarded as hereditary friends of the King. Having obtained these answers, but declining all gifts other than tokens of gratitude and affection,[44] he set out for home.

[31] The embassy increased the good will felt for Pelopidas on his return, both because of the resettling of Messene and the autonomy of the other Greeks. But when Alexander of Pherae, reverting to his true nature, devastated several cities in Thessaly and made all the Achaeans of Phthiotis and the people of Magnesia subject to garrisons, her cities, informed that Pelopidas had returned, immediately sent embassies to Thebes requesting a force under his command. When the Thebans eagerly passed the decree, and all preparations were made and the commander about to march out, an eclipse of the sun occurred and darkness enveloped the city in daytime. Seeing everyone distressed by the visitation, Pelopidas did not think he should exert pressure on men who were terrified and despondent, or venture out with seven thousand citizens. Instead, offering the Thessalians only himself, and taking three hundred volunteers from among the foreign horsemen, he set forth, though the seers would not give their permission and the other citizens withheld their help; for the eclipse was thought to be a great sign from heaven and to have reference to a preeminent man. But Pelopidas, angered by the insults he had received, was incensed with Alexander. . . . And the

42. The Spartan invasion of Persia is described in *Agesilaus* 6–15.
43. That is, that the new settlement established by the Thebans in Messenia, a home for the newly liberated helots, could continue to exist.
44. The Great King was fantastically wealthy, and Greek visitors to his court were often reviled by other Greeks for accepting his gifts.

beauty of the venture particularly encouraged him; for at a time when the Spartans were sending generals and governors to Dionysius, the tyrant of Sicily, and the Athenians had Alexander as their paymaster and had erected a bronze statue of him as their benefactor,[45] Pelopidas longed and aspired to show that now only the Thebans were waging war on behalf of peoples oppressed by tyrants, and were overthrowing Greece's unlawful and violent dynasties.

[32] When he reached Pharsalus and mustered his force,[46] he marched at once against Alexander. And when Alexander saw that Pelopidas had few Thebans with him, while he himself had more than twice as many hoplites as the Thessalians,[47] he advanced to the temple of Thetis to meet him. When someone remarked to Pelopidas that the tyrant was coming against him with many men, Pelopidas replied, "So much the better, since there will be more for us to vanquish."

At the place known as Cynoscephalae, high sloping hills jut out to the center of the plain; both men set out to occupy these with their infantry. Pelopidas sent his horsemen, a large company of brave men, against the enemy horsemen, and they routed and pursued them into the plain. But Alexander occupied the hills first, and when the Thessalian hoplites ascended later and tried to force their way to lofty and impregnable positions, Alexander attacked and killed the foremost, while the rest, sustaining blows, accomplished nothing. Observing this, Pelopidas recalled his horsemen and ordered them to charge at the enemy infantry where it was still in formation, while he himself, grabbing a spear, ran to join those who were fighting on the hills. And by thrusting himself from behind through the ranks to the front, he inspired so much might and zeal in all his men that the enemy thought them transformed in body and soul as they came on. Two or three of their assaults

45. The Athenians, less concerned than the Thebans about Alexander's tyrannical ways, had concluded an alliance with him in 368 BCE. The reference in the previous clause is probably to Dionysius I of Syracuse, though he was succeeded at about this time by his son, Dionysius II. Both men were aggressive, expansionist rulers with whom the Spartans maintained friendly relations.

46. Pelopidas had increased his numbers with recruits from the Thessalians. Though he was still outnumbered, he had far more troops than his original corps of three hundred; otherwise, his invasion would have been suicidal.

47. That is, the Thessalian forces fighting on Pelopidas' side. Alexander was largely supported by hired mercenaries.

were repulsed by the enemy; but when Pelopidas' soldiers saw that these men, too, were attacking vigorously and that the cavalry was returning from its pursuit, they yielded, retreating in good order. When Pelopidas, watching from the heights, saw that the entire enemy army, though not yet routed, was now full of disorder and confusion, he stood and looked about, searching for Alexander himself. And when he spotted him at the right wing, encouraging and arraying the mercenaries, his anger overpowered his judgment. Inflamed at the sight and surrendering himself and his command to passion, he leaped out far ahead of the others and charged forward, crying out and challenging the tyrant. Alexander did not receive or await his assault, but retreated and concealed himself among his guards. Of the mercenaries, the first to come to blows were beaten back by Pelopidas, and some were wounded and killed; but most of them, thrusting their spears through his armor from a distance, were wounding him, until the Thessalians, greatly distressed, raced to the rescue from the hills when he had already fallen, and the cavalry, charging up, routed the entire phalanx; they then engaged in a lengthy pursuit and filled the country with corpses, striking down more than three thousand men.

[33] The fact that the Thebans who were present were distressed at the death of Pelopidas, calling him their father and savior and teacher of the greatest and noblest blessings, was not at all surprising; but the Thessalians and allies, after surpassing in their decrees every honor that can properly be bestowed on human excellence, showed even more by their grief how grateful they were to him. They say that those who were present at the engagement neither took off their breastplates nor unbridled their horses nor bound up their wounds when they learned of his death, but, still heated and in their armor, came to the corpse, and as if it were still sentient, heaped enemy spoils around the body, sheared their horses' manes, and cut off their own hair; and when they departed to their tents, many neither kindled a fire nor took a meal, but silence and dejection overwhelmed the entire camp, as if they had not won the greatest and most conspicuous victory, but had been defeated by the tyrant and enslaved.

[35] Though Pelopidas' death grieved his allies deeply, it also benefited them. For the Thebans, when they learned of Pelopidas' death, did not defer their vengeance but marched out in haste with eight thousand hoplites and seven hundred horsemen under the command of Malcitas and Diogeiton. They came upon Alexander weakened and cut off from his forces, and compelled him to restore

to the Thessalians the cities he had taken, to release the Magnesians and Achaeans in Phthiotis, to withdraw his garrisons, and to swear to follow the Thebans' lead against any enemies they commanded him to fight.[48]

48. As Plutarch goes on to relate, shortly after this, Alexander of Pherae was assassinated by his wife.

Demosthenes

Demosthenes (384–322 BCE) is one of the only figures in Plutarch's Lives *who had no military achievements. Indeed, Plutarch repeats a story, possibly apocryphal, that Demosthenes threw away his shield and ran from the enemy on the only occasion when he fought in arms, at the battle of Chaeronea. Plutarch nevertheless admires Demosthenes for eloquence, tireless pursuit of political goals, and what he regarded as ideologic constancy (opinions have differed on this, as Plutarch acknowledges in chapter 13). He gave Demosthenes a noble, and highly moving, exit from the historical stage.*

The events of Demosthenes *give us our only Plutarchan narrative of the rise of Philip, king of Macedon and father of Alexander the Great, starting in 358. By any measure, Philip was an extraordinary leader who brought Macedonia from humble status to domination of the entire Balkan Peninsula in a single generation. Plutarch would have done well to compose a life of Philip but chose instead to take Philip's even more extraordinary son Alexander the Great as one of his subjects. As a result there is a gap in the historical record provided by Plutarch's* Lives, *between the death of Pelopidas in 364 and the point at which Demosthenes begins to speak against Philip in the Athenian assembly, about 351.*

[4] Demosthenes, the father of Demosthenes, was a member of the nobility, as Theopompus reports, and was nicknamed "the Sword-maker," as he owned a large workshop and slaves skilled in that trade. . . . When Demosthenes, at age seven, was left well provided for by his father (the value of his entire estate fell little short of fifteen talents), he was ill-used by his guardians, who embezzled part of his fortune and neglected the rest, and consequently even his teachers were robbed of their wages. That was one reason he appears not to have been instructed in the subjects suitable and proper for a freeborn lad; another was his physical weakness and delicacy, since his mother would not permit him to engage in physical exercise, nor did his instructors insist that he do so. For Demosthenes was scrawny and sickly from the start, and it is said that the boys who made fun of him for his physique gave him the derogatory nickname "Stutterer."

[6] When he came of age Demosthenes began by taking his guardians to court and writing speeches denouncing them, in response to which they devised many evasions and additional trials. Having gained practice by these exercises, in which, to use the phrasing of Thucydides, he took on challenges both boldly and

energetically, he achieved considerable success. Though he was unable to recover even a small portion of his patrimony, he acquired confidence and sufficient practice in public speaking; and once he had tasted the prestige and the feeling of power associated with contests, he ventured to come forth and take part in public affairs. . . .

Yet when he first appeared in the assembly he met with uproars and was laughed at for his inexperience, since his discourse seemed to have been muddied up by his long sentences and too harshly and immoderately strained by his rhetorical syllogisms. It also appears that the weakness of his voice, a tendency to slur his words, and shortness of breath further confused the sense of his remarks by throwing his complicated sentences into disarray.

[11] To overcome his physical disadvantages Demosthenes adopted the practices described by Demetrius of Phalerum,[1] who claims he heard about them from Demosthenes himself when the latter was an old man. Demosthenes corrected his lisp and the indistinctness of his speech by reciting with pebbles in his mouth; he exercised his voice at the racecourses, declaiming as he scaled a flight of steps, and reciting speeches or verses while holding his breath; and he had a large mirror at home, before which he would stand as he practiced his speeches.

[12] Demosthenes embarked on his public career when the Phocian War[2] was in progress, as he himself says, and as one may gather from his orations against Philip.[3] . . . Once he had adopted the noble civic purpose of pleading against Philip on behalf of the Greeks, and made a worthy success of that cause, he soon gained renown and was admired everywhere for his eloquence and outspokenness. He was revered in Greece, was courted by the Great King,[4] and won more respect from Philip than all the other public speakers.

1. Chief executive in Athens starting in 318 BCE, after the city had become a protectorate of the Macedonians.

2. A war that began around 355 BCE when the Phocians, in a bid for regional supremacy, took over the shrine of Apollo at Delphi and began using its wealth to hire mercenaries.

3. The so-called *Philippics*, which have given a new word to the English language, were a series of speeches calling on the Athenians to oppose Philip II of Macedon (father of Alexander the Great). The first was delivered in 351 BCE.

4. The king of Persia, at that time Artaxerxes III, had just as much reason as Demosthenes to oppose Philip, seeing that the rise of Macedon threatened Persia's interests as well as those of Athens.

Even those who disliked him considered him a worthy opponent; Aeschines and Hyperides[5] certainly expressed their regard even when they were attacking him.

[13] With this in mind, I cannot understand how it occurred to Theopompus to say that Demosthenes was of an unstable character and could not remain faithful for any length of time to the same policies or men. For it is clear that Demosthenes maintained to the very end the line and position to which he committed himself at the start of his public career. And not only did he *not* alter his position during his lifetime,[6] but he gave up his life in the cause of not altering it, unlike Demades,[7] who, when defending his change of policy, said that he often spoke at variance with himself but never at variance with the city's best interest. . . . As for Demosthenes, we cannot speak of him as we would of a man given to altering course and adapting to circumstance, either in word or deed. For just as he adhered to one unalterable conception of public policy, he held to one course in public affairs. Panaetius the philosopher states that most of Demosthenes' speeches share the premise that only the honorable is to be chosen for its own sake. Panaetius cites the speeches "On the Crown," "Against Aristocrates," "In Defense of Indemnities," and the speeches against Philip, in all of which Demosthenes guides the citizens not toward the pleasantest course or the easiest or the most profitable, but at many points deems that their security and safety ought to hold second place to honor and decency. And that is why, had martial courage and an unshakeable incorruptibility been added to the distinction of his principles and the nobility of his speeches, Demosthenes would have deserved to be ranked not with such orators

---

5. Aeschines, another leading Athenian orator during this era, was often on the opposite side from Demosthenes in matters regarding the Macedonians, and there was a deep personal hatred between the two men; Aeschines brought charges in 330 BCE that Demosthenes rebutted, successfully, in his famous speech "On the Crown" (see chapter 15). Hyperides, by contrast, was usually a political ally and friend of Demosthenes, but attacked him bitterly in a prosecutorial speech at Demosthenes' bribery trial in 323.

6. Plutarch goes unusually far out of his way to defend his biographical subject. In fact, Demosthenes' record is not nearly as uniform as Plutarch claims, since, though he started out as a bitter foe of Macedonian power, he made various accommodations with it in later life.

7. Another orator contemporary with Demosthenes, notorious for corruption and opportunism.

as Moerecles, Polyeuctus, and Hyperides, but on high with Cimon, Thucydides, and Pericles.[8]

[14] Among his contemporaries, at any rate, Phocion,[9] though he advocated a policy by no means praiseworthy and was reputed to favor Macedonia, was nevertheless, because of his courage and honesty, thought to be in no way inferior to Ephialtes, Aristides, or Cimon.[10] Demosthenes, on the other hand, was neither a reliable soldier (as Demetrius says) nor completely immune to bribery (though incorruptible by gold from Philip and Macedonia, he proved susceptible and was overwhelmed by the stream that flowed in from Susa and Ecbatana);[11] and while supremely adept at praising our noble forebears, he was unequal to emulating them.

But except for Phocion, Demosthenes surpassed the orators of his own day even in his manner of living. He clearly excelled at reasoning frankly with the people, resisting the inclinations of the multitude, and attacking their faults, as one may gather from his orations. . . . In the case of Antiphon,[12] his procedure was highly aristocratic. When the man was acquitted by the assembly, Demosthenes had him arrested and brought before the council of the Areopagus,[13] whereupon, taking no account of the fact that he was displeasing the

8. The same contrast between strength of arms and strength of judgment is found in the inscription that adorned Demosthenes' memorial statue at Athens. Unlike the leaders of a previous era, or his own contemporary Phocion, Demosthenes had eloquence and political skill but no military experience.

9. Phocion the Good, an aristocratic soldier-statesman educated by Plato, had a long and esteemed political career (see *Phocion* in this volume).

10. Three great leaders of fifth-century BCE Athens. See *Aristides* and *Cimon*; on Ephialtes, see *Pericles* 9–10.

11. That is, from the Persian king. Demosthenes was accused at Athens of taking Macedonian money as well, despite what Plutarch says here (and his own evidence in chapter 25).

12. Not the famous orator of the late fifth century BCE but a less prominent citizen of the mid-fourth century. Demosthenes himself refers to the incident related here in his speech "On the Crown" (132ff.).

13. That is, Demosthenes brought Antiphon to trial before a small, elite group of jurors (the Areopagus) after the broader citizen body (the assembly) had acquitted him.

people, he convicted Antiphon of having promised Philip to set the dockyards on fire.[14]

[15] As for Demosthenes' public orations,[15] his speeches against Androtion, Timocrates, and Aristocrates were written for others to deliver, as Demosthenes had not yet embarked on his public career. (He evidently produced those speeches when he was twenty-seven or twenty-eight.) He appeared in person in the action against Aristogeiton and delivered the speech about the indemnities. . . . It is not clear whether his speech denouncing Aeschines' dishonest embassy[16] was ever delivered, though Idomeneus says that Aeschines won acquittal by a mere thirty votes. But it appears unlikely that this is true, if one must judge by the "On the Crown" speeches written by both orators.[17] For neither of them refers to that conflict clearly and distinctly as one that ever came to trial. But that is a question for others to decide.

[16] Demosthenes' public policy was apparent even while the peace lasted,[18] as he allowed none of the Macedonian's[19] actions to go uncriticized, but stirred the Athenians up at each affront and

14. That is, to sabotage the Athenian navy, the principal bastion of Greek military strength.

15. In Athens, legal charges were often used to advance political agendas; indicting a public speaker on procedural grounds was an indirect way to challenge the positions he had taken. Defendants in such cases were called upon to justify their politics as much as their actions. Demosthenes wrote many speeches for such defendants, including the three referred to here, as well as for contestants in purely private legal actions. It was customary in all Athenian trials to hire a professional speechwriter, much as a modern defendant hires a lawyer.

16. In 346 BCE Demosthenes accused Aeschines of malfeasance in negotiating a peace treaty with Philip of Macedon. His oration "On the False Embassy" survives.

17. Plutarch refers here to the great showdown between Aeschines and Demosthenes in 330 BCE. Aeschines brought suit against Ctesiphon for proposing that an honorary crown be awarded to Demosthenes for public service; at issue was the propriety of Demosthenes' policies over the course of two decades. After a ringing rebuttal, Demosthenes won such a huge majority of the votes that Aeschines was forced into exile (see chapter 24).

18. The "peace" refers to an entente between Macedon and Athens, known as the Peace of Philocrates, negotiated in part by Aeschines in 346 BCE (see note 16).

19. Referring to Philip II, father of Alexander the Great.

inflamed them against him. Philip accordingly held Demosthenes in the highest regard, and when the orator arrived in Macedonia as one of an embassy of ten, though Philip listened to everyone, he responded to Demosthenes' speech with particular care. Yet when it came to other honors and friendly overtures, Philip did not treat Demosthenes equally well, but made a greater effort to win over Aeschines and Philocrates. Consequently, when these men praised Philip for being an excellent speaker, extremely good-looking, and a champion drinker, Demosthenes felt compelled to disparage him and joked that this was proper praise for a sophist, a woman, and a sponge—not for a king.

[17] When matters were tending toward war because Philip could not remain quiet, and the Athenians were stirred up by Demosthenes, the orator began by urging the Athenians to invade Euboea, which had been made subject to Philip by its tyrants.[20] When Demosthenes had written the decree, the Athenians sailed across the straits and expelled the Macedonians. Then, when Byzantium and Perinthus had been attacked by the Macedonians, Demosthenes lent aid to both cities,[21] having persuaded the Athenians to relinquish their enmity, forget the wrongs each people had committed in the allies' war,[22] and send out the force that saved both cities. Then, serving as an ambassador, he engaged the Greek states in an exchange of views, sharpened their resentment, and succeeded in setting all but a few against Philip. As a result, the Greeks mustered a mercenary force of fifteen thousand foot soldiers and two thousand horsemen (apart from the militias), and eagerly contributed money to pay their wages. . . .

When Greece had been stirred up about her future, and a league had been formed that included the tribes and cities of the Euboeans, Achaeans, Corinthians, Megarians, Leucadians, and Corcyraeans, Demosthenes was left with the most important challenge, namely to induce the Thebans to join the military alliance, since they occupied

20. Demosthenes in his third *Philippic* (341 BCE) called attention to the threat posed by Philip's incursions into Euboea. The island, lying just off Attica's shores, was of crucial strategic concern to Athens.

21. The Hellespont was even more vital to Athens than Euboea because many of the city's food supplies arrived by this route. Philip's attacks in 340 BCE on two Hellespont cities, Perinthus and Byzantium, were aggressive moves against Athenian interests. Demosthenes rallied Athens to send troops and ships, and, together with other forces sent by the Persians, these succeeded in driving Philip out of the region.

22. Byzantium had revolted from the Second Athenian League in 357 BCE.

a position that commanded a full view of Attica, possessed a force fully equal to the struggle, and were considered the finest warriors in Greece at the time. It was not easy to sway the Thebans, as they had been pacified by favors recently conferred by Philip during the Phocian War,[23] and particularly because, given the two cities' proximity, each skirmish reopened the wounds caused by their standing differences.

[18] But when Philip . . . launched a surprise attack on Elatea and occupied Phocis,[24] the Athenians were utterly taken aback. And when no one dared to ascend to the dais (as no one had any idea what should be said), and a puzzled hush fell on the assembly, Demosthenes alone came forward and advised the Athenians to stand by the Thebans. Raising his fellow citizens' spirits in various ways, and encouraging their hopes, as he was accustomed to do, he was sent with others as an ambassador to Thebes. According to Marsyas, Philip sent two Macedonians, Amyntas and Clearchus, Daochus the Thessalian, and Thrasydaeus to counter the Athenians' arguments.

Now the Thebans, as they deliberated, were not unmindful of their own interests. Each man possessed a clear vision of the horrors of war, their recent defeats in the Phocian War still fresh in their minds. But Theopompus reports that the orator's power stirred their spirits, fired their ambition, and blinded them to all other considerations. Inspired by his speech to embrace a noble cause, they cast aside fear, calculation, and gratitude. Demosthenes had achieved an effect so powerful and brilliant that Philip immediately sent ambassadors to treat for peace, and Greece was aroused and up in arms to face what lay ahead. And it was not only the generals who served Demosthenes and carried out his orders; the boeotarchs[25] did so as well. Demosthenes took charge of all the Thebans' assemblies no less than those of the Athenians, was greeted with affection by both

23. See note 2. Philip had carefully leveraged the antipathies in the Phocian War (also sometimes called the Third Sacred War) to his own advantage, so that he came out of it as both the ally of Thebes and the champion of Delphi.

24. In 339 BCE Philip swerved from his apparent route of march and seized Elatea, a town that commanded one of the routes through the mountains into southern Greece. By this gesture he proclaimed that he was willing to fight for hegemony of the Greek world rather than continue to nibble away at it by diplomacy and proxy wars. Athens and Thebes were both now directly in his line of advance.

25. The boeotarchs formed an annually elected executive board governing the whole Boeotian confederacy.

peoples, and exerted his power neither unfairly nor unworthily, but with great propriety.

[20] It is said that Demosthenes, who had complete confidence in the Greeks' armaments, and was clearly elated by the strength and zeal of so many men defying their enemy, forbade them to pay heed to oracles or listen to prophecies (he even suspected the Pythian priestess of siding with Philip), and reminded the Thebans of Epaminondas and the Athenians of Pericles,[26] pointing out that those men had believed such things to be pretexts for cowardice, and had grounded their calculations on reason. So in *that* sense Demosthenes was a brave man. But in the battle itself[27] he showed no valor and performed no deed in keeping with his words. Instead he deserted his post, bolted disgracefully, and flung away his weapons.[28] Nor did he even feel shame with regard to the inscription on his shield—"with good fortune"—engraved, as Pytheas says, in letters of gold.

Immediately after the victory, Philip gave insolent expression to his joy, and in a drunken state went about among the corpses with a party of revelers, chanting the opening line of Demosthenes' decree: "Demosthenes, son of Demosthenes, of Paeania, moves thus," having divided it into feet, and beating time to it.[29] But when he had slept off his drunkenness and realized the magnitude of the struggle in which he had involved himself, he shuddered at the cleverness and power of the orator who had forced him, in the small space of a single day, to risk his hegemony and his life.[30] Demosthenes' renown penetrated even to the Persian king, who sent letters to his satraps on the coast, commanding them to give Demosthenes money and to pay more attention to him than to all the other Greeks, as he had been capable of distracting the Macedonian and embroiling him in the Greek troubles.

26. The greatest leaders of each city.

27. The battle of Chaeronea, fought on the Boeotian plain near Thebes in 338 BCE (see *Alexander* 9).

28. Plutarch accepts without hesitation a story that might well have arisen as a slanderous attack by Demosthenes' enemies (see, for example, Aeschines, *Against Ctesiphon* 253). It is credible, however, that Demosthenes, who had never before this battle seen military action, might have turned and run from danger, as did many Athenian hoplites.

29. That is, Philip made the legal language of an assembly decree into a singsong poem.

30. By arranging the alliance with Thebes, Demosthenes had put Philip in a much weaker position than Philip would have liked.

[21] In the aftermath of the Greeks' misfortune, some political rivals, seeking to attack Demosthenes, prepared audits[31] and trumped up charges against him. The people, however, not only acquitted but continued to honor Demosthenes, and called on him again and again as a man sincerely concerned for the city's well-being. And when the bones of the fallen were conveyed from Chaeronea and honored with funeral rites, the people allowed Demosthenes to deliver the eulogy for their men.[32] Nor did they bear their misfortune basely or ignobly, as Theopompus reports in his lofty style, but made it evident, by taking special pains to revere and honor their counselor, that they did not regret having been guided by his advice. So Demosthenes delivered the eulogy, though he now stopped affixing his own name to decrees, inscribing instead the names of his friends, one after another, and avoiding the use of his own as ill-omened until after Philip's death, when he regained confidence. For Philip did not long survive his success at Chaeronea.[33]

[22] Demosthenes was informed in secret of Philip's death. Hoping to hearten the Athenians for what lay ahead, he came beaming to the council and declared that he had had a dream that he supposed foreshadowed some great good for Athens. Shortly afterward, the messengers arrived bringing word of Philip's death. The Athenians immediately performed thank offerings for good tidings and voted to award a crown to Pausanias. And Demosthenes came forward, crowned and wearing a bright cloak, though his daughter had died seven days earlier, according to Aeschines, who reviles him for this and accuses him of being a heartless father.

[23] Incited by Demosthenes, the cities again formed themselves into a league. The Thebans, whom Demosthenes had helped to supply with arms, attacked their Macedonian garrison and killed many guards,[34] while the Athenians, intending to join forces with them,

31. Since bribery was rife in Athenian politics, financial inquiries were often used as political weapons.

32. At Athens, a funeral oration over the war dead was delivered by a leading orator chosen by the people. The funeral oration of Pericles survives in Thucydides' famous version, but that given on this occasion by Demosthenes has perished.

33. Philip was assassinated in 336 BCE, two years after his great victory over Athens and Thebes (see *Alexander* 10).

34. The Theban revolt of 335 BCE began when a group of Thebans seized the Cadmeia, a piece of high ground garrisoned by Macedonian troops (see *Alexander* 11). Plutarch has here placed this episode directly after the death

were preparing to do so.[35] Demosthenes was constantly on the dais, and also wrote to the King's[36] generals in Asia, rousing them to make war on Alexander, whom he called a boy and a Margites.[37] But when Alexander, after settling affairs in his own country, reached Boeotia in person with his forces, the Athenians' courage failed, and Demosthenes was stifled, while the Thebans, betrayed by the Athenians, fought on their own and lost their city. . . . Alexander sent at once and demanded the surrender of ten public speakers, as Idomeneus and Duris have reported, though most writers (and the most reputable) say he demanded eight men: Demosthenes, Polyeuctus, Ephialtes, Lycurgus, Moerecles, Demon, Callisthenes, and Charidemus.

It was then[38] that Demosthenes told the people the story about the sheep that gave their dogs to the wolves,[39] likening himself and his colleagues to dogs fighting on behalf of the people, and calling Alexander a lone wolf. He went on to say, "Just as we see the merchants selling most of their produce by means of a few grains of wheat, which they carry about in a bowl as a sample, so in surrendering us you are selling yourselves, all of you, without realizing it." These incidents have been reported by Aristobulus of Cassandreia.

When the Athenians took counsel and were at a loss what to do, Demades, taking five talents from the men Alexander had named, agreed to go on an embassy and to petition Alexander on their behalf, either relying on his friendship or expecting to find him overfed, like

---

of Philip, whereas in fact it occurred a year later, after false reports reached Greece that Alexander too had died, killed in battle.

35. Demosthenes strongly encouraged Athens to join with Thebes in revolting from Macedon, a policy that was opposed by the cautious Phocion (see *Phocion* 17). It is not clear what course the assembly voted on, but in any case Athenian troops did not take part in the fight.

36. The Persian king (as indicated by uppercase "King").

37. Margites was the bumbling hero of a Greek comic poem.

38. That is, in the assembly session that deliberated over the response to Alexander's demands. See *Phocion* 17 for Phocion's role at the same assembly meeting.

39. This fable of Aesop describes a time when wolves were at war with an alliance of sheep and dogs. The wolves offered the sheep a favorable peace if they would betray the alliance. The sheep complied, but without the dogs they had no defense when the wolves broke the treaty and turned on them.

a lion sated with slaughter. Interceding for the men, Demades won Alexander over and reconciled him with the city.[40]

[24] When Alexander had departed[41] . . . Demosthenes played a modest role. He was briefly moved to lend assistance when Agis of Sparta was stirred up,[42] but then he shrank. The Athenians failed to help Sparta, whereupon Agis fell and the Spartans were crushed.

It was then that the suit connected with the affair of the crown was brought against Ctesiphon.[43] . . . The fame of the trial surpassed that of all other public events, both because of the speakers' renown and the integrity of the jurymen, who would not vote against Demosthenes, though his prosecutors were men of enormous influence and were siding with Macedonia. In fact, the jury acquitted so decisively that Aeschines failed to obtain the fifth part of the votes.[44] He left the city immediately and spent the rest of his life lecturing in Rhodes and Ionia.

[25] Shortly afterward, Harpalus[45] reached Athens from Asia. He had fled from Alexander, aware that his own prodigality had

40. Phocion also went to Alexander on this diplomatic mission, and indeed in *Phocion* 17 Plutarch gives him, rather than Demades, credit for placating Alexander.

41. He "departed" into Asia, to begin the invasion of the Persian empire that would consume the rest of his reign (334–323 BCE). Demosthenes played a very muted political role during this period, probably because Alexander's hold over Greece seemed too secure to challenge. As a result Plutarch moves very quickly through the decade following Alexander's departure.

42. In 331 BCE the Spartan king Agis launched a war against Macedonian forces in Europe, without Athenian support. Antipater, Alexander's guardian of the home front, crushed the Spartan forces the following year.

43. In the suit brought by Aeschines, Ctesiphon was ostensibly the defendant since it was he who had proposed (in 336 BCE) the award of a crown to Demosthenes. But the real target was Demosthenes himself.

44. To discourage frivolous lawsuits, the Athenians fined any prosecutor who failed to win even a fifth of the jury votes.

45. A close friend of Alexander and treasurer of his imperial revenues. In 324 BCE Harpalus fled his post, in Babylon, out of fear that he would be punished for mismanagement. He took with him a huge amount of embezzled money and six thousand hired mercenaries. Plutarch telescopes the events that followed: Harpalus came to Athens for refuge, bringing his whole force, but was turned away, largely at Demosthenes' urging; then he returned a few weeks later with only a few ships and a small amount of money and was admitted. On both occasions the Athenians were afraid of incurring the wrath of Alexander by harboring the fugitive Harpalus.

led him to perform base deeds; he also feared the king, who had by then been cruel to his friends. When he had taken refuge with the Athenian people, and surrendered himself with his property and ships, the other orators, as soon as they had cast longing glances at his wealth, sought to assist him, and tried to persuade the Athenians to receive the suppliant and keep him safe. At first Demosthenes advised them to drive Harpalus away and to take care not to embroil the city in an unnecessary war on an unjust pretext. But a few days later, when Harpalus' possessions were being examined, and their owner observed Demosthenes admiring a barbarian wine cup and giving close attention to its form and relief carving, he urged the orator to take it up and feel the weight of the gold in his hand. When Demosthenes marveled at its heaviness and inquired how much it cost, Harpalus smiled and said, "Twenty talents will bring it to you." And as soon as night fell, Harpalus sent Demosthenes the cup with the twenty talents.[46]

It turned out that Harpalus was clever at spotting a gold-lover by the look that overspread his face and his beaming eyes. For Demosthenes did not resist; smitten by the bribe, he went over to Harpalus like one who has welcomed a garrison. When it was day, and he had wrapped his neck well with woolen scarves, he went forth to the assembly; and when the people urged him to stand and speak, he indicated that he had lost his voice. The wits mockingly remarked that during the night the orator was afflicted not by a cold in the head but by gold in the head.[47] Later, when the whole populace learned of the bribe and refused to listen to Demosthenes when he sought to defend himself, but raged against him and raised an uproar, someone stood up and jestingly inquired, "Will you not listen, Athenians, to the man who holds the cup?"[48]

It was then that the people dismissed Harpalus from the city. And afraid that they might be required to account for the money the orators had seized,[49] they conducted a thorough investigation,

46. Turning his own words into a pun, Harpalus had made the money accompany the cup and therefore "bring" it.

47. The Greek wordplay has been loosely translated.

48. Punning on a custom at drinking parties by which, as a cup was passed, each man who received it had the right to speak.

49. Despite Plutarch's imputation of guilt to Athens' politicians, it is not clear what happened to the missing money, which belonged to Alexander but had been stolen by Harpalus. Harpalus allegedly gave 700 talents to city officials for safekeeping, but later only 350 talents were found in the cache.

visiting and searching all their houses except for that of Callicles, son of Arrhenidus. His was the only house they would not allow to be searched, as he had recently married and his bride was inside, as Theopompus reports.

[26] Addressing the issue head on, Demosthenes proposed a measure whereby the council of the Areopagus would investigate the matter, and those it found to have transgressed would suffer punishment. Demosthenes himself, however, was among the first to be condemned by the council. On coming before the court, he incurred a fine of fifty talents and was remanded to prison. But out of shame at the accusation, as he says, and because physical weakness made him unable to tolerate prison life, he ran away, escaping the notice of some of his guards, while others put it in his power to do so.[50]

[27] But while Demosthenes was still in the exile mentioned above, Alexander died and the Greek cities again formed themselves into a league, Leosthenes proving his valor and throwing a wall around Lamia, where Antipater was besieged.[51] . . . Demosthenes, joining Athenian diplomatic missions,[52] did his utmost to assist the envoys and supported their effort to attack the Macedonians and expel them from Greece. . . . Pleased by his conduct, the people of Athens voted to recall Demosthenes from exile. Demon of Paeania, Demosthenes' nephew, proposed the measure, and a trireme was sent to Aegina to fetch the exile home. When he journeyed up from the Piraeus, no archon or priest was absent, and all the citizens went together to meet Demosthenes and give him a hearty welcome. According to Demetrius of Magnesia, it was then that Demosthenes stretched out his hands and blessed himself on account of that day,

50. That is, gave him money to bribe his jailers. Demosthenes left Athens in 323 BCE, taking up a wandering life that brought him to Aegina, Troezen, and the tiny island of Calauria.

51. After Alexander's death became known at Athens, in mid-323 BCE, the city went into revolt from Macedonian control. A mercenary captain named Leosthenes took control of Athens' armed forces and won numerous other Greek cities over to his cause. The combined Greek armies defeated Antipater in battle and forced him to take refuge in the walled city of Lamia; the war in question has hence become known as the Lamian War.

52. Apparently on his own initiative and in violation of the law, Demosthenes attached himself to these Athenian state delegations as they made their way around Greece.

which brought him a nobler return than that of Alcibiades,[53] since the citizens had been persuaded, rather than compelled, to receive him. As for the fine that awaited him (since it was not possible, as a favor, to cancel damages awarded), the people devised a clever means of getting around the law. As it had been their custom to pay a sum of money to those who prepared and adorned the altar for the sacrifice to Zeus Soter, they now assigned the performance of those services to Demosthenes and gave him fifty talents, the amount he owed in damages.

[28] But after his return he did not enjoy his native city for long, since the Greeks' cause was soon crushed. In the month of Metageitnion, the battle of Crannon took place;[54] in Boadronion, the garrison entered Munychia;[55] and in Pyanepsion, Demosthenes ended his life in the following way.

When it was reported that Antipater and Craterus[56] were approaching Athens, Demosthenes and his associates, having anticipated their arrival, slipped out of the city. They were then indicted by Demades,[57] and the people sentenced them to death. As the fugitives had scattered in all directions, Antipater sent a force of men under the command of Archias, "the fugitive-hunter," to arrest them. Rumor has it that this man, a native of Thurii, had once been a tragic actor. . . . In any event, this Archias caught up with the orator Hyperides, Aristonicus of Marathon, and Himeraeus, the brother of Demetrius of Phalerum,[58] where they had fled to the shrine of Aeacus in Aegina; he dragged them away and sent them to Antipater at

53. For the heroic return of Alcibiades from exile, about ninety years before that of Demosthenes, see *Alcibiades* 32.
54. In August of 322 BCE, the Greek forces in the Lamian War fought Antipater, who had broken out of the Lamia siege, a second time and were defeated. Antipater forced a harsh settlement on Athens, requiring it to change its government to an oligarchy, install a Macedonian garrison in the Piraeus, and surrender Demosthenes and three other orators for punishment. The garrison took up its duties in September, and the fates of the orators were resolved in October.
55. Munychia was a fortified hill in the Piraeus from which Macedonian soldiers could control the whole port.
56. Leaders of the Macedonian army in Europe.
57. The Athenian orator was now collaborating with the Macedonians.
58. Three members of the anti-Macedonian faction at Athens who had fled after the city was defeated by Antipater.

Cleonae. There they were put to death. It is even said that Hyperides had his tongue cut out.

[29] On learning that Demosthenes was sitting as a suppliant in the temple of Poseidon at Calauria,[59] Archias sailed across in a dispatch boat, disembarked with some Thracian spearmen, and tried to persuade the orator to stand up and go with him to Antipater, claiming that he would not be ill-treated. . . . When Archias had made many friendly overtures, Demosthenes, just as he sat, looked Archias in the eye and said, "Archias, you never convinced me when you were an actor, nor will you convince me now with these promises." When Archias began to threaten him angrily, Demosthenes said, "*Now* you are speaking 'from the Macedonian tripod,'[60] whereas before you were acting a part. But wait a moment, so that I may send a message to those at home." So saying, he withdrew into the temple. Taking up a scroll as if he intended to write, he brought his pen to his mouth; and biting it, as he was accustomed to do when thinking or writing, he kept it there for some time. Then, covering his face, he leaned his head back. The spearmen standing by the door were deriding him for playing the coward, and were calling him soft and unmanly; then Archias entered, urged him to stand up, and repeated the same speeches, promising a reconciliation with Antipater. Aware that the poison was taking effect and overpowering him, Demosthenes uncovered his head, glanced at Archias, and said, "You'd not be getting ahead of yourself now, playing the role of Creon in the tragedy and casting this body out unburied.[61] Beloved Poseidon, I leave your temple still alive. But not even *your* shrine has been left undefiled[62] by Antipater and the Macedonians." So saying and bidding them support him, as he was now trembling and tottering, he came forward. And as he passed the altar he fell, and with a groan gave up his soul.

59. He had returned to the place he had spent much of his exile the previous year. Calauria is a tiny island in the Saronic Gulf, west of Attica.

60. A punning use of a contemporary cliché. To speak "from the Macedonian tripod" meant to speak pure truth.

61. In the play *Antigone* by Sophocles, Creon orders that the body of Antigone's brother Polynices be left unburied as a form of punishment.

62. It was considered a violation of religious taboo to allow a death to occur inside a shrine.

[30] Shortly afterward,[63] the people of Athens, rendering Demosthenes a worthy honor, erected a bronze statue of him[64] and decreed that the eldest member of his family should receive public maintenance in the Prytaneum.[65] And the well-known inscription was carved at the base of his statue:

> If you had had bodily strength equal to your judgment, Demosthenes, Macedonian Ares[66] would never have ruled the Greeks.

63. The rehabilitation of Demosthenes in fact took several decades.
64. The statue, by Polyeuctus, survives in several Roman-era copies.
65. Public support in the Prytaneum, a state building constructed for use by the boulē or council, was a high honor, usually awarded to Olympic victors and other public benefactors.
66. A personification of Macedonian military power in the form of the god of war, Ares.

Alexander

Plutarch's Alexander *is among the longest of his* Lives, *both because of Alexander's constant, unceasing activity and because of the complexity of his character. Plutarch seems to have admired Alexander immensely at the time he wrote his two speeches, "On the Fortune or Virtue of Alexander"— probably well before he wrote the* Lives—*referring to the Macedonian king as a "philosopher in arms" who tried to bring Greek enlightenment to the barbarian world. In the account below, Plutarch takes a more measured view of Alexander while still giving him the benefit of many doubts.*

Alexander (356–323 BCE) transformed Greece, and the ancient world as a whole, more thoroughly than any other leader. The league established by his father Philip, consisting of all the European Greek states except Sparta, would surely have come apart had Alexander not thrown himself into action upon taking the throne. Then the conquest of the Persian empire that followed— a project undertaken, at least ostensibly, as a Greek crusade—made Asia subordinate to European power for the first time ever. Hellenism became the dominant culture in urban centers from the Aegean to modern Afghanistan and Pakistan and would continue to hold sway over much of the world for centuries thereafter—the so-called Hellenistic Age. Had Alexander lived longer, he might have brought Greek culture westward to the Atlantic, but a fateful illness cut short his life in 323.

[2] That Alexander, on his father's side, was a descendant of Heracles by Caranus, and on his mother's a descendant of Aeacus by Neoptolemus,[1] has never been called into question. It is said that Philip was initiated into the Mysteries in Samothrace[2] at the same time as Olympias. Though he was still a boy and she an orphan child, he is said to have fallen in love with her and betrothed himself to her at once, on persuading her brother Arymbas. The night before they confined her in the bridal chamber, the bride dreamed that thunder was heard and that a thunderbolt fell on her belly and kindled a great

---

1. These two mythic genealogies were advanced by the royal houses of Macedon and Molossia, respectively. The Argeads of Macedonia, the line of Philip's father, was said to descend from Heracles, while the Molossian dynasty to which Alexander's mother belonged traced its descent from Neoptolemus, the son of Achilles and great-grandson of Aeacus. Both lines thus ultimately went back to Zeus, the father of both Heracles and Aeacus.

2. Samothrace, an island in the northern Aegean, was the center of a cult of deities called the Cabiri.

fire, which burst into flames that darted everywhere and finally died out.

[3] Alexander was born early in the month of Hecatombaeon (Lous is its Macedonian name), on the sixth[3]—the very day the temple of Ephesian Artemis was burned down. In referring to that event, Hegesias the Magnesian made a witty remark, the coolness of which might have extinguished that blaze. For he said that the temple was probably burned down because Artemis was occupied with Alexander's delivery. All the Magi who were currently residing in Ephesus,[4] believing that the destruction of the temple foreshadowed another disaster, ran through the town striking their faces and shouting that that day had given birth to ruin and dire misery for Asia.

[4] Alexander's physical appearance was best represented by the statues of Lysippus,[5] the only artist Alexander thought worthy to sculpt his likeness. And in fact the traits that many of his successors and friends tried to imitate later on—the tilt of his neck, which inclined slightly to the left, and the moistness of his eyes—have been accurately observed by the artist. . . .

When he was still a boy, his self-control manifested itself in the fact that, though violent and impetuous in other respects, he was unmoved by the pleasures of the body and indulged them very sparingly. His ambition kept his spirit grave and magnanimous beyond his years. For he was not eager for fame of every kind or from every quarter, unlike Philip, who prided himself like a sophist on his eloquence and had his Olympic victories in chariot-racing engraved on his coins.[6] Instead, when the men who attended Alexander asked if he wanted to compete in the footrace at the Olympic Games (for he was swift-footed), he replied, "Only if I can compete with kings."

3. It is impossible to precisely correlate dates on the ancient calendrical system with modern ones, but the date indicated here is around July 20. The year is 356 BCE.

4. The Magi were a caste of Persian priests. It is strange to find any of them near Ephesus, a Greek city of western Asia, when they were concentrated near the Persian royal capitals.

5. One of the greatest Greek sculptors, a contemporary of Alexander. His work survives only in Roman copies. The head of Alexander in the Louvre is probably a copy of one of his portraits.

6. Coins issued by Philip, Alexander's father, in the 340s BCE do indeed show a two-horse chariot on one side.

[5] In Philip's absence, Alexander entertained and became acquainted with envoys from the Persian king,[7] who were won over by his affectionate nature and impressed that he asked no childish or trivial question, but inquired about the lengths of the roads and the manner of their journey, and about the King himself,[8] his manner of dealing with enemies, and the Persians' power and prowess. The envoys were so dazzled that they thought nothing of Philip's famed severity as compared with the drive and high ambition of his son. . . . Whenever Philip was reported either to have captured a notable city or to have won a famous battle, Alexander appeared by no means elated, but would say to his comrades, "Boys, my father will get everything first, and will leave no great or glorious deed for *me* to perform with your help."

[6] When Philonicus of Thessaly had brought the horse Bucephalas[9] to Philip and offered to sell him for thirteen talents, they went down to the plain to make trial of him. Bucephalas seemed savage and altogether intractable: he let no rider approach him, and submitted to no one's voice among the men in Philip's suite, but reared up against everyone. In his annoyance, Philip ordered the animal to be led away, thinking him utterly wild and undisciplined, whereupon Alexander, who was present, said, "What a horse they are losing because in their inexperience and softness they cannot manage him!" At first Philip kept silent, but when Alexander continued to interrupt and to murmur indignantly, he said, "Do you criticize your elders in the belief that you are more knowledgeable and better able to manage a horse?" "I would manage this one, at any rate, better than anyone else," replied Alexander. "And if you fail, what penalty will you pay for your indiscretion?" "By Zeus," said he, "I'll pay the price of the horse." This raised a laugh, and they then came to an agreement as to the amount. Thereupon, running right up to the horse and taking hold of the rein, Alexander turned him toward the

7. Relations between Macedonians and Persians were complex. Macedonia had for a long time been part of the Persian empire, in the late sixth and early fifth centuries BCE, and had developed friendly ties with the Persian elite. More recently, suspicions had grown that Philip was planning to invade Asia, and no doubt the envoys Plutarch mentions here were seeking to prevent such an attack.

8. As always in this volume, "King" when capitalized refers to the Great King of Persia.

9. The name means "ox-head" in Greek, after the shape of a brand on the horse's shoulder.

sun, having apparently guessed that Bucephalas was confused by his own shadow as it fell in front of him and darted about. Alexander ran alongside him for a little way as he trotted, and stroked him with his hand. When he saw that Bucephalas was full of courage and spirit, he quietly flung off his cloak, leaped up, and bestrode him securely. . . . At first there was silence and anguish among the men of Philip's suite. But when Alexander had rounded the turning post properly and rode back to them, elated and swaggering, they all cheered, and his father is said to have wept for joy and to have kissed his son when he dismounted. "Son," said he, "seek a kingdom equal to yourself; for Macedonia cannot contain you."

[7] Observing that his son's nature was uncompromising and that he resisted the use of force but was easily led by reasoned argument to do what was proper, Philip tried to persuade rather than command him; and since he was by no means willing to entrust Alexander's training and discipline to the masters who were instructing him in the arts and general studies, understanding that this was of greater importance—a task for many bits and rudders, as Sophocles says—Philip sent for Aristotle,[10] the most celebrated and reputable of the philosophers, and paid him a handsome and suitable fee: though he had destroyed Stagira (Aristotle's native place), Philip resettled it and restored those of its citizens who had fled or been enslaved. As a resort for their leisure and study, Philip gave Aristotle and Alexander the precinct of the temple of the nymphs near Mieza,[11] where to this day they point out the stone seats and shaded walkways of Aristotle.

[9] While Philip was making war on Byzantium,[12] Alexander, who was sixteen years old and had been left behind in Macedonia as regent and master of the seal-ring, subdued the rebelling Maedians,[13] and after seizing their city expelled the barbarians, settled a mixed population there, and named the city Alexandropolis. Present at

10. Aristotle was a native of Stagira, a Greek city not far from Macedonia's borders. His father Nicomachus, a doctor, had served as physician to Philip's father, who was then king, so that Aristotle grew up partly at the Macedonian court. Later Aristotle went to Athens and studied with Plato and then to Asia Minor, where he did research in biology. He was called back to Macedonia by Philip in 343 BCE, to tutor Alexander, then thirteen.

11. A relatively rural area of Macedonia, where the distractions of court life would not interfere with instruction.

12. In 340 BCE Philip tried to get control of the Chersonese, a region vital to Athenian interests. See *Phocion* 14.

13. A Thracian tribe who had been forced into the Macedonian empire.

Chaeronea, Alexander took part in the battle against the Greeks and is said to have been the first to assault the Theban Sacred Band.[14] Even today in Cephisus they point out an ancient oak that is called Alexander's oak; for it stands near the spot where he pitched his tent on that occasion, not far from the Macedonians' common burial-place.

These exploits naturally endeared Alexander to Philip, who rejoiced to hear the Macedonians saying Alexander was their king, Philip their general. But Philip's domestic troubles, which were caused mainly by his marriages and love affairs, and which in some sense infected the kingdom with the concerns of the women's quarters, occasioned many accusations and serious quarrels. These were aggravated by the harshness of Olympias, a jealous and sullen woman, who egged Alexander on. Attalus precipitated a notorious clash at the wedding of Cleopatra, a young girl Philip was taking to wife[15] (he had fallen in love with her when well past his prime). Attalus was the bride's uncle. Having drunk deep at the carousal, he called on the Macedonians to ask the gods for a legitimate son to be born of Philip and Cleopatra, to be a successor to the throne. Provoked, Alexander cried, "Villain, do you take me for a bastard?" and threw a cup at Attalus.[16] Philip then rose up, his sword drawn, to confront Alexander. But luckily for both, owing to his anger and the wine, Philip slipped and fell. Alexander now insulted him, saying, "This man, gentlemen, was preparing to cross from Europe to Asia, yet

14. Plutarch gives strangely short shrift here to the battle of Chaeronea (338 BCE), one of the most important turning points in Greek history (*Demosthenes* 18–19 gives a bit more detail). Philip and Alexander crushed the combined armies of Athens and Thebes, proving decisively that the Greek phalanx could not stand up in battle to the Macedonian. The Greeks reluctantly organized themselves into a Panhellenic league that, though nominally independent, had little choice but to accept Philip's leadership. For the Theban Sacred Band, see *Pelopidas* 18.

15. Kings were permitted multiple marriages in Macedonia, and Philip in fact contracted seven, mostly in an effort to cement alliances with neighboring peoples. Olympias was fifth in the series. Cleopatra, the last, was Macedonian, so evidently Philip's reasons for marrying her had more to do with personal feelings than foreign policy.

16. Attalus may have been implying that Alexander was illegitimate, but also that his mixed parentage made him a poor heir to the throne. Olympias, Alexander's mother, was from neighboring Molossia, whereas Cleopatra, Philip's latest wife, was from native-born aristocracy.

he is overturned merely crossing from couch to couch." After this drunken episode, Alexander took Olympias away and settled her in Epirus. He himself took up temporary residence in Illyria.

Meanwhile, Demaratus the Corinthian, a plainspoken friend of the family, paid Philip a visit. After their first affectionate greetings, Philip asked Demaratus how the Greeks were getting along with one another. The latter replied, "How appropriate, Philip, for you to concern yourself about Greece, now that you have filled your own house with such strife and misery." Coming to his senses, Philip sent for Alexander and brought him home, having persuaded him through Demaratus to return.

[10] When Pausanias, who had been affronted through the machinations of Attalus and Cleopatra and had obtained no justice, assassinated Philip,[17] most of the blame was laid on Olympias, on the grounds that she had encouraged and whetted the young man's anger, though Alexander also came in for a share of discredit.[18] For it is said that when Pausanias encountered him after that affront and lamented it, Alexander quoted the iambic verse from *Medea:*

the giver of the bride, the groom, and the bride.[19]

Nevertheless, after seeking out the accomplices of the plot, Alexander punished them, and was angry with Olympias for treating Cleopatra cruelly in his absence.[20]

[11] Thus at twenty years of age Alexander succeeded to a kingship beset by serious jealousies, fearsome hatreds, and dangers from all quarters. . . . He brought a swift end to the barbarians' revolts

17. Philip was stabbed to death in 336 BCE by Pausanias, a young man who had formerly been Philip's lover but had been rejected by him and cruelly abused by Philip's cronies.

18. There is no evidence on which to accuse either Alexander or Olympias of involvement in Philip's death (assuming the anecdote Plutarch quotes here is spurious), but historians have often suspected one or both.

19. In Euripides' *Medea*, Medea reviles all three of these enemies after her husband Jason casts her off for a new wife. In Alexander's case, they would be Attalus, Cleopatra, and Philip. The implication behind the recitation of the quote, if it actually happened, was that Alexander planned to imitate Medea in slaying the three who had most injured him.

20. Other sources report that Olympias had Cleopatra and her infant executed.

and wars[21] by overrunning their country with an army as far as the Danube, where he also defeated Syrmus, the king of the Triballians, in a great battle. On learning that the Thebans had revolted[22] and that the Athenians were conspiring with them, he immediately led his force through Thermopylae. He declared that he wanted Demosthenes, who had called him a boy while he was among the Illyrians and Triballians, and a lad when he had reached Thessaly, to regard him as a man at the walls of Athens.

On reaching Thebes and offering her a chance to repent her actions, he demanded the surrender of Phoenix and Prothytes,[23] and proclaimed an amnesty for those who came over to his side. When the Thebans demanded Philotas and Antipater from him in return,[24] and proclaimed that all who wished to liberate Greece should range themselves on their side, Alexander directed the Macedonians to prepare for combat.

The battle was fought with courage and zeal on the Thebans' part against an enemy many times more numerous. But when the Macedonian guards, after abandoning the Cadmeia,[25] attacked them from the rear, most of the Thebans, finding themselves surrounded, fell in the battle itself, and the city was seized, plundered, and razed to the ground. This was done mainly because Alexander had expected that the Greeks, astonished by such a tragedy, would cower and keep quiet; but he also prided himself on gratifying his allies' complaints, since the Phocians and Plataeans had lodged accusations against the Thebans.[26] Having exempted the priests, all the Macedonians'

---

21. The "barbarians" at issue here are the peoples of eastern Europe— Thracians, Triballians, and others—who were prompted to rebel. The Triballians, a Balkan people, had submitted to Philip, but rebelled after his death.

22. In 335 BCE; see *Demosthenes* 23, *Phocion* 17.

23. Not otherwise known; presumably leaders of the revolt.

24. The Thebans' reply was a barb; Philotas and Antipater were two of Alexander's highest-ranked generals.

25. The Cadmeia was a fortified piece of high ground within the walls of Thebes. It had been garrisoned by the Macedonians after the battle of Chaeronea, but the Thebans seized the garrison troops at the outset of the revolt and were keeping them prisoner there.

26. Plutarch's assessment of mixed motives for Alexander's destruction of Thebes is probably correct. Other sources highlight either Alexander's anger and desire for revenge or his deference to the enemies of Thebes serving in his army.

hosts and guests, the descendants of Pindar,[27] and those who had opposed the citizens who voted for the revolt, he sold the rest, nearly thirty thousand, into slavery.[28] But the dead numbered upward of six thousand.

Having stunned the Greek cities into submission and stabilized his father's empire, Alexander took up the invasion of Asia his father had been preparing at the time of his death. Alexander won from the Greeks—with the exception of the Spartans, who held aloof—an appointment as supreme commander of the army of invasion, a largely Macedonian force to which most Greek cities, especially Athens, also contributed men, money, or ships.

[14] The Greeks had assembled at the Isthmus[29] and voted to march against Persia with Alexander, and Alexander was proclaimed commander. Since many statesmen and philosophers had met and congratulated them, Alexander was hoping that Diogenes of Sinope,[30] who was living near Corinth, would do the same. But as Diogenes had very little regard for the king, and remained quietly in Craneion, Alexander went to *him*, and came upon him lying in the sun. Diogenes sat up a little, at the approach of so many men, and squinted at Alexander, who greeted him and asked if there was anything he needed, to which Diogenes replied, "Only for you to move a little out of the sun." It is said that Alexander was so affected by this, and so admired the haughtiness and grandeur of the man who despised him, that when they were departing, and his attendants were laughing and making fun of the philosopher, Alexander said, "Well, had I not been Alexander, I'd have been Diogenes."

[15] As for the size of the expedition, those who give the smallest figures write that it included 30,000 foot soldiers and 4,000 horsemen; those who give the largest, 43,000 foot soldiers and 5,000 horsemen. For provisioning these men, Aristobulus says that Alexander had no more than seventy talents, Duris that he was in possession of only thirty days' sustenance, and Onesicritus that he was also two

27. Pindar was a famous Theban poet of the early fifth century BCE.

28. This mass enslavement of a large, populous city was an extremely harsh measure in the context of Greek warfare.

29. The Isthmus of Corinth was the designated meeting place for the league, a confederation of Greek states (Sparta excluded) established by Philip under Macedonian leadership.

30. A famous Cynic philosopher who rejected the values espoused by Greek society, especially the pursuit of power and wealth.

hundred talents in debt.[31] But though he started out with such small and meager means, he did not board his ship until he had looked into the circumstances of his Companions[32] and distributed to one a farm, to another a village, and to still another the revenue of some hamlet or harbor. And when almost all the royal property had been spent or allocated, Perdiccas[33] said, "But what, sire, do you leave for yourself?" When Alexander replied, "My hopes," Perdiccas said, "Then surely we too, who serve with you in the expedition, will share also in these." And when Perdiccas had declined the property that had been allotted to him, some of his other friends did the same. But Alexander eagerly gratified those who accepted or requested allotments, and most of what he possessed in Macedonia was spent in this way. With such ardor, and his mind thus disposed, he crossed the Hellespont.[34]

Ascending to Troy, he sacrificed to Athena and poured a libation to the heroes. And when he had anointed Achilles' gravestone with oil, he and his Companions ran a race around it, naked, as is the custom, and crowned it with a garland.[35]

[16] Meanwhile, since Darius' generals had mustered and arrayed a mighty force at the crossing of the Granicus,[36] it was necessary to fight at the gates of Asia, as it were, for an entrance and dominion there.

Most of the Macedonian officers feared the depth of the river and the unevenness and ruggedness of the farther banks, which they would have to scale during battle. . . . And when Parmenio[37] tried to

31. Plutarch here names three of the historians who had written about Alexander during his own time. There were many such primary sources that Plutarch was able to consult, but all have since perished, leaving modern historians with only the secondary sources that drew on them.

32. The inner circle of nobles and chiefs attending the Macedonian king were formally known as Companions.

33. One of Alexander's oldest Companions and highest officers.

34. In the spring of 334 BCE, almost two years after taking the throne.

35. One of many symbolic rites Alexander performed to evoke the ancestral link between himself and Achilles, and to portray his invasion of Asia as a new Trojan War.

36. A river in northern Turkey, the spot at which the regional Persian forces had elected to oppose Alexander's progress. The Persians had not defended the Hellespont crossing because Macedonian advance forces had well before established a beachhead there.

37. The senior general and right-hand man of Alexander's father and now of Alexander as well.

prevent Alexander from running risks, as it was late in the season, Alexander said that the Hellespont would be ashamed if, now that he had crossed *it*, he feared the Granicus. He then plunged into the stream with thirteen companies of cavalry.[38] Charging toward enemy missiles and steep positions fortified with infantry and cavalry, and across a stream that was surging around his men and sweeping them away, his actions seemed those of a mad and desperate commander, rather than one whose judgment was sound. But he persevered in the crossing, and when he had with difficulty scaled the opposite banks, though these were wet and slippery with mud, he was instantly forced to fight in disorderly, headlong haste, and to engage his attackers man by man, before his men who were crossing could form up in any order. For the enemy assaulted with a roar; and matching horse against horse, they made good use of their spears, and of their swords once the spears were shattered. Many thrust themselves at Alexander, who was easily distinguished by his light shield and the crest of his helmet, on either side of which was fixed a plume of marvelous size and whiteness. Though hit by a javelin at the joint of his breastplate, he was not wounded; and when the generals Rhoesaces and Spithridates rushed at him together, he avoided Spithridates and struck Rhoesaces, who was wearing a breastplate. After his own spear broke, Alexander used his sword. When the two men were engaged at close quarters, Spithridates rode up on one side, raised himself up on his horse, and brought his battle-axe down with main force on Alexander's helmet. His crest was broken off, along with one feather, and his helmet could barely and with difficulty resist the blow: the edge of the axe grazed Alexander's topmost hairs. And when Spithridates was rising up for another blow, Cleitus—the one known as Black Cleitus—anticipated him and ran him through with his spear. At that very moment Rhoesaces fell, struck by Alexander's sword.

While this dangerous cavalry combat was under way, the Macedonian phalanx completed its crossing of the river, and the two infantry forces came to blows. But the enemy infantry did not hold its ground firmly for long; it was routed and put to flight, except for the Greek mercenaries.[39] These men, making a stand on a certain

38. The heroic account given here of the battle of Granicus is one of two extant versions. Diodorus (*Library of History* 17.18.4–21) records a very different battle, in which Alexander approached the river cautiously, avoiding Persian strongpoints, and crossed more stealthily.

39. The Persians employed many thousands of Greek infantrymen, who were better trained and equipped than the native peoples from whom they

ridge, asked Alexander for quarter. But he, more in anger than by calculation, charged at them ahead of his men and lost his horse, which was struck through the ribs with a sword (this was not Bucephalas, but another). And it was there, as it turned out, that most of the Macedonians who died and were wounded fought and fell, engaging at close quarters with warlike and desperate men.[40]

It is said that twenty thousand barbarian foot soldiers fell, and twenty-five hundred horsemen. On Alexander's side, Aristobulus says that there were thirty-four dead in all, nine of whom were foot soldiers. Alexander ordered that bronze statues of these men be set up. (The statues were sculpted by Lysippus.) Wishing to share the victory with the Greeks, he sent the Athenians in particular three hundred shields taken from his captives; and on all the remaining spoils, grouped together, he ordered that this highly ambitious inscription be engraved: "Alexander, son of Philip, and the Greeks, except for the Spartans, from the barbarians who inhabit Asia."[41] But the drinking cups, purple robes, and any articles of that kind that he took from the Persians were sent, with a few exceptions, to his mother.

Alexander made a sweep through Asia Minor after the Granicus battle, "liberating" Greek cities (which meant transferring them from the Persian empire to his own) and chasing out Persian satraps. The following year (333 BCE) he brought his army deeper into Asia, a move opposed by a much larger Persian army than he had faced at the Granicus, commanded this time by the Great King, Darius III, himself. Darius had assembled forces many times as numerous as Alexander's and had chosen a level, open battlefield where he could deploy his superior numbers. But after Alexander delayed longer than expected in Cilicia, Darius grew impatient and decided to march out and meet the Macedonians rather than await them on his chosen ground.

---

could levy troops. Alexander had, before starting his invasion, gotten a decree passed by the Greek cities forbidding Greek soldiers to fight for the Persians.

40. Plutarch does not record the grim results of this attack: some ten thousand Greek mercenaries were slaughtered by Alexander's forces, partly as a warning to other Greeks serving the Persians.

41. This inscription was designed to highlight Alexander's self-proclaimed partnership with the Greek cities of the league, even if that alliance had been achieved only by his show of cruelty at Thebes. The omission of the Spartans, who were not league members, reinforced the point. By sending the spoils to Athens, Alexander hoped to curry favor with the most powerful and politically influential Greek city, which had thus far regarded him with deeply mixed feelings.

[20] In Darius' army there was a Macedonian, Amyntas, who had fled from Macedonia and was fairly well acquainted with Alexander's nature. This man, when he saw Darius eager to advance into the narrow passes against Alexander, begged him to stay where he was and contend, with his enormous numbers, against the inferior force of the enemy in plains that were broad and open. When Darius replied that he was afraid the enemy might escape by stealth and Alexander elude him, Amyntas replied, "Rest assured, sire, on that score; for this man will march against you, and indeed will soon be at hand." Despite what he had said, Amyntas failed to persuade the king. Setting forth, Darius marched into Cilicia, and at the same time Alexander advanced into Syria against him. Missing one another overnight, they turned back.[42] Alexander was delighted with this turn of events and eager to encounter Darius near the passes, while Darius was glad to extricate his forces from them and regain his previous encampment. For he now realized that it was not to his advantage to launch himself into a region flanked by the sea and mountains, bisected by a river (the Pinarus), and riddled with broken ground—a setting that favored the small numbers of his enemy. Alexander's good fortune provided the site,[43] though his victory was due more to generalship than luck. For though in numbers he was inferior to the barbarians by so large a multitude, Alexander gave them no chance to surround him, whereas he himself outflanked their left wing with his right, and on getting opposite their flank put the enemy to flight. Through it all he fought in the front ranks, and as a result was wounded in the thigh with a sword while contending with Darius at close quarters, according to Chares, though Alexander himself, in the letters about the battle that he dispatched to Antipater, does not say who wounded him, reporting only that he had been stabbed in the thigh with a dagger, but was not seriously inconvenienced by the wound.

Upon winning a splendid victory and destroying more than 110,000 of his enemies, Alexander nonetheless did not capture

42. Plutarch has not troubled to explain these movements clearly. The two armies marched past one another unawares, separated as they were by a tall mountain range. Darius' army thus got around to the north of Alexander, cutting him off from his supply lines and escape route. After realizing his unexpected good fortune, Darius turned southward again, hoping to trap and destroy Alexander's army, and Alexander moved northward to meet him.

43. Close to Issus, the city that has given its name to the battle.

Darius, who had got the start in the flight by half a mile or more;[44] but by the time Alexander had turned back he had captured Darius' chariot and bow.

[21] Among the captives were Darius' mother, wife, and two daughters. . . . But Alexander, considering it more kingly to master himself than to conquer his enemies, laid no hand on these women nor consorted with any other before marriage[45] besides Barsine, who had become a widow after the death of Memnon and was captured near Damascus.[46]

[23] Where wine was concerned he was less susceptible than was generally thought. He came by that reputation because of the time he spent, talking more than drinking, over each cup, always engaging in some long discussion when he had nothing else to attend to.[47] . . .

But though in other respects he was the pleasantest of all kings to consort with, and lacked none of the social graces, he had now become unpleasant in his arrogance and very much the rude soldier; not only was he carried away when it came to boasting, but he also allowed himself to be ridden by his flatterers, by whom the more refined among the company were irritated, since they wished neither to compete with these men nor to fall short of them in praising Alexander. For the former course seemed shameful, the latter dangerous. After the carousal, Alexander would bathe and then retire to sleep, often until midday; there were even times when he spent the entire day sleeping.

---

44. In the heat of the battle, Darius, standing in his war chariot at the center of the Persian line, had perceived that Alexander's forces were penetrating. Realizing that he was in danger of being captured, Darius turned and fled at top speed, escaping with his life but precipitating the total collapse of his army.

45. The romantic legends surrounding Alexander made much of his chivalrous treatment of Persian royal women. Alexander later married Stateira, the eldest daughter of Darius (see chapter 70).

46. Barsine was a half-Greek, half-Persian noblewoman with whom Alexander carried on an affair in the 330s BCE. With her he had a son, Heracles.

47. One of the many points on which Plutarch has trusted the more pro-Alexander sources, in this case Aristobulus, who was at pains to defend Alexander from charges of excessive drinking. When in the next paragraph Plutarch reports that Alexander sometimes slept the whole day through, one has to believe that overindulgence in wine was involved.

After defeating Darius and putting him to flight at Issus, Alexander swept down the coast of Phoenicia, taking over the port cities that the Persian navy might use as a base. The Persians were at this time using their naval superiority to good advantage in the Aegean, and Alexander recognized that he could not challenge them on the sea; indeed, he had already dismissed his Greek-led fleet. Instead he tried to neutralize Persian naval strength by taking over all the anchorages and harbors along the coast of Asia. This required him to fight a long, grueling siege at Tyre, a nearly impregnable island city, in 332 BCE.

After capturing the entire Phoenician coast, Alexander turned westward, toward Egypt. This province of the Persian empire was happy to welcome him, having long hated its Persian masters. Here Alexander's army spent a cheerful and restful sojourn in late 332 and early 331. During this time Alexander founded the most famous of the many cities that were to bear his name.

[26] They say that on conquering Egypt Alexander wanted to found a large and populous city and to name it after himself, and on the advice of his architects was just about to measure off a certain site and build a wall around it. Then, one night in his sleep he saw an astonishing vision: a man of majestic appearance, with a great thatch of grey hair, stood beside him and uttered these epic verses:[48]

> An island lies in the high-surging sea
> Before Egypt; Pharos is what men call it.

As soon as he had risen, he went to Pharos, which at the time was still an island (it lay a short distance off the Canopic mouth), though today it is connected by a pier to the mainland. When he saw a surpassingly fertile spot—a strip of land, nearly equivalent in breadth to an isthmus, that separates a large lagoon and an arm of the ocean that terminates at a large harbor—he declared that Homer was not only admirable in other respects, but also the cleverest of architects, and he gave orders for his builders to trace the city's outline to conform to that site. . . . He ordered his contractors to get the work under way, while he himself set out for Ammon.[49] This was a long journey, one that furnished considerable trouble and hardship.

[27] When Alexander had crossed the desert and reached the site of the oracle, the prophet hailed him with a greeting from the god as from a father, whereupon Alexander inquired whether any of the

---

48. Homer's *Odyssey* 4.354–55.

49. Ammon was an Egyptian god, equated with Zeus by the Greeks. The oracle of Ammon, in a remote oasis west of Egypt, was considered one of the most reliable sources of prophecy.

murderers of his father had escaped him. When the prophet urged
him to guard his tongue, as his father was not mortal,[50] Alexander
rephrased the question and inquired whether the murderers of Philip
had all been punished; he then inquired about his own empire, asking
whether the god had granted him supreme power over all mankind.
When the god had answered that this too had been granted, and that
Philip had been fully avenged, Alexander presented the god with
splendid votive offerings, and the priests with gifts of money.

That is what most writers report about the oracles. But Alexander
himself, in a letter to his mother, says that he received certain secret
prophecies, which on his return he will reveal to her alone. Some say
that the prophet, wishing to hail him with the affectionate Greek
greeting, "*O paidion*," misspoke, owing to his barbarian accent, and
pronounced the last word with an "s" instead of an "n," saying, "*O
pai Dios*," and that the slip delighted Alexander, whereupon the story
spread abroad that the god had addressed him as "son of Zeus."[51]

[28] On the whole, Alexander treated the barbarians haughtily
and behaved as if he actually believed in his divine begetting and
birth, but to the Greeks he was moderate and restrained when it came
to assuming his own divinity.[52] But when writing to the Athenians
about Samos[53] he said, "I cannot have given you that free and famous
city, for you received it from the man who was then your master and
was called my father," meaning Philip. . . .

[29] When Darius sent a letter to Alexander and his friends,
requesting him to accept ten thousand talents in return for his captives, to keep all the territory east of the Euphrates, to marry one of

50. The oracle hereby implied that Alexander was the son of a god rather
than of Philip.

51. In Greek, *paidion* is a way of hailing a friend, "hey, young man,"
whereas *pai Dios*, heard as two words, means "son of Zeus."

52. Alexander's Greek subjects were much more wary of human preten-
sions to divinity than were Egyptians and Asians. The Greeks eventually
passed resolutions giving Alexander divine worship, but the measures were
very controversial.

53. In 323 BCE, near the end of his life, Alexander decreed that all those
exiled by the Greek cities must be returned to their homes, a measure that
would have resulted in Athens losing Samos, a territory from which it had
expelled all the native inhabitants. The Athenians appealed to Alexander to
exclude them from the decree, but were denied.

his daughters, and to be his friend and ally,[54] Alexander shared the letter's contents with his Companions. When Parmenio said, "Well, if *I* were Alexander, I would accept these terms," Alexander replied, "And so would *I*, by Zeus, if I were Parmenio." He accordingly wrote in reply that if Darius came to him, he would be shown every courtesy; if not, Alexander would march against him at once.

In the spring of 331 BCE, Alexander left Egypt and headed east, having heard that Darius had gathered a new army to defend his empire. Plutarch says this force numbered one million, but that is doubtless an exaggeration. By any measure, though, it was huge and included Darius' most fearsome weapons: expert Bactrian cavalrymen, scythed chariots with blades protruding from their wheels, and even a handful of trained Indian war elephants. Determined to preserve the advantage of favorable ground, Darius brought this force to an open plain near Gaugamela, in what is now Iran, and cleared the land of rocks and obstructions so that his cavalry would not be impeded. Alexander approached this battleground cautiously, in late September 331, and prepared for his most important showdown yet.

[33] And now, after Alexander had addressed the Thessalians and the other Greeks at great length, and they had urged him, with a roar, to lead them against the barbarians, he shifted his spear to his left hand and with his right called on the gods, as Callisthenes[55] says, beseeching them, if he was truly the offspring of Zeus, to defend and strengthen the Greeks. The seer Aristander, wearing a white shawl and a golden crown, rode by and pointed out an eagle soaring over Alexander's head and flying straight toward the enemy, at the sight of which the men grew bold and encouraged one another, the cavalry charged at full speed against the enemy, and the phalanx surged forward like a wave. But before the first ranks had come to blows, the barbarians gave ground and there was a relentless pursuit, Alexander driving the conquered force toward their center, where Darius was. For Alexander saw him from a distance—a tall, handsome man mounted on a high chariot, fenced about with many splendid horsemen, who stood in compact array around the chariot to

54. The different Alexander sources give varying accounts of what Darius offered Alexander and when, but all of them make clear that the price Darius was willing to pay to buy Alexander off was huge.

55. The expedition's official historian, a Greek intellectual and kinsman of Aristotle, Callisthenes was later killed on Alexander's orders, after defying the king's policies, in an episode not included in this volume.

resist the enemy's attack. But once Alexander, formidable when seen at close range, had charged after the fugitives toward the ranks who were standing their ground, he astounded and scattered almost all of them. The best and noblest, however, who were slain in front of their king and falling in heaps on one another, hindered the Macedonians' pursuit, struggling convulsively and flinging themselves around the men and horses.

But Darius, faced with all these horrors and seeing his defenders retreating toward him and making it impossible to turn his chariot around and drive through easily, since its wheels were obstructed and jammed by the large numbers of fallen bodies, while his horses, overcome and hidden by the masses of corpses, were rearing up and alarming his charioteer, abandoned his chariot and weapons, mounted a mare that, according to report, had just foaled,[56] and fled. But it is thought that he would not have escaped had other horsemen not come from Parmenio, summoning Alexander with the plea that a large enemy force was still in formation there and would not give ground. In fact Parmenio is generally criticized for having been sluggish and idle in that battle, either because old age was already impairing his courage, or because he was oppressed by the arrogance and pomp, as Callisthenes phrases it, of Alexander's sovereignty, and regarded it with envy. At the time, though the king was vexed by the summons, he did not tell his men the truth, but signaled retreat, declaring that he would refrain from further slaughter since darkness was falling. And as he drove toward the division that was in danger, he heard on the way that the enemy had been roundly defeated and was fleeing.[57]

56. Mares that had recently given birth were thought by the Greeks to have extra speed.

57. Plutarch had little interest in military history, and his account of the battle of Gaugamela is only a rough outline. Interested readers should consult the battle plans given in *The Landmark Arrian: The Campaigns of Alexander*, ed. James Romm and trans. Pamela Mensch (New York: Pantheon, 2010). The outcome at least is clear: Darius once again turned his chariot and fled the field, rather than risk being taken prisoner by Alexander. The center of his line followed him in flight, but his right wing had already made good inroads against Alexander's left, led by Parmenio, and continued to threaten it. Alexander had to turn back from pursuit of Darius in order to aid Parmenio, allowing the Persian king to get away unscathed with a few followers.

[34] The battle having had this outcome, the empire of the Persians appeared to have been utterly destroyed, and Alexander, proclaimed king of Asia,[58] performed splendid sacrifices to the gods and presented his friends with large sums of money, houses, and commands. In his eagerness to be honored by the Greeks, he wrote that all their tyrannies had been abolished and that they might govern themselves autonomously.[59]

[36] On becoming master of Susa,[60] Alexander came into possession, in the palace, of forty thousand talents of coined money and all the other trappings of untold wealth.[61]

[38] After this, when he was about to march against Darius,[62] he chanced to take part in a playful carousal with his Companions that was also attended by women who came to revel with their lovers. The most popular among them was Thais, an Athenian by birth, and the mistress of Ptolemy, who subsequently became king.[63] Partly wishing to praise Alexander properly, and partly in jest, she was moved during the carousal to make a speech in keeping with the character of her native land, though it was too high-flown for a person of her sort. She said that for all she had suffered wandering about Asia she was on that day receiving her reward, enjoying a luxurious party in the splendid

58. Alexander assigned himself this unprecedented title.

59. Upon gaining control of Asia Minor three years earlier, Alexander had removed the Persian-installed puppet governments in the Greek cities and installed democracies. In theory these cities were now free, but in practice, of course, they could not defy Alexander, and many had to pay "voluntary" tribute to him. The idea that Alexander's campaign was in fact a Greek war of liberation from Persia was thereby maintained.

60. Susa was the principal Persian capital, though Babylon, Persepolis, and Pasargadae were also royal seats.

61. A fantastic sum of money, and yet this was only a small portion of the total that Alexander captured after all the Persian treasuries had been emptied. The Persians had been hoarding the tribute money collected from all of Asia for more than two centuries.

62. After resting his troops and enjoying the pleasures of Babylon and Persepolis, Alexander set out for Bactria in the spring of 330 BCE to find and capture Darius.

63. Ptolemy, son of Lagus, was one of Alexander's oldest friends and top commanders. After the death of Alexander in 323 BCE, Ptolemy became satrap of Egypt, and some sixteen years later, after Alexander's royal family had been killed off by those competing for control of the empire, he and several other former generals crowned themselves kings.

palace of the Persians. But it would be pleasanter still to go on a revel and burn down the house of Xerxes, who had burned Athens,[64] she herself kindling the fire while Alexander looked on, so that a legend might be preserved for mankind that the women of Alexander's entourage imposed a greater punishment on the Persians on behalf of Greece than all her naval and infantry commanders. This speech was received with uproarious applause, and the king's Companions eagerly cheered him on. Captivated, the king leaped up with a garland and a torch and led the way. The other revelers, following with a merry shout, stood around the palace, and other Macedonians who learned of it ran there with torches and were filled with joy. For they were hoping that the burning and destruction of the palace were the acts of a man who had fixed his thoughts on home and would not settle among barbarians. Some say that these events came about in this way, while others say they were planned;[65] but it is agreed that Alexander quickly repented and gave orders for the fire to be extinguished.

[42] Alexander now marched out in the belief that he would again do battle with Darius. But on hearing that the king had been captured by Bessus,[66] Alexander sent the Thessalians home, giving the mercenaries a gift of two thousand talents over and above their pay. And in the course of the pursuit, which proved troublesome and prolonged (in eleven days he covered upward of four hundred miles on horseback), most of his men gave out, mainly from lack of water.

[43] It is said that only sixty rushed together into the enemy's camp, where they actually rode over much silver and gold that had been discarded, passed many wagons of children and women being carried this way and that, bereft of drivers, and pursued the first fugitives, thinking that Darius was among them. They finally found Darius lying in a wagon, his body full of javelins, on the point of death. Yet he asked for something to drink, and on taking some cool

---

64. In 480 BCE, when the Athenian population had been evacuated to Salamis; see *Themistocles* 10.

65. Plutarch gives a nod to the alternative, and in most historians' eyes more likely, version recorded in Arrian's *Anabasis:* Alexander soberly decided to burn the palace, as a signal to the Persians that the Achaemenid dynasty was over and also as a sign to the Greeks that the promised revenge on the Persians had been achieved.

66. Bessus, satrap of Bactria, had accompanied Darius in flight, but when it was clear that Alexander was overtaking the fugitives, Bessus and his followers staged a coup and put Darius in chains and eventually killed him. Thereafter Bessus tried to claim the throne that Darius had lost.

water said to Polystratus, who had given it to him, "This, my good fellow, is the climax of all my bad luck—to be treated well without being able to make a return. But Alexander will thank you for the favor, and the gods will reward Alexander for his kindness to my mother, wife, and children. To him, through you, I give this right hand." So saying, and taking Polystratus' hand, he died. When Alexander arrived, he was visibly grieved by the man's death; loosening his own cloak, he threw it over the body and shrouded it. And later on, when he found Bessus, he had him dismembered. Bending two straight trees toward each other, he attached a part of the man's body to each; then, when the trees were let go, and swung back with a rush, the part attached to each went with it.[67]

[45] From there, after moving the army into Parthian territory, Alexander found himself at leisure, and for the first time donned barbarian attire, either because he wanted to adapt himself to the local customs (in the belief that community of race and custom is a great humanizer of men), or as an attempt to introduce the practice of ritual bowing[68] to the Macedonians by gradually accustoming them to tolerate changes in his way of life and habits.[69] . . . And the sight pained the Macedonians. But since they admired all his other virtues, they supposed they should forgive some of the things he chose to do for the sake of his own pleasure and renown.

[47] Alexander now adapted his way of life more and more to that of the local inhabitants, and encouraged the latter to adopt Macedonian customs, thinking that by means of assimilation and fellowship—by good will rather than by force—he would ground his authority more securely while he himself was far away. That was why, upon selecting thirty thousand boys, he gave orders that they were to

67. This version of Bessus' death is probably fanciful, but it is clear from other sources that Alexander had Bessus tortured and mutilated before execution. Arrian's *Anabasis* takes Alexander to task for this, but it seems to be in line with Persian (though not Macedonian or Greek) norms.

68. In one of his most controversial moves, Alexander attempted to have his officers bow down to him in greeting as the Persians did before the Great King.

69. Plutarch presents the two contrasting views of his sources, some of which excused Alexander's Asianizing dress as an attempt to gain authority among his new Asian subjects, while others blamed him for arrogance and pomp. This was the first of many steps in Alexander's "fusion" program, his attempt to meld European and Asian political cultures and even force their aristocratic families to intermarry.

study Greek literature and be trained in Macedonian warfare, having
assigned them several instructors.[70] As for his union with Roxane,[71]
while it is true that, charmed by her youth and beauty, he fell in love
when he saw her dancing at a drinking party, the match was also
thought to accord well with his immediate aims. For the barbarians
were heartened by the fellowship his marriage created, and admired
Alexander beyond measure because he had proved so temperate in
these matters that he would not even consent to touch, without legal
right, the only woman by whom he had been vanquished.

*Once Darius and Bessus were dead, Alexander was the unchallenged ruler
of the former Persian empire, but he elected not to stop his campaign. He
spent two years in Bactria and Sogdiana (modern Afghanistan, Tajikistan, and
Uzbekistan), the wild frontier of the Persian world, subduing tribes that had
no inclination to respect his authority. Here, several incidents occurred that
revealed tensions, or even breakdown of unity, in Alexander's army. Two plots
against Alexander's life were uncovered during these two years, and purges
were conducted after each. Alexander personally punished a grumbling dis-
sident, a high officer named Cleitus, by killing him with a spear in full view
of the whole senior staff. But ultimately Alexander's authority stood the test,
and his army, now reorganized to give the king added security, held together.*

*In 327 BCE Alexander left Bactria, headed not homeward but farther east.
He had accepted an alliance with Taxiles, a ruler near the Indus River, and
took his army across the Hindu Kush mountains and into the land he knew
as India (modern northern Pakistan). This region had once belonged to the
Persian empire, so Alexander had a slight political pretext for entering it. But
he also needed to give his army, now indisputably the world's most powerful,
something to do, and he himself longed to make a journey that only the gods
Heracles and Dionysus, according to Greek legend, had made before him.*

[57] When Alexander was about to cross the mountains into India,
he saw that his army was overburdened, its mobility impaired by its
vast spoils. At dawn, when the wagons had been packed up, he burned
his own wagons first, along with those of his Companions, and then
commanded that those of the Macedonians be set on fire. And the
ambition that prompted this exploit seemed greater and more formidable than the deed itself. For though a few of his soldiers were

70. This corps of select Asian youths had been trained to fight in
Macedonian fashion, beginning probably in 327 BCE.
71. Alexander's first wife Roxane was the daughter of a Bactrian chieftain.
Alexander married her in 327 BCE, largely in an effort to make allies and
willing subjects of the recalcitrant Bactrian tribes.

vexed, most of them, raising an impassioned war cry, shared their necessities with those who needed them, and burned and destroyed their own superfluous goods, thereby filling Alexander with zeal and eagerness. By then he had also become a fearsome and implacable punisher of any who misbehaved. For after appointing Menander, one of his Companions, as chief of a garrison, he had the man killed for declining to remain in office, and personally dispatched Orsodates, one of the barbarians who revolted from him, with a bow shot.

[59] Taxiles is said to have been in possession of a portion of India no smaller in size than Egypt—a region especially rich in pastures and land that bore fine fruit, and to have been, in his own way, a clever man. Welcoming Alexander, he said, "What need have we, Alexander, to fight with one another if you have come intending to deprive us neither of water nor of necessary sustenance, the only things for which sensible men are compelled to fight? As for the other riches and possessions so-called—if I prove the stronger man, I am ready to treat you well, but if the weaker, I do not hesitate to show my gratitude when treated well." Delighted, Alexander clasped Taxiles by the hand and said, "Do you somehow imagine that after such friendly words our meeting will not lead to a battle? But you will not get the better of me; for I shall contend against you and fight on behalf of the favors *I* bestow, that you may not surpass me in generosity." Receiving many gifts, and giving more, Alexander finally made Taxiles a present of 1,000 talents of coined money. In doing so, though he greatly pained his friends, he made many of the barbarians regard him more kindly.

But the most warlike of the Indians, who were mercenaries, went about to the various cities, defending them stoutly and doing Alexander great harm. Eventually, after making a truce with them in a certain city, Alexander caught them on the road as they were departing and killed them all.[72] And this adheres like a stain to his military record; in all other instances he waged war lawfully and in a manner worthy of a king. No less than the mercenaries, the philosophers[73]

72. This occurred at the town called Massaga, near the end of 327 BCE. According to Arrian's account (*Anabasis* 4.27), Alexander attacked the mercenaries after learning that they intended to break their oath and desert him.

73. Like many Greeks, Plutarch was deeply impressed by the religious ascetics of India, known to the Greeks variously as Brahmans, gymnosophists, wise men, or (as here) philosophers. The various religious orders in the region—Hindus, Jains, and perhaps also early Buddhists—were opposed to Alexander's occupation.

made trouble for him by abusing any kings who allied themselves with him, and by encouraging free peoples to revolt—which was why he had many of these men hanged as well.

[60] Alexander himself, in his letters,[74] has described his campaign against Porus.[75] He says that their two camps were separated by the river Hydaspes, and that Porus, stationing his elephants on the opposite bank, kept constant watch on the crossing. Accordingly, day after day Alexander created plenty of noise and uproar in his camp, and thereby accustomed the barbarians not to be alarmed. And then, one stormy, moonless night, taking a detachment of his infantry and his best horsemen, he marched a distance from the enemy and crossed to a smallish island. Rain poured down furiously there, and many hurricanes and lightning bolts assailed his men. But though he saw some of them perishing and burned to death by the lightning, he nevertheless set forth from the island toward the opposite banks. But the Hydaspes, swollen and agitated by the storm, forced a large breach in its bank, and a large part of the stream surged through it; and the ground between the two channels was too slippery and jagged to provide any secure footing. At that point Alexander is said to have cried, "Athenians, can you believe the dangers I undergo to earn your praise?" . . . Alexander himself says that after abandoning their rafts they crossed the breach with their armor on, the water coming up to their chests; and that after getting across he led his horsemen two and a half miles in advance of his infantry, calculating that if the enemy attacked with their cavalry, he would prove superior, whereas if they advanced their phalanx, his own infantry would arrive in time. And his expectation was justified. For after routing a thousand horsemen and the sixty chariots that had attacked him, he seized all the chariots and killed four hundred of the horsemen. As Porus now guessed that Alexander himself had crossed the river, he advanced against him with his entire force, except the party he left behind to prevent the Macedonians from crossing.[76] But Alexander, dreading

74. Plutarch evidently had access to a collection of Alexander's letters, of uncertain authenticity. They have become almost entirely lost.

75. An important local leader, an enemy of Taxiles, with whom Alexander had allied.

76. A detachment of Macedonians had been left in position on the riverbank opposite Porus while Alexander led the rest to the crossing point. Porus wanted to deter this squadron, which included cavalry horses, from crossing, so he left some of his elephants there, knowing that horses were not willing to approach elephants. Alexander in fact never reached the Ganges.

the beasts and the enormous numbers of the enemy, attacked the left wing himself, and ordered Coenus to assault the right. A rout occurring at each wing, Porus' men, forced back, retreated in each case toward the beasts, and crowded in among them. From then on the battle was a scramble until, in the eighth hour, the enemy gave up. This is the account the victor himself gives in his letters.

Most of the historians agree that Porus' height exceeded four cubits by a span,[77] and that because of his stature and the dignity of his physique, his size in relation to his elephant was proportional to that of a horseman's to his horse. Yet his was the largest elephant; and it showed a wonderful understanding and concern for the king, angrily warding off his attackers and repulsing them while the king was still vigorous. But when it sensed that he was wearied by scores of missiles and wounds, and dreaded that he might slip off, it lowered itself gently to its knees; and gently grasping the spears with its proboscis, drew each of them from Porus' body. When Alexander asked the captive Porus how he should treat him, Porus replied, "Like a king"; and when Alexander then asked whether he had anything else to say, Porus answered, "Everything is comprehended in 'like a king.'" Accordingly, Alexander not only allowed Porus to rule the territories over which he had been reigning, appointing him as satrap, but added another territory, having subdued its autonomous tribes, in which there were said to be fifteen peoples, five thousand noteworthy cities, and a great many villages. And he appointed Philip,[78] one of his Companions, as satrap over a territory three times as large.

[62] The battle with Porus sapped the Macedonians' vigor, and discouraged them from advancing farther into India. After barely repelling Porus, who had arrayed twenty thousand infantry and two thousand cavalry against them, they firmly opposed Alexander when he insisted on crossing the river Ganges;[79] for they had learned that it was four miles wide and one hundred fathoms deep, and that the opposite banks were concealed by enormous numbers of infantry, horses, and elephants. For it was said that the kings of the Gandarites and Praesii were awaiting him with 80,000 horsemen, 200,000 foot

77. Making him over six feet tall, large for his time.
78. No relation to Alexander's father.
79. Plutarch's error for the Hyphasis River. Alexander's army refused his order to cross this river and proceed toward what he claimed was the eastern edge of the world.

soldiers, 8,000 war chariots, and 6,000 warrior elephants.[80] And this was no idle boast. For Androcottus,[81] who reigned shortly thereafter, made Seleucus a present of 500 elephants, and with any army of 600,000 invaded and subdued all of India.

At first, in his despair and anger, Alexander shut himself up in his tent and lay there, claiming no satisfaction with what he had accomplished unless he crossed the Ganges and regarding retreat as an admission of defeat. But when his friends, who gave him suitable consolation, and his men, who stood weeping and wailing by his door, appealed to him, he relented and broke up camp, fashioning many false and deceptive devices to enhance his renown; for he ordered the manufacture of armor that was larger than usual, taller horse stalls, and heavier bridles,[82] and left these items behind, scattered about, and built altars of the gods, which to this day are held sacred by the kings of the Praesii, who cross the river and perform sacrifices on them in the Greek manner.[83]

[63] From there, eager to see the outer sea,[84] he built many rafts and ferry boats furnished with oars and was transported down the rivers[85] in a leisurely manner. But the voyage was not free of toil or even of battles: on landing and disembarking at the cities, he subdued them all.[86] Against the so-called Malli, whom they say were the most

---

80. The Nanda kingdom in the Ganges valley, the people apparently known to the Greeks as the Praesii, was indeed quite powerful at this time, and reports of their resources may well have played a part in the unwillingness of the troops to proceed.

81. Chandragupta, the founder of the Mauryan empire.

82. The outsized gear was intended to give the impression that the realm was ruled by giants, to deter potential invaders.

83. A fascinating statement, though how Plutarch could have known this is unclear. The altars of Alexander, if they ever really existed, have disappeared entirely today.

84. With his vague notions of geography, Alexander imagined that the Arabian Sea, the body of water by the Indus River mouth, was in fact part of the world-encircling Ocean or "outer sea" that stretched around both Africa and northern Asia to join the Atlantic.

85. That is, the tributaries of the Indus and the Indus itself.

86. The army's voyage down the Indus and its tributaries saw some of the hardest fighting, and harshest treatment of enemies, in all of Alexander's campaigns. Either Alexander wanted to terrorize the region in hopes of keeping it tractable, or he wanted to punish his men for defying him at the Hyphasis, or both.

warlike of the Indians, he just missed being cut to pieces. For he dispersed the Indians from their walls with spears, and was the first to mount the wall by a ladder; and when the ladder was shattered, and he was sustaining blows from the barbarians who were resisting from below, he wheeled about, though he had few companions, and leaped down into the midst of his enemies, and luckily landed on his feet.

When he brandished his weapons, the barbarians imagined that some flamelike specter hovered before his body, which was why they fled at first and scattered. But when they saw him with two of his shield-bearers, they rushed at him, some of them trying to wound him with their swords and spears as he defended himself; and one, standing a little way off, released from his bow an arrow so forceful and steady that on piercing Alexander's breastplate it lodged in the bones near his chest. He himself yielded to the blow, his body bending double, whereupon his assailant, having hit him, advanced with his scimitar drawn, while Peucestas and Limnaeus[87] stood over the king. When both of these men were struck, Limnaeus perished, but Peucestas held out, and Alexander slew the barbarian.

After sustaining many wounds, Alexander was finally hit on the neck with a cudgel, at which point he planted his body against the wall and merely gazed at his enemies. Thereupon the Macedonians crowded around him, and he was seized, already unconscious, and carried to his tent. And at once there was a rumor in the army that he had died. When with great difficulty and effort they had excised the arrow's shaft, which was made of wood, and succeeded in removing his breastplate, they had to excise the barb that had entered one of his bones. It is said that the barb was three finger breadths wide and four long. That was why, as it was being extracted, he fainted repeatedly and nearly died; but he nonetheless recovered. And when he was out of danger, but still weak and receiving prolonged care and treatment, he became aware, from the disturbance outside, that the Macedonians were longing to see him. He then donned a cloak and went out.[88] After sacrificing to the gods, he again set sail and voyaged along the coast, subjugating great cities and extensive territory.

87. The two men who had accompanied Alexander over the wall. Other writers say the second was not Limnaeus but Leonnatus, or they include a third man, Abreas.

88. Plutarch's brief finale does little justice to the intensely emotional episode. According to Arrian, Alexander's troops were ready to riot, believing him dead, until he summoned enough strength to mount a horse and ride out among them. The response of the troops was ecstatic.

[66] His voyage down the rivers to the sea took seven months.[89] When he surged into the ocean with his fleet, he sailed out to an island that he called Scillustis, though others call it Psiltucis.[90] Disembarking there, he sacrificed to the gods and observed the natural features of the sea and the points on the coast that were accessible. Then, on praying that no man after him might travel beyond the bounds of his own expedition, he turned back. Appointing Nearchus as admiral, and Onesicritus as chief pilot, he gave orders for the fleet to sail along the coast, keeping India on its right.[91] He himself, advancing on foot through the Oreitans' territory, was led into the direst hardship and lost an enormous number of men, so that not even a fourth of his fighting force was brought back, though his infantry had numbered 120,000, and his cavalry 15,000.[92] Virulent diseases, bad food, the burning heat, and famine destroyed most of them, as they were crossing the untilled country of men who lived poorly and owned only a few miserable sheep whose flesh was inferior and foul-smelling, since the animals had been fed on ocean fish. After crossing the region with great difficulty in sixty days, he reached Gedrosia, where he suddenly had all things in abundance, since the nearest satraps and kings had provided them.

[68] When Nearchus and his men reached him from the coast, Alexander so enjoyed hearing in detail about their voyage that he himself decided to sail down the Euphrates with a large armament, and then, after circumnavigating Arabia and Africa, to pass through

89. Roughly, the first half of 325 BCE.

90. Arrian gives the name as Cilluta (*Anabasis* 6.19.3). Its location is unknown.

91. With these orders, Alexander gave his old friend Nearchus a formidable task. The coast of Carmania, in modern eastern Iran, was nearly barren, harborless, and totally unexplored. Alexander's plan was for a portion of the army to march along the coast and keep in contact with the fleet, finding water and anchorages for the sailors, while the ships supplied the land army with food. But the fleet and army became separated early on and both endured terrible hardships. Nearchus' account of his voyage has been largely preserved in Arrian's *Indica*.

92. The numbers and the scale seem fantastic, but some historians have found Plutarch's figures—the only surviving estimate for Gedrosia losses—credible. Hard evidence is lacking, but there is no doubt that the trip (in 325 BCE) was a harrowing ordeal.

the Pillars of Heracles and into the inner sea.[93] He had vessels of all sorts built for him at Thapsacus, and sailors and helmsmen were assembled from all quarters. But his difficult return march, the wound he sustained among the Malli, and the reports of his army's heavy losses raised doubts about his survival, which in turn incited his subject peoples to revolt and occasioned great iniquity, greed, and insolence among his generals and satraps. In short, unrest and revolutionary impulses spread everywhere. . . . For these reasons he sent Nearchus back to the coast (for he was determined to fill the entire seaboard with wars), while he himself proceeded to punish the rogues among his generals.[94] He himself killed one of Abuletes'[95] sons, Oxyartes,[96] by running him through with a spear; and when Abuletes failed to furnish him with the necessary provisions, bringing him three thousand talents of coined money instead, Alexander ordered the money to be thrown to the horses. When they would not touch it, he said, "What use to us are these provisions of yours?" and cast Abuletes into prison.

[70] Holding a wedding for his Companions at Susa, he himself married Darius' daughter Stateira and assigned the noblest women to the noblest men;[97] and for the Macedonians who had already married[98] he provided a public wedding feast at which he is said to have given each of the nine thousand invited guests a golden drinking cup for the libations. Distinguishing himself admirably in every way, he

93. Other sources also credit Alexander with this plan, to reach home by circumnavigating Africa and entering the Mediterranean (the "inner sea") at the strait of Gibraltar ("Pillars of Heracles"), but it is doubtful that he really entertained it.

94. This purge of unreliable satraps in 324 BCE resulted in the flight of Harpalus to Athens, among other upheavals; see *Demosthenes* 25.

95. Abuletes the Persian was satrap of Susiana, first under the Persians, then under Alexander.

96. His name was Oxathres; Plutarch has confused him with Oxyartes, Roxane's father.

97. The mass marriage Plutarch refers to occurred in the spring of 324 BCE. Alexander matched nearly a hundred of his high officers with Persian and Bactrian brides, selected from the royal and noble families of Asia. The goal was to create a closer collaboration between the elites of the Greek and Persian worlds. Alexander himself married not only Stateira, as Plutarch says here, but also Parysatis, daughter of the Persian king who had preceded Darius. Alexander remained wedded to Roxane.

98. That is, those who had Asian mistresses.

even cleared the debts his men had incurred, which amounted to 9,870 talents.

[71] Since the thirty thousand boys he had left behind for training and exercises[99] had acquired manly physiques and handsome looks, and displayed a wonderful ease and lightness in their drills, Alexander was delighted, though the Macedonians grew despondent and feared that he would regard *them* as less valuable. That was why, when he sent the weak and disabled to the coast,[100] they said it was insulting and humiliating that after using men in every capacity he discarded them in disgrace and cast them back to their native cities and parents, no longer the men they had been when he recruited them. They therefore urged him to send them *all* away and to consider all the Macedonians useless, since he now had these young dancers of the war dance[101] with whom he could go forth and conquer the world.

To this Alexander responded harshly, and in his anger showered them with abuse. On driving them away, he gave his guard posts to Persians, out of whom he chose his bodyguards and heralds. When the Macedonians saw him escorted by Persians, while they themselves were excluded and dishonored, they were humbled; and in talking among themselves, they realized that they had been almost mad with envy and rage. Coming to their senses at last, they visited Alexander's tent, unarmed and wearing only their tunics. . . . For two days and nights they persisted in standing at his door, weeping and appealing to him as their master. On the third day, coming forth and seeing them humbled and sobbing pitiably, he wept for a long time;[102] then, after duly scolding them, he addressed them kindly and released the men who were unfit, giving them splendid gifts and

99. For Alexander's decision some years earlier to train a corps of Asian youths to fight with the Macedonians, see chapter 47 and note 70.

100. Alexander decommissioned not only the "weak and disabled" but also many of the most egregious troublemakers from the Hyphasis mutiny. About ten thousand Macedonian veterans were to be sent "to the coast," that is, the west coast of Asia, and then home to Macedonia by ship, under the leadership of Craterus. The events described here occurred at the town of Opis, on the Tigris River, in the spring of 324 BCE.

101. Evidently a sarcastic reference to the youth and vigor of the new recruits. The veterans taunting Alexander were in their fifties and sixties.

102. Arrian, in his account of the same episode (*Anabasis* 7.11), does not show Alexander behaving nearly so emotionally.

writing to Antipater[103] that at all public games and theaters they were to occupy the front seats, crowned with laurel. He also awarded pensions to the children, now orphans, of the men who had died.

[73] As he was advancing to Babylon, Nearchus, who had rejoined him after sailing through the ocean to the Euphrates,[104] said that some Chaldaeans[105] had met him and recommended that Alexander keep away from Babylon. But Alexander ignored this advice and proceeded onward. . . . He was also perturbed by many other signs. For example, a tame ass, attacking the largest and most beautiful lion in his menagerie, kicked it to death. And when he had stripped to anoint himself and exercise, and was playing ball, and the young men who were playing went to put on their clothes, they found a fellow sitting silently on the throne, wearing the diadem and cloaked in the royal robe. The man, when asked who he was, was silent for a long time. Then, collecting himself, he said that his name was Dionysius, a Messenian by birth, and that charged with some crime he had been brought there from the coast and kept in chains for a long time; but just now the god Sarapis,[106] standing before him, had removed his chains, led him to that spot, and told him to don the robe and diadem, sit on the throne, and remain silent.

[74] On hearing of this, Alexander obeyed the seers and did away with the man. He himself now lost heart, and grew dubious about divine protection, and suspicious of his friends. He particularly feared Antipater and his sons, one of whom, Iolaus, was his chief cup-bearer; the other, Cassander, had lately arrived.[107] And when Cassander, on catching sight of some barbarians performing a ritual

103. Antipater was in command of the Macedonian home front in Alexander's absence.

104. That is, through the Persian Gulf.

105. A caste of Mesopotamian priests, famous for their powers of divination.

106. Sarapis was a god worshiped primarily in Egypt during the post-Alexander period, thought by some to have been invented by Ptolemy, the ruler there. But the mention of Sarapis here and of a temple called the Sarapeion in chapter 76 predate Ptolemy's sovereignty. The problem has been variously dealt with by modern historians.

107. Antipater was presumably an enemy because Alexander had ordered him to step down from his post in Macedonia and report to Babylon. But it is unclear whether Alexander was displeased with Antipater or meant him harm. Antipater did not comply, indicating he felt at least some misgivings, but sent his son Cassander to Babylon in his place. Those who suspected Alexander was poisoned (see chapter 77) largely believed that Cassander

bow, could not help laughing, since he had been reared in the Greek manner and had never seen such a thing before, Alexander flew into a rage, grasped Cassander's hair firmly with both hands, and knocked his head against the wall.

[75] Once Alexander had permitted himself to believe in divine influences, his mind grew so troubled and apprehensive that he regarded any odd or unusual occurrence, no matter how trivial, as a sign or portent; and his palace was full of people sacrificing, performing ritual purifications, and prophesying. . . .

After entertaining Nearchus and his men with a brilliant banquet, he bathed, as was his habit before going to bed; but then he joined Medius[108] in a carousal, at the latter's invitation. Then, after drinking all the next day, he fell into a fever.

[76] The royal diaries[109] give the following account of his disease. On the eighteenth of the month of Daesius[110] he slept in the bathhouse because of his fever. On the next day, after bathing, he moved back to his bedroom and spent the day playing at dice with Medius. Then, after bathing late in the day, he performed his sacrifices to the gods, took a little food, and was feverish during the night. On the twentieth, after bathing again, he performed his customary sacrifice; reclining in the bathhouse, he devoted himself to Nearchus, listening to his account of his voyage and of the Great Sea.[111]

On the twenty-first, spending the day in the same way, his fever worsened; he passed a difficult night, and on the next day was in a raging fever. After being carried outside, he lay down beside the great bath, where he talked with his officers about the vacant posts of his

---

had brought poison with him to Babylon, at his father's behest; but Plutarch rejects that theory.

108. This man, evidently a trusted friend of Alexander, is unknown apart from the large role he played in Alexander's final days.

109. There is great dispute as to what this document was or how much it can be trusted. Apparently a set of diaries was kept throughout Alexander's campaign, recording events day by day. Whether the account of Alexander's illness that Plutarch drew on here actually came from that set is unclear. Arrian claims to quote from the same royal diaries in his narrative of Alexander's fever (*Anabasis* 7.25–26), but the two versions differ in some details.

110. The beginning of June of 323 BCE. Alexander died, as we know from a Babylonian record, on June 11.

111. Plutarch refers to the Arabian Sea as though it were a part of the world-encircling Ocean.

realm and how they might be filled by able men. On the twenty-fourth, though in a high fever, he had himself carried out to perform his sacrifices. He gave orders for his most important officers to wait in the courtyard, and for the taxiarchs and pentakosiarchs[112] to pass the night outside. On the twenty-fifth, he was carried to the palace on the other side of the river, where he slept a little, though his fever did not let up. When his officers came to him, he could not speak. His condition was unchanged on the twenty-sixth, which was why the Macedonians, thinking he had died, came shouting to his door, threatened his companions, and forced their way in. And when the doors had been thrown open to them, they all filed past his couch, one by one, wearing only their tunics. . . . And on the twenty-eighth, toward evening, he died.

[77] Most of these details have been set down here exactly as recorded in the diaries. In the immediate aftermath, no one suspected poisoning; but five years later, they say, when information was given, Olympias had many persons put to death,[113] and cast out the ashes of Iolaus,[114] alleging that he had administered the poison. . . . But most think that the story about the poisoning is a complete fabrication.[115]

112. The various commanders and subcommanders of the army brigades. It is unclear why Alexander wanted them all present. In Arrian's account of the fatal illness, which overlaps closely with that of Plutarch but is not identical, Alexander was about to launch an invasion of Arabia.

113. Olympias, Alexander's mother, got power in Macedonia in 317 BCE by a strange series of twists and turns; see James Romm, *Ghost on the Throne: The Death of Alexander the Great and the War for Crown and Empire* (New York: Knopf, 2011), for a fuller account of this turbulent period. While in power Olympias had one of Cassander's brothers, and many of his supporters, executed. Rumors that had spread through the Greek world accused Cassander and his father Antipater of having poisoned Alexander.

114. Iolaus was Cassander's brother, and had been serving as the royal wine pourer at the time of Alexander's illness.

115. Of the surviving sources, several support the theory that Alexander was poisoned, while only Plutarch explicitly rejects it; Arrian implies that he believes Alexander died of illness. Modern historians remain divided on this question, or on whether it can even be answered.

Phocion

Phocion is one of Plutarch's less-known Greek lives, just as Phocion himself is a little-known historical figure—largely because he came to a full leadership role only after the death of Alexander the Great, that is, beyond the point at which most surveys of classical Greece reach their end. Yet Phocion (406–318 BCE) is a fascinating personality, and his later life illuminates the period after Alexander's death, when Athens faced some of its greatest challenges and weathered its stormiest political turbulence.

Plutarch deeply admired Phocion as an ideal soldier–statesman, the last of the breed once represented by Pericles and Cimon. In Phocion's day, as Plutarch observes, the combination of political and military skills in a single individual was becoming a rarity. The Athenians clearly valued this combination, since they reelected Phocion to the office of stratēgos *or general nearly continuously over the course of six decades. They also awarded him the epithet* chrēstos, *a word sometimes translated simply as "good" but referring especially to benefit and service. In the end, though, those qualities did not spare him their wrath, as Plutarch describes in one of his most moving and tragic closing sequences.*

[5] Though Phocion was exceedingly gentle and kind, his countenance resembled that of a man both gloomy and forbidding, so that anyone who did not know him would not have been inclined to converse with him alone. That was why, when Chares once raised a laugh among the Athenians by referring to Phocion's brow, Phocion said, "This brow has never done you any harm; but the laughter of these men has often made the city shed tears." Likewise Phocion's language was instructive in its sound insights and conceptions, but had an imperious, austere, and unsweetened brevity.

[6] As a young man Phocion attended and attached himself to the general Chabrias,[1] gaining much useful experience in warfare and even at times correcting his chief's uneven and inconsistent nature. For though at other times Chabrias was sluggish and hard to move, in the heat of battle he was so agitated and ardent that he would dash recklessly into danger with the boldest, which doubtless cost him his life in Chios when he drove his own trireme ahead of

---

1. An important Athenian military leader of the early fourth century BCE. By that time, the roles of *stratēgos* ("general") and politician, usually united in one person in the fifth century, had begun to separate, as Plutarch discusses below.

the rest to force a landing.[2] And as his unerring and efficient officer, Phocion would be seen either rousing Chabrias' zeal when the general procrastinated, or, alternatively, blunting his ill-timed impulses. For this reason Chabrias, who was warm-hearted and good, adored Phocion and promoted him for actions and commands, making him well-known to the Greeks and employing him in his most important ventures.

[7] Though he saw that the public men of his day had divided among themselves (as if by lot) the functions of the general and the orator; that some only spoke in the assembly and wrote decrees, while [others] were advancing themselves by serving as commanders and waging war, Phocion wished to adopt and restore the political system of Pericles, Aristides, and Solon, which had been regulated perfectly so that men could function in both capacities.[3] For indeed each of those men, in Archilochus' words, had been

> Both a servant of divine Enyalius,
> And versed in the lovely gifts of the Muses.[4]

And he saw that the city's patron goddess was the goddess both of war and of statecraft, and was referred to by both titles.

[8] Having thus positioned himself, Phocion conducted state affairs always with an eye to peace and tranquility, though he led more campaigns than any man of his day—more, in fact, than any previous general. And though he did not pursue or canvass for that office, neither did he avoid or shun it when the city called on him. It is agreed that he obtained the post of general forty-five times,[5] though he was never present at the election, but always abroad when the citizens summoned and elected him. And consequently men who do not reason soundly marvel at the Athenian populace, since Phocion

---

2. During the so-called Social War of the 350s, in which Athens was seeking to force its rebellious allies to remain in its naval league.

3. See the *Lives* of these three figures. The main office held by all three was *stratēgos*, member of the board of ten generals elected each year for one-year terms. Holders of that office were highly respected, not least because they were almost always from upper-class backgrounds, and so gained a hearing whenever they rose to speak in the assembly.

4. Archilochus was a poet of the seventh century BCE who also fought numerous times in regional wars.

5. A remarkable record, attesting both to Phocion's stamina—he continued active military service even past the age of eighty (see chapter 24)—and to the esteem in which the people held him.

opposed it more than anyone else and never spoke or acted to win its favor. Just as people think it right for kings to fraternize with their flatterers at dinnertime, so the Athenian people made use of their more gracious and pleasant politicians on unserious occasions; but when they needed a commander, they were invariably sober and earnest, and called on their severest and most prudent citizen, who alone, or more than the others, tended to oppose their desires and impulses. And when an oracle from Delphi was published, declaring that when all the other Athenians were of the same mind, one man would oppose the city's wishes, Phocion came forward and urged the people not to worry about the oracle, since *he* was the man to whom it referred, for he alone disapproved of everything they did.[6]

[11] Allies of Athens and islanders[7] regarded as enemies the ambassadors from Athens who arrived in the ship of any *other* commander, and would strengthen their walls, bank up their harbors, and convey their cattle, slaves, women, and children from the country to their cities. But if Phocion were in command, they would go out to meet him in their own ships, wearing garlands, and delighted to be escorting him to their homes.

[14] When Philip, who was making ambitious plans, reached the Hellespont with his entire force, intending to gain possession of the Chersonese, Perinthus, and Byzantium,[8] the Athenians were eager to aid their allies, and their orators argued for Chares to be sent out as general. But on sailing there, Chares accomplished nothing worthy of his force, nor would the cities even receive his army. Regarded with suspicion by everyone, he wandered about trying to raise funds from his allies and incurring the enemy's contempt. Meanwhile, when the people, spurred on by the orators, voiced their displeasure and regretted having sent aid to Byzantium, Phocion stood up and said that they should be angry not at their distrustful allies, but at their

6. This portrait of Phocion's relationship to the people is derived from that of Socrates in Plato's *Apology*. Phocion was a student of Plato in his youth, according to Plutarch.

7. Referring to the members of the Second Athenian League, the naval federation Athens established in the fourth century BCE. Its treatment of these states was gentler than in the days of its fifth-century empire, but still coercive.

8. See *Demosthenes* 17. Philip of Macedon's moves against the Chersonese, in 341 BCE, posed a direct threat to Athenian interests and broke the treaty between himself and Athens.

distrusted commanders: "For these men make you suspected even
by those who lack the power to save themselves without your help."

Moved by his argument, the people changed their minds and
urged Phocion to take another force and hasten in aid to their
Peloponnesian allies; and this measure, more than any other, proved
decisive in saving Byzantium. For Phocion's renown was already
great; and when Leon, a foremost citizen of Byzantium who was
esteemed for his virtue and had been an acquaintance of Phocion's
at the Academy, personally vouched for him to the city, his fellow
citizens would not let Phocion encamp outside their walls as he
wished, but opened their gates and received and kept company with
the Athenians, who proved not only blameless and moderate in their
conduct, but exceedingly zealous in combat because of Leon's pledge.
And thus Philip was driven from the Hellespont and held in contempt, though he had been thought to be invincible and irresistible,[9]
and Phocion seized some of Philip's ships and recovered a number
of cities that had been garrisoned. Landing in many parts of the
country, he plundered and overran it until he was wounded by those
who came to Philip's aid, and sailed home.

[16] By now the Athenians had become altogether hostile to
Philip, and in Phocion's absence appointed other generals for the war.
After sailing home from the islands, Phocion at first tried to persuade
the people, on the grounds that Philip was peaceably inclined and
averse to risk, to accept the terms he was offering.[10] . . . When he
could not persuade them, and Demosthenes, who carried the day,
urged the Athenians to join battle as far away from Attica as possible,
Phocion said, "My good friend, let us not consider *where* we'll fight
but *how* we'll win. For the war itself may be fought at a distance; but
war's horrors always press the defeated very closely." . . .

In general, Phocion thought that the Athenians should accept
Philip's governance and his generous overtures, but when Demades[11]
had written a decree stating that the city should participate in the

9. Philip's reverse at Perinthus and Byzantium was the first defeat the
Macedonian king had suffered in many years of constant campaigning.

10. Despite his many terms as general, Phocion was temperamentally dis-
inclined toward warfare, especially when Athens' chances were not clearly
favorable; see chapter 21.

11. An Athenian politician of Phocion's day, who was notoriously susceptible to bribes and therefore willing to support the Macedonian cause in the
assembly.

joint peace and in the Hellenic council,[12] Phocion would not allow them to commit themselves until they learned what Philip expected of them. But owing to the crisis Phocion's opinion was overruled. And as soon as he saw the Athenians repenting (since they were required to furnish Philip with triremes and cavalrymen), Phocion said, "This is what I was afraid of when I opposed you; but since you agreed to it, you mustn't be grieved or disheartened, remembering that your ancestors sometimes ruled and sometimes submitted to rule, doing both honorably and thereby saving both their city and the Greeks." And when Philip had died,[13] Phocion would not allow his fellow citizens to make a thank offering for good tidings, saying that it would be ignoble to rejoice and that the force that had arrayed itself against them at Chaeronea[14] was now smaller by only one man.

[17] When Demosthenes was reviling Alexander, who was already on his way to Thebes,[15] Phocion said, "'Wretch, why would you seek to provoke a savage man,'[16] who yearns for great renown? Or do you wish, with such a conflagration nearby, to engulf the city in flames? But I shall not permit my fellow citizens, regardless of their wishes, to perish, since it was to that end that I assumed the office of general." When Thebes had been destroyed, and Alexander demanded the surrender of Demosthenes, Lycurgus, Hyperides, and Charidemus,[17] the assembly gazed steadfastly at Phocion; and when he had been called upon many times by name, he stood up. Drawing

12. Referring to the league formed after the Greek defeat at Chaeronea (338 BCE). Athens and other Greek states were required to settle their quarrels with one another and accept Macedonian leadership.

13. In 336 BCE, Philip was assassinated, giving Athens the illusion that Macedonian power had been destroyed. See *Alexander* 10.

14. At the battle of Chaeronea, Philip's forces, co-generaled by Philip's son Alexander, had defeated the combined armies of Athens and Thebes. See *Demosthenes* 19.

15. The context is the first year of Alexander's reign, 335 BCE, when Thebes revolted from Macedonian rule. See *Alexander* 11 and *Demosthenes* 23, as well as Arrian's *Anabasis* 1.7–10.

16. The quote is from Homer's *Odyssey* 9.494. The warning was spoken by Odysseus' crew to stop their captain from taunting the Cyclops—a taunt that led to disaster later on.

17. See *Demosthenes* 23. Plutarch gives varying versions of how many orators were on the list of those demanded by Alexander, or who they were, but Demosthenes was certainly among them, having done his utmost to support the Theban revolt.

to his side one of his oldest friends, whom he loved and trusted above all others, he said, "These men have so misled the city that if someone should ask for Nicocles here, I would surrender him. For my own part, I would consider it a piece of good fortune to die on your behalf. I also feel pity, men of Athens, for those who have fled here from Thebes. But it is enough for the Greeks to have Thebes to lament.[18] And that is why it is better for both parties if we supplicate and conciliate our conquerors rather than go to war with them."

It is said that when Alexander received the Athenians' original decree, he tossed it aside and turned away from the envoys. But he accepted the second because it was brought by Phocion,[19] since Alexander had heard from his elders that Philip had admired the man. And he not only granted Phocion an audience and heard his petition, but even listened to his advice. And Phocion advised Alexander that if he yearned for peace he should bring the war to an end; but if he aimed at renown, he should change course and turn his attention from the Greeks to the barbarians.

[18] As for the story about the money, there is general agreement that Alexander sent Phocion a present of one hundred talents. When this sum had been carried to Athens, Phocion asked the bearers why, out of so many Athenians, Alexander was offering so much money to him alone. When they replied, "Because he judges you to be the city's only good and honorable man," Phocion said, "Then let him allow me to be so always, and to be thought so." When on following him home they saw the great modesty of his household—his wife kneading bread and Phocion himself drawing water from the well to wash his feet[20]—they were indignant and pressed the money on him even more urgently, saying that it was dreadful for a man who was the king's friend to live so poorly.

[21] When Alexander wrote demanding that the Athenian send him triremes, and the orators objected, the council urged Phocion to state his opinion. "Well, I maintain," said he, "that one must either prevail over the powerful by force of arms, or be their allies."

18. Implying that Alexander might destroy Athens if his will was thwarted, just as he had destroyed Thebes.

19. In *Demosthenes* Plutarch gave Demades the lead role in assuaging Alexander.

20. In a well-off household like Phocion's, slaves would normally do these jobs.

[22] When Asclepiades, son of Hipparchus, first announced that Alexander had died,[21] Demades urged the Athenians to pay no attention to him, since if the report were true the whole world would long ago have been reeking of the corpse. But Phocion, seeing that the people were incited to revolt, tried to appease and restrain them. And when many leaped onto the dais and shouted that Asclepiades had reported the truth and that Alexander was dead, Phocion said, "Well, if he's dead today, he'll be so tomorrow and the next day, and we may therefore deliberate in peace, and with greater safety."

[23] When Leosthenes,[22] after plunging the city into the Lamian War,[23] mockingly asked Phocion, who was disgusted, what good *he* had done the city in all his years serving as general, Phocion replied, "No small good, since the citizens are now buried in their own tombs."[24] And when Leosthenes was talking boldly and boastfully in the assembly, Phocion said, "Your speeches, lad, resemble cypress trees: though lofty and sublime, they do not bear fruit." And when Hyperides, on rising to speak, asked, "When, Phocion, will you advise the Athenians to go to war?" Phocion replied, "Whenever I see the young men willing to defend their posts, the wealthy to contribute money, and the politicians to refrain from stealing public funds."

When many marveled at the forces assembled by Leosthenes, and asked Phocion what he thought of the preparations, he answered, "They seem excellent for a quarter-mile race; but I worry about the war's long run, when the city has no more money, ships, or men-at-arms." And the event justified him. For at first Leosthenes succeeded brilliantly, overpowering the Boeotians in battle and driving Antipater into Lamia; it is even said that the city, harboring high hopes, was constantly holding festivals and sacrifices in honor of good tidings. But when people thought to prove that Phocion had been mistaken, and asked him whether *he* would not like to have

21. In the summer of 323 BCE. For one version of Alexander's death in Babylon, see *Alexander* 75–76, and Arrian, *Anabasis* 7.25–26. Other sources claim Alexander was poisoned.

22. An Athenian mercenary captain appointed by the war party at Athens to lead the coalition of cities rebelling from Macedon in the wake of Alexander's death. Plutarch is wrong to say he plunged the city into war, though he certainly helped push the assembly in that direction.

23. The rebellion against Macedonian control, launched in 323 BCE; see *Demosthenes* 27.

24. Instead of on foreign battlefields.

performed such feats, he replied, "Oh, by all means! Yet I stand by my earlier advice."

[24] When the Athenians were determined to make war on the Boeotians,[25] Phocion at first opposed them; and when his friends said that he would be put to death if he offended the Athenians, he said, "Unjustly, if I act in their best interests; justly, if I do not." When he saw that the people would not relent but were raising an uproar, he ordered the herald to proclaim that all the Athenians between the ages of sixteen and sixty were to take rations for five days and follow him straight from the assembly. An enormous uproar ensued, with the elderly men leaping up and shouting, at which point Phocion said, "Have no fear. For I, who will be your general, am in my eightieth year." And thus, for the time being, he restrained them and changed their minds.

[25] When the coast was being ravaged by Micion, who had disembarked at Rhamnous with many Macedonians and mercenaries and was overrunning the countryside, Phocion led the Athenians out against him.[26] . . . When he had attacked the enemy forces and routed them decisively, he killed Micion along with many others. As for the Greek army in Thessaly, when Leonnatus and the Macedonians from Asia had joined forces with Antipater,[27] the Greeks prevailed in battle. And with Antiphilus leading the Greek phalanx, Menon the Thessalian the cavalry, Leonnatus fell.

[26] Shortly thereafter, when Craterus had crossed to Greece from Asia with a large force,[28] and another battle was fought at Crannon, the Greeks were defeated, though the defeat was not serious, nor were there many casualties. But because they had disobeyed their commanders, who were young and good-natured,[29] and because

25. The Boeotians supported the Macedonian side, so that Leosthenes had to first vanquish them before advancing to meet his main foe, Antipater, the Macedonian commander.

26. These actions occurred during the Lamian War of 323–322 BCE. Phocion was given charge of the home guard during that war, defending Attica from Macedonian invasion.

27. Leonnatus, one of Alexander's top generals, came over from Asia late in 323 BCE to help rescue Antipater from Lamia.

28. See note 27. Craterus followed the same route as Leonnatus, after the latter failed to help Antipater.

29. Leosthenes by this time had been killed in a skirmish, and his successors were not nearly as revered by the troops.

at the same time Antipater succeeded in suborning a number of their cities, the Greeks melted away disgracefully and surrendered their liberty.

As soon as Antipater led his force to Athens, Demosthenes and Hyperides left the city,[30] but Demades, who was unable to pay even a fraction of the money he owed the city for damages (he had been convicted on seven counts; and since he had been disenfranchised he was barred from speaking in public), managed on that occasion to obtain immunity, whereupon he wrote a decree endorsing an autonomous embassy to negotiate a peace treaty with Antipater. But when the people had misgivings and summoned Phocion, maintaining that he was the only man they trusted, he said, "Well, if I had been trusted when I gave you my advice, we would not now be deliberating about such matters." When the decree had been ratified, Phocion was sent to Antipater, who had encamped at the Cadmeia and was preparing to march into Attica immediately. Phocion's first request was that Antipater remain where he was and make the treaty. And when Craterus said that it was unfair of Phocion to try to persuade them to remain in the territory of friends and allies and plunder it, when it was in their power to avail themselves of enemy lands, Antipater took his hand and said, "We must grant this favor to Phocion." But as for the treaty's other terms, he urged the Athenians to leave those up to the conquerors.

[27] When Phocion had returned to Athens, and the Athenians decided, under duress, to do as he advised, he returned to Thebes with the other ambassadors. . . . But when Phocion tried to discuss the treaty, Antipater replied that there would be a friendship and an alliance with the Athenians only if they surrendered Demosthenes and Hyperides, restored their city's ancestral constitution (according to which a man's property determined his eligibility for office),[31] accepted a garrison at Munychia,[32] and paid the Macedonians' war costs in addition to a fine.

30. The fate of these two from this point forward can be followed in *Demosthenes* 28–29.

31. This characterization of the new constitution as a return to ancient forms is a bit disingenuous. Athens had, for much of the fifth century, limited certain offices to the top one or two property classes (out of four). But the new rules laid down by Antipater stripped the poor of rights they had always enjoyed.

32. Munychia was a nearly impregnable hill in the harbor town of Piraeus. With that position occupied, the Macedonians could, if they desired,

[28] Thus the Athenians accepted a Macedonian garrison under the command of Menyllus, an honest man who was friendly to Phocion. But the measure seemed arrogant, and more a display of insolent power than an occupation made necessary by circumstances. And the timing added not a little to the people's suffering. For the garrison was brought in on the twentieth of the month of Boedromion, when the Athenians, in the course of celebrating the Mysteries, conduct Iacchus from the city to Eleusis,³³ and accordingly the disruption of those rites moved most people to recall the gods' earlier visitations and those of recent times. . . . The garrison, under Menyllus' command, did not harass the people; but when more than twelve thousand citizens had been disenfranchised because of their poverty, those who remained in the city appeared to be suffering grievous and undeserved harm, while those who, for the same reason, departed and migrated to Thrace (Antipater having provided them with land and a city) were like men who had been forced to surrender after a siege.

[29] It now occurred to many to recall that those kings—Alexander and Philip—had been magnanimous and capable of a noble forgiveness, unlike Antipater.³⁴ . . . Yet by interceding with Antipater, Phocion succeeded in exempting many men from exile, and for those who *were* banished he saw to it that instead of being expelled from Greece beyond the Ceraunian Mountains and Taenarum,³⁵ they were permitted to settle in the Peloponnese. (One of these was the public informer Hagnonides.) Managing civic affairs gently and lawfully, Phocion kept the men of education and culture constantly in office;³⁶ as for those who were inclined to meddle or to engage in revolutionary activities, and who were fading into obscurity from the

---

interdict Athens' food imports. Athens had never before had a Macedonian garrison on its territory, though several other cities received one after the battle of Chaeronea in 338 BCE.

33. The procession of the Mysteries cult was an important ritual in which the Athenians took great pride; see *Alcibiades* 34.

34. Alexander and Philip had both treated Athens with great deference, hoping to win the city's voluntary allegiance rather than force it into submission.

35. That is, into what is now Albania and North Africa.

36. A euphemistic way of saying that the rich and near rich wielded power in this new Athens while the poor had none.

fact that they were not holding office or raising any uproars, Phocion taught them to be fond of home and to delight in farming their land.

[30] When the Athenians earnestly begged Phocion to approach Antipater and persuade him to remove the garrison, he invariably rejected the mission, either because he did not expect to succeed or because he observed that the people, under the influence of fear, were behaving more temperately and conducting their public affairs in a more orderly manner (though he did persuade Antipater not to exact the war costs and fine, but to allow the Athenians to defer payment).

[31] When Antipater died (after appointing Polysperchon as general and Cassander as chiliarch), Cassander immediately rose up,[37] took charge of state affairs, and hastily dispatched Nicanor to be Menyllus' successor as garrison commander, with orders to gain possession of Munychia before Antipater's death became common knowledge.[38] When this was done, and the Athenians learned a few days later that Antipater was dead, Phocion was censured and maligned, since it was assumed that he had known of Antipater's death beforehand and had kept silent as a favor to Nicanor. But Phocion paid no attention to these charges; and by visiting Nicanor and conferring with him, he not only secured his good will and kindness for the Athenians, but even persuaded him to undertake various costly exhibitions as director of games.

[32] In the meantime Polysperchon, who had personal charge of the king[39] and was seeking to frustrate Cassander's schemes, sent the people of Athens a letter saying that the king was restoring their democracy and urging all the Athenians to live as citizens according to their ancestral customs.[40] This was part of a plot against Phocion.

---

37. Cassander, who was Antipater's son, bitterly resented the decision by his father to hand down power to Polysperchon, a veteran of Alexander's campaigns who was not a blood relation. Cassander's refusal to accept this decision precipitated a civil war.

38. Cassander's move was designed to secure the Piraeus for his own use in the coming war, by placing a trusted associate, Nicanor, in charge of it. The fortified harbor of the Piraeus was the Greek world's best naval base.

39. The Macedonian king referred to here was Philip III, the mentally debilitated son of Philip II, and the half brother of Alexander the Great. Philip III, sometimes known as Arrhidaeus, was put on the throne despite the fact that he needed a regent (in this case Polysperchon) to manage him.

40. This decree promised not only Athens but the Greeks generally that they could return to the liberal governments they had enjoyed in former times, before the rise of Macedonian power. Polysperchon, pressed by the

For Polysperchon, who was planning to arrange matters in the city to suit his own interests (as he soon made clear by his actions), did not expect to accomplish his ends unless Phocion was banished; and he assumed the man *would* be banished once the disenfranchised had overwhelmed the government, and the demagogues and paid informers had regained control of the dais. Since the Athenians were stirred up by his letter, Nicanor wished to converse with them, and when a council met in the Piraeus he came forward, relying on Phocion to ensure his personal safety. But when Dercyllus, the district general, tried to arrest him, Nicanor escaped (he became aware of the attempt just in time).[41]

As the civil war between rival Macedonian leaders Cassander and Polysperchon heated up, Phocion found himself caught in the middle. He was a natural ally of Cassander, who favored keeping Athens an oligarchy as his father Antipater had fashioned it; but Polysperchon, who was nominally in control of Macedonian policy, had passed a decree restoring to Athens, and other Greek cities, their former democratic constitutions. After this decree took effect and Athens' oligarchic government fell, Phocion was kicked out of the city, along with several followers. He went north to see Polysperchon and ask for support, but the Macedonian leader, desperately clinging to power himself, chose not to make an exception to his new freedom decree.

[34] A guard now surrounded Phocion and his associates; and all of his friends who were not standing nearby, on seeing this, covered their faces and saved themselves by fleeing. Cleitus[42] brought the captives to Athens, ostensibly to stand trial, but in fact already sentenced to die. And the manner of their conveyance was also distressing, since they were carried on wagons through the Cerameicus to the theater.[43] After bringing them there, Cleitus kept them confined until the magistrates had filled the assembly—opening the dais and

---

revolt of Cassander, was hoping to win the Greeks' support by appearing to liberate them (while retaining full military control of the region).

41. It was widely believed that Phocion had tipped off Nicanor to save his life, meaning that Phocion was again colluding in Cassander's attempt to make the Piraeus his base.

42. A top Macedonian officer.

43. The theater of Dionysus at Athens was normally the site of performances of tragedies and comedies, but it was occasionally used as space for political proceedings. It is not clear what disgrace was involved in bringing Phocion there by cart rather than on foot.

the theater to everyone, male and female, even slaves, foreigners, and criminals.[44] And when they had read the king's letter[45] aloud, in which he said that though he had determined that these men had betrayed him, he was handing them over to be tried by their fellow citizens, who were free and autonomous, Cleitus brought the men in.

The noblest citizens, when they saw Phocion, covered their faces, hung their heads, and wept. One of them, rising to his feet, had the courage to say that since the king had entrusted so important a trial to the people, it was just as well that slaves and foreigners leave the assembly. And when the multitude bridled at this, and shouted that the oligarchs and haters of democracy should be stoned, no one else ventured to speak on Phocion's behalf, whereupon Phocion himself, though he could hardly make himself heard, said, "Do you want to put me to death unjustly or justly?" When some answered, "Justly," he said, "And how will you reach a decision unless you have listened?" But when they would hear no more, he drew near and said, "Then I admit that I have done wrong, and I accept the death penalty for the policies I enacted. But why, men of Athens, will you kill *these* men, who have done no wrong?" When the crowd replied, "Because they are your friends," Phocion stood apart and remained silent. And Hagnonides,[46] holding the decree he had written, read it aloud. It said that the people should vote as to whether they thought these men had done wrong; and if convicted, they should be put to death.

[35] When the decree had been read aloud, a number of people demanded an additional clause, that Phocion should be tortured before execution, and said that the rack should be brought in and the executioners summoned. But Hagnonides, who felt that such a proceeding was barbaric and abominable, and saw that even Cleitus was disgusted by it, said, "When we catch that rogue Callimedon,[47] gentlemen of Athens, let us torture *him*. But where Phocion is concerned I shall not write such an order." At this some decent fellow called out in answer, "You do right! For if we torture Phocion, what are we to do to *you*?" When the decree had been ratified and a vote by show of hands was taken, no one remained seated; all stood up,

44. Against constitutional law, the leaders of the new democracy had allowed noncitizens into the assembly.
45. That is, the letter of King Philip III of Macedon, the mentally incompetent monarch then under the control of Polysperchon.
46. Leader of the democratic counterrevolution.
47. A fugitive member of the fallen oligarchic regime.

many having donned garlands,[48] and voted to condemn the prisoners to death.

[36] When the assembly was dismissed, the condemned men were led to the prison. The rest of them, receiving the embraces of their friends and relatives, walked along weeping and wailing; but the onlookers who gazed at Phocion's face, which looked just as it had on those occasions when he was sent forth from the assembly to serve as general, marveled at the man's impassivity and greatness of heart.

[37] It was the nineteenth day of the month of Munichion,[49] and the cavalry, conducting the procession in honor of Zeus, was passing by the prison. Some of the horsemen removed their garlands, while others, gazing at the prison door, shed tears. And it was clear to persons not altogether savage or debased by spite and envy that it was terribly impious for the city not to exercise restraint on that day and keep itself unpolluted by a public execution while holding a festival. Nevertheless, as if their triumph over him left something to be desired, Phocion's enemies passed a decree stipulating that Phocion's body was to be sent beyond the border and that no Athenian was to kindle a pyre in honor of his burial. Accordingly, no friend dared to touch his body. But a certain Conopion, a man in the habit of rendering such services for a fee, conveyed the corpse beyond Eleusis, obtained fire in Megara, and burned it. Phocion's wife, who was present with her female slaves, heaped up an empty tomb there and poured a libation. Putting the bones in the fold of her dress and conveying them home by night, she buried them beside the hearth, saying, "Dear hearth, I entrust you with the remains of a good man. Restore them to his ancestral tombs once the Athenians have come to their senses."

[38] And indeed, when a short time had elapsed, and their state affairs taught them what sort of steward and guardian of temperance and justice they had lost, the people erected a bronze statue of Phocion and buried his bones at public expense.

48. As a gesture of celebration.
49. The day of an Athenian festival in honor of Zeus. The year was 318 BCE.

Glossary of Names, Places, Peoples, and Military Terms

All dates are BCE unless otherwise indicated.

Aegae: Important Macedonian city (modern Vergina), originally the capital of the country, where Philip II, father of Alexander III, was assassinated and where members of the royal family were interred. Recent excavations have brought to light a tomb there that may well be that of Philip.

Aegina: An island off the coast of Attica, frequently at war with Sparta, Athens, or both.

Agesilaus: Long-lived Spartan king whose aggressive pursuit of power dominated Spartan policy throughout the first half of the fourth century. Agesilaus led an expedition into Asia, the forerunner of Alexander the Great's anabasis, that for a time posed a serious threat to the Persian empire. He later tangled with the Thebans in the era of Epaminondas.

Agis II: Spartan king during most of the Peloponnesian War and its immediate aftermath. Succeeded by Agesilaus when his eldest son, Leotychides, was thought to have been fathered by Alcibiades.

Alcibiades: Athenian general and politician who rose to prominence at an early age in about 420. A former disciple of Socrates, he was a man of enormous charm and great wealth. He talked the Athenians into the expedition to Sicily; after he was removed from command of the expedition and indicted for impiety he fled to the Spartans and gave them tips on conducting the war against Athens. He returned to the Athenian side in 411 but was exiled in 406 and died two years later under mysterious circumstances. He is best known to modern readers through a stunning speech he gives at the end of Plato's *Symposium*.

Alcmaeonids: Descendants of Alcmaeon; a wealthy family whose members (including Cleisthenes, Pericles, and Alcibiades) exerted great political influence at Athens.

Alexander I: King of Macedon at the time of Xerxes' invasion of Greece, when he generally supported the Persians; ancestor of Alexander III.

Alexander II: King of Macedon from 371 to 369.

Alexander III, "the Great": Born to Philip II and Olympias in 356, ascended the throne after his father's murder in 336; died in Babylon, probably of disease, in 323. Inherited from his father the most powerful army in the world, along with a plan to use it in an invasion of western Asia. From

334 to 327 Alexander conquered all the territories that had comprised the Persian empire, and then spent two more years marching through India until compelled by his troops to turn homeward.

Alexander of Pherae: Tyrant who took power in Thessaly in the fourth century, using mercenary troops and terror tactics to dominate the Thessalians.

Ammon: Egyptian deity generally identified with Zeus. Alexander III consulted the oracle of Ammon in Egypt in 331 and claimed, possibly out of sincere belief, that he was descended from the god.

Amphipolis: City in Thrace in northern Greece that was of strategic importance because it guarded access by river to major sources of timber (for shipbuilding) and precious metals. Originally settled by Thracians, it was made a colony of Athens in 437 but was lost to the Spartans in 424. The historian Thucydides held a command in the area at the time of its loss; he was held accountable and exiled. After this time Amphipolis maintained its independence until Philip of Macedon (Alexander's father) took it in 357.

Anaxagoras: Philosopher and natural scientist living at Athens until he was sent into exile in the mid-fifth century, the victim of hatreds directed against his most famous student, Pericles.

Antipater: Father of Cassander, Alexander's boyhood friend; appointed by Alexander to govern Macedonia's European empire while the Asian campaign was under way.

Archidamus: Spartan king during the first phase of the Peloponnesian War, the so-called Archidamian War (431–421).

Aristides: Athenian political leader during the early fifth century, nicknamed "the Just" because of his reputation for fair dealing. Aristides' conservative politics and aristocratic background contrasted sharply with the more populist Themistocles, with whom he often clashed and competed.

Aristotle: Greek philosopher and head of Peripatetic school, appointed Alexander's tutor for three years starting near the end of 343.

Arrian: Greek writer who studied with the Stoic sage Epictetus in his youth, then served Rome as governor of an eastern province and commander of a sizable army. Sometime before the middle of the second century CE, he wrote the *Anabasis* of Alexander, along with several other works dealing with both military and spiritual topics.

Artabanus: Persian noble at the time of Xerxes' invasion of Greece (480); brother to Darius and uncle to Xerxes; depicted by Herodotus as an elder sage.

Artaxerxes II: King of Persia from 404 to 358. His long reign spanned from the end of the Peloponnesian War through the series of confrontations between Thebes and Sparta. Artaxerxes played arbiter of Greek affairs after the signing of the Peace of Antalcidas in 387.

Artemisia: Carian queen who ruled Halicarnassus for the Persians and accompanied Xerxes on his invasion of Greece in 480.

Aspasia: Milesian courtesan living at Athens who became the consort of Pericles. Her influence over her husband was said to have helped spark the Peloponnesian War.

assembly: The primary decision-making body of the Athenian democracy. Any citizen could attend its meetings, where speakers addressed the policy choices the city faced and votes were taken. Over time the assembly took on greater powers, especially in the constitutional reforms of Ephialtes in 462 and 461.

Attalus: Macedonian noble from the fourth century and son-in-law of Parmenio and uncle of Cleopatra, Philip II's last wife. Alexander perceived him as an enemy and had him assassinated shortly after coming to power.

Babylon: Mesopotamian city that became one of the capitals of the Persian empire after its conquest by Cyrus the Great in the sixth century. Alexander captured it after his victory at Gaugamela in 331 and celebrated the rites of Bel, its chief deity. He returned there in 324 and died there in June of 323.

Bactria: Northeastern province of the Persian empire encompassing modern northern Afghanistan and southern Uzbekistan and Tajikistan.

Bessus: Satrap of Bactria in the mid-fourth century and fierce foe of Alexander the Great.

boeotarch: Officer of the Boeotian League, elected for a one-year term. A board of boeotarchs, usually seven in number, directed affairs of the league, a regional hegemony headed by Thebes.

Boeotia: Region of northern Greece centered on Thebes; base of operations for Mardonius' army in 480 and 479.

boulē: The executive board at Athens that supervised the agenda and schedule of the assembly. At first 400 in number, the boulē was expanded to 500 in the fifth century and its powers increased as Athens' constitution evolved.

Chaeronea: City in Boeotia, the site of a battle that in 338 ended an attempt by Thebes and Athens to prevent Philip II from dominating mainland Greece. Alexander led the decisive cavalry charge that smashed the Theban infantry and defeated the Sacred Band.

Chersonese: Long peninsula in the eastern Aegean, modern Gallipoli; largely dominated by Athens starting in the mid-sixth century; ruled by Miltiades (the younger) before his escape to Athens.

Chios: Eastern Aegean island that remained loyal to Athens until 413, after which it resisted Athens until the end of the war. Chios was one of the very few members of the Delian League that retained its own fleet.

Cimon: Athenian political and military leader who came to prominence after the Persian wars (470s and 460s). Cimon took the lead role in foreign policy after Themistocles fell from grace, and advocated a more friendly and collaborative stance toward Sparta. Cimon in turn fell from favor after the Spartans revealed their mistrust of Athens at Mount Ithome.

Cleisthenes: Alcmaeonid politician who spearheaded a democratic reform of the Athenian constitution in 508.

Cleombrotus: Spartan king of the early fourth century, killed in the battle of Leuctra.

Cleon: Athenian politician and demagogue who rose to power after the death of Pericles. He was responsible for the brilliant Athenian success at Sphacteria in 425 but was killed soon afterward at the battle of Amphipolis.

Cleopatra: (1) Last wife of Philip II of Macedon and mother of his son Caranus, whom some viewed as a rival to Alexander for the Macedonian throne; killed after Philip's death. (2) Daughter of Philip and Olympias, and sister of Alexander, whose wedding festivities in 336 were the occasion of her father's murder.

Coenus: High-ranking officer under Alexander who led a decisive cavalry movement at the battle of the Hydaspes. In the Hyphasis mutiny of 325 he served as spokesman for the troops who did not want to proceed farther eastward. He died of disease shortly thereafter.

Companions: Alexander's trusted inner circle of advisers and friends, consisting of less than a hundred Macedonian nobles.

Corinth: Greek city located near the isthmus where the Peloponnese joins mainland Greece.

Craterus: A revered officer in Alexander's army who executed many crucial commissions for Alexander, serving virtually as second in command after Parmenio's death. Appointed to lead the veterans homeward from Opis and assume command of the home front from Antipater (323), he played a crucial role in the Lamian War and died in battle in 321.

Cyrus ("the Great"): Founder of the Persian empire in the mid-sixth century. His tomb at Pasargadae was restored by Alexander in 324.

Cyrus (the Younger): Brother of the Persian king Artaxerxes II and satrap of Lydia in the late fifth century. He died in an attempt to overthrow his brother in 401.

Darius I: King of Persia who ordered first invasion of Greece in 490.

Darius II: King of Persia during much of the Peloponnesian War, in which he supported the Spartans. He reigned from 423 to 405.

Darius III: King of Persia starting in 336, the same year Alexander came to the throne; portrayed by Arrian as a coward and a bungler whose flight from battle lost the engagements at Issus and Gaugamela. Assassinated in exile by a group of usurpers led by Bessus, Darius was given burial with full royal honors by Alexander.

Datis: Persian general and a leader in the invasion of Greece culminating in the battle of Marathon (490).

Delian League: Alliance of Greek city-states led by Athens, formed in 477 as a counterweight to Persian power after the Greek victories at Salamis and Plataea. Though it began as a strictly cooperative venture, the league became dominated by Athens to a degree that effectively made it an Athenian empire.

Delos: Sacred Greek island at the center of the Aegean, supposedly Apollo's birthplace.

Delphi: Greek oracular shrine where the priestess of Apollo, known as the Pythia, answered questions about the future; repository of vast wealth.

Demades: Athenian politician of the late fourth century; an advocate of collaboration with Alexander and the Macedonians.

Demosthenes: Leading Athenian orator and politician in the third quarter of the fourth century. Led the opposition to Philip II's expansion, and then, after Philip's death, worked quietly behind the scenes to oppose Alexander. After the defeat of Athens in the Lamian War, he was exiled and hunted as an enemy of Macedonia; he killed himself in 322.

Epaminondas: Theban general who led the military and political resurgence of Thebes in the 370s and 360s. His brilliant tactics, and the newly constituted infantry forces he had helped train (together with his co-leader Pelopidas), enabled Thebes to defeat Sparta at the battle of Leuctra (371), drive deep into Spartan territory, and liberate the enslaved Messenians.

Ephialtes: Athenian political leader who, together with Pericles, introduced a set of radical democratic constitutional reforms in 462 and 461. Ephialtes was killed shortly thereafter, evidently by conservative opponents.

Epipolae: Strategic height overlooking Syracuse, site of the night battle that turned the tide against the Athenians in 413.

Euboea: Long island off the north coast of Attica. Athenian military and economic strategy depended on retaining control over Euboea.

Gedrosia: Desert region spanning the coast of modern Pakistan and eastern Iran. Alexander marched his army through this land on his return from India in 325, at huge cost.

Harpalus: Boyhood friend of Alexander who was appointed to the important post of royal treasurer on the Asian campaign. He defected and fled to Greece in 333 but was welcomed back by Alexander and granted amnesty. During the satrapal purge of 324 he again decamped from Babylon, where he had been spending lavishly out of purloined funds, and tried, unsuccessfully, to stir up a revolt against Alexander in Greece. Exiled from Athens, he was murdered by an associate on Crete in 323.

Hellespont: Modern strait of Dardanelles and surrounding region; used as a crossing point between Europe and Asia, first by Xerxes marching his armies toward Greece in 480, then by Alexander in 334 leading his forces in the opposite direction.

Heracles: Son of Zeus by Alcmene, a mortal; by legend, an ancestor of Alexander as well as the kings of Sparta. The mythic labors of Heracles were echoed in Athenian legends about Theseus, and Heracles was thought to have befriended and helped Theseus on numerous occasions.

Herodotus: Greek historian of the mid-fifth century, originally from Halicarnassus in Asia Minor. His work, today known as the *Histories*, gives an account of the Persian empire from about 560 to 479, focusing on its conflicts with the Greeks.

hoplites: Heavy-armed infantry who formed the backbone of Greek armies during the Classical Age. As they were expected to pay for their own armor, hoplites, in most cases, were moderately well-off citizens.

Hyperides: Athenian orator and politician known for his opposition to Macedonian power in the era of Philip and Alexander the Great.

Ionia: A term usually used to refer to the Greek-populated coast of Asia Minor. The uprising of the Greek cities on that coast in 499 is known as the Ionian Revolt.

Lacedaemon: South-central region of the Peloponnese, centered on and politically dominated by Sparta. "Lacedaemonians" is the more common Greek term for the people commonly (though less precisely) called Spartans.

Lamachus: Athenian general who was given shared command of the Sicilian expedition with Nicias and Alcibiades in 415 and was killed in battle in 414.

Leonidas: Spartan king (489–480) who led the Greek forces at Thermopylae and died there.

Lesbos: The largest of the islands off the coast of Asia Minor. Its main city is Mytilene.

Lycurgus: Legendary Spartan lawgiver, credited with the constitutional reforms that produced Sparta's uniquely closed and militarized society. If he in fact existed, Lycurgus can best be dated to the eighth century.

Lydia: Non-Greek kingdom in western Anatolia; imperial master of various Ionian Greek cities starting in the early sixth century.

Lysander: Spartan admiral during the last phase of the Peloponnesian War (late fifth century), victor at the battle of Aegospotami, and arbiter of the terms of Athenian surrender. Lysander attained power not through royal birth but through the patronage of King Agesilaus, reportedly his lover.

Macedonia: Partly Hellenic or Hellenized kingdom situated in the north of mainland Greece.

Malli: An Indian people usually identified with the Malavas mentioned in Sanskrit literature. Their fierce resistance to Alexander during his trip down the Indus in 325 resulted in much bloody fighting, including one siege in which Alexander, trapped almost alone within a town's walls, was badly wounded by an arrow in the chest.

Marathon: Coastal plain about twenty-five miles northeast of the city of Athens; site of the battle in 490 in which Athenian troops defeated the invading Persians.

Mardonius: Persian noble who commanded the land army of Darius in the invasion of Xerxes (480–479).

Medes: An Asian people who became powerful starting in the seventh century, participating in the defeat of the Assyrians at Nineveh in 612, thereafter masters of the northern and eastern segments of the Assyrian empire; subjugated by the Persians in 550, they became integrated into Persian society, such that Greek authors often call the Persians "Medes."

Megara: City located between Athens and Corinth and a member of the Peloponnesian League. The Megarian Decree of the Athenians barred Megara from commerce with Athens and its empire, and was one of the causes of the war.

Messenians: Inhabitants of Messenia, the district of the Peloponnesus west of Sparta. Conquered by Sparta in the eighth and seventh centuries, most of the Messenians were forced to work their own land for Spartan landlords. Something between serfs and sharecroppers, they were known as helots.

Miletus: Ionian Greek city located on the coast of Asia Minor; intellectual and economic capital of the Asian Greeks, prior to its destruction by Persia in 494.

Miltiades (the younger): Athenian nobleman who ruled the Chersonese on behalf of Athens in the late sixth and early fifth centuries; escaped Persian pursuit and arrived at Athens in time to serve as one of ten generals at the battle of Marathon. His son Cimon became an important Athenian leader.

Minos: Mythic king of Crete in the time of Theseus, said to have demanded tribute from Athens in the form of young men and women to be fed to the monstrous Minotaur.

Nicias: Athenian politician and general. He helped negotiate the peace treaty of 421 between Athens and Sparta that bears his name. Opposed to the expedition against Sicily, he was nevertheless made one of its three commanders in 415, and became principal commander after the defection of Alcibiades.

Olympias: Philip II's fifth wife, a princess of the kingdom of Epirus east of Macedonia, and mother of Alexander the Great.

ostracism: Ten-year banishment and disenfranchisement inflicted occasionally on a leading Athenian, by popular referendum. Such banishments were intended to resolve power struggles or eliminate the threat of an autocratic coup.

Parmenio: Senior Macedonian general and right-hand man to both Philip and Alexander, until 331 when Alexander posted him to a lesser command in Media; murdered in 330 on Alexander's orders.

Pelopidas: Theban political and military leader who teamed up with Epaminondas to lead Thebes in its brief sojourn as superpower of Greece, 371–362. Pelopidas helped defeat the Spartans on several occasions and tangled ineffectually with Alexander of Pherae, a Thessalian tyrant.

Peloponnese: Peninsula comprising the southern half of mainland Greece; dominated militarily and politically by Sparta.

Pericles: Leader of Athens during the period of its greatest expansion and most explosive cultural developments. First active in 462 as supporter of Ephialtes, Pericles assumed leadership of the democratic political wing after Ephialtes' death. Athens looked to Pericles to set policies toward Sparta that were uncompromising enough to provoke war in 432; Pericles died of illness in the second year of the war.

Persepolis: One of several capital cities of the Persian empire, site of magnificent palaces built under Darius I and Xerxes. The central palace of the complex was destroyed by fire while occupied by Alexander's forces in 331.

Persians: An Iranian people who seized power from their kinsmen, the Medes, in the mid-sixth century. Under the so-called Achaemenid dynasty established by Cyrus the Great, the Persians built an immense empire, which by 500 encompassed all of Asia from Turkey to the Indus River, Egypt and North Africa, and parts of eastern Europe. Their attempts to conquer Greece in 490 and 480 were unsuccessful, however. By the fourth century their empire was thought to be in decline, tempting Agesilaus of Sparta to lead a partly successful invasion in 396; later Alexander succeeded in capturing the entire empire and ending the Achaemenid dynasty.

phalanx: Rank-and-file formation of infantry soldiers designed to present a solid wall of weaponry to an opponent in battle. Devised by the Greeks, perhaps in the ninth century, the phalanx was radically altered in the fourth century, first by Thebes, which experimented with its size and configuration, and then by Macedonia, which armed its soldiers with long *sarissas* (lances) and small, shoulder-hung shields.

Philip II: Born 382, assumed the Macedonian throne in 359. A gifted leader, diplomat, and military strategist, Philip transformed his country from a weak provincial backwater to superpower status in two decades. Philip was assassinated by Pausanias in 336, two years after his victory over Athens and Thebes at Chaeronea, and succeeded by his son Alexander III, "the Great."

Phocion: Athenian general and statesman whose long life spanned most of the fourth century. A famous moderate with regard to policy toward Macedon, Phocion was appointed one of two puppet leaders of the government imposed on Athens by Antipater in 322.

Phoebidas: Spartan general of the early fourth century who led an unprovoked attack on the Theban stronghold called the Cadmeia. By seizing this fort, Phoebidas and his Spartan troops gained control over Thebes, until they were overthrown in a revolt led by Pelopidas and others.

Phoenicians: Seafaring people inhabiting the cities of the Levantine coast (principally Tyre, Sidon, and Gaza) as well as parts of North Africa and the western Mediterranean. Phoenicians served the principal naval arm of the Persian empire, but did so without great loyalty to Persia; many deserted to Alexander's side during the early phase of the Asian campaign.

Piraeus: Port system on the west coast of Attica; after 493, the harbor serving Athens.

Pisistratus: Tyrant of Athens starting around 560, after the reforms of Solon had failed to resolve class conflicts. Ejected and returned to power numerous times; died in 527, leaving power to his sons.

Plataea: Greek city on the border between Attica and Boeotia.

Plutarch: Greek essayist and biographer of the late first and early second centuries CE who composed *Parallel Lives of the Greeks and Romans* as well as many short ethical treatises, dialogues, and speeches collectively known as the *Moralia*.

Pnyx: Hill next to the Acropolis at which the Athenian assembly met.

Porus: Indian ruler of territories between the Hydaspes and Acesines rivers; Alexander's last great opponent, defeated in 326 at the battle of the Hydaspes.

Ptolemy, son of Lagus: Boyhood friend of Alexander and member of the Companions who held various minor commands during the Asian campaigns. After Alexander's death he established himself as ruler of Egypt, where he was crowned king in 305 and ruled as Ptolemy I.

Pythia: Greek term for the priestess through whose mouth the oracular responses were given at Delphi.

Roxane: Iranian princess, daughter of Oxyartes (ruler of the Sogdian Rock), married to Alexander in 327.

Sacred Band: Elite infantry corps created at Thebes in the 370s, finally destroyed by the Macedonians at the battle of Chaeronea in 338. The band consisted of 150 male homosexual couples, on the theory, first propounded in Plato's *Republic*, that men would fight more vigorously if their lovers were looking on.

Salamis: Island in the gulf offshore from Attica. Site of the naval battle in which the Greek navy defeated the navy of the invading Persians in 480.

Samos: Island off the coast of Asia Minor not far from Miletus. A strong member of the Delian League, Samos tried to quit in 440, but was brought to heel by Pericles. In the second phase of the war, after 412, Samos became a major Athenian naval base.

Solon: Athenian wise man and lawgiver whose political leadership commenced in 594; died about 560. Solon was empowered to alter the constitution to address the extreme strife between rich and poor in archaic Athens.

He carved out a famously moderate path between the interests of the two factions.

Sparta: Leading Greek city in the Peloponnese, and for centuries (until the rise of Athens) the military superpower of the Greek world. Its constitution preserved a monarchy (actually a diarchy, with two kings sharing rule) until well past the time when other Greek cities had rejected that institution. A system of military training and strict social discipline, the *agoge*, was ascribed by Spartans to an early leader they called Lycurgus.

Sphacteria: Tiny island offshore of Pylos on the west coast of the Peloponnese; site of a Spartan defeat in 327 that resulted in a large contingent of prisoners being brought to Athens.

Sphodrias: Spartan general of the fourth century who led a failed raid on the Athenian port, the Piraeus.

stratēgos: "General," a military officer elected annually at Athens by a vote in the assembly. Ten generals served at any one time, sometimes acting together as a board, other times leading separate expeditions or assignments. Because the *stratēgoi* were chosen from among the leading citizens, they also exercised great influence in the assembly and other political bodies.

Susa: One of the imperial capitals of Persia, captured, with its vast wealth, by Alexander in 331.

Syracuse: Colony of Corinth and the most prosperous of the Greek cities on the island of Sicily. It was the main target of Athens' ill-fated expedition of 415–413.

Thebes: Infantry superpower of the Greek world in the mid-fourth century, thanks to the military innovations of Epaminondas. Defeated by Philip II at the battle of Chaeronea and thereafter secured by a Macedonian garrison. Destroyed by Alexander after a revolt in 335.

Themistocles: Athenian statesman in the early fifth century who charted the course that led to Athens becoming a naval power. Themistocles led the Athenian contingent of the Greek fleet at Salamis and engineered the Greek victory there almost single-handedly. Despite this victory Themistocles later fell into disfavor at Athens, was exiled, and ended his career as a satrap of the Persian empire.

Thermopylae: Land pass leading into central Greece from the north. In a battle in 480, a small Spartan force, led by Leonidas, was wiped out defending the pass of Thermopylae against the invading Persian army.

Theseus: Legendary Athenian king who was believed to have urbanized Athens by aggregating the disparate settlements of Attica. Theseus' mythic career in many ways parallels that of Heracles, but also includes a period of reign that was famously wise and moderate.

Thirty Years' Peace: Treaty that kept a kind of peace between the Athenians and the Lacedaemonians and their respective allies from 446/5 to 432/1, when the Spartans voted to go to war.

Thrace: Tribal region to the northwest of Macedonia, stretching across the northern Aegean to the Danube. The Thracians were subdued by Philip II and contributed a cavalry contingent to the Macedonian army.

Thucydides: Athenian general and historian of the late fifth century, exiled from Athens in 424 for a military lapse in the Peloponnesian War. His historical narrative, *The Peloponnesian War*, written while in exile, covers the period 432–410 in remarkable detail.

trireme: Large Greek warship of the Classical period. A trireme carried a crew of two hundred, of which most were rowers, plus a few marines and officers. Triremes fought either by ramming each other at high speed or by placing themselves close enough to other vessels that the marines on board could fire off javelins, arrows, or slings.

Xenophon: Athenian general, mercenary captain, historian, and essayist of the late fifth and early fourth centuries. His works *Agesilaus* and *Hellenica* were especially valuable to Plutarch as sources for his biographies of fourth-century subjects.

Xerxes: Persian king who commanded the great land-and-sea invasion of Greece in 480, resulting in the sacking of Athens. He retreated from Europe after the naval defeat at Salamis.

Index

Cynosarges, 39
Cynoscephalae, 209
Cyprus, 59, 79, 84
Cyrus the Younger, 150, 156, 157
Cythera, 111, 186
Cyzicus, 142 *n.*, 147, 176;
    Cyzicenians, 142

Damocleidas, 197
Darius I, 41, 61, 64 *n.*
Darius II, 155, 172–74, 177–78,
    181
Darius III, 230, 238–48, 255
Datis, 61
decarchies, 157, 161, 172
Decelea, 50, 141, 148, 149 *n.*
Delian League, 73 *n.*, 77, 78 *n.*,
    92 *n.*
Delos, 73, 77, 92
Delphi, 1 *n.*, 12, 25, 46 *n.*, 53,
    83, 162, 167, 169, 262. *See also*
    Pythia
Demades, 214, 221–22, 225, 263,
    265–66, 268
Demaratus of Corinth, 177, 233
Demetrius of Phalerum, 5, 213
Demosthenes (fifth-century gen-
    eral), 111–13, 122–24, 127–28,
    137
Demosthenes (fourth-century
    orator), 212–27, 234, 263–64,
    268
Diogenes of Sinope, 26, 235
Dionysius of Sicily, 209
Diopeithes, 103
Dioscuri, 22 *n.*, 162
Dioscurides, 103
Diphridas, 179
Dodona, 167
Dolopians, 8
Dorians, 166, 186
Doris, 45
Draco, 32

Ecbatana, 177, 208, 215
Egypt, 10–11, 59, 83 *n.*, 83, 85, 97,
    113, 191, 241
Eion, 76
Elaeus, 158
Elatea, 218
Elatus, 13
Eleius, 81
Eleusis, 50, 148, 149 *n.*, 269. *See
    also* Mysteries
Eleutheria, 71
Elis, 202; Elians, 116, 134
Elpinice, 81 *n.*
Epaminondas, 182, 184–89,
    192–94, 201–7, 219
Ephesus, 150, 155, 156 *n.*, 157,
    173, 174, 229
Ephialtes, 33 *n.*, 80, 82, 88, 90–91
Ephorus, 167
Epicrates of Acharnae, 56
Epicydes, 42
Epicydidas, 177
Epidaurus, 106
Epipolae, 120, 122 *n.*, 123
Epirus, 55, 233
Erechtheus, 1
Eretria, 48
Ergoteles, 56
Erianthus, 162
Eteocles, 163
Euboea, 7, 44, 98, 141, 172, 217
Euphemidius, 42
Euphrates, river, 242, 254, 257
Eupolis, 100, 132
Euripides, 35, 130, 132, 162
Europe, 51, 64 *n.*, 96
Eurotas, river, 19, 187, 189, 203
Eurybiades, 43–44, 47–48, 64, 66
Eurycles, 128
Eurymedon, river, 79, 80 *n.*, 124
Eurypontids, 166
Euryptolemus (cousin of Pericles)
    88, 148